Praise for the First Four Books in T. J. Stiles's *In Their Own Words*

The Colonizers

"To enliven this collection of writings by th̶̶̶̶warriors of eastern North America, Stiles pr̶̶̶̶ally waggish introductions. Arranged chro̶̶̶̶ogically, his selections reach from the founding of Jamestown to the defeat of France in 1759, and many are taken from annals set down by the period's most famous founding figures. . . . An interesting assemblage of original material." —*Booklist*

"An entertaining page-turner . . . The gripping narratives bring this amazing period to life. The excerpts represent slaves, women, farmers, and scouts, as well as more prominent figures in colonial history. . . . Stiles then takes readers deeper to show how each colony's demographics, philosophy, leaders, and relations with both Native Americans and Europe impacted on their survival, their future, and the future of North America." —*School Library Journal*

Robber Barons and Radicals

"Powerful . . . The genius of Stiles's approach is his panoramic view of post–Civil War America fighting for identity on many fronts. . . . A book of surprising passion." —*Library Journal*

"Interweaving revealing and often moving excerpts from contemporary documents with his own lucid narrative, T. J. Stiles has fashioned a compelling account of the Reconstruction era that followed the Civil War." —Eric Foner, DeWitt Clinton Professor of History, Columbia University

"T. J. Stiles has once again made history come alive." —Louis P. Masur, author of *The Real War Will Never Get in the Book: Selections from Writers During the Civil War*

Warriors and Pioneers

"Unique . . . A thorough and accurate history of the westward expansion that began en masse in 1843. . . . Stiles presents history as a living thing, infused with life. Even if you have read a great deal about the conquest of the West, *In Their Own Words* might make that turbulent half century, for the first time, real." —*Statesman Journal* (Salem, OR)

"The next best thing to oral histories are contemporary writings. . . . T. J. Stiles includes white and Indian accounts for most of the major conflicts in the settlement of the West, including the gold rush, the war for the Black Hills, and the major campaigns to conquer the Indians." —*The Denver Post*

Civil War Commanders

"This skillful compilation of firsthand accounts by participants of the Civil War's most important battles offers readers rewarding fare. . . . *Civil War Commanders* is a valuable addition to the literature of the American *Iliad*." —James M. McPherson, author of *Battle Cry of Freedom: The Civil War Era*

"Treats the reader to a detailed perspective that is often lost. . . . This makes for interesting reading. . . . Overall, this is a well-organized and concise overview of the Civil War that is allowed to unfold through the words and actions of the participants." —*Library Journal*

"A chronological history of decisive events in a critical chapter in American history. Highly recommended." —*Booklist*

About the Author:

T. J. Stiles is the author of a number of books about American history, including the four previous volumes of *In Their Own Words*. His articles and essays have appeared in the *Smithsonian* magazine, the *Los Angeles Times, The Denver Post*, and the *New York Daily News*, among other publications. He is currently working on a book about the career of Jesse James and the politics of Reconstruction. He lives in Park Slope, Brooklyn.

About the Introducer:

William Pencak, Professor of History at the University Park Campus of the Pennsylvania State University, edits *Pennsylvania History: A Journal of Mid-Atlantic Studies*, which publishes *McNeil Center Annual: Explorations in Early American Culture* as a supplement. His books most relevant to the American Revolution are *War, Politics, and Revolution in Provincial Massachusetts; America's Burke: The Mind of Thomas Hutchinson;* and (coedited with John B. Frantz) *Beyond Philadelphia: The American Revolution in the Pennsylvania Hinterland.*

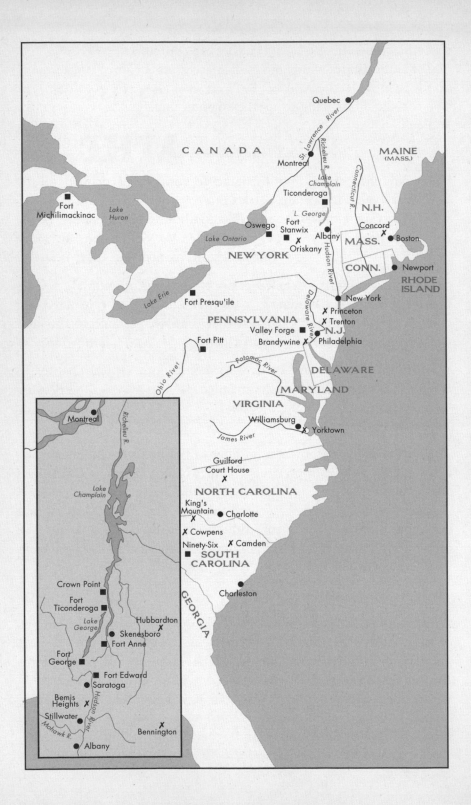

IN THEIR OWN WORDS

FOUNDING FATHERS

Collected and Edited by

T. J. Stiles

Introduction by William Pencak

A PERIGEE BOOK

A Perigee Book
Published by The Berkley Publishing Group
A division of Penguin Putnam Inc.
375 Hudson Street
New York, New York 10014

First edition: June 1999

Published simultaneously in Canada.

The Penguin Putnam Inc. World Wide Web site address is
http://www.penguinputnam.com

Library of Congress Cataloging-in-Publication Data

Founding fathers / collected and edited by T. J. Stiles. — 1st ed.
      p. cm. — (In their own words)
   "A Perigee book."
   Includes bibliographical references (p.xvii–xviii).
   ISBN 0-399-52513-0
   1. United States—History—Revolution, 1775–1783—Sources. 2. United
States—History—Revolution, 1775–1783—Personal narratives. I. Stiles, T. J. II. Series: In
their own words (Berkley Publishing Group)
   E203 .F68 1999
   973.3'092'2—dc21
                                                                          98-55448
                                                                             CIP

Printed in the United States of America

10 9 8 7 6 5 4 3 2 1

CONTENTS

IV: Victory

PREFACE

When my editor spoke to me about this, the fifth and last title in the *In Their Own Words* series, I gathered that he was hoping for a book on the intellectual origins of the American republic. This is not that book. Fortunately, if anyone is reading this, I was paid and the book was published anyway.

It's not that I am uninterested in the intellectual history of the American Revolution, or that I've left it out. Rather, I have structured this collection of first-person accounts to reflect my deeply held belief that ideas are inseparable from events in the course of history. In an episode like the American Revolution, ideas are enormously important—but they grow and change in response to concrete actions. As Samuel Adams wrote during the debate over independence in early 1776, "Mankind are governed more by their feelings than by reason. Events which excite those feelings will produce wonderful effects. . . . One battle would do more towards a Declaration of Independency than a long chain of conclusive arguments in a provincial convention or the Continental Congress."

Of course, reason—encompassing convictions, beliefs, and arguments—was necessary (or a *conflict* of reason was necessary) for these events to occur in the first place; but once they did, they radicalized the colonists' ideas in turn. My purpose is to show this interrelationship, how it shaped the winding, dramatic path toward independence. A purely intellectual history, by removing the element of accident, of contingency, could make the Revolution seem inevitable, or the American victory unstoppable, when that was far from the case. On the other hand, a purely military or political history would reduce the story to a mere struggle for power, without revealing the sweeping change that (as Gordon Wood demonstrated in *The Radicalism of the American Revolution*) truly revolutionized American society.

The question I address in this book is a simple one: How did the colonies come to be independent? The answer, of course, is quite complex (as my little discussion of events and ideas has already hinted); in my pursuit of it, I have attempted only to note the major landmarks along the way, and some of the guides who brought (or resisted bringing) much of a continent along the path to nationhood. I must honestly state that this book is not an attempt to break new ground in the field. I have steered clear of many important but difficult issues, such as the role of women, local politics, class divisions, religious influences and debates, and the awkward, contradictory positions the Founders took on slavery. I kept the issue of independence foremost throughout, concentrating on political and military events and ideas. This book is aimed at the general reader, after all; it requires no specialized knowledge, nor was it created to please a scholarly audience.

Having lowered the reader's expectations, I had best perk them up a bit. By tracing this period through the words of the participants, I hope to recapture something that is inevitably lost in the best works of history—and the last twenty years have seen some excellent works of history. From Robert Middlekauff's *The Glorious Cause* to David Hackett Fischer's *Paul Revere's Ride*, from Pauline Maier's *American Scripture* to Benson Bobrick's recent *Angel in the Whirlwind*, the narratives and analyses of recent times have been outstanding (anyone interested enough to read this author's preface should rush out and start buying them). But there is a quality of insight, a depth of experience, that comes from reading Samuel Adams's letters, as he moved from loyal opponent of the Stamp Act to fire-breathing radical; John Adams's intimate reflections on his times and the men who shaped them; Washington's resilient reports of defeat, and exuberant accounts of victories; and the piercing words of men who stood in battle, locked shoulder to shoulder, as bullets and cannon balls tore through the ranks. In letters and diaries and autobiographies, they struggled to make sense of the great events they helped shape; to read their words is to come as close as we can to actually *knowing* this age.

Of course, there are numerous anthologies of original writings covering the age of the Revolution, ranging from authoritative collections of personal papers and political pamphlets to narrowly edited works on the clash of arms. For my own part, I have not sought to provide comprehensive coverage: this is, inevitably, an idiosyncratic collection, and any knowledgeable reader will bemoan the absence of some accounts, as well as delight (I hope) in some unexpected gems. But this book has certain strengths that many other anthologies lack. First, it offers in-depth selections in every chapter, rather than the paragraph or two featured in many such books. I find the greater length offers readers a chance to truly gather the story from the writer's perspective, to follow an important event or development in a relatively complete episode. Second, I have tried to create a cohesive narrative of the struggle toward independence, by tying these first-person accounts together with my own writing. I not only introduce the selections and provide critical commentary (for an inevitable amount of self-justification and distortion creeps in here and there, especially in the case of defeated generals), but I also offer actual narrative, to offer the reader a single overarching history in this one volume.

As I mentioned, I stick to the issue of independence itself: how Americans settled on the idea in principle, and how they won it in fact. That means this book offers a parade of Dead White Males, because they, after all, were calling the shots in the 1770s. A more complete and nuanced account of the age would simply be a different (and far larger) book. Besides, the principles these fellows established have served as the foundation of the American mansion of liberty— not a flawless structure, but one that has been able to grow far beyond anything those men could envision when they laid the first stones.

This book is not a comprehensive collection of the writings of all, or even most, of the Founding Fathers. I have stuck with only a few: the ever-quotable John Adams (a brilliant diarist); his hell-raising older cousin, Samuel Adams; Thomas Paine, whose *The Crisis* provided an opinionated take on current events; and George Washington, who wrote from the battlefield. I also offer a few key arguments from Thomas Jefferson and Alexander Hamilton. Despite the limited selection of authors, these relatively lengthy excerpts of their writings will (I hope) offer an understanding of the views and world of the

Founders as a whole, and impart a more intimate knowledge of the lives of these select few.

I have also included the words of other men who staked their lives on the outcome of the battle for independence. Here is a surgeon who served at Valley Forge; a captain who dug trenches outside Yorktown; and a legendary cavalry officer who fought in the bitter war for the South. Here, too, are the British officers who made command decisions or stood in the storm of musketry at Concord, Freeman's Farm, Camden, and Yorktown. Their accounts are an essential ingredient in this book; they offer the real life-and-death flavor of the struggle, as well as insight into the forces arrayed against American independence.

As with my selection of authors, my selection of events is limited. I do not cover every point of conflict in the decade before the outbreak of hostilities, but I try to evoke both the changing ideology of the struggle and the diminishing ground for compromise. Halfway through the book, the war emerges as the center of the action, gradually leaving Congress behind, but I have restricted my coverage to a few key campaigns. In so doing, I have tried to provide insight into the ebb and flow of events, the decisions of the commanders, and the experience of the men—an experience that was shared by the nation.

A few acknowledgments are in order. I must thank my wife, Nadine T. Spence, for her limitless reservoir of wisdom, of grace, of wit, of common sense. She has guided me forward at all times, and in all things, and without her I am lost. Next, I must pay a heartfelt tribute to my editor, Mr. John Schline, who has done so much to foster my career from its very beginnings. I will forever be in debt to him for his confidence in my work, his enthusiasm for my writing, and his passion for both history and books. His support has been invaluable to me personally as well as professionally.

I have grown accustomed to writing acknowledgments once a year over the last five years—the rate at which I have been completing anthologies for this series. On the realization that I may not write another for a few years, it is tempting to list everyone who has been helpful and supportive. Perhaps I should just leave off with those who first nourished my love of history: my teacher back at Foley High

School, Kenneth Anderson; and the history faculty of Carleton College, especially Professor Robert Bonner—a model of dignity and humanity, as much as fine scholarship. All students should be so fortunate as to have such instructors.

—T. J. Stiles

SOURCES

Charles Francis Adams, ed., *The Works of John Adams, Second President of the United States* (Boston: 1850)

Ethan Allen, *The Narrative of Colonel Ethan Allen* (Philadelphia, 1779)

Thomas Anburey, *Travels in the Interior of America* (Boston: Houghton Mifflin Company, 1923)

Edward C. Boynton, ed., *General Orders of George Washington, Commander-in-Chief of the Army of the Revolution, Issued at Newburgh on the Hudson, 1782–1783* (Newburgh: News Company, 1883)

John Burgoyne, *A State of the Expedition from Canada, as Laid Before the House of Commons* (London: J. Almon, 1780)

Clarence Edwin Carter, ed., *The Correspondence of General Thomas Gage with the Secretaries of State*, 1763–1775 (New Haven: Yale University Press, 1931)

Correspondence of George Washington and Comte de Grasse, August 17–November 4, 1781 (Washington, D.C.: United States Government Printing Office, 1931)

Harry Alonzo Cushing, ed., *The Writings of Samuel Adams*, Volumes 1–4 (New York: G. P. Putnam's Sons, 1904)

James Duncan, "Diary of Captain James Duncan, of Colonel Moses Hazen's Regiment, in the Yorktown Campaign, 1781," *Pennsylvania Archives*, Second Series, Vol. XV (Harrisburg: E. K. Meyers, 1890)

Paul Leicester Ford, ed., *The Works of Thomas Jefferson* (New York: G. P. Putnam's Sons, 1904)

James Hadden, *A Journal Kept in Canada and Upon Burgoyne's Campaign in 1776 and 1777* (Albany: Joel Munsell's Sons, 1884)

Henry Lee, *Memoirs of the War in the Southern Department of the United States* (Philadelphia: Bradford and Inskeep, 1812)

Jeremy Lister, *Concord Fight* (London: Oxford University Press, 1931)

Benjamin Franklin Stevens, ed., *The Campaign in Virginia, 1781: An Exact Reprint of Six Rare Pamphlets on the Clinton-Cornwallis Controversy* (London: 1888)

Banastre Tarleton, *A History of the Campaigns of 1780 and 1781, in the Southern Provinces of North America* (Dublin: 1787)

Albigence Waldo, "Valley Forge, 1777–1778: Diary of Surgeon Albigence Waldo, of the Connecticut Line," in *The Pennsylvania Magazine of History and Biography*, Volume 21 (Philadelphia: Historical Fund of Pennsylvania, 1897)

William W. Wright et al eds., *The Papers of George Washington*, Revolutionary War Series (Charlottesville: University Press of Virginia, 1983); by permission of the Mount Vernon Ladies' Association of the Union and the University Press of Virginia

THE WRITERS AND THEIR POSITIONS AT THE TIME

Americans and French

John Adams, lawyer, delegate to the Massachusetts General Court, delegate to the Continental Congress, United States peace commissioner

Samuel Adams, delegate to the Massachusetts General Court, founder of the Boston committee of correspondence, delegate to the Continental Congress

James Duncan, captain in a Continental light infantry regiment in the Yorktown campaign

François-Joseph Paul de Grasse, commander of the French Atlantic fleet

Alexander Hamilton, student at King's College and pamphleteer (later an officer in the American army)

Thomas Jefferson, planter, delegate to the Continental Congress (later governor of Virginia)

Henry Lee, lieutenant colonel and commander of Lee's Legion

Thomas Paine, soldier and pamphleteer

Albigence Waldo, surgeon in a Connecticut Continental infantry regiment at Valley Forge

George Washington, general and Commander in Chief of the American army

British

Thomas Anburey, lieutenant in the 29th Regiment in the Saratoga campaign

John Burgoyne, general and commander of the British forces in the Saratoga campaign

Henry Clinton, general and last Commander in Chief in America

Charles Cornwallis, general and commander in the South

Thomas Gage, general, military governor of Massachusetts, and first Commander in Chief in America

James Hadden, lieutenant of artillery in the Saratoga campaign

Jeremy Lister, ensign (a junior officer) at the battles of Lexington and Concord

Barry St. Leger, lieutenant colonel and commander of British forces at the siege of Fort Stanwix in the Saratoga campaign

Banastre Tarleton, lieutenant colonel and commander of Tarleton's Legion

INTRODUCTION
A Tale of Two Wars

I

In 1842, the young Bostonian lawyer Mellen Chamberlain, later an important historian of the American Revolution, conducted an interview with ninety-one-year-old Levi Preston. Preston had turned out with his fellow Minute Men from Danvers and throughout eastern Massachusetts on April 19, 1775, to harass the British army that had set out from Boston to seize munitions, John Hancock, and Samuel Adams. Were oral history as popular in the nineteenth century as it is today, thousands of such interviews would exist. But exceptional as it is, Chamberlain's conversation with Preston cuts to the heart of why America rebelled:

> Chamberlain: "My histories tell me that you men of the Revolution took up arms against 'intolerable oppressions.' What were they?"
> Preston: "Oppressions? I didn't feel them."
> Chamberlain: "What, were you not oppressed by the Stamp Act?"
> Preston: "I never saw one of those stamps, and always understood that Governor Bernard [of Massachusetts] put them all in Castle William [on an island in Boston Harbor]. I am certain I never paid a penny for one of them."
> Chamberlain: "Well, what then about the tea tax?"
> Preston: "Tea tax! I never drank a drop of the stuff, the boys threw it all overboard."
> Chamberlain: "Then I suppose you had been reading [English political writers] James Harrington, [Algernon] Sidney, and [John] Locke about the eternal principles of liberty."
> Preston: "Never heard of 'em. We read only the Bible, the Catechism, Watts's Psalms and Hymns, and the Almanack [probably that of Nathaniel Ames of Dedham, New England's answer to Benjamin Franklin's Poor Richard].

Chamberlain: "Well, then, what was the matter? What did you mean in going to the fight?"

Preston: "Young man, what we meant in going for those Redcoats was this: we always had governed ourselves, and we always meant to. They didn't mean we should."[1]

Although a farmer with a limited education living over three thousand miles from the Houses of Parliament, Preston had a better understanding of the British Empire's constitution than the lawmakers who claimed the right "to bind the colonies in all cases whatsoever," as the Declaratory Act of 1766 proclaimed. Historian Jack P. Greene has stressed that British law had traditionally recognized diverse sources of political authority; the Common Law, the Bill of Rights promulgated after the Glorious Revolution of 1688, and charters granting governing powers to corporations and colonies around the world set the limits Parliament itself had recognized it needed to respect.[2]

"The Great War for Empire," as historian Lawrence Henry Gipson has aptly rechristened the French and Indian War of 1754–1763 (to stress that it included a world war for global supremacy between Britain and France), changed perceptions of the British Constitution. A proud and victorious Britain, guided by the great legal theorist Sir William Blackstone—famous for his dictum that Parliament could do "everything that is not naturally impossible"[3]—considered the colonies' insistence on the right to consent to the laws that governed them "obsolete." "No maxim of policy was more universally admitted, than that a supreme and uncontrollable power must exist somewhere in every state," wrote the anonymous author of *Colonising*. In the Empire, that power belonged to the "King, Lords, and Com-

[1]Reprinted in Elinor Lenz and Rita Riley, eds., *The American Revolutionary Experience* (Los Angeles: The Western Humanities Center, UCLA), pp. 78–79.

[2]Jack P. Greene, "Origins of the Revolution: A Constitutional Interpretation," in *Understanding the American Revolution: Issues and Actors* (Charlottesville: University Press of Virginia, 1995), pp. 72–95.

[3]See Gareth Jones, ed., *The Sovereignty of the Law: Selections from Blackstone's Commentaries on the Laws of England* (Toronto: University of Toronto Press, 1973), p. 64.

mons, under the collective appellation of the Legislature," or Parliament.[4]

The colonists disagreed. Even when they granted Parliament the right to regulate their commerce, they always stressed that their consent was required and thus revokable. As Samuel Adams wrote in 1772: "If the trade of the colonies is protected by the British navy, there may *possibly* be . . . a just right in the Parliament of Great Britain to restrain them from carrying on their trade to the injury of the trade of Great Britain. It may be the wisdom of the colonies, under present circumstances to acquiesce in *reasonable* restrictions."[5] Note the qualifiers: "if" and "acquiesce" in addition to the words Adams himself emphasized through the use of italics. Thomas Jefferson considered the Navigation Act a treaty between two nations, in which one contracts to furnish protection in return for the other's agreeing to restrict its trade voluntarily.[6] Observe that even before independence, Jefferson considered the North American colonies a "nation" possessing a common identity.

This identity was forged in the common experience first of war, then of conservative resistance to Parliament's radical threat to traditional self-government through taxes, trade regulations, quartering troops in Boston, and the unilateral modification of the Massachusetts Charter imposed by Parliament from 1761 to 1774. Like the British at home, the British Americans—as they styled themselves until the moment of independence—emerged from the Great War for Empire full of high hopes for a glorious future. As Nathaniel Ames—author of the best-selling almanac in North America at some 60,000 copies a year to Poor Richard's 10,000—predicted in 1758, when the war finally began to go Britain's way:

> The Curious have observ'd, that the Progress of Humane Literature
> (like the Sun) is from the East to the West; thus it has travelled thro'
> Asia and Europe, and now is arrived at the Eastern Shore of America.

[4]Quoted in Greene, "Origins of the Revolution," p. 88.
[5]Harry A. Cushing, ed., *Writings of Samuel Adams* (New York: G. P. Putnam's Sons, 1904–1906), vol. 2, pp. 322–326.
[6]Andrew A. Liscomb, ed., *Writings of Thomas Jefferson* (Washington: Thomas Jefferson Memorial Association), vol. 17, pp. 126–128.

As the Celestial Light of the Gospel was directed here by the Finger of GOD, it will doubtless finally drive the long! long! Night of Heathenish Darkness from America:—So Arts and Sciences will change the Face of Nature in their Tour from Hence over the Appalachian Mountains to the Western Ocean; and as they march thro' the vast Desert, the Residence of wild Beasts will be broken up, and their obscene Howl cease for ever—Instead of which, the Stones and Trees will dance together at the music of Orpheus.—The Rocks will disclose their hidden Gems—and the inestimable Treasures of Gold & Silver be broken up. Huge Mountains of Iron Ore are already discovered, and vast Stores are reserved for future generations. . . . *O! Ye unborn Inhabitants of America! . . . when your Eyes behold the Sun after he has rolled the Seasons round for two or three Centuries more, you will know that in* Anno Domini 1758 *we dream'd of your Times.*[7]

Similarly, Philip Freneau and Hugh Henry Brackenridge foretold in their *Poem on the Rising Glory of America*, published in Philadelphia in 1772, that "here fair freedom shall forever reign." History will enter its "final stage where time shall introduce renowned characters, and glorious works of high invention and of wond'rous art."[8]

In previous colonial wars—King William's (1689–1697), Queen Anne's (1702–1713), and The War of Jenkins' Ear[9] (which merged with King George's War of 1739–1748)—New England, particularly Massachusetts, did most of the fighting. But in the 1750s and 1760s all the colonies raised thousands of soldiers and mustered over two and one-half million pounds sterling in supplies to assist British forces. Britain acknowledged these exertions by reimbursing the colonies just over a million pounds, about 40 percent of their expenses: some £350,000 went to Massachusetts alone.[10] Of the authors

[7]William Pencak, "Nathaniel Ames, Sr., and the Political Culture of Provincial New England," *Historical Journal of Massachusetts* 22 (1994), pp. 141–158, quotation p. 153–154.

[8]Quoted in Max Savelle, ed., *The Colonial Origins of American Thought* (Princeton: D. Van Nostrand, 1964), p. 186.

[9]So named because an English Captain Jenkins appeared before Parliament pretending that his own ear, which he supposedly had preserved in a jar, had been cut off by the Spaniards.

[10]Jack P. Greene, "The Seven Years War and the American Revolution: The Causal Relationship Reconsidered," *The Journal of Imperial and Commonwealth History*, 8 (1980), pp. 85–105, esp. p. 98.

included in this collection, John Adams, Thomas Jefferson, and Thomas Paine stress the colonists' contributions to their own defense, denying the major premise of Britain's plans to tax the colonies and regulate their trade.[11] So did James Otis,[12] the New York Assembly,[13] Benjamin Franklin in his examination before the House of Commons in 1766,[14] and loyalist Governor of Massachusetts Thomas Hutchinson in private letters sent to England in a futile effort to prevent new taxes.[15] These arguments had a special force in Massachusetts, which had raised the most men and money for the common cause even though it had not been directly under attack since the beginning of the century. Isaac Royall, an absentee West India sugar planter who resided in Medford, Massachusetts, and ultimately became a loyalist, spoke almost universally for his fellow countrymen when he pleaded with Lord Dartmouth that they should not be punished for the Boston Tea Party: "This province Sir has always been foremost even beyond its ability and notwithstanding the present unhappy disputes would perhaps be so again if there should be the like occasion for it in promoting the Honour of their King and Nation. Witness . . . the reduction of Louisbourg[16] and many other expensive and heroic expeditions against the common enemy."[17]

Most current scholarly interpretations of why the American Revolution happened take one of two approaches. Bernard Bailyn, Pauline Maier, and Gordon Wood have argued that the colonists' "country" or "New Whig" ideology predisposed them to regard British efforts to regulate the empire as evidence that a corrupt min-

[11]See pp. 16–18, 48, and 115–120 of this volume.

[12]James Otis, *The Rights of the British Colonies Asserted and Proved* (1764), reprinted in Merrill Jensen, ed., *Tracts of the American Resolution, 1763–1776* (Indianapolis: Bobbs-Merrill, 1967), p. 33.

[13]Quoted in Jack P. Greene, ed., *Colonies to Nation, 1763–1789* (New York: McGraw-Hill, 1967), p. 34.

[14]*Ibid.*, p. 72.

[15]Edmund S. Morgan, "Thomas Hutchinson and the Stamp Act," *New England Quarterly*, 21 (1948), pp. 488–489.

[16]In 1745, Massachusetts conquered the French fortress of Louisbourg on Cape Breton Island, which guarded the mouth of the St. Lawrence River in French Canada. In 1748, Britain returned the fort to France in return for Madras in India when the peace of Aix-la-Chapelle was signed.

[17]Isaac Royall to Lord Dartmouth, January 18, 1774, Large Manuscripts, Massachusetts Historical Society, Boston.

istry was plotting to extinguish their liberties.[18] Alfred F. Young, Edward Countryman, and Gary B. Nash, on the other hand, emphasize the presence of internal divisions in which groups excluded from political power—both elites and the urban lower orders suffering from a postwar depression—turned on the loyalists associated with British rule.[19] Each interpretation explains something different; they are complementary rather than contradictory. Political ideas account for why the colonies perceived postwar Parliamentary regulation as so threatening. Even future loyalists such as Hutchinson and Pennsylvania's Joseph Galloway[20] shared their opponents' opinions, although not their method of obtaining redress. Nearly all colonists opposed British measures. An understanding of the colonies' own internal conflict is required to understand why some people took the lead in the resistance movement, while others confined their protests to the printed word. As James Allen, member of a Pennsylvania family that opposed British policy until violence ensued, wrote: "I love the Cause of Liberty, but cannot heartily join in the prosecution of measures totally foreign to the original plan of Resistance. The madness of the multitude is but one degree better than submission to the Tea-Act."[21]

To accompany these explanations, I would expand Lawrence Henry Gipson's portrayal of "The American Revolution as an Aftermath of the Great War for Empire, 1754–1763," in an article of that

[18]Bernard Bailyn, *The Ideological Origins of the American Revolution* (expanded ed., Cambridge: Belknap Press of Harvard University, 1992); Pauline Maier, *From Resistance to Revolution: Colonial Radicals and the Development of American Opposition to Britain, 1765–1776* (New York: Knopf, 1972); *idem, The Old Revolutionaries: Political Lives in the Age of Samuel Adams* (New York: Knopf, 1980); Gordon Wood, *The Creation of the American Republic, 1776–1787* (Chapel Hill: University of North Carolina Press, 1969).

[19]Alfred F. Young, ed., *The American Revolution* (DeKalb: Northern Illinois University Press, 1976); *idem,* ed., *Beyond the American Revolution: Explorations in the History of American Radicalism* (DeKalb: Northern Illinois University Press, 1993); Edward Countryman, *The American Revolution* (New York: Hill and Wang, 1985); Gary B. Nash, *The Urban Crucible: Social Change, Political Consciousness, and the Origins of the American Revolution* (Cambridge: Harvard University Press, 1979).

[20]William Pencak, *America's Burke: The Mind of Thomas Hutchinson* (Lanham: University Press of America, 1982); John E. Ferling, *The Loyalist Mind: Joseph Galloway and the American Revolution* (University Park: Penn State Press, 1977).

[21]Quoted in Morton and Penn Borden, eds., *The American Tory* (Englewood Cliffs: Prentice-Hall, 1972), p. 2.

title. The war did more than free the mainland colonies from the French and Native American menace, thereby permitting "politically mature, prosperous, dynamic, and self-reliant" provincials to oppose the Empire when it failed to act in their interests.[22] Britons at home and those in the New World experienced the war in radically different ways.

European Britons argued, correctly, that they had sent thousands of soldiers to protect over one million colonists from some 80,000 French habitants assisted by several thousand Native American allies. The homeland ended the war in debt by some £130 million, necessitating an income or land tax of some 15 percent, a huge amount for premodern times. In Britain, unlike most of Europe, everyone, including the nobility (but not the royal family), paid taxes.[23] Meanwhile, colonial soldiers had mutinied, refused to fight away from their respective provinces, and resented taking orders from British regulars. Colonial merchants traded with the enemy; colonial farmers only reluctantly supplied the soldiers who risked their lives for the common cause; assemblies refused to comfortably quarter troops in cities during the winter (since they thought so many single men would threaten public order, female virtue, and jobs held by local laborers).[24]

In turn, the colonies maintained, also correctly, that they had defended themselves for a century or more without British assistance. They had greatly increased the wealth of the empire through commerce, frontier expansion, and demand for British manufactured goods. Furthermore, during the Great War, arrogant British officers had relegated them to tedious support work, all the while failing to win a major victory during the first four years.[25]

[22]Lawrence Henry Gipson, "The American Revolution as an Aftermath of the Great War for Empire, 1754–1763," *Political Science Quarterly*, 75 (1950), pp. 86–104.

[23]J. H. Plumb, *England in the Eighteenth Century (1714–1815)* (revised ed., Baltimore: Penguin, 1963), p. 126.

[24]Douglas Edward Leach, *Roots of Conflict: British Armed Forces and Colonial Americans, 1677–1763* (Chapel Hill: University of North Carolina Press, 1986), pp. 87–99; Charles Brodine, "Civil-Military Relations in Pennsylvania, 1758–1760," *Pennsylvania History*, 62 (1995), pp. 213–219.

[25]Fred Anderson, *A People's Army: Massachusetts Soldiers and Society in the Seven Years War* (Chapel Hill: University of North Carolina Press, 1984); Alan Rogers, *Empire and Liberty: American Resistance to British Authority, 1755–1763* (Berkeley: University of California Press, 1974).

Familiarity had produced mutual contempt. In peacetime, there was almost no British presence (except for the royal governors and just a handful of officials, soldiers, and occasional naval personnel) in the mainland colonies. Law and order was assured because the colonies basically ran their own affairs, as attested by hundreds of letters from exasperated royal governors who depended on the local assemblies for their salaries.[26] As thousands of military and support personnel crossed the Atlantic during the 1750s, a largely middle-class, self-governing society confronted a highly stratified military where aristocratic officers demanded unquestioning obedience from lower-class troops. Neither side was impressed with the other, but despite these divergent experiences, Britain and the colonies both emerged proud and triumphant from the struggle. Therein lay the seeds of the Revolution, for the colonies and the Mother Country had very different plans for the postwar world.

During the early 1760s, George III was one of four young monarchs who came to power determined to correct those abuses in their states that had hampered their success in the great global conflict. On the European continent, Catherine the Great of Russia, King Charles III of France, and Josef II of Austria—numbered among those rulers known as "Enlightened Despots"—tried to establish supremacy over nobles and the "constituted bodies" that represented them.[27] In Britain, King George III—who ascended the throne in 1760 at the age of twenty-two—took seriously the admonition of the late Lord Bolingbroke that his nation required a "Patriot King." Such a ruler would ideally eliminate the corruption of the Whig aristocracy and leading merchants who dominated Parliament. He would also compel colonies that had flouted the Navigation Acts and failed to

[26]Evarts B. Greene, *The Provincial Governor in the English Colonies of North America* (New York: Longmans, 1898). See also the relevant letters in W. Noel Sainsbury, *et al.*, eds., *The Calendar of State Papers, Colonial Series* (London: The Public Record Office, 1860–1969), 45 volumes.

[27]The phrase "constituted bodies" and their comparison to the colonial legislatures is that of Robert R. Palmer, *The Age of the Democratic Revolution, 1760–1801*, vol.1 (Princeton: Princeton University Press, 1959); for a survey of the reactions of early American historians to Palmer's thesis of parallel developments in different nations in the late eighteenth century, see William Pencak, "R. R. Palmer's *The Age of the Democratic Revolution: The View from America after Thirty Years*," *Pennsylvania History*, 60 (1993), pp. 73–92.

contribute what was perceived as their fair share of imperial defense to obey the law. The colonists got it wrong: the corruption and conspiracy of Britain to destroy liberty did not bring down the empire, but rather the sincere efforts of King George and his ministers to counter corruption in the customs service and disorder in the streets, modernize the empire, and render the colonies subservient to the sort of unified sovereign state prevalent among the dominant European powers.[28]

Britons in North America viewed the glory of the empire precisely in the fact that the home government guaranteed their liberty to govern themselves. If allowed to do so, the Reverend Thomas Barnard of Salem, Massachusetts, preached: "Here shall be the . . . Seat of Peace and Freedom. Here shall our indulgent Mother, who has most generously rescued and protected us, be served and honoured by growing numbers till Time shall be no more."[29] When Britain followed the war by decreasing colonial freedom, including the longed-for opportunity to expand west of the Appalachians, a pattern of mutual provocation and response replaced the short-lived euphoria of the late fifties and early sixties. The Stamp Act led to crowd resistance, which produced repeal, accompanied, however, by the assertion of Parliamentary supremacy. The Townshend Acts caused the colonies to enforce nonimportation of British goods. The appointment of customs officers in Boston who went after smugglers provoked crowds to chase them out of town, which in turn inspired Britain to send troops to protect these detested officials. Hostility toward the soldiers then led to the Boston "Massacre," producing seven out of no more than a dozen casualties inflicted by British tyrants on the American population during the decade before the Revolution. The Tea Act began a chain of events that included the Tea Party, the British Coercive Acts, the Continental Congress, and popular mobilization for the looming military conflict. Every measure

[28]For an interesting perspective on George III, see the interview of H.R.H. Prince Charles and Alistair Cooke, " 'A Much Maligned Monarch': A Conversation on King George III," in William M. Fowler, Jr., and Wallace Coyle, eds., *The American Revolution: Changing Perspectives* (Boston: Northeastern University Press, 1979), pp. 213–231.

[29]Quoted in Greene, "The Seven Years War and the American Revolution," p. 99.

was a real affront, yet also a symbol in the struggle over "who was to govern" that compelled Levi Preston to turn out on the morning of April 19, 1775. The contest only ended with what became the fifth world war in a hundred years.

II

Catherine Drinker Bowen wrote of the United States Constitution as *The Miracle at Philadelphia*. She described the amazing fact that thirteen loosely linked states—almost alone among modern nations that have experienced revolutions or fought wars for independence—established a stable, united government that forestalled internal strife and has endured for over two centuries.[30] Yet, an earlier miracle had preceded that at Philadelphia: the very fact that the states had won their revolutionary struggle in the first place. Any smart gambler comparing the thirteen colonies with Britain in the quarter-century before 1776 would probably have bet his last dollar on the Mother Country.

In the Great War for Empire, Britain had stood alone with Prussia against the far more populous powers of Russia, Austria, and France, later joined by Spain. Victory had been secured because Frederick the Great's ruthlessly drilled army (supported by British pounds sterling) and William Pitt's brutally disciplined navy were the greatest military machines of the eighteenth century. The colonies, despite their substantial effort, had often performed abysmally in the war. Furthermore, in the 1760s and early 1770s, they were frequently fighting among themselves. Regulator movements tried to secure justice for the recently arrived backcountry settlers of the Carolinas.[31] What is

---

[30]Catherine Drinker Bowen, *Miracle at Philadelphia: The Story of the Constitutional Convention May to September 1787* (Boston: Little, Brown, 1966).

[31]George R. Adams, "The Carolina Regulators: A Note on Changing Interpretations," *North Carolina Historical Review*, 49 (1972), pp. 345–352; James P. Whittenburg, "Planters, Merchants, and Lawyers: Social Change and the Origins of the North Carolina Regulation," *William and Mary Quarterly*, 3d ser., 34 (1977), pp. 215–238; Richard Maxwell Brown, *The South Carolina Regulators* (Cambridge: Harvard University Press, 1963); Rachel H. Klein, "Ordering the Backcountry: The South Carolina Regulators," *William and Mary Quarterly*, 3d ser., 38 (1981), pp. 661–680.

now the state of Vermont was contested between New Yorkers and New Englanders.[32] Land rioters challenged proprietors in New Jersey and New York, where the British army had to defend the Livingston family's interests.[33] Pennsylvania and Connecticut settlers fought over the Wyoming Valley, in what is now northeastern Pennsylvania.[34] British soldiers, having saved the colonists from the French, had to fight the Cherokees in South Carolina and a confederation of Native Americans led by Pontiac to preserve even the prewar boundaries of the "victorious" colonists.[35]

The colonists, however, had advantages that only became apparent as the War for Independence progressed. Unsuited to protracted garrison duty or building roads and forts on the frontier, they were tenacious in defending their homes. It is a myth that the American Revolution was a guerrilla war, in which colonists hiding behind trees or in trenches fought Indian-style to pick off the foolish British who marched closely packed together in open fields. George Washington's Continental army trained, maneuvered, and engaged much as any contemporary European force. However, it was supplemented by the militia of the regions wherever British and Hessian troops appeared. Only serving for short periods like the men of eastern Massachusetts who turned out for Lexington and Concord, these "Minute Men"

[32]Chilton Williamson, *Vermont in Quandary, 1763–1825* (Montpelier: Vermont Historical Society, 1949); Michael A. Bellesiles, *Revolutionary Outlaws: Ethan Allen and the Struggle for Independence on the Early American Frontier* (Charlottesville: University of Virginia Press, 1993).

[33]Brendan McConville, *"Those Daring Disturbers of the Public Peace": Agrarian Unrest and the Struggle for Political Legitimacy in New Jersey, 1701–1776* (Ithaca: Cornell University Press, 1999); Thomas Humphrey, "Agrarian Rioting in Backcountry New York: Tenants, Landlords, and Revolution in the Hudson Valley, 1750–1800" (Ph.D. thesis, Northern Illinois University, 1996); see also their articles in the *McNeil Center Annual: Explorations in Early American Culture: A Supplement to Pennsylvania History,* 65 (1998); McConville, "Conflict and Change on a Cultural Frontier: The Rise of Magdalena Valleau, Land Rioter," pp. 120–138, and Humphrey, " 'Extravagant Claims' and 'Hard Labour': Perceptions of Property in the Hudson Valley, 1750–1790," pp. 139–164.

[34]Frederick J. Stefon, "The Wyoming Valley," in John B. Frantz and William Pencak, eds., *Beyond Philadelphia: The American Revolution in the Pennsylvania Hinterland* (University Park: Penn State Press, 1998), pp. 133–152.

[35]Lawerence Henry Gipson, *The British Empire Before the American Revolution* (Caldwell, Idaho: The Caxton Printers [vols. 1–3] and New York: Knopf [vols. 4–15], 1936–1965), 9: 55–87; Howard Peckham, *Pontiac and the Indian Uprising* (Princeton: Princeton University Press, 1947).

would indeed harass British columns and forts. The militiamen of northern New York and western New England, for instance, were critical in defeating General Burgoyne's 1777 invasion from Canada. They also ensured that the British, much like the Americans in the Vietnam War,[36] could only be secure in well-defended cities. For a good deal of the war, British control was confined to the area immediately around New York City, with briefer occupations of Boston, Newport, Philadelphia, Charleston, and Savannah.

Yet, for several reasons, the British had to establish effective control over much of the countryside or lose the war. First, nearly all Americans lived on farms or in small towns. Philadelphia with 40,000 inhabitants, New York with 20,000, and Boston with 15,000 were the largest communities in a new nation of some two million people. American forces and revolutionary governments could easily withdraw inland, where narrow river valleys such as the Schuylkill and the Hudson permitted the Americans to take impregnable positions at Valley Forge and West Point, effectively sealing off the interior. Second, Committees of Safety—a term later used in the French Revolution— and various legal or informal bodies effectively neutralized the numerous loyalists found throughout the colonies except in New England and Virginia.[37] Although the British organized loyalist regiments, including a band of African-American guerrillas in the New York City area who fought their former masters,[38] they were not able to effectively mobilize domestic supporters who may have numbered 20 percent of the population. Native Americans—who knew the British were their only defense against a rapidly expanding

[36]Piers Mackesy, "The Redcoat Revived," in Fowler and Coyle, eds., *The American Revolution,* pp. 169–188, thoughtfully compares the British failure in the Revolution with the American debacle in Vietnam.

[37]The best discussion of loyalists and estimates of their strength are by Robert M. Calhoon, *The Loyalists in Revolutionary America, 1760–1781* (New York: Harcourt Brace Jovanovich, 1973) and *idem. et al.,* eds., *The Loyalist Perception and Other Essays* (Columbia: University of South Carolina Press, 1989). See also Wallace Brown, *The King's Friends: The Composition and Motives of American Loyalist Claimants* (Providence: Brown University Press, 1965); *idem., The Good Americans: The Loyalists in the American Revolution* (New York: Morrow, 1969).

[38]Graham Russell Hodges, "Black Revolt in New York City and the Neutral Zone, 1775–1783," in Paul A. Gilje and William Pencak, eds., *New York in the Age of the Constitution* (Rutherford: Fairleigh Dickinson University Press, 1992), pp. 20–47.

frontier—were one example of distant loyalists who could only oc-casionally be united with a major British army.[39] (It is ironic that Indians and blacks, the people most in need of "life, liberty, and the pursuit of happiness" in colonial America, overwhelmingly supported the British.) Finally, the British—having brought thousands of troops to North America—were saddled with the women, servants, wagon drivers, and other people who accompanied them, and with large numbers of loyalist refugees; as a result, they had only two means to feed, clothe, and arm their forces. They usually attempted to buy or confiscate supplies in the countryside, but the redcoats frequently resorted to pillaging, thereby alienating the very people they had hoped to protect from what they considered a revolutionary minority (yet another similarity with the American experience in Vietnam).[40] Most British supplies had to be imported across the Atlantic Ocean at considerable risk and expense.[41]

The great cost of the war to Britain gave the Americans another advantage. As Britons' hopes of achieving the easy, inevitable victory foreseen at the outset faded (a further Vietnam parallel), they began to wonder whether conquering America was worth the price. What had started the quarrel in the first place was the Americans' refusal to pay taxes: the price of victory would exceed whatever taxes could be collected in the indefinite future. Opposition to the war developed both within and without Parliament, and acquired organized form through The Friends of America and The Society of the Supporters of the Bill of Rights.[42] In 1776, the year America declared independence from Britain, Adam Smith provided Britain with the reasoning that would enable it to accept the independence of America. In *The Wealth of Nations*, he argued that by ridding itself of the colonies:

[39]Colin G. Calloway, *The American Revolution in Indian Country* (Cambridge: Cambridge University Press, 1995); Sylvia R. Frey, *Water from the Rock: Black Resistance in the Revolutionary Age* (Princeton: Princeton University Press, 1991); Gary B. Nash, "The Forgotten Experience: Indians, Blacks, and the American Revolution," in Fowler and Coyle, eds., *The American Revolution*, pp. 27–46.

[40]Linda Grant DePauw, "Politicizing the Politically Inert: The Problem of Leadership in the American Revolution," in Fowler and Coyle, eds., *The American Revolution*, pp. 3–26.

[41]David Syrett, *Shipping and the American War: A Study in British Transport Organization* (London: Athlone Press of the University of London, 1970).

[42]Michael Durey, *Transatlantic Radicals and the American Revolution* (Lawrence: University of Kansas Press, 1997).

> Great Britain would not only be immediately freed from the whole
> annual expence of the peace establishment of the colonies, but might
> settle with them such a treaty of commerce as would effectually se-
> cure to her a free trade, more advantageous . . . than the monopoly
> she now enjoys. By thus parting good friends, the natural affection
> of the colonies to the mother country would quickly revive. It might
> dispose them . . . to favor us in war as well as in trade, and instead
> of turbulent and factious subjects, to become our most faithful, af-
> fectionate, and generous allies.[43]

Smith here offers a fairly accurate picture of Anglo-American relations
after the War of 1812. Colonies now cost more to defend and to
govern than they were worth. The real wealth of the British nation
lay in the demand America created, by earning money selling its food-
stuffs as freely as possible. As only Britain manufactured what America
needed, its trade and wealth would gravitate naturally toward the
Mother Country whether it retained political control of the colonies
or not.

As the war expanded throughout the world and seemed increasingly unwinnable, Smith's position, advocated by the opposition led
by the Earl of Shelburne and the Marquis of Rockingham, gained
ground. In 1782, following the news of Yorktown, Lord North received the only no-confidence vote of any British prime minister before the Reform Bill passed in 1832.[44] The new ministry approved a
peace treaty extremely favorable to the new United States, abandoning its Indian allies east of the Mississippi River so France or Spain
would not control the region.

Supporters of the Vietnam War have suggested that America
might have been able to win had we continued to fight and used all
the weapons at our disposal. The war ended not with a genuine defeat, they argue, but in a lack of willingness to pursue it caused by
dissension at home. The flaw with that position appears if we look at
the Revolution. After the Battle of Yorktown, the British Army in
New York was still formidable. But it was under orders not to fight

---

[43]Adam Smith, *An Inquiry into the Nature and Causes of the Wealth of Nations*,
ed. Edward Canaan (New York: The Modern Library, 1937), p. 582.

[44]Vincent T. Harlow, *The Founding of the Second British Empire, 1763–1793*
(London: Longmans, Green, 1952, 1964), vol. 1: pp. 203–210, 308–311.

unless attacked: at some point, the British, like the Americans in the 1970s, decided that whatever might be gained by victory was not worth the price in life and money or the risks entailed in expanding the scope of the war. Had the United States used atomic weapons in Southeast Asia, invaded North Vietnam or China, or attacked Russian convoys, the global implications would have been incalculable. The enemy could have also expanded the war as it saw fit. Similarly, beginning in 1780, The League of Armed Neutrality—which included Russia, Prussia, Austria, the Netherlands, and nearly every other maritime state in Europe—made it clear to the British that attacks on their ships would be considered declarations of war.[45] And by this time, Britain was fighting not only the United States but its ally France, and France's (although not America's) ally Spain. Just as Britain had intervened less than a century earlier against Louis XIV's France to preserve the European balance of power, the rest of Europe combined against a Britain whose global empire and superior economy made it far more powerful than any of its adversaries.[46]

Many Americans are familiar with the results of the French Alliance of 1778 on their own soil. Rochambeau's army and de Grasse's fleet were instrumental in bottling up Cornwallis at Yorktown and thus ending the war. French troops were also indispensable in besieging the British in New York during the last two years of the war: Washington's army was drifting away and a change of ministry (Shelburne only lasted until 1783), combined with weak American forces, might have renewed hostilities. Less familiar is that France's entry turned the American Revolution into a world war. Immediately, Britain dispatched half its forces in North America to the West Indies. These sugar islands were far more lucrative and important to Britain than its colonies on the mainland. War continued in the islands after Yorktown, successfully for the British, as Admiral Rodney decisively defeated de Grasse at the Battle of the Saints in 1782. A British garrison at Gibraltar withstood a combined French-Spanish siege for two years, ensuring Britain free access to its important Mediterranean and

[45]Samuel Flagg Bemis, *The Diplomacy of the American Revolution* (Bloomington: Indiana University Press, 1967), pp. 149 163.

[46]Ludwig Dehio, *The Precarious Balance: Four Centuries of the European Power Struggle* (New York: Knopf, 1962).

Middle Eastern trade. A French force tried unsuccessfully to reestablish a foothold in India. Perhaps most important of all, Britain had to hold many of its regiments and much of its navy in readiness at home, as France and Spain were building a second armada. Although never launched, it threatened to take the war to British territory, limited the forces available for America, and allowed John Paul Jones to raid the relatively undefended west coast of Britain with impunity.[47]

Yet allies did not win the war for the young United States. The Americans possessed substantial advantages of their own. First and foremost, there was George Washington. While making potentially fatal mistakes early in the war—such as dividing his army between New York and Brooklyn in 1776—Washington learned to preserve his army intact and block British advances into the interior even when he technically lost a battle. He was a master of the unexpected, as his victory at Trenton, his dispatch of Horatio Gates with part of his army to defeat Burgoyne at Saratoga, and his masquerading of his march to Yorktown as an attack on New York prove. He was also a superb administrator, functioning in effect as the new nation's nonelected chief executive. He advised Congress and the states on foreign and domestic policy, and the ever-vexatious problems of supplying and paying the army and enlisting troops. He commanded enough respect among his officers and men to keep the army together even when it was defeated and went unpaid for months at a time. And with the help of "Baron" von Steuben at Valley Forge, Washington molded the Continental Army into a well-drilled fighting force that could hold its own with the British regulars in a traditional open-field battle.[48]

Washington was also fortunate that none of his British counterparts measured up to the great generals, such as Marlborough, Wolfe, and Wellington, that Britain produced in its other eighteenth-century

---

[47]Piers Mackesy, *The War for America* (Cambridge: Harvard University Press, 1964), fully explains the world war.

[48]Good accounts of Washington's leadership are Marcus Cunliffe, *George Washington: Man and Monument* (New York: New American Library, 1960), and Don Higginbotham, *George Washington and the American Military Tradition* (Athens: University of Georgia Press, 1985).

wars. Sir William Howe, reluctant to risk his forces by leaving his urban supply bases at New York and Philadelphia, conceived his role as a diplomat as well as a military leader. He hoped that defeating the American army would cause the rebels to negotiate a peace.[49] His successor, Sir Henry Clinton, similarly feared to leave New York, abandoning Burgoyne's army at Saratoga and Cornwallis's at York-town to their fates. Burgoyne and Cornwallis, for their part, as if to overcompensate for their Commanders in Chief's timidity, boldly struck out into hostile country, where their forces were picked to pieces by regular troops who had joined local militia.[50]

But perhaps the greatest credit for victory goes to the rank-and-file American troops. Historian Charles Royster has effectively argued that they were motivated by a genuine patriotism and a desire to defend their homes against outsiders. If it was money they wanted, the British had pounds sterling rather than depreciated Continental paper dollars. If it was comfort, they could have joined the British in the cities instead of shivering with Washington in the mountains. The Continentals may have gone home on occasion, but they rarely deserted to the enemy. Even the men suffering on British prison ships in New York Harbor, when offered food, money, and a chance to escape the disease-infested hulks by switching sides, proved immune to these blandishments.[51]

To return to Levi Preston: the men in one army were fighting so they could govern themselves, the troops on the other side fought because they were sent to a foreign land to subdue people seeking independence. To draw a final analogy with Vietnam: in Southeast Asia our troops were a mixture of career soldiers and draftees, the modern counterparts of the eighteenth-century British army's officer class and enlisted men from the lower social classes (exactly six grad-

---

[49]Ira D. Gruber, *The Howe Brothers and the American Revolution* (Chapel Hill: University of North Carolina Press, 1972).

[50]See articles on all these generals in George A. Billias, ed., *George Washington's Opponents: British Generals and Admirals in the Revolutionary War* (New York: Morrow, 1969).

[51]Charles Royster, *A Revolutionary People at War: The Continental Army and the American Character, 1775–1783* (Chapel Hill: University of North Carolina Press, 1979), pp. 373–378; Robert Middlekauff, *The Glorious Cause: The American Revolution, 1763–1789* (New York: Oxford University Press, 1982), pp. 496–510.

uates of Princeton University died in Vietnam, all officers).[52] The Vietnamese had previously fought for independence against the French and, for hundreds of years, intermittently against the Chinese, and they would fight again until they had defeated our forces. The American colonists had expanded their territory in the face of French, Spanish, and Native American resistance for over a century before Britain sent forces to back them, and the new nation would successfully withstand new invasions in the War of 1812. If we wish to learn from history, we might compare the British Empire, the world's economic and military superpower for much of the eighteenth and nineteenth centuries, with the American New World Order of the post–Cold War era, and see that we too will have to decide under what circumstances the fruits of military intervention outweigh the price.[53]

—William Pencak

[52]Nearly all the major universities in the United States have "rolls of honor" that list graduates who died in various wars. The great number of elite men who enlisted and perished in World Wars I and II and the Civil War, although they could have evaded military service, contrasts vividly with the handful who fought and died in Vietnam.

[53]Paul M. Kennedy, in *The Rise and Fall of the Great Powers: Economic Change and Military Conflict from 1500 to 2000* (New York: Random House, 1987), sees a cyclical pattern in history. Nations such as sixteenth-century Spain and eighteenth-century Britain obtained great wealth through overseas expansion. They thus acquired both the desire and the means to protect their empires, and turned from economic into military powers. At some point, the cost of preserving worldwide empires while competing economically with nations that did not have that burden led to their decline. However, it is unwise to draw easy conclusions from Kennedy's sensible argument. The British Empire survived the American Revolution by over a century and a half, and in fact achieved its greatest extent in the nineteenth century. Similarly, an American economy being overtaken by Japan and Germany in the 1980s appears in 1998 to be in better shape despite its military commitments.

A NOTE TO THE READER

In addition to providing introductions to the first-person accounts in this book, the editor has included original narrative to connect the selections and offer critical commentary. A heavy line appears at the beginning and end of these sections, marking off the editor's words from those of the historical writers. Within the first-person accounts, of course, the editor's insertions appear in brackets.

I

TYRANNY

1

THE STAMP ACT

On June 2, 1763, a ball sailed through the air in front of Fort Mich-ilimackinac. After it darted scores of Indian warriors, shouting and cheering in the Ojibwa language; they crowded together, arms atan-gle, as they reached out with their long, netted lacrosse sticks.

A few British soldiers idled outside the gate among a number of Ojibwa women, watching the strange game and chatting amiably among themselves. They had good reason to be so relaxed: they were conquerors, recent victors in a global war with France that had raged for most of a decade. The prize had been France's North American colony of Canada, including the Great Lakes and the Ohio valley. This fort itself had been a strategic French outpost, located on the very tip of the Michigan peninsula where it controlled the channel between lakes Michigan and Huron. Now these British troops held its walls and (they thought) the thickly wooded wilderness beyond; and so they watched the indigenous lacrosse players with fatherly in-dulgence.

A stick leaped up and snared the ball; then a quick snap lofted it once more, right up to the gate of the fort, and the exuberant players converged on it like iron filings to a magnet. Amused, the soldiers watched as the Indians crowded around them, even into the fort itself. The British had little time to react as the warriors dropped their lacrosse sticks and pulled hatchets and knives out of the baskets car-ried by the women. In a few moments of brutal, efficient, intensely personal combat, the Ojibwa killed fifteen out of the thirty-five sol-diers in the garrison, and took the rest prisoner.

All across the Great Lakes and Ohio valley wilderness, Native American warriors swept over British posts. The offensive began on May 9 with an assault on Detroit by the Ottawa, led by the man known as Pontiac; this first attack was one of the few to fail, turning into a close and bitter siege. Almost everywhere else Indian forces triumphed: Fort Sandusky fell on May 16, St. Joseph on May 25, Miami on May 27, Ouiatenon on June 1, Green Bay on June 15, Venango on June 16, Le Boeuf on June 18. At the end of June, Seneca warriors combined with Huron, Ottawa, and Ojibwa war parties to surround and capture Fort Presqu'île, using trenches and other sophisticated European siege tactics.

That ball game at Michilimackinac, with its accompanying multitribal offensive, may be seen as the starting point of the long dispute between Britain and the American colonies—the dispute that would end in war and independence. Other events, it is true, might just as easily mark the beginning: the capture of the French city of Quebec in 1759; or the coronation of George III in 1760; or the passage of the Stamp Act five years later. But the Indian offensive will do nicely as the opening act in the great drama, because it forced the royal government to make systematic changes in its colonial policies— changes that would soon crystallize American resentment and resistance.

To understand why, it is necessary to go back even farther, to three years before the Indian attacks. Under the leadership of William Pitt, the ministry (as the parliamentary leadership, or government, was known) was waging a long but brilliantly successful struggle against France. To Europeans, the conflict would be known as the Seven Years War, for obvious reasons; to the American colonists, it was the French and Indian War.[1] In Boston, Albany, Philadelphia, and Williamsburg the war was seen as the final showdown with New France (as Paris's colony of Canada was called), as well as with France's many Indian allies; in London, it looked like a single worldwide struggle between the two great empires. With fighting raging in Europe and India, Pitt boldly decided to stake everything on a victory in North America. After much hard fighting, the French surrendered their last Canadian stronghold in 1760, even as George III ascended the throne.

After the conquest of New France, Pitt hungered for more victories—but the new king had other ideas. George III was an unusual

[1]See *The Colonizers*, the previous volume in the *In Their Own Words* series, for an account of the French and Indian War.

monarch. He was the grandson of his predecessor, George II, and during his childhood he naturally expected to succeed his father, Frederick, the Prince of Wales. With kingship seemingly far over the horizon, he had led a somewhat isolated life—until Frederick suddenly died in 1751 at the age of thirty-nine, thrusting the awkward youth into the unlooked-for role of heir. His mother, however, continued to shield him, placing him in the care of an overbearing tutor named John Stuart, the Earl of Bute. A complex, intelligent, but brittle Scotsman, Bute imparted to the young prince a vision of becoming an enlightened king who would rise above the personal and party disputes that racked the House of Commons.

As noble as this ideal might have seemed, it made George particularly ill prepared for the messy reality of British politics. Parliament stood ascendant in the country's mixed form of government—it had been since the Glorious Revolution of 1688, when it had helped oust the absolutist King James II. The monarchy, while still quite powerful, had no choice but to cooperate with the House of Commons, a chamber riddled with factional infighting.

And to cooperate meant to manipulate. Parliament in the late 1700s was no model of democracy: the great aristocratic families filled the House of Lords, while the Commons, the more important chamber, was elected by a narrow segment of landowners. A number of electoral districts, known as pocket boroughs, had only a handful of electors, or none at all, allowing certain families to pass down seats from generation to generation. And members of the Commons hungered after prestigious and lucrative government offices, pensions, and military commissions; the ministry relied on a lavish distribution of gifts to control their votes.

So when the twenty-two-year-old George III received the crown in 1760, his rigid principles about public service gave him little traction in the slippery world of Westminster, where Parliament sat. As king, he was able to press for peace, push Pitt out, and insert Bute as his first minister; but his boyhood tutor had no political base whatsoever. Nor did the king and his confidant wish to stoop to the petty corruption needed to drag the Commons behind them. Fortunately for Britain, Pitt secured a profitable peace before he left office in

1762, forging a treaty with France that was formally signed and sealed the next year.

Bute came to power with peace in hand, but the burdens of war on his back. In the remote wilds of North America, British troops took over French posts under the suspicious eyes of Native Americans. Along the eastern seaboard, colonial legislatures issued demands for reimbursement from London for heavy war expenses; the northern colonies in particular had spent vast sums raising their own regiments and building their own forts. But Bute's particular worry was the government's debt: at the end of the war, London owed more than £137 million. Interest alone equaled 60 percent of the peacetime budget.[2]

Then came the sweeping Native American offensive of 1763. It followed close on the heels of a costly war with the Cherokees to the south—but this new conflict proved far more humiliating to British arms, and far bloodier on American frontiers. Perhaps two thousand colonists died in attacks on settlements, as thousands of refugees fled into the colonial interior. Eventually the situation was reestablished, less by fighting than by patient diplomacy; despite some bitter skirmishing by columns of troops (including the infamous use of infected blankets to spread smallpox among the Indians), peace delegations did the real work.

The conquest of French North America, and the Indian war that followed, forced the British government to think systematically about its policies toward its American colonies. For a century and a half, London had largely coped with them on an ad hoc, one-by-one basis: in Connecticut and Rhode Island, corporate governments ruled, with elected governors; in Pennsylvania, Delaware, and Maryland, hereditary proprietors appointed the governors, who worked with elected assemblies; in the other colonies, chief executives named by the king shared power with small councils and elected legislatures. Britain's only uniform laws for America generally related to trade and

[2]Ian K. Steele, *Warpaths: Invasions of North America* (New York: Oxford University Press, 1994), p. 225. Massachusetts alone, Steele notes, spent £818,000 on the war, and received £352,000 in repayment from the British government. Steele also offers the most up-to-date discussion of the Indian war of 1763–1765, pp. 226–247.

other external matters. And except for the recently concluded war, London had never stationed troops there; the colonies themselves had paid for their own defense. But now Britain faced the task of controlling tens of thousands of conquered French Canadians—as well as dozens of Indian tribes that had just demonstrated their military power.

Bute faced two contradictory problems: to keep America at peace, and to reduce the overwhelming public debt. The answer to the first was obvious: he would station, for the first time, regular soldiers in North America. The idea pleased the king immensely. The long war with France had led to a dramatic expansion of the British army: ten new regiments had been raised, creating positions for influential gentry and aristocrats who fancied military titles and careers. George III wanted their continued political support (and the prestige of the larger force), which meant the army couldn't possibly shrink to its prewar level. The answer was to keep most of the regiments active and ship them across the Atlantic, where they could keep an eye on the Indians.

The ministry took one more step as well, something it had contemplated before the Indian attacks but now rushed into action. In October 1763, the king issued a proclamation banning any settlement by the colonists west of the Appalachian Mountains. Everything beyond the "proclamation line," as it was known, was reserved to Native Americans forever. The announcement was designed to reduce the chance of future wars (and it went far toward ending the war already raging). But it also proved to be one of the first government actions that aroused widespread resentment in the land-hungry colonies.

Bute (ground into uselessness by his Parliamentary enemies) had already left the office by the time George III signed the proclamation; in his place came George Grenville. An experienced politician and a member of Parliament since 1741, Grenville knew the world of committees, coalitions, and corruption, of income and interest payments. So as he grappled with the second—and larger—problem left by the war, he cast a grim and jaded eye over the empire's accounts, and soon discovered that the populous, prospering American colonies contributed virtually nothing.

It's not that mechanisms were lacking to collect money from these distant subjects of George III: there were potentially lucrative customs duties already in place, most notably the molasses tax. The Americans, however, circumvented the fees with rampant smuggling. They relied on thousands of miles of unguarded beaches and inlets; customs officials who rarely bothered to leave England; and a widespread system of bribery for those who did. But Grenville determined to shake things up with the Sugar Act, signed into law on April 5, 1764. He actually cut the molasses duty in half, to make it less onerous; but he also forced customs officials to go to America or quit, and he arranged for smuggling cases to be tried in admiralty courts (which lacked juries—American juries rarely convicted smugglers).

As far as Grenville was concerned, the Sugar Act merely sorted out the mess of customs collection; he expected a substantial rise in revenue, but to truly bury Britain's debt he conceived an entirely new tax. In March 1764, even before the Sugar Act became law, he casually mentioned that "it may be proper to charge certain Stamp Duties in the said Colonies and Plantations."[3]

In London, the colonial agents (lobbyists, essentially, hired by the colonial legislatures) reacted with alarm to Grenville's proposed stamp duty. They were already wary, thanks to the Sugar Act, which immediately proved to be immensely unpopular in America (where smuggling had come to be seen virtually as a basic right). Anger at the Sugar Act centered in the merchant community, but the law's provisions for nonjury trials had disturbed a much broader segment of the population. The stamp duty, however, looked like something far more dangerous: rather than merely levying fees on the colonies' external commerce, it imposed a direct tax on the population, without their direct assent.[4]

Rumors of the forthcoming tax worried well-connected Americans both at home and in London throughout the year. In early

[3]Quoted in Robert Middlekauff, *The Glorious Cause: The American Revolution, 1763–1789* (New York: Oxford University Press, 1982), p. 70. Middlekauff's excellent work offers a detailed account of the controversies over the Sugar Act and the Stamp Act.

[4]The tax was to apply to all official documents, including wills and deeds. The plan was for certain local officials to collect the duty and distribute the stamp that indicated that the tax had been paid.

1765, four leading colonial agents (including Benjamin Franklin) met with Grenville to convince him to abandon the idea. The king's first minister dismissed their objections with scarcely a thought. The immense public debt had been incurred to protect the colonies, he reasoned; the continuing military expense had the same purpose; surely the king's American subjects could contribute something toward their own safety. And as far as he was concerned, the colonies were as much a part of the kingdom as Cornwall—they might not send representatives directly to Parliament, but they were "virtually" represented there.

On February 6, 1765, the House of Commons met to discuss the proposed stamp tax. Charles Townshend summed up the government's case: "And now will these Americans, children planted by our care, nourished up by our indulgence until they are grown to a degree of strength and opulence, and protected by our arms, will they grudge to contribute their mite to relieve us from the heavy weight of the burden which we lie under?" He spoke for the majority of the house: protests against taxing the unrepresented colonists were brushed aside. On March 22 the Stamp Act landed on the king's desk, and he promptly signed it into law.

Perhaps three weeks later, news of the Stamp Act crossed the Atlantic. There it came to the attention of a middle-aged, failed tradesman named Samuel Adams. It would be safe to say that the forty-two-year-old Bostonian was cantankerous, if not downright belligerent: when his many creditors tried to foreclose on his estate, he showed up at the sheriff's auction and intimidated all concerned with his fierce and believable threats. Then he did it again. And again. And again. After four attempts to collect their debts, his creditors gave up.

Adams was inept with accounts. After failing repeatedly in business, he won election to the office of tax collector for Boston, which he quickly ran into the ground. In 1765, the year of the Stamp Act, he left the post to serve in the colonial legislature, leaving behind a balance sheet that showed £8,000 unaccounted for. The town, like everyone else, gave up any effort to collect. But Samuel Adams had other talents: he boasted an excellent education (Harvard College, Class of '40), and a pen as sharp as his tongue. A passion for politics had been bubbling inside him for years; it now boiled over, thanks to this news from London.

Samuel Adams, and Boston, did *not* take the lead in America's response to the Stamp Act. That chore fell to Virginia's Patrick Henry and that colony's elected House of Burgesses; and they executed the task to Adams's admiration. It was rather remarkable that Virginia assumed this role; until that time, the American colonies had no common identity, no common institutions (apart from the post office), and little trade with each other. The plantation culture of this Southern, tobacco-growing province, with its thousands of slaves and rich Anglican landowners, differed dramatically from Congregationalist Massachusetts, with its farmers, merchants, fishermen, and other middling sorts. But the Stamp Act was so alien to American sensibilities, and so universal in its effect, that it caused an immediate polarization, pitting all the colonies against the government in London.

On May 31, 1765, the House of Burgesses passed the Virginia Resolves, which crystallized the American case against the Stamp Act. Copies of the declaration swiftly filtered through every other colony. In distant Massachusetts, a small group of men soon formed an organization to follow where Virginia had led. They called themselves the Loyal Nine—a name they soon dropped in favor of something more resonant: the Sons of Liberty. Samuel Adams certainly met with the group and took part in its activities, though he was probably not one of its initial members.

Early on August 14, the Sons of Liberty went to a tree in Boston and hung an effigy of the local stamp distributor (the official responsible for collecting the tax). That night, a mob carried the effigy to the man's home, which the angry public ransacked. When they finally cornered him, he quickly agreed to step down. Not quite two weeks later, they attacked the home of Thomas Hutchinson—a prominent politician known to favor the Stamp Act—and methodically destroyed it.

Similar scenes erupted all along the Atlantic coast. From New Hampshire to Georgia (the newest and most conservative of the colonies), stamp distributors resigned under threat of imminent harm, perhaps even death. Mobs filled the streets, packed with Americans from all levels of society. In October, a Stamp Act Congress gathered in the city of New York, bringing together representatives of nine colonies; it passed resolutions and petitions to the king that echoed those issued by virtually all the colonial legislatures. The British government had accomplished something the French and Indians had never been able to achieve: they had given the Americans unity, identity, a common cause.

Why were the Americans so upset? The English asked themselves this very question; it seemed to them as if (as Charles Townshend had said) "they grudge to contribute their mite" to the government that ruled over them all—to the nation they belonged to. But to the colonists, the Stamp Act was not a question of money. Rather, they saw it as a threat to their fundamental rights as British subjects.

As the tumultuous year wound down to a close, Samuel Adams wrote a letter to a friend in England that pleaded the American case. Written with Adams's characteristic passion and eloquence, it offers a more personal expression of the colonial view than any formal resolve or petition. It reveals how the Americans came to define themselves as Americans, and not as New Yorkers, Virginians, or Carolinians, as they had for so long; how they understood the (unwritten) British constitution, and their rights under it; and how Adams himself began his long, personal journey toward a career as a revolutionary.

The Unhappy Controversy
by Samuel Adams

TO JOHN SMITH   DECEMBER 19, 1765

I should have taken the liberty of writing to you by vessels which have already sailed, had I known your intention to spend the winter in England. Your acquaintance with this country . . . makes you an able advocate on her behalf, at a time when her friends have everything to fear for her.

Perhaps there was never a time when she stood in greater need of friends in England, & had less reason to expect them: not because

she has forfeited them but from the nature of the unhappy controversy, which has of late arisen between Great Britain & her colonies,
while the prosperity of both depends on mutual affection & harmony.

The nation [Britain], it seems, groaning under the pressure of a
very heavy debt, has thought it reasonable & just that the colonies
should bear a part; and over & above the tribute which they have been
continually pouring into her lap, in the course of their trade, she now
demands an internal tax. The colonists complain that this is both bur-
densome & unconstitutional. They allege, that while the nation has
been contracting this debt solely for her own interest, detached from
theirs, *they* have [been] subduing & settling an uncultivated wilderness, & thereby increasing her power & wealth at their own expense,
which is eminently true with regard to New England.

This must certainly be esteemed of very great weight in point of
equity; for it has always been usual for mother states to put themselves
to great expense in settling their colonies, expecting to reap the advantage of it in the extent of trade & empire. But Britain reaps all
this advantage without any expense of her own & solely at theirs.

But it is said that this tax is to discharge the colonies' proportion
of expense in carrying on the [French and Indian] war in America,
which was for their defense. To this it is said, that it does by no means
appear that the war in America was carried on solely for the defense
of the colonies. Had the nation been only on the defensive here, a
much less expense would have been sufficient; there was evidently a
view of making conquests, & by means thereof establishing an advantageous peace for the nation, or perhaps advancing her dominion
& glory. But admitting that the whole expense was necessary (barely)
for the defense of the colonies, they [the colonists] say they have
already born their full share in the aids they afforded for the common
cause, & even much beyond in their ability—which the Parliament
seem to have been sensible of, when they made us reimbursements
from year to year, to relieve us from the burden under which we must
otherwise have sunk.

But is there no credit to be given to the New England colonies
who not only purchased these territories of the [Indian] nations &
settled them, but have also defended & maintained them for more
than a century past, against the encroachments or rather incursions

of those warlike savages, with a bravery & fortitude scarcely to be equaled, & without a farthing's expense to the nation? Besides which they have always readily joined their forces, when any attempts have been made by the government at home [in England], in former wars, against His Majesty's enemies in this part of the world. . . .

But there are other things which perhaps were not considered when the nation determined this to be a proportionate tax upon the colonies. . . . The nation constantly regulates their [the colonies'] trade, & lays it under what restrictions she pleases. The duties upon the goods imported from her & consumed here, together with those which are laid upon almost every branch of our trade all which center in dry cash in her coffers, amount to a very great sum. The moneys drawn from us in the way of actual direct tax, by means of these regulations, it is thought will very soon put an end in a great measure to trade. . . . [5] The Stamp Duty, if the act should be enforced, will probably in two or three years take off the whole of their remaining cash, and leave them none to carry on any trade at all. . . .

But there is another consideration which makes the Stamp Act obnoxious to the people here, & that is, that it totally annihilates, as they apprehend, their essential rights as Englishmen. The first settlers of New England were very cruelly persecuted in their native country at a time when the nation was infatuated with bigotry, & in consequence the public religion reduced to mere form & ceremony.[6] This induced them to cross an untried ocean & take shelter in this dreary wilderness. Immediately after their arrival here they solemnly recognized their allegiance to their sovereign in England, & the Crown graciously acknowledged them, granted them charter privileges, & declared them & their heirs forever entitled to all the liberties & immunities of free & natural born subjects of the realm. The other colonies are by charter or other royal institution thus acknowledged. . . .

[5]This passage is a reference to the Sugar Act, which sparked noisy protests in Boston and other major seaports. Adams's complaints about the customs duties possibly ending overseas trade seem exaggerated, but they reflect the fact that an economic depression had set in following the war.

[6]Samuel Adams was a devout Congregationalist, steeped in the traditions of his Puritan ancestors; he viewed the founding of Massachusetts as an act of the righteous, who fled from the persecution of a corrupt church in England.

To talk of British subjects free, & of other British subjects not so free, is absurd; they are all alike free. The British Constitution is founded in the principles of nature and reason—it admits of no more power over the subject than is necessary for the support of government which was originally designed for the preservation of the unalienable rights of nature. It engages to all men the full enjoyment of these rights, who take refuge in her bosom. . . .

The question then is, what the rights of free subjects of Britain are? Without entering into a nice disquisition of the full extent of these rights, which would require much greater ability than I have, it is sufficient for the present purpose to say, that the main pillars of the British Constitution are the right of representation & trial by juries, both of which the Colonists lose by this act. Their property may be tried at the option of informers, the most detestable set of men, in a court of Admiralty, where there is no jury, & which courts to say no more of them, have been little reverenced by his Majesty's good subjects in America.

Great pains have been taken by party writers in England . . . to have it understood that we are represented in Parliament, but I trust to little purpose. No man of common sense can easily be made to believe that the colonies all together have one representative in the House of Commons, upon their *own free election*. I am sure this province never returned a single member. If the colonists are free subjects of Britain, which no one denies, it should seem that the Parliament cannot tax them consistent with the Constitution, because they are not represented—& indeed it does not appear to me practicable for them to be represented there.

———

"THE BRITISH CONSTITUTION is founded in the principles of nature and reason," Adams stated: clearly he had no thought of independence when he wrote those words. Less than a decade later, he would deservedly win a reputation as the most radical of revolutionaries; if this man gloried in his status as a British subject in 1765, then certainly most other Americans did as well.

Indeed, the arguments against the Stamp Act were rooted in the colonists' very Englishness. They took pride in what they saw as the greatness of the British constitution, and they were appalled to see their constitutional rights violated. They also drew on a deeper English legacy of dissent and protest. The Puritans who settled in Massachusetts and Connecticut had been involved in the greatest protest of all, the English Civil War of the 1640s, which climaxed in the execution of King Charles I. The next generation had feared and resented James II forty years later, and revolts in numerous colonies mirrored the Glorious Revolution in 1688. They rejoiced in the result of that great rebellion: the final ascendancy of the elected legislature. All of these very English traditions shaped the colonists' views. The rub came in the fact that they saw their own legislatures as equivalents to Parliament—a view that Parliament itself did not share.

Something more than constitutionalism, however, kept the Stamp Act crisis at the level of protest rather than rebellion. Britain—and, by extension, America—was still a hierarchical society. To countries ruled by absolute monarchs, such as France, Austria, Spain, and Prussia, teeming, commercial Britain looked more like a soiled democratic pit than a gleaming aristocratic pyramid; but the kingdom and its colonies remained a monarchical realm, with clear social strata defined largely by heredity. As historian Gordon Wood has shown, there was less distance from bottom to top in America, yet life there was still marked by deference to gentlemen "of quality," by vertical lines of obligation and respect, by reverence for the king. In 1765, the colonists were far from abandoning this traditional view of the world.

As the year ended and 1766 began, Americans eagerly awaited the results of their earnest petitions and angry protests. The crisis, now months old, continued to permeate public discussion and private thought. For most colonists, the crisis was a dramatic experience, a series of raw events: the secret meetings, the erection of symbolic poles or "liberty trees," the swelling excitement felt by the men and women who marched in crowds, shouting with one voice. Personal habits changed, as many of the three million Americans refused to buy British goods. They were a people who avidly participated in politics and government—and in this moment, politics absorbed them utterly.

For a taste of the flavor of those expectant, fearful days, no better source can be found than the famous diary of Samuel Adams's famous cousin, John Adams. He was thirty years old as 1766 began, ten years out of Harvard College and seven years into his law practice in the town of Braintree, Massachusetts. As full of fire as his older cousin, John hungered for reputation and respectability—and he would achieve both sooner than he thought, as the controversy with Britain continued to grow. Indeed, in 1765 he had already won attention by drawing up Braintree's instructions to its delegate to the legislature on how to oppose the Stamp Act; the same year he published an account of how liberty had been threatened by tyranny throughout history.

The following passage traces two weeks in John Adams's life, as the Stamp Act crisis neared its conclusion. It reveals interesting details of the daily rhythms of existence in colonial Massachusetts, and shows how the people gathered to debate the events of the day. Most important, it gives us critical insight into the mind of a politically active American, and into the minds of his compatriots, as they took to heart the issues of the moment. The level of personal involvement (and social unity) witnessed here would prove a critical ingredient in years to come, as future crises deepened the rift between Britain and her colonies.

This Year Brings Ruin or Salvation
by John Adams

JANUARY 1, 1766. WEDNESDAY. Severe cold, and a prospect of snow. We are now upon the beginning of a year of greater expectation than any that has passed before it. This year brings ruin or salvation to the British colonies. The eyes of all America are fixed on the British Parliament. In short, Britain and America are staring at each other; and they will probably stare more and more for some time.

At home all day. Mr. Joshua Hayward, Jr., dined with me; town politics the subject. Doctor Tufts here in the afternoon; American politics the subject. Read in the evening a letter from Mr. Deberdt, our present agent [from the colony to the British government], to

Lord Dartmouth, in which he considers three questions: 1. Whether in equity or policy America ought to refund any part of the expense of driving away the French in the last war? 2. Whether it is necessary for the defense of the British plantations [colonies] to keep up an army here? 3. Whether in equity the Parliament can tax us? Each of which he discusses like a man of sense, integrity, and humanity, well informed in the nature of his subject.

In his examination of the last question, he goes upon the principle of the Ipswich instructions,[7] namely, that the first settlers of America were driven by oppression from the realm, and so dismembered from the dominions, till at last they offered to make a contract with the nation, or the Crown, and to become subject to the Crown upon certain conditions, which contract, subordination, and conditions were wrought into their charters, which gave them a right to tax themselves. This is a principle which has been advanced long ago. . . .

And, indeed, it appears from Hutchinson's History and the Massachusetts Records, that the colonies were considered formerly, both here and at home, as allies rather than subjects. The first settlement, certainly, was not a national act; that is, not an act of the people nor the Parliament. Nor was it a national expense; neither the people of England nor their representatives contributed anything towards it. Nor was the settlement made on a territory belonging to the people nor the Crown of England. . . .

It is said at New York, that private letters inform [that] the great men are exceedingly irritated at the tumults in America, and are determined to enforce the [Stamp] act. This irritable race, however, will have [need] good luck to enforce it. They will find it a more obstinate war than the conquest of Canada and Louisiana.

JANUARY 2. THURSDAY. A great storm of snow last night; weather tempestuous all day. Waddled through the snow driving my cattle to water at Doctor Savil's; a fine piece of glowing exercise. Brother spent the evening here in cheerful chat.

At Philadelphia, the Heart-and-Hand Fire Company has expelled

---

[7]A reference to the instructions given by the town of Ipswich to its representative, Dr. John Calef, on October 2, 1765. These instructions formulated a basic argument about the colonies' virtually coequal relationship with Britain.

Mr. Hughes, the stamp man for that colony. The freemen of Talbot county, in Maryland, have erected a gibbet before the door of the court-house, twenty feet high, and have hanged on it the effigies of a stamp informer in chains, *in terrorem* till the Stamp Act shall be repealed; and have resolved, unanimously, to hold in utter contempt and abhorrence every stamp officer, and every favorer of the Stamp Act, and to "have no communication with any such persons, not even to speak to him, unless to upbraid him with his baseness."

So triumphant is the spirit of liberty everywhere. Such a union was never before known in America. In the wars that have been with the French and Indians a union could never be effected. . . .

JANUARY 10. FRIDAY. Went in the afternoon, with my wife, to her grandfather's. Mr. Cleverly here in the evening. He says he is not so clear as he was that the Parliament has a right to tax us; he rather thinks it has not. Thus the contagion of the times has caught even that bigot to passive obedience and non-resistance; it has made him waver. It is almost the first time I ever knew him converted, or even brought to doubt and hesitate about any of his favorite points— as the authority of Parliament to tax us was one. Nay, he used to assert positively that the king was as absolute in his plantations as the Great Turk in his dominions.

Mr. Quincy gave me some anecdotes about John Boylston and Jo. Green, &c. Green refused to sign the resolutions of merchants at first, but was afterwards glad to send for the paper. They were at first afraid of Salem, Newbury, Marblehead, and Plymouth, but these towns have agreed unanimously with the same resolutions.

What will they say in England, when they see the resolves of the American legislatures, the petitions from the united colonies, the resolutions of the merchants in Boston, New York, Philadelphia, &c.?

JANUARY 13. MONDAY. At Boston. . . . Dined at brother Dudley's, with Gridley, Swift, Lowell, and Mr. Fayerweather. Fayerweather is one of the genteel folks; he said he was dressed in black as mourning for the Duke of Cumberland; he said he was wearing out his black clothes as fast as he could, and was determined to get no more till the Stamp Act was repealed. He designed to wear out all his old clothes and then go upon our own manufactures, unless the Stamp Act was repealed. . . .

JANUARY 15. WEDNESDAY. Dined at Mr. Isaac Smith's—no company, no conversation. Spent the evening with the Sons of Liberty, at their own apartment in Hanover Square near the tree of liberty. It is a counting-room in Chase and Speakman's distillery; a very small room it is.

John Avery, distiller or merchant, of a liberal education; John Smith, the brazier; Thomas Crafts, the painter; Edes, the printer; Stephen Cleverly, the brazier; Chase, the distiller; Joseph Field, master of a vessel; Henry Bass; George Trott, jeweler, were present. I was invited by Crafts and Trott to go and spend an evening with them and some others. Avery was mentioned to me as one. I went, and was very civilly and respectfully treated by all present. We had punch, wine, pipes and tobacco, biscuit and cheese, &c.

I heard nothing but such conversation as passes at all clubs, among gentlemen, about the times. No plots, no machinations. They chose a committee to make preparations for grand rejoicings upon the arrival of the news of a repeal of the Stamp Act, and I heard afterwards they are to have such illuminations, bonfires, pyramids, obelisks, such grand exhibitions and such fireworks as were never before seen in America. I wish they may not be disappointed.

EVEN AS ADAMS wrote in his diary, outrage flowed through Parliament. The reaction in America looked like outright rebellion, pure and simple: the king's stamp distributors threatened, a tax rendered inoperative by mob action, a continentwide refusal to abide by laws passed according to constitutional form. George Grenville was most outraged of all—but he was no longer the first minister. Thanks to a personal dispute with the king, he had been replaced by Lord Rockingham (as Charles Watson-Wentworth, Second Marquess of Rockingham, was known). Nevertheless, Grenville kept a seat in the House of Commons, which he used to publicly berate the government for failing to suppress the anarchy in America.

Rockingham no doubt disliked the resistance to the stamp duty just as much as his predecessor, but he now had the troublesome task of actually governing the empire. The simple fact was, Americans were no longer buying British goods, causing an economic catastrophe.

English merchants could not be bothered with constitutional arguments when faced with ledgers of unpaid debts and warehouses of unsold products. They made sure that Rockingham felt their pain, as they demanded the repeal of the nettlesome Stamp Act.

On March 17, 1766, George III signed a repeal of the act, ending the great crisis. It had not been easy for Rockingham to push the legislation through Parliament, or past the king; both were outraged by Americans' claims that Britain's legislature had no authority over the colonies. To secure the repeal, he had relied on the volumes of protests by British merchants as evidence of the real harm caused by the controversial law.

Rockingham did, however, soften the blow with a second piece of legislation. To make clear that the Stamp Act repeal was a purely practical measure—that the British government, and people, refused to accept the Americans' constitutional arguments—the ministry prepared a document known as the Declaratory Act. It easily won passage in both houses, as well as George III's signature, for it voiced the sentiments of all but a noisy handful. The Declaratory Act stated that the laws passed by the Parliament in London were binding on all the king's subjects, in all cases whatsoever. It was, in short, a flat rejection of Americans' most deeply held beliefs about their rights under the British constitution.

John Adams and the Sons of Liberty would have their celebration, but the unhappy controversy was far from over.

2

THE INTOLERABLE

Revolutions often begin with backward glances. A conservative impulse most often moves the mass of humankind—a fear of change, a dread that what little one has will soon be taken away. Rarely have governments been overturned by a bold vision of the future; rather, popular radicalism often rises from the churning tide of events. A ruler's initiative prompts a protest; a protest sparks repression; repression stirs resistance; and on and on in a cycle of polarization, anger, and revolt. Never has this process been more clear than in the American Revolution.

From the start of the Stamp Act crisis to the outbreak of actual war ten years later, Americans believed that they were fighting to assert their ancient rights—to stop successive British ministries from overturning a long-established constitutional balance. When they learned the news of the Stamp Act's repeal, they poured into the streets, celebrating in mass demonstrations up and down the continent. It seemed as if their point had been made—the world had returned to the way it was. If George III's government had only left things undisturbed—if it had realized that taxing the colonists was more trouble than it was worth—it is likely that Samuel Adams, John Adams, and the other Founders would have continued their obscure careers in local politics, law, and trade.

But Parliament had conceded nothing: in the Declaratory Act it asserted the absolute right to make Americans pay taxes—indeed, to rule over them in all cases whatsoever. So the crisis would continue—but the furor over the Stamp Act had already changed the situation, ensuring that future conflicts would be even more intense. The colonists had felt unity for the first time; they had refined their arguments; they had tasted the exhilaration of popular defiance of authority; and they had honed methods for communicating and organizing across colonial boundaries that would serve them well in the years ahead. The Sons of Liberty—that small knot of men who organized the riots in Boston—gathered members throughout Massachusetts and in other colonies as well, becoming a major force in colonial politics.

Back in London, George III continued to churn through first ministers. William Pitt returned to power, but he soon endured a complete collapse of his health, leaving Charles Townshend (the Chancellor of the Exchequer, or finance minister) the de facto leader of the government. Townshend was an aristocrat, a witty man experienced in government, but he still faced the same problems that had overwhelmed Bute, Grenville, and Rockingham: a heavy public debt, and the ongoing expense of stationing troops in North America. In January 1767, the army declared that it needed no less than £400,000 for its overseas regiments. To make matters worse, a coalition in Parliament pushed through a 25-percent reduction in the land tax (the government's main source of income, paid by the very landowners who filled both the House of Commons and the House of Lords).

Townshend wanted to avoid a crisis like the one that the unbending Grenville had set off with the Stamp Act, but he also needed the money that three million prosperous colonists could provide. At the same time, he yearned to strip the Americans of their power to protest—to force them to acknowledge the supremacy that Parliament had asserted in the Declaratory Act. From the perspective of almost everyone in London, from the most obscure member of the opposition in the Commons to the king himself, Parliament was the supreme authority for the entire British Empire. Townshend dreaded a humiliating repeat of the Stamp Act crisis, but he would never let go of that principle.

The Chancellor believed that he knew a path through this political thicket. As he understood the American protests of the previous two years, the colonists objected to *direct* taxes; they would accept duties on overseas trade. In the Revenue Act of 1767, the government imposed taxes on lead, glass, paper, painter's colors, and tea shipped to North America. Townshend sincerely believed that the Americans would accept the new duties; to effectively collect them, he created an American Board of Customs Commissioners, with its headquarters in the colonies.

He also secured the passage of a third measure as well, to assert Parliament's supremacy. Two years earlier, the Quartering Act had gone into effect, requiring the colonies to provide housing for British troops.[8] At the time, most of the army in America was fighting Indians or occupying forts in the wilderness. As the Stamp Act crisis erupted into mob violence, however, the military command moved a substantial body of men into settled districts to cope with the unrest; most of these soldiers arrived in New York. There the legislature refused to comply with the act.[9] So Parliament voted for the Suspending Act, stripping New York's assembly of its right to pass its own acts, from October 1, 1767, until it ended its defiance.

What Townshend failed to understand, when he crafted what would soon be known as the Townshend Acts, was that the key distinction to Americans was *not* between internal and external taxes. In the constitutional arguments developed through the Stamp Act controversy, they articulated a view that Parliament had no right to *raise money* from the colonists, whether through direct or indirect taxes; they accepted customs duties (indirect taxes) only as a measure to regulate trade. And Townshend made clear that his duties were designed purely to collect cash. Direct or indirect, this was still taxation without representation, at least in American eyes.

If Townshend had passed his duties a few years earlier they *might* have been grudgingly accepted in the colonies. But the crisis of 1765–1766 had heightened Americans' sensitivities, polished their thinking, strengthened their ability to resist. Even worse, he bundled them with measures that seemed explicitly threatening to colonial liberty and self-government: the formation of the Board of Customs Commis-

[8]The act did not provide for putting troops in private housing, but in barracks, taverns, and vacant buildings.

[9]The irony of this dispute is that New York's legislature was one of the most conservative of all the colonial assemblies. Unlike the other Northern colonies, New York had a large number of tenant farmers—whose landlords dominated the legislature. In that respect, New York and its assembly were not so different, socially, from the House of Commons; it even faced a revolt by tenant farmers in 1766. Yet such was the public feeling against the Stamp Act that it refused to abide by the Quartering Act.

sioners, and the suspension of the New York legislature. The first looked to Americans like a tyrannical institution designed to steal their property; the second, the indefensible destruction of one representative body by another. None of the colonists had voted for a member of Parliament—so they refused to accept its right to suspend one of their assemblies.

Resistance to the Townshend Acts began with the publication of *Letters from a Pennsylvania Farmer* by John Dickinson. Dickinson was no radical: his calmly stated arguments both crystallized the opposition to the acts and reflected the mainstream of American thought. The *Boston Gazette* chimed in with a specific means of fighting the new duties: nonimportation of British goods. Economic pressure had worked against the Stamp Act—surely it would work against a tax that applied specifically to imports. The newspaper's slogan: "Save your money, and save your country." On November 5 (Guy Fawkes Day, a traditional time of public carousing), the customs commissioners arrived in Boston; a crowd greeted them with effigies labeled "Devils, Popes, & Pretenders," while they wore signs declaring "Liberty & Property & no Commissioners."

In 1768, the assemblies took a hand in the controversy. In Massachusetts, Samuel Adams coauthored a circular letter to the other colonies, calling for coordinated action (meaning continent-wide nonimportation). In Virginia, the House of Burgesses asserted its equality, as a legislature, to Parliament; it joined in the call for united action against any steps taken by the ministry in London that "have an immediate tendency to enslave them."

In Boston, attempts by the customs commissioners to enforce the law led to repeated run-ins with John Hancock, one of the wealthiest merchants in America and a vocal opponent of the Townshend Acts. In June, a massive crowd composed of "sturdy boys and Negroes," according to one official, as well as gentlemen, fought a pitched battle against sailors of the Royal Navy as they tried to impound the aptly named *Liberty*, one of Hancock's ships.[10] The Sons of Liberty effectively took control of the town, as the customs commissioners dis-

[10]Quotes in this and the previous paragraphs appear in Middlekauff, pp. 155, 157, 161, and 167.

patched a desperate request for troops. On October 1, 1768, soldiers of the 14th and 19th Regiments marched off transports onto the wharves of Boston Harbor.

As British troops occupied the capital of Massachusetts, a wave of patriotism swept over the colonies. Indeed, the remarkable thing is that the colonists now began to think of their resistance to the British government *as* patriotism—that their "country" comprised the thirteen colonies. Such feelings should not be exaggerated into a desire for independence; but clearly colonists of all stripes felt they were defending a common set of liberties against the aggressions of the ministry. Nonimportation emerged as an article of faith; Americans made tremendous efforts to manufacture what they needed, rather than buy from the British.

Wherever troops went among the population, tension followed. In New York, the local Sons of Liberty gained strength when the legislature voted to comply with the Quartering Act. The army became a constant presence in the city; occasional brawls erupted, especially when the soldiers cut down the liberty tree (actually a pine pole) that the Sons repeatedly erected in the public commons. The Sons urged the local population to stop providing jobs to off-duty members of the poorly paid garrison; the troops responded with insults and provocations of their own. In January 1770, a riot between the soldiers and a few thousand New Yorkers resulted in one death and scores of other casualties.

The atmosphere in Boston was even worse; historian Robert Middlekauff describes it as "poisonous." Insults and street fights marked the garrison's days; frequently the troops found themselves in local courts for offenses both real and imagined. The pressure began to rise toward an explosion on March 2, 1770, when an off-duty soldier went to a ropemaker's shop, looking for a job; the tradesman offered to let him "clean my shithouse."[11] The predictable result: a series of brawls between friends of the two men, extending over the next two days.

On the brisk, snowy evening of March 5, 1770, a British sentinel, Private Hugh White, found himself under siege by an angry group

[11]Quoted in Middlekauff, p. 203.

of Bostonians. He had struck a local man for insulting an officer of his regiment, and now he faced a barrage of snowballs and chunks of ice. Word of the skirmish flew down the streets, and the crowd rapidly swelled. At nine o'clock, Captain Thomas Preston decided to rescue White with a party of seven men. What followed was a tragedy, forever remembered as the Boston Massacre.

For the events of March 5, Captain Preston and his men would stand trial in the courts of Massachusetts. Their defending attorney was John Adams, "full of honest conviction that every Englishman deserved a fair trial, not to mention self-righteous satisfaction at taking on an unpopular case."[12] Adams did an excellent job: all but two of Preston's detachment were found innocent of any wrongdoing.

The verdict outraged the people of Boston. They saw the Massacre as more than an act of violence—it was the culmination of a conspiracy to deprive the colonists of their most sacred rights. But a better description of the Massacre, the trial, and the meaning of these events can be found in the works of Samuel Adams, John's radical older cousin. In the space of five years, Samuel had come far from his temperate protests against the Stamp Act: he had been radicalized, and he now employed his prodigious skills to radicalize others. His own account of these events (written for publication after the verdict was delivered) reveals both the direction of his thinking, and his effectiveness in arousing public fury.

The Boston Massacre
by Samuel Adams

As the lives of five of his Majesty's subjects were *unfairly* lost on the evening of the 5th of March last [1770], it follows that some persons must have been in fault. The unhappy sufferers, for ought that has ever appeared, were in the peace of God and the King; let their memories, then, so far at least as respects this matter, remain unreproach'd. It appeared by the evidence in court, that all the prisoners were present in King Street; that they all discharg'd their muskets but one, and

[12]Middlekauff, p. 206.

his flash'd in the pan; and that the deceas'd were all kill'd by musket balls. Six of the prisoners were acquitted by the jury, and two found guilty of *manslaughter*.

In ordinary cases, the public ought to rest satisfied with the verdict of a jury; a method of trial, which an Englishman glories in as his greatest security. It is a method peculiar to the English; and as a great writer observes, has been a probable means of having supported their liberties thro' so many ages past. . . . I am not about to arraign the late jurors before the bar of the public: They are accountable to God and their own consciences, and in *their* day of trial, may God send them good deliverance. But in times when politics runs high, we find by the experience of past ages, it is difficult to ascertain the truth even in a court of law. At such times, witnesses will appear to contradict each other in the most essential points of fact; and a cool conscientious spectator is apt to shudder for fear of perjury. . . .

While the soldiers were passing from the main guard to the custom-house, it did not appear by any of the witnesses that they were molested by the people. . . . It is agreed by the witnesses for the prisoners, who mention'd their seeing the soldiers upon their first coming down, that they had loaded their guns, leveled them at the people, & began to insult & abuse them (as indeed they did upon their march) before any just provocation had been offer'd to them.

Mr. Hinckley saw the party come down—they loaded—push'd their bayonets and pricked the people. Mr. Wilkinson also saw the party come down; did not see anything thrown at them, tho' he stood at two or three yards distance. Mr. Murray said they came down and cried, "Make Way." Andrew declared, that the party planted themselves at the custom-house—the people gave three cheers—he heard one of the soldiers say, "Damn you stand back." One of them had like to have prick'd a man as he was passing by, and swore by God he would stab him. Several persons were talking with the captain, and a number pressing on to hear what they said; one of the persons talking with the officer said, "He is going to fire"; the people shouted and said, "He dare not fire." And *then they began* to throw snowballs.

Even by Andrew's account, the people were rather curious to know what the soldiers design'd to do, than intent upon doing them any hurt, until they were assaulted by them; which I am apt to think is true, because Newtown Prince, another Negro, of whom for my own part I conceive a better opinion of than Andrew, declared that the soldiers planted themselves in a circle—their guns breast high. And the people crowded on to speak with Capt. Preston—and further, several of the witnesses swore that they themselves talked with the Captain, and one of them caution'd him against firing. . . .

I shall now take notice of what the witnesses for the crown testified concerning the behavior of the soldiers, upon their first arrival at the custom-house. Mr. Austin saw the party come down; the captain was with them. McCauley, one of the prisoners, loaded his gun, push'd at him with his bayonet, and damn'd him. He did not observe the people press on. Mr. Bridgham declared, that about a dozen surrounded the soldiers and struck their guns with their sticks. But he also said that the soldiers were loading at the same time. He further added, that he did not apprehend himself or the soldiers in any danger by anything he saw; from whence it may be suppos'd, that as the people struck their guns only, when they might as easily have knocked them down, their intention was not to hurt them, but rather to prevent their loading. . . .

Mr. Bayley testified, that when the party came down, Carrol, one of the prisoners, *put his bayonet to his breast*. Mr. Wilkinson stood at about two yards distance from the soldiers all the while they were there—*he saw no ice nor snowballs thrown*; in which he agreed with Mr. Austin. Mr. Fosdick testified, that he *was push'd as the party came down*—that afterwards they wounded him in the breast—two different bayonets were thrust into his arm—*all this while there had been no blows that he saw*, nor did he know the cause of their firing. . . .

And by their testimonies the reader will judge, whether the soldiers had just provocation to fire upon the people; or whether they were in danger of their lives or had any reason to think they were. On the contrary, whether they did not themselves first assault the people as they were coming from the main guard; and afterwards, by leveling their guns loaded with ball in an exasperating manner at the people; pushing their bayonets at some of them, wounding others, and threatening all, even before any injury had been offer'd them. . . .

It is I believe the general opinion of judicious men, that *at present* there are good grounds to apprehend a settled design to enslave and ruin the colonies; and that some men of figure and station in America have adopted the plan, and would gladly lull the people to sleep, the easier to put it into execution. . . . The true patriot will constantly be jealous of those very men, knowing that power, especially in times of corruption, makes men wanton, that it intoxicates the mind. And unless those with whom it is entrusted are carefully watched, such is the weakness or the perverseness of human nature, they will be apt to domineer over the people, instead of governing them according to the known laws of the state, to which alone they have submitted. . . .

In the state of nature there was subordination. The weaker was *by force* made to bow down to the more powerful. This is still the unhappy lot of a great part of the world, under government. So among the brutal herd, the strongest horns are the strongest laws. Mankind have entered into political societies, rather for the sake of restoring *equality*; the want of which, in the state of nature, rendered existence uncomfortable and even dangerous.

I am not of leveling[13] principles; but I am apt to think, that constitution of civil government which admits equality in the most extensive degree, consistent with the true design of government, is the best.

———

CLEARLY SAMUEL ADAMS had gone beyond local politics when he wrote about the Massacre: the chain of provocations (as he saw them) by successive British ministries had led him to think, and write, about the nature of government itself. Like most prominent Americans, he was experienced in the reality of government, thanks to his public service; like most prominent Americans, he was also familiar with the major writings on the philosophy of government, by John Locke and others. Events drove him to examine not just how the colonies' rights were being violated, but why—what basic prin-

———

[13]"Leveling" was a pejorative term for a radical belief in complete social, economic, and political equality; the term had its origins in the Levellers, a group that briefly flourished in the English Civil War of the mid-1600s, until they were suppressed by Cromwell. Despite a strong belief in government by consent, pre-Revolutionary American society was strongly influenced by older, aristocratic values.

ciples were at stake, to bring on crisis after crisis. His thinking took
him in an increasingly republican direction, long before most colonists were ready to consider anything close to independence.

Meanwhile, the current crisis faded. No more violence followed
the Massacre. The latest leader of the British government, Lord Frederick North, repealed all the Townshend duties except for the one
on tea. Tempers on both sides of the Atlantic slowly cooled.

Samuel Adams, however, was not content. The ministry intended
to make royal officials—governors, justices, and others—independent
of colonial legislatures; the tax on tea was now used to pay their
salaries. As others settled into contentment, he saw this as another
sign of the "settled design to enslave and ruin the colonies." Most
alarming to him was the active participation in this "design" by local
officials—most notably Thomas Hutchinson, the old defender of the
Stamp Act who was now governor of Massachusetts. Bitter factional
disputes ran deep in the colony, but a long-standing hatred of Hutchinson now merged with distrust of London.

Adams convinced the town of Boston to form a committee of
correspondence, "to state the rights of the colonists and of this province in particular, as men, as Christians, and as subjects; to commu-
nicate and publish the same to the several towns in this province and
the World as the sense of this town, with the infringements and violations thereof that have been, or from time to time may be
made."[14] Boston's example was soon followed by half the towns in
Massachusetts, and committees of correspondence began to appear
elsewhere as well. Hutchinson's opposition to the committees heightened his unpopularity.

Then came another blow from across the Atlantic. The East India
Company had sunk into a dire financial condition; to rescue it, Parliament passed the Tea Act of 1773, giving the company a monopoly
on the export of tea to America. The colonists reacted with fury. To
have the British legislature deny American merchants access to the
tea trade seemed outrageous. Furthermore, the act rekindled opposition to the tax on tea. For three years after the repeal of the other
import duties, the colonists had chosen to ignore the one duty left;

[14]Quoted in Middlekauff, p. 216.

the Tea Act did nothing to change it. But Parliament's gift of a monopoly to the well-connected East India Company drew Americans' attention back to it, reminding them that Parliament still claimed the right to tax the colonies.

Under the leadership of Samuel Adams, the Boston committee of correspondence leaped into action. Eight years had passed since they first confronted the Stamp Act; five since the arrival of the customs commissioners; three since the Boston Massacre. Despite the turnover in Britain's Parliamentary leadership, it seemed that the successive ministries had one continuing goal: to force America to submit to the rule of a legislature they had not elected, in order, as Adams wrote, "to introduce arbitrary government and slavery." The committee quickly agreed with Adams's own summation of the sense of the town of Boston.

The Sense of the Town
by Samuel Adams

Whereas it appears by an Act of the British Parliament passed in the late sessions, that the East India Company are by the said Act allowed to export their teas into America, in such quantities as the Lord of the Treasury shall judge proper; and some people with an evil intent to amuse the People, and others thro' inattention to the true design of the Act, have so construed the same, as that the tribute of three pence on every pound of tea is not to be enacted by the detestable task master there—upon the due consideration thereof, *Resolved*, That the sense of the town cannot be better expressed on this occasion, than in the words of certain judicious resolves lately entered into by our worthy brethren the citizens of Philadelphia. Wherefore

Resolved, that the disposal of their own property is the inherent right of freemen; that there can be no property in that which another can of right take from us without our consent; that the claim of Parliament to tax America, is in other words a claim of right to lay contributions on us at pleasure—

2nd. That the duty imposed by Parliament upon tea landed in America is a tax on the Americans, or levying contributions on them without their consent—

3rd. That the express purpose for which the tax is levied on the Americans, namely for the support of government, the administration of justice, and the defense of His Majesty's dominions in America, has a direct tendency to render assemblies useless, and to introduce arbitrary government and slavery—

4th. That a virtuous and steady opposition to the ministerial plan of governing America is absolutely necessary to preserve even a shadow of liberty, and is a duty which every freeman in America owes to his country, to himself, and to his posterity—

5th. That the resolutions lately come by the East India Company, to send out their teas to America subject to the payment of duties on its being landed here, is an open attempt to enforce the ministerial plan, and a violent attack upon the liberties of America—

6th. That it is the duty of every American to oppose this attempt—

7th. That whoever shall directly or indirectly countenance this attempt, or in any wise aid or abet in the unloading, receiving, or vending of the tea sent or to be sent out by the East India Company while it remains subject to the payment of a duty here is an enemy to America—

8th. That a committee be immediately chosen to wait on those gentlemen who, it is reported, are appointed by the East India Company to receive and sell said tea, and to request them from a regard to their own characters and the peace and good order of this town and province immediately to resign their appointment.

ON NOVEMBER 28, 1773, the *Dartmouth* arrived in Boston with the first load of East India Company tea. Elsewhere in America, in Philadelphia and New York, local Sons of Liberty organizations had successfully threatened company agents who intended to receive the tea; in Charleston, South Carolina, the tea was landed but never sold. But in Boston, Governor Hutchinson convinced the consignee to accept his shipment. At least 5,000 people gathered at the Old South

Meeting House on November 29, 30, and December 14, demanding that the tea go back to England. Hutchinson refused to allow the ship to leave.

On the evening of December 16, 1773, a crowd of people filled the Boston waterfront. Fifty men, dressed in Indian costumes, boarded the ships containing tea and dumped the hated cargo into the harbor waters. They harmed nothing else. The raiders destroyed at least 90,000 pounds of tea—£10,000 worth—in one night's work. The famous Boston Tea Party was over.

Once again, the diary of John Adams offers a glimpse of the day's events, as they played out in the daily lives and conversations of the colonists. The brief selection below comes from the months following the Boston Tea Party, as the resistance continued—and as the force of Parliament's reaction began to be felt. Adams (by now a member of the colony's legislature) and his fellows thought themselves to be at the forefront of a great fight—one in which their local political enemies (Governor Hutchinson and his circle) were indistinguishable from their opponents in London.

After the Party
by John Adams

MARCH 5, 1774. SATURDAY. Heard the oration, pronounced by Colonel [John] Hancock, in commemoration of the massacre. An elegant, a pathetic, a spirited performance. A vast crowd, rainy eyes, &c. The composition, the pronunciation, the action, all exceeded the expectations of everybody. They exceeded even mine, which were very considerable. Many of the sentiments came with great propriety from him. His invective, particularly, against a preference of riches to virtue, came from him with a singular dignity and grace.[15]

Dined at neighbor Quincy's with my wife. Mr. John Denny and

[15]John Hancock was most likely the wealthiest man in Massachusetts, and thus one of the wealthiest in all the American colonies.

son there. Denny gave a few hints of [the British government soon] vacating the [colony's] charter and sending troops, and depriving the province of advantages, quartering troops, &c., but all pretty faint. The happiness of the family where I dined, upon account of the Colonel's justly applauded oration, was complete. . . .

MARCH 6. SUNDAY. Heard Dr. Cooper in the morning. Paine drank coffee with me. Paine is under some apprehension of troops, on account of the high proceedings. He says there is a ship in today with a consignment of tea from some private merchants at home, &c.

Last Thursday evening, March 3d, died Andrew Oliver, Esq., Lieutenant-Governor. This is but the second death which has happened among the conspirators, the original conspirators against the public liberty, since the conspiracy was first regularly formed and begun to be executed, in 1763 or 1764. . . .

MARCH 7. MONDAY. This morning brought us news from South Carolina, of the destruction of the tea there, and from England . . . that three regiments are ordered to Boston and New York . . . and great things to be laid before Parliament, &c., &c. Twenty-eight chests of tea arrived yesterday, which are to make an infusion in water at seven o'clock this evening. This evening there has been an exhibition in King Street, of the portraits of the soldiers and the massacre. . . .

MARCH 8. TUESDAY. Last night twenty-eight chests and a half of tea were drowned. . . .

MARCH 12. SATURDAY. The enmity of Governor Bernard [the previous governor], Hutchinson, and Oliver, and others, to the constitution of this province, is owing to its being an obstacle to their views and designs of raising a revenue by parliamentary authority, and making their own fortunes out of it. The constitution of this province has enabled the people to resist their projects so effectually, that they see they shall never carry them into execution while it exists. . . .

There is so much of a republican spirit among the people, which has been nourished and cherished by their form of government, that they never would submit to tyrants or oppressive projects. The same spirit spreads like a contagion into all the other colonies, into Ireland and into Great Britain too, from this single Province of Massachusetts

Bay, that no pains are too great to be taken, no hazards to great to be run, for the destruction of our charter.

IN ONE BREATH, Adams spoke of the glories of the Massachusetts colonial charter, and the "republican spirit" felt by the people. Truly he had come far since 1765: now, as then, he looked to existing rights and institutions—but now he saw them as the basis for republican principles. He had gone from defending the status quo to implicitly rejecting the very heart of British society—the monarchy. John Adams, like Samuel, was more radical than most; but the movement toward outright revolution had begun, driven by the tide of events.

Even as Adams commented on the spirit of America, the spirit of Parliament turned ugly. All debate over the justice of taxing the colonists dissolved into outrage at the destruction of tea in Boston Harbor. In the spring of 1774, the ministry of Lord North pushed through five bills that came to be known as the Intolerable Acts— marking the final hardening of Parliament's position in the great controversy.

The first four acts were designed to punish Massachusetts, and force the Americans in general to admit the supremacy of Parliament. The first closed the port of Boston to virtually all trade until the town repaid the East India Company for its lost tea. The second altered the charter of the Massachusetts colony, stripping away most local control and strengthening the power of the king in its government: the council—the upper house of the legislature—was to be named by the crown; the governor could appoint and remove local officials; town meetings could no longer be held without royal permission; and sheriffs would now select juries. The third act allowed magistrates indicted for capital crimes in America to stand trial in England. The fourth gave royal governors the power to "quarter" or house troops in private dwellings. The fifth less direct than the others—recognized Roman Catholicism as an official religion in Quebec, and extended the conquered province's boundaries to the Ohio River (forestalling any extension of the other colonies' territory over the Appalachian Mountains).

The thrust of the Intolerable Acts was clear: the British government, king and legislature alike, was determined to force the Americans to succumb to the supremacy of Parliament in all things. As Lord North said, "We are not entering into a dispute between internal and external taxes, not between taxes laid for the purpose of revenues and taxes laid for the regulation of trade, not between representation and taxation, or legislation and taxation; but we are now to dispute whether we have, or have not any authority in that country."[16]

How did the colonists react? Their fears and sensitivities had only been heightened over the preceding decade, as one crisis followed another. Now that the British ministry had abandoned all attempts at compromise—now that the king himself had called for the use of force to subdue the colonists—they felt that their deepest suspicions about a "conspiracy" to "enslave" their country had been true all along. And no sooner had news of the Intolerable Acts crossed the Atlantic than Samuel Adams issued a call for unified action in "the common cause of America."

Letter from the Town of Boston to the Colonies, May 13, 1774
by Samuel Adams

I am desired by the freeholders and other inhabitants of this town to inclose you an attested copy of their vote passed in town meeting legally assembled this day. The occasion of this meeting is most alarming: We have received the copy of an Act of the British Parliament (which is also inclos'd) wherein it appears that the inhabitants of this town have been tried and are to be punished by the shutting up of the harbor, and other ways, without their having been called to answer for, nay, for aught that appears without their having been even accused of any crime committed by them; for no such crime is alleged in the Act.

[16]Quoted in Middlekauff, p. 228.

The town of Boston is now suffering the stroke of vengeance in the common cause of America. I hope they will sustain the blow with a becoming fortitude; and that the effects of this cruel act, intended to intimidate and subdue the spirits of all America will by the joint effort of all be frustrated.

The people receive this edict with indignation. It is expected by their enemies and feared by some of their friends, that this town singly will not be able to support the cause under so severe a trial. As the very being of every colony, consider'd as a free people, depends upon the event, a thought so dishonorable to our brethren cannot be entertain'd, as that this town will now be left to struggle alone.

General [Thomas] Gage is just arrived here, with a commission to supersede Gov. Hutchinson. It is said that the town of Salem about twenty miles east of this metropolis is to be the seat of government—that the commissioners of the Customs and their numerous retinue are to remove to the town of Marblehead, a town contiguous to Salem, and that this if the General shall think proper is to be a garrison'd town. Reports are various and contradictory.

A MILITARY GOVERNMENT. A charter altered by edict. A port closed by a body of men that contained no representatives from America, let alone Boston. Such arbitrary acts startled not only Massachusetts, but all the thirteen colonies. The sense of crisis in Samuel Adams's letter can be felt in the final line, "Reports are various and contradictory": It breathes fear, confusion, and indignation.

For years, the colonies had been officially responding to the British initiatives on an individual basis, even though popular action (such as nonimportation, or the creation of the Sons of Liberty) had long since stretched across the provincial boundaries. Now the Intolerable Acts had driven the various legislatures to finally combine with each other. They did not need Adams's letter to tell them that their last hope was in unity—in a Continental Congress to speak for them all.

3
THE ARGUMENTS

In the early summer of 1774, the various colonies agreed to send delegates to a Continental Congress. The Intolerable Acts had driven matters almost to the final extremity: a unified body of Americans must meet, to meet the malice of Parliament. And one of the men selected by the people of Massachusetts was an outspoken lawyer named John Adams.

Adams's private thoughts have already been heard in this volume, reflecting the deepening crisis and his own slow rise to prominence. But when the Congress met in Philadelphia, this obscure son of a farmer would emerge as a truly continental figure: a determined leader in the American battle against the British ministry—and eventually against Britain itself.

Historians Stanley Elkins and Eric McKitrick best express the reasons for that dramatic rise: they have identified "a governing theme in Adams's life, his almost rabid insistence on independence—usually in opposition to somebody, and sometimes to everybody. It was better if there were costs and obstacles. . . . Adams always thirsted for fame, but it had to be on his terms, and his terms seldom fitted anyone else's. He could never put himself out to flatter others or to court popularity, these things being in any case a matter of instinct, and Adams had no such instinct. He talked too much, was too opinionated and too censorious, too often said what he thought (though he fretted about it afterwards); was too irritable and irritated too many others. He rather expected to be unpopular; indeed, he was all but determined to be so, and in large part he was. What renown he acquired was certainly not for commanding manner of person . . . but rather for the fruits of his pertinacious industry."[17]

[17]Stanley Elkins and Eric McKitrick, *The Age of Federalism: The Early American Republic, 1788–1800* (New York: Oxford University Press, 1993), pp. 532–533.

To the people of Massachusetts, John Adams was less liked than respected, less loved than trusted, and that made him the perfect representative. In an age when the colonists saw themselves as the virtuous children of an earlier and better age, pitted against the flatterers and courtiers who gathered around the throne, against the corrupt pursuers of offices and pensions who piled into Parliament, Adams was known as a man who spoke his mind (usually quite well) and who could never be bought. Who better to stand for the Puritans' descendants in the Continental Congress?

Two passages follow from Adams's writings, passages that capture both his own tumultuous but determined heart, and the spirit of the times. In public, he never wavered, never showed the first flutterings of weakness; but in his own mind and spirit, he steeled himself against despair at the enormity of the task. What was to be done? What good could they possibly accomplish? With General Thomas Gage in command of his colony, he must have secretly wondered if the dispute would end in blows.

Whatever fears he may have felt were surely dampened by the public response to the meeting of the Congress—an enormous outpouring of support that he discovered as he traveled to Philadelphia. And once he arrived, he found a gathering of men fluent in the philosophy of government, who wished to establish for themselves the very basis of their beliefs, rather than recite a list of petty complaints. The previous ten years of public debate and organization would show in the rapidity and unanimity of the Congress's work.

The second passage comes from Adams's autobiography, written decades after the events it describes. Unlike the diary, it was written with the benefit of hindsight, after the importance and effects of the Congress's work were well established. Nevertheless, it offers the valuable reflections of one of the most important Founding Fathers.

In Congress
by John Adams

JUNE 20, 1774. MONDAY. There is a new and a grand scene open before me: a Congress. This will be an assembly of the wisest men upon the continent, who are Americans in principle; that is, against the taxation of Americans by the authority of Parliament. I feel myself unequal to this business. A more extensive knowledge of the realm, the colonies, and of commerce, as well as of law and policy, is necessary, than I am master of. What can be done? Will it be expedient to propose an annual congress of committees? to petition? Will it do to petition at all?—to the King? to the Lords? to the Commons? What will such consultations avail? Deliberations alone will not do. We must petition or recommend to the Assemblies to petition, or—

The ideas of the people are as various as their faces. One thinks, no more petitions—formerly having been neglected and despised; some are for resolves, and some are for bolder counsels. I will keep an exact diary of my journey, as well as a journal of the proceedings of Congress.

JUNE 25. SATURDAY. Since the [General] Court[18] adjourned . . . this afternoon, I have taken a long walk through the Neck, as they call it, a fine tract of land in a general field. Corn, rye, grass, interspersed in great perfection this fine season. I wonder alone and ponder. I muse, I mope, I ruminate. I am often in reveries and brown studies. The objects before me are too grand and multifarious for my comprehension. We have not men fit for the times. We are deficient in genius, in education, in travel, in fortune, in everything. I feel unutterable anxiety. God grant us wisdom and fortitude! Should the opposition be suppressed, should this country submit, what infamy and ruin! God forbid. Death in any form is less terrible! . . .

BOSTON. AUGUST 10. WEDNESDAY. The committee for the Congress took their departure from Boston, from Mr. Cushing's house, and rode to Coolidge's, where they dined in company with a large number of gentlemen, who went out and prepared an entertainment for them at that place. A most kindly and affectionate meeting we had, and about four in the afternoon we took our leave of them, amidst the kind wishes and fervent prayers of every man in the company for our health and success. The scene was truly affecting, beyond all description of affecting. . . .

AUGUST 15. MONDAY. Mr. Silas Deane of Weathersfield came

[18]The General Court was Massachusetts's colonial legislature.

over to Hartford to see us. He is a gentleman of a liberal education, about forty years of age; first kept a school, then studied law, then married the rich widow of Mr. Webb, since which he has been in trade. Two young gentlemen, his sons-in-law, Messrs. Webbs, came over with him. They are genteel, agreeable men, largely in trade, and are willing to renounce all their trade. Mr. Deane gave us an account of the delegates of New York. Duane and Jay are lawyers. Livingston, Low, and Alsop are merchants. . . .

Mr. Deane says the sense of Connecticut is, that the resolutions of the Congress shall be the laws of Medes and Persians; that the Congress is the grandest and most important assembly ever held in America, and that the *all* of America is intrusted to it and depends upon it. . . .

AUGUST 16. TUESDAY: At four we made for New Haven. Seven miles out of town, at a tavern, we met a great number of carriages and of horsemen who had come out to meet us. The sheriff of the county, and the constable of the town, and the justices of the peace, were in the train. As we were coming, we met others to the amount of I know not what number, but a very great one. As we came into the town, all the bells in town were set to ringing, and the people, men, women, and children, were crowding at the doors and windows, as if it was to see a coronation. At nine o'clock the cannon were fired, about a dozen guns, I think. . . . No governor of a province, nor general of an army, was ever treated with so much ceremony and assiduity as we have been throughout the whole colony of Connecticut. . . .

AUGUST 20. SATURDAY. Arrived in the city of New York at ten o'clock, at Hull's, a tavern, the sign the Bunch of Grapes. We rode by several very elegant country seats before we came to the city. This city will be a subject of much speculation to me. . . .

AUGUST 23. TUESDAY. We went up on the new Dutch church steeple, and took a view of the city. You have a very fine view of the whole city at once, the harbor, East River, North [Hudson] River, Long Island, New Jersey, &c. The whole city is upon a level, a flat. The houses in general are smaller than in Boston, and the city occupies less ground. . . .

The way we have been in, of breakfasting, dining, drinking coffee,

&c., about the city, is very disagreeable on some accounts. Although it introduces us to the acquaintance of many respectable people here, yet it hinders us from seeing the college, the churches, the printers' offices, and booksellers' shops, and many other things which we should choose to see.

With all the opulence and splendor of this city, there is very little good breeding to be found. We have been treated with an assiduous respect; but I have not seen one real gentleman, one well-bred man, since I came to town. At their entertainments there is no conversation that is agreeable; there is no modesty, no attention to one another. They talk very loud, very fast, and all together. If they ask you a question, before you can utter three words of your answer, they will break out upon you again, and talk away. . . .

SEPTEMBER 5. MONDAY [Philadelphia]. At ten the delegates all met at the City Tavern, and walked to the Carpenters' Hall, where they took a view of the room, and of the chamber where is an excellent library. . . . The general cry was, that this was a good room, and the question was put, whether we were satisfied with this room? and it passed in the affirmative. A very few were negative, and they were chiefly from Pennsylvania and New York. Then Mr. Lynch arose, and said there was a gentleman present who had presided with great dignity over a very respectable society, greatly to the advantage of America, and he therefore proposed that the Honorable Peyton Randolph, Esquire, one of the delegates from Virginia, and the late Speaker of their House of Burgesses, should be appointed Chairman, and doubted not it would be unanimous.

The question was put, and he was unanimously chosen. . . .

DEBATES.

Mr. Henry. Government is dissolved. Fleets and armies and the present state of things show that government is dissolved. Where are your landmarks, your boundaries of colonies? We are in a state of nature, sir. I did propose that a scale should be laid down; that part of North America which was once Massachusetts Bay, and that part which was once Virginia, ought to be considered as having a weight. Will not people complain? Ten thousand Virginians have not outweighed one thousand others.

I will submit, however; I am determined to submit, if I am over-ruled. A worthy gentlemen near me seemed to admit the necessity of obtaining a more adequate representation.

I hope future ages will quote our proceedings with applause. It is one of the great duties of the democratical part of the constitution to keep itself pure. It is known in my province that some other colonies are not so numerous or rich as they are. I am for giving all the satisfaction in my power.

The distinctions between Virginians, Pennsylvanians, New Yorkers, and New Englanders, are no more. I am not a Virginian, but an American.

Slaves are to be thrown out of the question, and if the freemen can be represented according to their numbers, I am satisfied.

Mr. Lynch. I differ in one point from the gentleman from Virginia, that is, in thinking that numbers only ought to determine the weight of colonies. I think that property ought to be considered, and that it ought to be a compound of numbers and property that should determine the weight of the colonies. I think it cannot be now settled.

Mr. Rutledge. We have no legal authority; and obedience to our determinations will only follow the reasonableness, the apparent utility, and necessity of the measures we adopt. We have no coercive or legislative authority. Our constituents are bound only in honor to observe our determinations. . . .

Mr. Gadsden. I can't see any way of voting, but by colonies.

Colonel Bland. I agree with the gentleman who spoke near me, that we are not at present provided with materials to ascertain the importance of each colony. The question is, whether the rights and liberties of America shall be contended for, or given up to arbitrary powers. . . .

Mr. Lee. Life, and liberty which is necessary for the security of life, cannot be given up when we enter into society.

Mr. Rutledge. The first emigrants could not be considered as in a state of nature; they had no right to elect a new king.

Mr. Jay. I have always withheld my assent from the position that every subject discovering land [does it] for the state to which he belongs.

Mr. Galloway. I never could find the rights of Americans in the distinction between taxation and legislation, nor in the distinction between laws for revenue and for the regulation of trade. I have looked for our rights in the law of nature, but could not find them in a state of nature, but always in a state of political society.

I have looked for them in the constitution of the English government, and found them. We may draw them from this source securely. . . .

It is the essence of the English constitution that no laws shall be binding, but such as are made by the consent of the proprietors in England.

How, then, did it stand with our ancestors when they came over here? They could not be bound by any laws made by the British Parliament, excepting those made before. I never could see any reason to allow that we are bound to any law made since, nor could I make any distinction between the sorts of law.

I have ever thought we might reduce our rights to one—an exemption from all laws made by British Parliament since the emigration of our ancestors. It follows, therefore, that all the acts of Parliament made since are violations of our rights. . . .

I am well aware that my arguments tend toward an independency of the colonies, and militate against the maxims that there must be some absolute power to draw together all the wills and strengths of the empire.

Reflections on the Congress
by John Adams

The more we conversed with the gentlemen of the country, and with the members of Congress, the more we were encouraged for a general union of the continent. . . . After some days of general discussions, two committees were appointed of twelve members each, one from each state, Georgia not having yet come in. The first committee was instructed to prepare a bill of rights, as it was called, or a declaration of the rights of the colonies; the second, a list of infringements or violations of those rights. Congress was pleased to appoint me on the first committee, as the member for Massachusetts. . . .

After several days deliberation, we agreed upon all the articles excepting one, and that was the authority of Parliament, which was indeed the essence of the whole controversy; some were for a flat denial of all authority; others for denying the power of taxation only; some for denying internal, but admitting external, taxation. After a multitude of motions were made, discussed, negatived, it seemed as if we should never agree upon anything.

Mr. John Rutledge of South Carolina, one of the committee, addressing himself to me, was pleased to say, "Mr. Adams, we must agree upon something; you appear to be as familiar with the subject as any of us, and I like your expressions—'*the necessity of the case,*' and '*excluding all ideas of taxation, external and internal.*' I have a great opinion of that same idea of the necessity of the case, and I am determined against all taxation for revenue. Come, take the pen and see if you can't produce something that will unite us."

Some others of the committee seconding Mr. Rutledge, I took a sheet of paper and drew up an article. When it was read, I believe not one of the committee was fully satisfied with it; but they all soon acknowledged that there was no hope of hitting on anything in which we could all agree with more satisfaction. All therefore agreed to this, and upon this depended the union of the colonies. . . .

The articles were then reported to Congress, and debated, paragraph by paragraph. The difficult article was again attacked and defended. Congress rejected all amendments to it, and the general sense of the members was, that the article demanded as little as could be demanded, and conceded as much as could be conceded with safety; and certainly as little as would be accepted by Great Britain; and that the country must take its fate, in consequence of it. . . .

The committee of violations of rights reported a set of articles which were drawn by Mr. John Sullivan of New Hampshire, and these two declarations, one of rights and the other of violations . . . were two year afterwards recapitulated in the Declaration of Independence, on the Fourth of July, 1776.

AS THE FIRST Continental Congress met in Philadelphia, a Boston silversmith named Paul Revere arrived with a set of resolves passed by the town of Suffolk, Massachusetts. Designed to fight the Intolerable Acts, they called for the colonists to ignore the royal governments and courts; for the creation of provincial congresses, and for the payment of all taxes to those congresses; and for local militia to prepare for action. On October 8, 1774, the Congress adopted the resolves unanimously.

John Adams and his fellow representatives took other steps as well: they voted for a Declaration of Rights and Grievances on October 14, and the creation of the Continental Association (to cut off all trade with Britain and its dependencies) on October 18. They issued petitions to the king and addresses to the people of Britain, the inhabitants of Canada, and the Americans themselves. They also voted to convene a second Congress on May 10, 1775.

The colonies had spoken with one voice. It was not the voice of revolution; rather, it was a stern, uncompromising voice of a people who still saw themselves as the king's subjects—but as badly wronged subjects. Whether they would be heard or not remained to be seen. Meanwhile, the colonists beyond the circle that met in Philadelphia continued to pour out pamphlets stating the American case—and driving it farther in the direction of republicanism. One of these writers was a young Virginia planter named Thomas Jefferson.

Stanley Elkins and Eric McKitrick offer one of the most insightful looks at the mind of this man, who would soon become known as one of the greatest Americans. "Jefferson," they observe, "was not a systematic theorist, nor indeed a system-builder of any kind. . . . His many legislative achievements in Virginia [accomplished some years later] as well as his innumerable practical inventions, tabulations, and measurements attest to an exceptionally wide-ranging mind. But it was a mind that habitually worked on two quite different levels. One was that of broad general statement, the other that of specific technical detail. He was both a utopian and something of a gadgeteer."[19]

[19]Elkins and McKitrick, pp. 196–197.

In 1774, just before the Continental Congress met, Jefferson published a tract titled *A Summary View of the Rights of British North America*. Formulated as a proposed set of instructions to Virginia's delegates to the Congress, it demonstrates exactly those qualities Elkins and McKitrick identify: a fascination with sweeping generalization, and with specific detail. It contains grand statements of human rights, and detailed analyses of colonial and British history to support those statements; it aggressively challenges the very basis of British assumptions about their power in North America, and ticks off a list of offensive acts by Parliament.

In grace and power, it is far from the later Declaration of Independence; but it offers rare insight into Jefferson's thinking, a year before the first shot of the Revolution. It also reveals the view taken by colonists far from Boston, the scene of the actual events that had crystallized the ministry's repression and American resistance. Here we see the reasons why virtually all of the colonies saw their fate wrapped up with that of their distant brethren in Massachusetts Bay.

A Summary View of the Rights of British North America
by Thomas Jefferson

Resolved, that it be an instruction to the said deputies, when assembled in general congress with the deputies from the other states of British America, to propose to the said congress that an humble and dutiful address be presented to his Majesty, begging leave to lay before him, as Chief Magistrate of the British empire, the united complaints of his Majesty's subjects in America; complaints which are excited by many unwarrantable encroachments and usurpations, attempted to be made by the Legislature of one part of the empire, upon those rights which God and the laws have given equally and independently to all. . . .

And this his Majesty will have reason to expect when he reflects that he is no more than the chief officer of the people, appointed by the laws, and circumscribed with definite powers, to assist in working the great machine of government, erected for their use, and consequently subject to their superintendence. And in order that these our rights, as well as the invasion of them, may be laid more fully before his Majesty, to take a view of them from the origin and first settlement of these countries.

To remind him that our ancestors, before their emigration to America, were the free inhabitants of the British dominions in Europe, and possessed a right which nature has given to all men, of departing from the country in which chance, not choice, has placed them, of going in quest of new habitations, and of there establishing new societies under such laws and regulations as to them shall seem most likely to promote public happiness. That their Saxon ancestors had, under this universal law, in like manner left their native wild and woods in the north of Europe, had possessed themselves of the island of Britain. . . .

And it is thought that no circumstance has occurred to distinguish materially the British from the Saxon emigration. America was conquered, and her settlement made, and firmly established, at the expense of individuals, and not of the British public. Their own blood was spilt in acquiring lands for their settlements, their own fortunes expended in making that settlement effectual; for themselves they fought, for themselves they conquered, and for themselves alone they have right to hold. No shilling was ever issued from the public treasures of his Majesty, or his ancestors, for their assistance, till, of very late times, after the colonies had become established on a firm and permanent footing.

That then, indeed, having become valuable to Great Britain for her commercial purposes, his Parliament was pleased to lend them assistance against the enemy, who would fain have drawn to herself the benefits of their commerce, to the great aggrandizement of herself, and danger of Great Britain. Such assistance, and in such circumstances, they had often before given to Portugal and other allied states with whom they carry on a commercial intercourse; yet these states never supposed that by calling in her aid they thereby submitted themselves to her sovereignty. . . .

That settlements having been thus effected in the wilds of America, the emigrants thought proper to adopt that system of laws under which they had hitherto lived in the mother country, and to continue their union with her by submitting themselves to the same common Sovereign, who was thereby made the central link connecting the several parts of the empire thus newly multiplied.

But that not long were they permitted, however far they thought themselves removed from the hand of oppression, to hold undisturbed the rights thus acquired, at the hazard of their lives and loss of their fortunes. A family of princes was then on the British throne, whose treasonable crimes against their people brought on them afterwards the exertion of those sacred and sovereign rights of punishment reserved in the hands of the people for cases of extreme necessity. . . . [20] Accordingly that country, which had been acquired by the lives, the labors, and the fortunes of the individual adventurers, was by these princes several times parceled out and distributed among the favorites and followers of their fortunes. . . .

That the exercise of a free trade with all parts of the world, possessed by the American colonists as of natural right, and which no law of their own had taken away or abridged, was next the object of unjust encroachment. . . . Upon the restoration of his majesty king Charles the second [in 1660], their rights of free commerce fell once more a victim to arbitrary power; and by several acts of his reign, as well as of some of his successors, the trade of the colonies was laid under such restrictions as show what hopes they might form from the justice of a British Parliament, were its uncontrolled power admitted over these states.

History has informed us that bodies of men, as well as individuals, are susceptible of the spirit of tyranny. A view of these acts of parliament for regulation, as it has been affectedly called, of the American trade, if all other evidence were removed out of the case, would undeniably evince the truth of this observation. . . .

To heighten still the idea of parliamentary justice, and to shew with what moderation they are like to exercise power, where themselves are to feel no part of its weight, we take leave to mention to

---

[20]This is a reference to the house of Stuart, which was twice thrown out of England (first during the Civil War and Interregnum, 1642–1660, then in the Glorious Revolution of 1688).

his majesty certain other acts of British parliament, by which they would prohibit us from manufacturing for our own use the articles we raise on our own lands with our own labor. By an act passed in the 5th year of the reign of his late majesty king George the second, an American subject is forbidden to make a hat for himself of the fur which he has taken perhaps on his own soil; an instance of despotism to which no parallel can be produced in the most arbitrary ages of British history. By one other act passed in the 23rd year of the same reign, the iron which we make we are forbidden to manufacture, and heavy as that article is, and necessary in every branch of husbandry, besides commission and insurance, we are to pay freight for it to Great Britain, and freight for it back again. . . . From which one of these conclusions must necessarily follow, either that justice is not the same in America as in Britain, or else that the British parliament pay less regard to it here than there. . . .

Scarcely have our minds been able to emerge from the astonishment into which one stroke of parliamentary thunder had involved us, before another more heavy, and alarming, is fallen on us. Single acts of tyranny may be ascribed to the accidental opinion of the day; but a series of oppressions begun at a distinguished period, and pursued, unalterably through every change of ministers, too plainly prove a deliberate and systematical plan of reducing us to slavery.

That the act, passed in the 4th year of his majesty's reign, entitled, "An act for granting certain duties in the British colonies and plantations in America, &c."

One other act, passed in the 5th year of his reign, entitled, "An act for the better securing of the dependency of his majesty's dominions in America upon the crown and parliament of Great Britain"; and one other act, passed in the 7th year of his reign, entitled, "An act for granting duties on paper, tea, &c." form that connected chain of parliamentary usurpation, which has already been the subject of frequent applications to his majesty, and the houses of lords and commons of Great Britain; and no answers having yet been condescended to any of these, we shall not trouble his majesty with a repetition of the matters they contained.

But that one other act, passed in the same 7th year of the reign, having been a peculiar attempt, must ever require particular mention;

it is entitled, "An act for suspending the legislature of New York." One free and independent legislature hereby takes upon itself to suspend the powers of another, free and independent as itself; this exhibiting a phenomenon unknown in nature, the creator and creature of his own power. Not only the principles of common sense, but the common feelings of human nature, must be surrendered up before his majesty's subjects here can be persuaded to believe that they hold their political existence at the will of a British parliament.

Shall these governments be dissolved, their property annihilated, and their people reduced to a state of nature, at the imperious breath of a body of men whom they never saw, in whom they never confided, and over whom they have no powers of punishment or removal, let their crimes against the American public be ever so great? Can any one reason be assigned why 160,000 electors in the island of Great Britain should give law to four millions in the states of America, every individual of whom is equal to every individual of them, in virtue, in understanding, and in bodily strength? Were this to be admitted, instead of being a free people, as we have hitherto supposed, and mean to continue ourselves, we should suddenly be found the slaves not of one but of 160,000 tyrants, distinguished too from all others by this singular circumstance, that they are removed from the reach of fear, the only restraining motive which may hold the hand of a tyrant. . . .

An act of parliament had been passed imposing duties on teas, to be paid in America, against which the Americans had protested as inauthoritative. The East India Company, who till that time had never sent a pound of tea to America on their own account, step forth on that occasion the assertors of parliamentary right, and send hither many shiploads of that obnoxious commodity. The masters of their several vessels, however, on their arrival to America, wisely attended to admonition, and returned with their cargoes. In the province of Massachusetts alone the remonstrances of the people were disregarded, and a compliance, after being many days waited for, was flatly refused. Whether in this the master of the vessel was governed by his obstinacy, or his instructions, let those who know say.

There are extraordinary circumstances which require extraordinary interposition. An exasperated people, who feel that they possess power, are not easily restrained within limits strictly regular. A number of them assembled in the town of Boston threw the tea into the ocean, and dispersed without doing any other act of violence. If in this they did wrong, they were known and were amenable to the laws of the land. . . . But that ill-fated colony had formerly been bold in their enmities against the house of Stuart, and were now devoted to ruin by that unseen hand which governs the momentous affairs of this great empire [and so the port of Boston was closed by an act of Parliament, impoverishing the town]. . . .

That we next proceed to consider the conduct of his majesty, as holding the executive powers of the laws of these states, and mark out his deviation from the line of duty. . . . In order to force the arbitrary measures before complained of, his majesty has from time to time sent among us large bodies of armed forces, not made up of the people here, nor raised by the authority of our laws. Did his majesty possess such a right as this, it might swallow up all other rights whenever he should think proper. But his majesty has no right to land a single armed man on our shores, and those whom he sends here are liable to our laws made for the suppression and punishment of riots, and unlawful assemblies; or are hostile bodies, invading us in defiance of the law. . . .

Open your breast, sire, to liberal and expanded thought. Let not the name of George the third be a blot in the page of history. You are surrounded by English counselors, but remember that they are parties. You have no minister for American affairs, because you have none taken up from among us nor amenable to the laws on which they are to give you advice. It behooves you, therefore, to think and to act for yourself and your people. The great principles of right and wrong are legible to every reader; to pursue them requires not the aid of many counselors. The whole art of government consists in the art of being honest. Only aim to do your duty, and mankind will give you credit where you fail. No longer persevere in sacrificing the rights of one part of the empire to the inordinate desires of another; but deal out to all equal and impartial right. . . .

The God who gave us life gave us liberty at the same time; the hand of force may destroy, but cannot disjoin them. This, sire, is our last, our determined resolution; and that you will be pleased to interpose with that efficacy which your earnest endeavors may ensure to procure redress of these our great grievances to quiet the minds of your subjects in British America, against any apprehensions of future encroachment, to establish fraternal love and harmony through the whole empire, and that these may continue to the last ages of time, is the fervent prayer of all British America.

JEFFERSON WROTE BEFORE the Continental Congress met; but he aptly expressed the convictions the delegates carried into the great conference, and the resolutions they carried out of it. He appealed to the king as a loyal subject; but he pointed to "a series of oppressions" that "too plainly prove a deliberate and systematical plan of reducing us to slavery." These were strong words, barely short of outright rebellion; yet they were still couched in an appeal for relief, rather than the language of revolution.

The king and his ministry, of course, read such words—and the actions of the Continental Congress—as explicit rebellion. As historian Robert Middlekauff has written, the government in London had long viewed the colonies with a mixture of condescension and neglect. As the colonists knew, the kingdom had rarely been troubled with great expenses on their behalf, and so it had rarely given them much thought. When it had, it was in the form of fitful efforts to force them to better serve the needs of the home islands. Various acts had been passed to restrict what the Americans could manufacture, to limit where they could buy and sell their goods overseas, to tax what they imported, to define where they could settle. The only real rebellion against such actions took place against the sweeping reforms of King James II, who was so loathed (for other reasons) in England itself that the colonists' own concerns were barely noted. In short, Parliament and the crown took America for granted—and when the Americans protested against London's arbitrary alteration of the status quo, their complaints were abruptly dismissed.

The colonists fought harder and harder to return to the past, ironically moving faster and faster into a radically new future. Like Jefferson, most leaders of the antiministerial movement argued that they were defending the existing constitutional structure—but they created a completely unconstitutional body, the Continental Congress, to do so. As they met with intransigence from Britain, they felt fewer qualms about the implications of their dramatic actions, and they turned the Congress into a quasi-governmental organ.

What were the implications of this unheard-of Congress, and where could the protest possibly go? Petition after petition, address after address, had been turned down by the rulers in London. The only response had been occupying soldiers, a major port sealed shut, a military governor for one of the oldest and proudest colonies. In the days after Congress met, one brilliant young writer faced those questions with startling lucidity.

His name was Alexander Hamilton; at the time, he was a student at King's College in the city of New York.[21] Perhaps twenty years old, Hamilton may well have merited the title of genius. A native of the West Indian island of Nevis, he grew up on the island of St. Croix, where (as a teenager) he managed a prosperous mercantile business. He moved to the North American mainland, enrolling in King's College after Princeton turned him down (he favored the New Jersey school because it had a reputation for republicanism).

Hamilton matched John Adams in energy and eagerness for fame—but he was younger, possibly smarter, and definitely more charismatic. As a student, he engaged in a remarkable debate (carried on in dueling pamphlets) with Samuel Seabury, a prominent Anglican priest, who was sharply criticizing the Continental Congress and the general drift toward republicanism and independence. If things continued as they were, Seabury warned, war would certainly follow. The passage that follows represents Hamilton's response—a full vindication of the Continental Congress. In this document, he looks the implications of Congress's actions square in the face, and assesses them with almost prophetic clarity.

---

[21]King's College, after some renaming and growth, eventually became Columbia University.

A Full Vindication
by Alexander Hamilton

The only distinction between freedom and slavery consists in this: In the former state a man is governed by the laws to which he has given his consent, either in person or by his representative; in the latter, he is governed by the will of another. In the one case, his life and property are his own; in the other, they depend upon the pleasure of his master. It is easy to discern which of these two states is preferable. No man in his senses can hesitate to be free, rather than a slave.

That Americans are entitled to freedom is incontestable on every rational principle. All men have one common original: they participate in one common nature, and consequently have one common right. No reason can be assigned why one man should exercise any power or pre-eminence over his fellow-creatures more than another; unless they have voluntarily vested him with it. Since, then, Americans have not, by any act of theirs, empowered the British Parliament to make laws for them, it follows they can have no just authority to do it.

Besides the clear voice of natural justice in this respect, the fundamental principles of the English constitution are in our favor. It has been repeatedly demonstrated that the idea of legislation or taxation, when the subject is not represented, is inconsistent with *that*. Nor is this all; our charters, the express conditions on which our progenitors relinquished their native countries, and came to settle in this, precludes every claim of ruling and taxing us without our assent. . . .

What, then, is the subject of our controversy with the mother country? It is this: Whether we shall preserve the security to our lives and properties, which the law of nature, the genius of the British constitution, and our charters afford us; or whether we shall resign them into the hands of the British House of Commons, which is no more privileged to dispose of them than the Great Mogul.

What can actuate those men who labor to delude any of us into an opinion that the object of contention between the parent state and the colonies is only three pence duty upon tea; or that the commotions in America originate in a plan, formed by some turbulent men, to erect into it a republican government? The Parliament claims a right to tax us in all cases whatsoever; its late acts are in virtue of that claim. How ridiculous, then, to affirm that we are quarreling for the trifling sum of three pence a pound on tea, when it is evidently the principle against which we contend.

The design of electing members to represent us in general Congress was that the wisdom of America might be collected in devising the most proper and expedient means to repel this atrocious invasion of our rights. It has been accordingly done. Their decrees are binding upon all. . . .

The only scheme of opposition suggested by those who have been and are averse from a non-importation and non-exportation agreement is by REMONSTRANCE and PETITION. . . . In the infancy of the present dispute, we had recourse to this method only. We addressed the throne in the most loyal and respectful manner, in a legislative capacity; but what was the consequence? Our address was treated with contempt and neglect. The first American Congress did the same, and met with similar treatment. The total repeal of the stamp act, and the partial repeal of the revenue acts, took place not because the complaints of America were deemed just and reasonable, but because these acts were found to militate against the commercial interests of Great Britain. . . .

We can have no resource but in a restriction of our trade, or in a resistance *vi et armis* [under arms]. It is impossible to conceive any other alternative. Our Congress, therefore, have imposed what restraint they thought necessary. Those who condemn and clamor against it do nothing more nor less than advise us to be slaves. . . .

Should Americans submit to be the vassals of their fellow-subjects in Great Britain, their yoke will be peculiarly grievous and intolerable. A vast majority of mankind is entirely biased by motives of self-interest. Most men are glad to remove any burdens off themselves and place them upon the necks of their neighbors. We cannot, therefore, doubt but that the British Parliament, with a view to the ease and advantage of itself and its constituents, would oppress and grind the Americans as much as possible. Jealousy would concur with selfishness; and for fear of the future independence of America, if it should be permitted to rise to too great a height of splendor and opulence, every method would be taken to drain it of its wealth and restrain its prosperity. We are already suspected of aiming at independence, and that is one principal cause of the severity we experience. The same cause will always operate against us, and produce a uniform severity of treatment. . . .

It is evident that she [Britain] must do something decisive. She must either listen to our complaints and restore us to a peaceful enjoyment of our violated rights, or she must exert herself to enforce her despotic claims by fire and sword. To imagine she would prefer the latter implies a charge of the grossest infatuation, of madness itself. Our numbers are very considerable; the courage of Americans has been tried and proved. Contests for liberty have ever been found the most bloody, implacable, and obstinate. The disciplined troops Great Britain could send against us would be but few. Our superiority in number would overbalance our inferiority in discipline. It would be a hard, if not impracticable, task to subjugate us by force.

Besides, while Great Britain was engaged in carrying on an unnatural war against us, her commerce would be in a state of decay. Her revenues would be decreasing. An armament, sufficient to enslave America, would put her to an insupportable expense. She would be laid open to the attacks of foreign enemies. Ruin, like a deluge, would pour in from every quarter. After lavishing her blood and treasure to reduce us to a state of vassalage, she would herself become a prey to some triumphant neighbor.

These are not imaginary mischiefs. The colonies contain above three millions of people. Commerce flourishes with the most rapid progress throughout them. . . . The conquest of so numerous a people, armed in the animating cause of liberty, could not be accomplished without an inconceivable expense of blood and treasure.

We cannot, therefore, suspect Great Britain to be capable of such frantic extravagance as to hazard these dreadful consequences; without which, she must necessarily desist from her unjust pretensions, and leave us in the undisturbed possession of our privileges.

Those who affect to ridicule the resistance America might make to the military force of Great Britain, and represent its humiliation as a matter most easily to be achieved, betray either a mind clouded by the most irrational principles, or a total ignorance of human nature.

However, it must be the wish of every honest man never to see a trial.

————

"THESE DREADFUL CONSEQUENCES": few other writers dared to broach the likelihood of armed action. Hamilton did; and he was only one of a growing number who accepted the possibility—though others did so less publicly, and with more dread. Many refered to a possible war not as a revolution or rebellion, but as a "civil war," for most colonists still thought of themselves as members of the larger nation.

But those feelings were fading in the white heat of events. The Intolerable Acts, the imposition of a general as governor of Massachusetts—such things were driving the political tide far faster than any arguments ever could. Even as Jefferson and Hamilton wrote their pamphlets, little-known men in New England were gathering gunpowder, cleaning their muskets, drilling in companies of militia. The British troops were on their very doorsteps; the long-discussed conspiracy to enslave America had materialized as a military occupation of Boston. The distance to open war could be measured in the space between a gun flint and the firing pan.

————

II

BATTLE

4
TO ARMS

As the sun burned west across the Atlantic on the first day of 1775, the king's fury came with it. News of the Continental Congress of the previous year had flabbergasted the ministry; and word of the Suffolk Resolves had infuriated George III. "The New England governments are in a state of rebellion," the king fumed. "Blows must decide whether they are to be subject to this country or independent."[22]

From where General Thomas Gage sat in Boston, things seemed rather more complicated. As the military governor of Massachusetts and commander of the king's troops on these shores, he had the thankless task of translating royal rage into actual policy—amid equally infuriated colonists. A serious, well-informed officer of the British army, he could boast long years of service in North America. He respected the Americans, and thought that he understood them. But Gage had no doubt that the supremacy of Parliament was a principle worth fighting for, even if it meant fighting fellow British subjects. To that end, he had taken the reins of the government; he had dismissed public officials, appointing outspoken loyalists in their place; he had forbidden the General Court (the colony's legislature) to meet; and now he gathered information from spies about his opponents' activities.

Those activities troubled him deeply. The Continental Congress had proved to be a truly unifying force, rallying all thirteen colonies behind the cause of Boston. The Congress had concluded its session with a call for armed resistance, should Gage's troops march out of the city. His authority within Massachusetts faced a challenge by the new Provincial Congress; it had set itself up as a rival government as soon as he dismissed the General Court. Even worse, he heard per-

[22]Quoted in Middlekauff, p. 262.

sistent reports of militia companies training in the countryside—of hidden stores of arms, ammunition, even artillery.

One of the leaders arrayed against him, as the first dawn of 1775 cracked over Boston, was the redoubtable Samuel Adams. Upon returning from Philadephia, Adams took the measure of the explosive situation, and he found it exhilarating. For ten years, he had been arguing with increasing vehemence for the rights of the colonies— struggling to inflame his fellow Americans with his own passion for liberty and country. He had thundered out speeches, rallied together committees and congresses, written unending reams of addresses and resolves. Now things had come to a head: with the charter of Massachusetts suspended and troops in the streets of Boston, he believed that no one could doubt the existence of a conspiracy to enslave the colonies.

At the end of the month, Samuel Adams summarized the circumstances in a letter. The document seethes with his hatred for Thomas Hutchinson and the other colonial leaders who had sided with the ministry; it comes close to blaming them personally for the military occupation of Massachusetts's capital. But such flashes of anger aside, this letter is notable for two things. First, it speaks of a lingering willingness—even by one of the most rebellious of American rebels— to come to some sort of terms with Lord North's government. He still held a shred of hope that an accommodation could be reached, that war might be avoided. Actually, Adams himself may have had no such hope, but he acknowledged that most Americans did.

The second thing worth noting is a fascinating reference to the militiamen who were preparing for the worst. After the failure of so many petitions to king and Parliament, Samuel Adams had little enthusiasm for those the First Continental Congress had just issued; instead, he rubbed his hands with satisfaction at the determination of his fellow New Englanders to defend their liberties literally to the death. The militia companies had been formally organized by the Committee of Public Safety set up by the Provincial Congress, and chaired by John Hancock—but they built on a long-standing tradition of military preparedness in the colony. Ready for action on a moment's notice, they were known as the Minutemen.

Minute Men
by Samuel Adams

TO ARTHUR LEE   JANUARY 29, 1775

Upon my return from the Continental Congress at Philadelphia I had
the pleasure of receiving your letter. . . . I beg you would attribute
my not having acknowledg'd the favor before this time, to continual
avocations which the necessity of the times have required.

When this cruel edict for shutting up this harbor took place,
which was in a very short time after we had any notice that such a
measure was intended, the inhabitants of the town met in Faneuil
Hall and, as you have long ago heard, resolv'd to suffer all the hardships intended by it, rather than submit to its unrighteous as well as
ignominious terms. Supported by the most liberal donations from
their brethren in all the colonies, they suffer the suspension of their
trade & business with patience and even laugh at this feeble effort of
their enemies to force them to make the concessions of slaves.

The Act for regulating the government of this province and the
Murder Act, as it is commonly called, soon follow'd the Port Act;
and General Gage, whether from his own motives or the instructions
of the minister, thought proper to assemble all the King's troops then
on the continent in this town and has declared to the selectmen &
others his resolution to put the Acts in execution. The people on the
other hand resolve that they will not submit to them and the continent applauds them herein. The new-appointed councillors and others who have openly avow'd the measures of administration, being
conscious that Mr. Gage was not mistaken when he publicly declared
under his hand that the opposition to these Acts was general through
the Province, have fled to this town for protection.

Thus we appear to be in a state of hostility. The General with . . .
[his] regiments [and] with a very few adherents on one side & all the
rest of the inhabitants of the Province back'd by all the colonies on
the other! The people are universally dispos'd to wait till they can
hear what effect the applications of the Continental Congress will
have, in hopes that the new Parliament will reverse the laws & measures of the old, abolish that system of tyranny which was plan'd in

1763 (perhaps before), confirm the just rights of the colonies, and restore harmony to the British Empire. God grant they may not be disappointed!

Lest they should be, they have been, & are still, exercising themselves in military discipline and providing the necessary means of defense. I am well informed that in every part of the Province there are selected numbers of men, called Minute Men, that are well disciplined & well provided—and that upon a very short notice they will be able to assemble a formidable army. They are resolv'd however not to be the aggressors in an open quarrel with the troops; but animated with an unquenchable love of liberty they will support their righteous claim to it, to the utmost extremity. . . .

I earnestly wish that Lord North would no longer listen to the voice of faction. Interested[23] men whose very being depends upon the emoluments deriv'd to them from the American revenue have been artfully deceiving him. Such men as these, some of them, under a mere pretence of flying to the army for protection, have got themselves about General Gage.

———

THE RADICAL'S RADICAL had spoken: with events rushing toward an explosive climax, he wrote that the colonists' goal was still to "restore harmony to the British Empire." These were hardly the words of a convinced revolutionary; but perhaps Adams already knew that the situation was out of his control. He was certainly capable of putting his own fury aside long enough to burrow into the mantle of the aggrieved party—to repeat what his less ferocious countrymen truly believed, that the goal was still to restore normal relations with the home country. But there can be little doubt that he placed his real faith in the farmers and artisans who were preparing to fight for their rights.

Later generations have hallowed the memory of those self-proclaimed Minutemen, depicting them as a people in arms, prepared

———

[23]By "interested" he means those with a financial stake, or interest, in the tax revenue from America. Since the ministry had started paying the salaries of the governors and other colonial officers out of the tea duty, this reference implicates Thomas Hutchinson and his circle.

to snatch up their squirrel guns on a moment's notice to battle invading Britons. A part of this image is accurate: certainly they came from a broad swath of the population of the towns around Boston; they were not professional soldiers, but musket-carrying civilians. However, as historian David Hackett Fischer has recently noted, they were carrying on a tradition as old as New England itself. Ever since the first English settlement, each town had maintained a "training band" or militia company. The institution was no mere formality: repeated wars with neighboring Indians filled the 1600s, and the 1740s and 1750s had brought a string of conflicts with the French. Many of the Minutemen could boast real military experience, and many of their companies were well-drilled and reasonably well-equipped units.

The First Continental Congress had issued an appeal to the militiamen to fight any British incursion into the countryside—but the Massachusetts Committee of Public Safety needed no urging from Philadelphia. An intricate network of spies and messengers kept the Minutemen informed of General Gage's deployments, as they waited for the word to turn out and defend their homes. Foremost among those watchmen was a public-spirited silversmith named Paul Revere—the man who had carried the Suffolk Resolves to Congress in October. Revere formed an essential link in the patriotic movement, passing easily between its various social layers, from farmers and artisans to merchants and lawyers.

Inside the town, General Gage found himself in an impossible situation. His letters to the ministry took on an increasingly nervous tone; every day, his troops were mocked, insulted, even attacked in the street. Every day, word came from his own spies and informers of the heightened preparations of the militia in the surrounding towns. He was worried, uncertain, indecisive. At one point, he told London that he needed 20,000 reinforcements; then he declared that the time had come for a powerful military strike; then he urged the ministry to suspend the Intolerable Acts.

Part of his problem, as historian Pauline Maier has pointed out, was that he had been reared in much the same political tradition as the colonists themselves. He knew that a very heavy hand indeed would be needed to suppress the Americans by force—and he drew back in horror at the prospect. As an Englishman, he shared the colonists' dread of arbitrary power. On the other hand, he knew that the king's patience was growing short. Gage's pleas for reinforcements met nothing but astonishment in London, and his suggestion that the Intolerable Acts be suspended brought only an indignant huff from Lord North and George III. Already the king had decided to send a trio of major generals to *assist* Gage in Boston.

Gage deeply felt the presure to strike a real blow. His repression of dissent became increasingly reflexive; at one point, he refused to call for a day of fasting and prayer (an old Congregationalist tradition in troubled times), fearing the ministers would preach sedition from the pulpits. Meanwhile he looked for an opportunity to destroy the caches of arms and ammunition collected in the countryside beyond Boston.

One of the British soldiers who served in Boston during those tense days was a young ensign named Jeremy Lister. A bright, alert, and professional junior officer, Lister struggled to cope with the grinding indignity of occupation duty. Though he scarcely realized it, the steady succession of insults and blows he traded daily with the hostile townspeople was slowly eroding his soul. He grew to hate the residents of Boston as much as they hated him, and he delighted in their discomfort.

When an opportunity came to strike back at his tormentors, he eagerly took it, volunteering for a dangerous mission. The word came almost at the last moment on the evening of April 18, 1775; General Gage had taken every precaution to ensure complete secrecy. The troops were to file silently down to the water, then cross the Back Bay from the Boston peninsula to the mainland in boats already collected for the purpose. Once across, they would march to the town of Concord, where the militia had collected a large store of arms and ammunition.

Young Ensign Lister and venerable General Gage little realized that news of the march would cross the bay before them. In legend-making fashion, Paul Revere rowed a small boat across the water— right under the guns of a powerful man-of-war—to spread the word to the Committee of Public Safety in Concord that the redcoats were coming. As both Lister and Gage later reported, many of them never returned.

___

Mission to Concord
by Jeremy Lister

I come now to that part where I experienc'd the chief part of my difficulties and distresses. We instituted several amusements which helped the winter [of 1774–1775] to pass tolerably, tho. not without being in imminent danger every evening of being insulted by the inhabitants. The worst of language was continually in our ears, often dirt thrown at us. They even went so far as to wound some officers with their watch crooks. Capt. [Hugh] McGinnis of the 28th Regt. was one of those unfortuante gentlemen, amongst many more.

We constituted a club of Yorkshire officers . . . and was one night oblig'd to sally out to rescue an officer, Lt. [William] Myers of 38th Regt., from the hands of the populace, who had nothing to lay to his charge only he was walking in the streets alone, therefore [they] thought him an easy prey. The consequences was very near being dreadful indeed but however the mob which was rais'd happily subsided without further mischief.

The 5th of March this year 1775 happen'd on a Sunday, therefore the annual oration [commemorating the Boston Massacre] was the day following. Just about the conclusion, the 43rd Regt., who had been a few miles in the country, return'd. When opposite the church they halted a few minutes. The congregation imagin'd they was going to fire into the church, or at least take them all prisoners, [and] jump'd out the windows as fast as possible, and was quite in confusion. The Regt. then march'd forward. To be sure the scene was quite laughable.

This evening was intended to have been a grand exhibition representing the Massacre in the year 1769 [actually 1770] by the 29th Regt., as the Boston people term'd it. But Genl. Gage represented to the selectmen, he should deem it an insult to his Majesty himself, and the army then at Boston, therefore if they persisted in their intentions, he should take proper steps to prevent them being put in execution. Consequently the army had orders to be in readiness to be under arms at a moment's notice. It was generally expected there would be some work that night, but fortunately nothing particular happened.

Things begun now to draw near a crisis, and we expected daily coming to blows, which was soon the case. For on the 18th of April, in the evening, there was a detachment ordered under arms to go on a secret expedition, under the command of Lt. Col. Smith of our Regt. The detachment consisted of the light infantry and grenadiers of the army.[24]

Lt. [James] Pettigrew being one of the lieutenants of our grenadiers and lodging in the same house with me, and [I] being anxious to know the reason of this order with the destiny of this armament, I went with him down to the parade, when I met Captn. [Lawrence] Parsons of our company of light infantry, who seem'd rather uneasy at Lt. Hamilton's not coming after being repeatedly sent for, who sent word at last he was sick. I immediately offered myself a volunteer in the room of Hamilton, and was accepted. . . . I immediately return'd to my lodgings to equip myself for a march, and met the company on their way through the town in order to embark in boats to cross the bay above Charlestown.

When we was just embarking, Lt. Col. Smith wish'd me to return to town again and not go into danger for others, particularly Hamilton, whose illness was suppos'd by everybody to be feign'd, which was clearly prov'd to be the case afterwards; but [I was] wishing much to go for the honor of the Regt. thinking it would be rather a disgrace for the company to march on an expedition, more especially it being the first, without its complement of officers, therefore my offer was accepted.

We got all over the bay and landed on the opposite shore betwixt

---

[24]Gage chose wisely when he selected these troops for the mission. The grenadiers were composed of the largest men in the army—they would make an imposing sight, he calculated, for the inexperienced American militia. The light infantry were specially trained to operate in broken terrain—amid woods and hills—and in dispersed formation.

twelve and one o'clock, and was on our march by one, which was at first through some swamps and slips of the sea, till we got into the road leading to Lexington. Soon after which the country people begun to fire their alarm guns, light their beacons, to raise the country. However, to the best of my recollection, about 4 o'clock in the morning, being the 19th of April, the 5 front companies was ordered to load, which we did. About half an hour after we found that precaution had been necessary, for we had then to unload again [that is, to fire] and then was the first blood drawn in this American rebellion.

It was at Lexington when we saw one of their companies drawn up in regular order. Major Pitcairn of the Marines, second in command, call'd to them to disperse. But their not seeming willing he desired us to mind our space,[25] which we did, when they gave us a fire then run off to get behind a wall. We had one man wounded of our company in the leg. His name was Johnson. Also Major Pitcairn's horse was shot in the flank. We return'd their salute, and before we proceeded on our march from Lexington, I believe we kill'd and wounded either 7 or 8 men.

We march'd forward without further interruption till we arriv'd at Concord. Tho' large bodies of men was collected together and with arms, yet as we approach'd they retired. Lt. Col. Smith remain'd at Concord to destroy military stores collected there, but detach'd Capt. Parsons forwards with 6 companies of light infantry in order to do the same business at another place, the name I don't now recollect. Capt. Parsons left one company of the 43rd at Concord Bridge, two companies, viz. 4th and 10th, upon two hills to command the road he had to go [on], then proceeded with the other two companies, viz. 23rd and 52nd, to execute the purpose of his detachment.

We had not been long in this situation when we saw a large body of men drawn up with the greatest regularity[26] and approach'd us

---

[25]Pitcairn here spoke like a true professional soldier. His men were meeting the Americans in combat for the first time, after a long, tedious occupation; he reminded them to maintain their formation ("to mind our space") as the uncertain situation developed, and not crowd in like a mob.

[26]"The greatest regularity" is a phrase that indicates Lister's surprise at seeing the American militia, who were so often described by the British as a "rabble." They came forward in a tight, well-drilled formation, indicating a high level of training and

seemingly with an intent to attack; when Lt. Kelly, who then commanded our company with myself, thought it most proper to retire from our situation and join the 4th Company, which we did. They still approach'd, and in [such] force that it was thought proper by the officers, except myself, to join the 43rd Company at Concord Bridge, commanded by Captn. [Walter Sloane] Laurie. My reason for objecting the joining of the 43rd Company was we had to go down a steepish hill, and just in a manner under the muzzles of the rebels' pieces. . . .

Luckily for us we joined the 43rd Company, and not a shot fired. I was then not sorry at my situation. Captn. Laurie of 43rd then commanded the three companies. He sent Lt. Robertson of his company to Lt. Col. Smith to beg [that] a reinforcement might be sent immediately. The answer brought back was Lt. Col. Smith thought the 3 companies must be the equal to the defense of the bridge; but he would see this message had no sooner arriv'd than the rebels begun their march from the hill we before had retired from. [They advanced] with as much order as the best disciplined troops.

I proposed destroying the bridge, but before we got one plank off they got so near as to begin their fire, which was a very heavy one. Tho. our company was drawn up in order to form for street firing,[27] yet the weight of their fire was such that we was oblig'd to give way, then run with the greatest precipitance at this place. There was 4 men of the 4th Company killed. . . . There was a good number wounded, amongst which was a Lt. Hull, 43rd, through the right breast, of which with other wounds received that day he died three or four days after. . . . [28]

Fortunately for us, in consequence of the message sent to Lt. Col.

---

discipline. The British were taken aback, and Lister comments later about the surprising "good order" of their opponents.

[27]Historian David Hackett Fischer calls street firing "a typically complex 18th-century maneuver, designed to dominate a small space with overwhelming firepower." The men formed a narrow column; the first three ranks would fire and file to the rear, allowing the next three to fire. David Hackett Fischer, *Paul Revere's Ride* (New York: Oxford University Press, 1994), p. 212.

[28]The British and Americans here met and fought in regular formation—marching in tight lines and firing in volleys. As this paragraph has described, however, it was the redcoats who broke formation and fled in the face of the heavy fire from the men of Massachusetts.

Smith, he had considered to send the 47th Company of grenadiers to our assistance, tho' too late to be of any service at the bridge. Yet they serv'd as a cover for us to draw up our scattered company again. We then retired in regular order to Concord, I mean the 10th and 43rd Companies with the 47th grenadiers. I don't know that the 4th Company was collected again that day, some of them join'd our company and was permitted to remain some time.

After we had got to Concord again my situation with the remains of the company was a most fatiguing one. Being detached to watch the motions of the rebels, we was kept continually running from hill to hill as they chang'd their position; but however after some hours Capt. Parsons return'd, after executing the purpose of his command. . . . On Capt. Parsons's joining us begun our march toward Boston again from Concord. The light infantry march'd over a hill above the town, the grenadiers through the town. Immediately as we descended the hill into the road the rebels begun a brisk fire, but at so great a distance that it was without effect. But as they kept marching nearer, when the grenadiers found them within shot they return'd their fire. Just about that time I received a shot through my right elbow joint which effectually disabled that arm.

It then became a general firing up on us from all quarters, from behind hedges and walls. We return'd the fire every opportunity which continued till we arriv'd at Lexington, which from what I could learn is about 9 miles. We was then met by a reinforcement of 4 battalions under Lord Percy. To our great joy, our ammunition being then nearly expended, there was also two field pieces; but our great commander of artillery, to his disgrace be it said, only sent 7 rounds of ammunition for each gun. Had we had plenty of that commodity they would have been of the greatest use to us on our march, which was then 13 miles to Bunker Hill, under a continual fire from all quarters as before. . . .

I got Mr. Simes, Surgeon's Mate to 43rd Regt., to examine my arm, when he extracted the ball, it having gone through the bone and lodg'd within the skin. From our long fatiguing march and loss of blood for 9 miles, want of provisions, having not had a morsel since the day before, I begun to grow rather faint. Seeing Lt. Col. Smith borrow a horse from an officer of Marines, he having been wounded some time before in the leg, I apply'd to him to lend me his horse, which he did. . . .

When I had rode about 2 miles I found the balls whistled so smartly about my ears I thought it more prudent to dismount; and as the balls came thicker from one side or the other, so I went from one side of the horse to the other for some time. When a horse was shot dead close by me, that had a wounded man on his back and three hanging by his sides, they immediately begged the assistance of my horse, which I readily granted, and soon after left him wholly to their care.

When we got to Charlestown neck, the rebels' fire ceas'd, they not having it in their power to pursue us any further in their skulking way behind hedges and walls.

Bottled Up in Boston
by Thomas Gage

TO DARTMOUTH[29]   BOSTON, APRIL 22, 1775

I am to acquaint your Lordship that having received intelligence of a large quantity of military stores being collected at Concord, for the avowed purpose of supplying a body of troops to act in opposition to His Majesty's Government, I got the grenadiers and light infantry out of town under the command of Lieut. Col. Smith of the 10th Regt. and Major Pitcairn of the Marines with as much secrecy as possible, and the 18th at night and with orders to destroy the said military stores; and supported them the next morning by eight companies of the 4th the same number of the 23rd, 47th, and Marines, under the command of Lord Percy.

It appears that from the firing of alarm guns and ringing of bells that the march of Lieutenant Colonel Smith was discovered, and he was opposed by a body of men within six miles of Concord [at Lexington]; some few of whom first began to fire upon his advanced

[29]William Legge, Earl of Dartmouth, was the secretary for the colonies.

companies which brought on a fire from the troops that dispersed the body opposed to them; and they proceeded to Concord where they destroyed all the military stores they could find. And on the return of the troops they were attacked from all quarters where any cover was to be found, from whence it was practicable to annoy them, and they were so fatigued with their march that it was with difficulty they could keep out their flanking parties to remove the enemy to a distance, so that they were at length a good deal pressed.

Lord Percy then arrived opportunely to their assistance with his brigade and two pieces of cannon, and notwithstanding a continual skirmish for the space of fifteen miles, receiving fire from every hill, fence, house, barn, &c. His Lordship kept the enemy off, and brought the troops to Charlestown, from whence they were ferried over to Boston. . . .

The whole country was assembled in arms with surprising expedition, and several thousand are now assembled about this town threatening an attack, and getting up artillery. And we are very busy making preparations to oppose them. . . .

TO DARTMOUTH   BOSTON, MAY 13th, 1775

Ever since the skirmish of the 19th the avenues to this town have been possessed by large bodies of men from all places in this province, Connecticut, New Hampshire, &c., and they have collected artillery and military stores that had been deposited in various parts of the country.

All supplies from the country have been stopped, and the inhabitants of the town desired to remove out with their effects, which was consented to, but it was demanded that they should immediately deliver up their arms. This was approved at first by all, for there would be fewer months left to be fed, and the danger from enemies within removed. It has since occasioned great clamor amongst some people who say that none but the ill-inclined will go out, and when they are safe with their effects, the town will be set on fire, and there is a demurr about the meaning of the word effects, whether merchandise is therein included. . . .

I apprehend that the resolves of the Continental Congress, which was to meet on the 10th instant, will regulate the future operations of the whole, and I have sent a gentleman to Philadelphia with dispatches to Lieutenant Governor Penn, in which I give him a true account of all that has passed, and desire him to make it known; that the Congress, whatever they do, may proceed upon facts, and not be biased by the false and inflammatory accounts that have been spread with great industry through the continent. In the meantime tho' reconciliation is pointed out, we are preparing for all events, and are threatened with attacks in various ways by great multitudes. . . .

I have issued precepts for the calling of the General Court [the colonial legislature of Massachusetts], but don't find that any regard has been paid to them. A late resolve of the Provincial Congress, which I transmit your Lordship, will shew you that they have set all my authority aside.

———

WAR HAD BEGUN. General Gage's long-delayed blow—his attempt to destroy the military stores at Concord—had ended in catastrophe. The mission had begun successfully enough: the militia company drawn up at Lexington had acted indecisively; someone, no one knows who, opened fire; and the redcoats easily dispersed their opponents with disciplined and well-directed volleys. But when they arrived at Concord, the expedition turned into a nightmare. In the end, the royal forces suffered 273 casualties—almost triple the American losses.

The battle of Concord is best remembered for the long march back to Boston, as the men of Massachusetts sniped from behind walls, trees, and hedges at the retreating British soldiers. Lister's account describes that humiliating episode in bloody detail; but the ensign also reveals the shocking moment when things first turned against the king's troops. At the North Bridge at Concord, the light infantry encountered not an uncertain crowd of men, as at Lexington, but a well-drilled and determined detachment. The Minutemen stood up to the British regulars on their own terms, in a battle of formal lines and precise drill. Firing from a tight formation, they caused the professional elite of the Royal Army to break formation and run.

As historian David Hackett Fischer has noted, this part of the battle stands apart from the legend of Concord; the harassment of the British retreat is the more famous part of the fighting that day. But it was the skirmish at the bridge that would set the pattern for later battles in the Revolution. The methods used by European armies were not a product of hidebound tradition or whimsy; they reflected decades of experience with existing military technology—and the Americans would soon find themselves hard-pressed to improve upon them. Though the image of citizens sitting safely under cover, plunking away at British troops in the open, is an appealing one, the retreat from Concord would prove to be virtually the only time that such circumstances occurred.

Lord Percy later warned his British colleagues to take the rebels seriously. "Whoever looks upon [them] as an irregular mob will find himself much mistaken," he wrote. "They have men amongst them who know very well what they are about."[30]It is an admonishment for us as well, lest we forget that many of these militiamen and their officers understood the military profession fairly well.

In the meantime, those militamen swarmed to the outskirts of Boston on the heels of the beaten redcoats. As General Gage wrote in his report to the ministry, at least 10,000 hastily gathered troops besieged the town, trapping half as many British troops. The day after the battle of Concord, General Artemas Ward assumed command of this spontaneous New England army. With the aid of the militia officers, he sorted out the various detachments, fortified their positions, and set up a headquarters in Cambridge.

When the Second Continental Congress gathered in Philadelphia on May 10, its members felt almost as helpless before the tide of events as General Gage did in Boston. War had begun without them, leaving them to improvise in a situation not of their own making. Ironically, the ever realistic General Gage accepted a simple fact that Congress itself failed (at first) to grasp: it was now the de facto government of the colonies.

But even before Congress met, others far from Philadephia

[30]Quoted in Benson Bobrick, *Angel in the Whirlwind: The Triumph of the American Revolution* (New York: Simon & Schuster, 1997), p. 120.

moved decisively ahead. A strapping, bellowing native of Connecticut named Ethan Allen had organized a militia in the New Hampshire Grants (now Vermont), called the Green Mountain Boys. Intelligent, well read, and extremely bellicose, Allen yearned to get into the fight after he heard about Lexington and Concord; so when a group of men from the Connecticut River valley approached him with a plan to seize Fort Ticonderoga, he quickly agreed.

Perhaps no other fortification held so strategic a position as Ticonderoga. Originally built by the French (who called it Fort Carillon) during the French and Indian War, it commanded the portage between Lakes George and Champlain. It dominated Lake Champlain in particular—which meant that it controlled the key bottleneck in the natural military corridor between Canada and the Hudson River. If the Americans were to prevent the British from bringing down troops from the north, they would have to control Ticonderoga. Only days after Concord, Allen led his Green Mountain Boys through the rugged passes to seize that fort.

Allen wrote about his experiences a few years later, in a much-reprinted autobiography. His account is direct and colorful, but it leaves out one critical fact: he shared command of the expedition with another hard-fighting Connecticut man by the name of Benedict Arnold. Arnold tagged along with the militia leader, claiming to be in charge by virtue of a commission issued by the Massachusetts Committee of Public Safety. Despite constant squabbling, Allen and Arnold kept the operation moving toward the unsuspecting garrison of Ticonderoga.

Ticonderoga
by Ethan Allen

Ever since I arrived to a state of manhood, and acquainted myself with the general history of mankind, I have felt a sincere passion for liberty. The history of nations doomed to perpetual slavery, in consequence of yielding up to tyrants their natural born liberties, I read with a sort of philosophical horror; so that the first systematical and bloody attempt at Lexington, to enslave America, thoroughly electrified my mind, and fully determined me to take part with my country.

And while I was wishing for an opportunity to signalize myself in its behalf, directions were privately sent to me from the then colony (now state) of Connecticut, to raise the Green Mountain Boys (and if possible) with them to surprise and take the fortress Ticonderoga. This enterprise I cheerfully undertook; and, after first guarding all the several passes that led hither, to cut off all intelligence between the garrison and the country, made a forced march from Bennington, and arrived at the lake opposite to Ticonderoga on the evening of the ninth day of May, 1775, with two hundred and thirty valiant Green Mountain Boys; and it was with the utmost difficulty that I procured boats to cross the lake.

However, I landed eighty-three men near the garrison, and sent the boats back for the rear guard commanded by Col. Seth Warner; but the day began to dawn, and I found myself under a necessity to attack the fort, before the rear could cross the lake; and as it was viewed hazardous, I harangued the officers and soldiers in the manner following: "Friends and fellow soldiers, you have, for a number of years past, been a scourge and terror to arbitrary power. Your valor has been famed abroad, and acknowledged, as appears by the advice and orders to me (from the general assembly of Connecticut) to surprise and take the garrison now before us. I now propose to advance before you, and in person conduct you through the wicket-gate; for we must this morning either quit our pretensions to valor, or possess ourselves of this fortress in a few minutes; and, in as much as it is a desperate attempt (which none but the bravest men dare undertake) I do not urge it on any contrary to his will. You that will undertake voluntarily, poise your firelocks [muskets]."

The men being (at this time) drawn up in three ranks, each poised his firelock. I ordered them to face to the right; and, at the head of the center-file, marched them immediately to the wicket gate aforesaid, where I found a sentry posted, who instantly snapped his fusee at me,[31] I ran immediately toward him, and he retreated through the

---

[31]That is, he pulled the trigger on his musket, which misfired.

covered way into the parade [ground] within the garrison, gave a halloo, and ran under a bomb-proof. My party who followed me into the fort, I formed on the parade [ground] in such a manner as to face the two barracks which faced each other.

The garrison being asleep (except the sentries), we gave three huzzas, which greatly surprised them. One of the sentries made a pass at one of my officers with a charged bayonet, and slightly wounded him. My first thought was to kill him with my sword; but, in an instant, altered the design and fury of the blow to a slight cut on the side of the head; upon which he dropped his gun and asked quarter, which I readily granted him, and demanded of him the place where the commanding officer kept. He shewed me a pair of stairs in front of a barrack, on the west part of the garrison, which led up to a second story in said barrack, to which I immediately repaired, and ordered the commander (Capt. Delaplace) to come forth instantly, or I would sacrifice the whole garrison; at which the Capt. came immediately to the door with his breeches in his hand, when I ordered him to deliver to me the fort instantly, who asked me by what authority I demanded it. I answered, "In the name of the great Jehovah and the Continental Congress" (the authority of the Congress being very little known at that time). He began to speak again; but I interrupted him, and with my drawn sword over his head, again demanded an immediate surrender of the garrison; to which he then complied, and ordered his men to be forthwith paraded without arms, as he had given up the garrison.

In the meantime some of my officers had given orders, and in consequence thereof, sundry of the barrack doors were beat down, and about one-third of the garrison imprisoned, which consisted of said commander, a Lieut. Feltham, a conductor of artillery, a gunner, two sergeants, and forty-four rank and file; about one hundred pieces of cannon, one 13-inch mortar, and a number of swivels [swivel-mounted light cannon].[32]

This surprise was carried into execution in the gray of the morn-

[32]The greatest immediate benefit of conquering Ticonderoga was not control of Lake Champlain, but the capture of its many artillery pieces, which were put to good use in the rebel army.

ing of the 10th day of May, 1775. The sun seemed to rise that morn-ing with a superior luster; and Ticonderoga and its dependencies smiled on its conquerors, who tossed about the flowing bowl, and wished success to Congress, and the liberty and freedom of America.

THE SAME DAY that Ticonderoga fell, the Second Continental Congress met in Philadelphia. When the delegates had voted in 1774 to convene again the next year, they little imagined that they would return to find a war on their hands. But a war is what they had. And with war would come the responsibilities of government; and with government, nationhood itself.

5

AN ARMY, A COUNTRY

John Adams itched for a fight. As the Second Continental Congress collected in Philadelphia on May 10, 1775, war fever gripped the countryside—and this stocky little lawyer from Braintree, this outspoken champion of the colonies, was not immune. News of the victory at Concord swept down the Atlantic coast, and the population roared its approval. The long dispute had finally come to blows; volunteers poured out into the streets to join hastily organized units in colony after colony. "Oh that I was a Soldier!" Adams exclaimed in a letter. "Every Body must and will, and shall be a soldier."[33]

And so the Continental Congress met, and discovered a war on its doorstep: a war springing from a cause shared by all the colonies, a war that would be jointly waged by all the colonies. That was the consensus of the American public, of all ranks, stations, and occupations—but the delegates in Philadelphia weren't so sure. They had planned to meet for the purpose of protest, to serve as a large coordinating committee that would petition for all the provinces. But now they had a war on their hands, and they didn't know quite what to do with it.

For the first week or two, they spent much of their time preparing yet another petition to the king—the same king, of course, who was insisting on force to suppress them. Their aimlessness was not helped by one of the newest faces among them: a man named Thomas Jefferson, now a representative for Virginia. He felt rather awkward in public, so he held back, saving his energy for his pen as the delegates dithered. John Adams and his cousin Samuel, on the other hand, forced themselves to speak less brazenly than was their custom; they saw that the force of events would drive the assembly toward real action.

[33]Lyman H. Butterfield, ed., *Adams Family Correspondence* (Cambridge: Harvard University Press, 1963), vol. I, p. 207.

And so the delegates struggled for several days, gazing with some trepidation over the precipice of war that had suddenly opened at their feet. As outraged as they were, many still clutched at a last desperate hope for reconciliation (especially John Dickinson, the author of *Letters from a Farmer in Pennsylvania*). Uncertain about independence, the delegates hesitated to act as the government they had suddenly become. The Congress balked at actually waging war; it merely urged the colonies to "repel force by force."[34] Even General Gage recognized that the Continental Congress was the de facto government of America—but in Philadelphia, hesitation held the reins.

Then came news of Ticonderoga: "An act," as Robert Middlekauff writes, "that no one could call defensive." Congress still remained in some confusion, but gradually its members accepted responsibility for the great events unfolding around them. They received a request for guidance from the Massachusetts Provincial Congress; other colonies followed suit, forcing them to respond. The Continental Congress had been created as a mouthpiece—but it was the only institution available to direct a unified military effort. There seemed little doubt that it would have to adopt the army that had spontaneously gathered around Boston. By so doing, it became a government—and the colonies began to look very much like a nation.

After the delegates cleared their heads and grasped the task before them, they leaped into action. Perhaps *hunkered down* into action is the best way to put it, because they soon established numerous committees to attend to the volumes of papers and long hours needed to sort out the affairs of this newly created state. If Congress was to adopt the army in New England, it would have to pay for it and supply it. If it was to do those things, it would have to raise money. And if it was to have an army at all, it had to have a commander.

As Congress moved ahead, John and Samuel Adams returned to their old aggressive selves, arguing, pressing, proposing new steps. Despite the universal enthusiasm for the war, the delegates often quarreled and whispered among themselves. They had never imagined that they would find themselves the rulers of a continent: sometimes they rose to the occasion with great public spirit, and sometimes

[34]Quoted in Middlekauff, p. 280.

they descended into all-too-human pettiness. John Adams grew impatient with it all as he pushed for thoroughgoing measures to build a powerful army and to appoint a powerful commander.

Decades later, he recalled those critical first weeks of war in his autobiography. He looked back, of course, with eyes colored by the partisan disputes of more recent years in his life (and Adams always hated partisanship). Far from mythologizing his fellows in Congress, he judged them rather harshly. Even so, his autobiography offers a fascinating look at the birth of the Revolution from one of its creators, a man whose own life was re-created by those events. In the selection that follows, Adams found himself able to reach beyond the sectional and personal divisions among his colleagues, and nominate the man best suited to be general of the Continental Army.

Congress Adopts an Army
by John Adams

The battle of Lexington, on the 19th of April, changed the instruments of warfare from the pen to the sword.

A few days after this event, I rode to Cambridge, where I saw General Ward, General Heath, General Joseph Warren, and the New England army. There was great confusion and much distress. Artillery, arms, clothing, were wanting, and a sufficient supply of provisions not easily obtained. Neither the officers nor men, however, wanted spirits or resolution.

I rode from thence to Lexington, and along the scene of action for many miles, and inquired of the inhabitants the circumstances. These were not calculated to dimish my ardor for the cause; they, on the contrary, convinced me that the die was cast, the Rubicon passed, and, as Lord Mansfield expressed it in Parliament, if we did not defend ourselves, they would kill us.

On my return home, I was seized with a fever, attended with alarming symptoms; but the time was come to repair to Philadelphia to Congress, which was to meet on the fifth [tenth] of May. I was determined to go as far as I could, and instead of venturing on horseback, as I had intended, I got into a sulky, attended by a servant on horseback, and proceeded on the journey. This year Mr. Hancock was added to our number. I overtook my colleagues before they reached New York. At Kingsbridge we were met by a great number of gentlemen in carriages and on horseback, and all the way their numbers increased, till I thought the whole city was come out to meet us. The same ardor was continued all the way to Philadelphia.

Congress assembled and proceeded to business, and the members appeared to me to be of one mind, and that mind after my own heart. I dreaded the danger of disunion and divisons among us, and much more among the people. It appeared to me that all petitions, remonstraces, and negotiations for the future would be fruitless, and only occasion a loss of time, and give opportunity for the enemy to sow divisions. . . . My heart bled for the poor people of Boston, imprisoned within the walls of their city by a British army, and we knew not to what plunders or massacres or cruelties they might be exposed.

I thought the first step ought to be . . . to recommend to the people of all the states to institute governments for themselves, under their own authority, and that without loss of time; that we ought to declare the colonies free, sovereign, and independent states. . . .

I was also for informing Great Britain, very frankly, that hitherto we were free; but, if the war should be continued, we were determined to seek alliances with France, Spain, and any other power of Europe that would contract with us. That we ought immediately to adopt the army in Cambridge as a Continental army, to appoint a general and all other officers, take upon ourselves the pay, subsistence, clothing, armor, and munitions of the troops. This is a concise sketch of the plan which I thought the only reasonable one; and, from conversation with the members of Congress, I was then convinced, and have been ever since convinced, that it was the general sense of at least of a considerable majority of that body. . . .

In the meantime the New England army investing Boston, the New England legislatures, congresses, and conventions, and the whole body of the people, were left without munitions of war, without arms, clothing, pay, or even countenance and encouragement. Every post brought me letters from my friends, Dr. Winthrop, Dr. Cooper, General James Warren, and sometimes from General Ward and his aides, and General Heath and many others, urging in pathetic terms the impossibility of keeping their men together without the assistance of Congress.

I was daily urging all these things, but we were embarrassed with more than one difficulty, not only with the party in favor of the petition to the King, and the party who were jealous of independence, but a third party, which was a Southern party against a Northern, and a jealousy against a New England army under the command of a New England general. Whether this jealousy was sincere, or whether it was mere pride and a haughty ambition of furnishing a Southern general to command the northern army (I cannot say); but the intention was very visible to me that Colonel Washington[35] was their object, and so many of our staunchest men were in the plan, that we could carry nothing without conceding to it.

Another embarrassment, which was never publicly known, and which was carefully concealed by those who knew it: the Massachusetts and other New England delegates were divided. Mr. Hancock and Mr. Cushing hung back; Mr. Paine did not come forward; and even Mr. Samuel Adams was irresolute. Mr. Hancock himself had an ambition to be appointed commander-in-chief. . . . In canvassing this subject out of doors [outside the formal meeting of Congress], I found too that even among the delegates of Virginia there were difficulties. The apostolical reasonings among themselves, which should be greatest, were not less energetic among the saints of the ancient dominion than they were among us of New England. In several conversations, I found more than one very cool about the appointment of Washington, and particularly Mr. Pendleton was very clear and full against it.

Full of anxieties concerning these confusions, and apprehending daily that we should hear very distressing news from Boston, I walked with Mr. Samuel Adams in the State House yard, for a little exercise and fresh air before the hour of Congress, and there represented to him the various dangers that surrounded us. He agreed to them all, but said, "What shall we do?" I answered him, that he knew I had

---

[35] In the French and Indian War, George Washington had been a colonel of the Virginia militia.

taken great pains to get our colleagues to agree upon some plan, that we might be unanimous; but he knew that they would pledge themselves to nothing; but I was determined to take a step which should compel them and all the other members of Congress to declare themselves for or against something. "I am determined this morning to make a direct motion that Congress should adopt the army before Boston, and appoint Colonel Washington commander of it." Mr. Adams seemed to think very seriously of it, but said nothing.

Accordingly, when Congress had assembled, I rose in my place, and in as short a speech as the subject would admit, represented the state of the colonies, the uncertainty in the minds of the people, their great expectation and anxiety, the distresses of the army, the danger of its dissolution, the difficulty of collecting another, and the probability that the British army would take advantage of our delays, march out of Boston, and spread desolation as far as they could go. I concluded with a motion, in form, that Congress should adopt the army at Cambridge, and appoint a general; that though this was not the proper time to nominate a general, yet, as I had reason to believe this was a point of the greatest difficulty, I had no hesitation to declare that I had but one gentleman in my mind for that important command, and that was a gentleman from Virginia who was among us and very well known to all of us, a gentleman whose skill and experience as an officer, whose independent fortune, great talents, and excellent universal character, would command the approbation of all America, and unite the cordial exertions of all the colonies better than any other person in the union. Mr. Washington, who happened to sit near the door, as soon as he heard me allude to him, from his usual modesty, darted into the library room. . . .

In the meantime, pains were taken out of doors to obtain a unanimity, and the voices were so generally clearly in favor of Washington, that the disentient [dissenting] members were persuaded to withdraw their opposition, and Mr. Washington was nominated, I believe by Mr. Thomas Johnson of Maryland, unanimously elected, and the army adopted. . . .

General Ward was elected second [in command], and [Charles] Lee the third. Gates and Mifflin, I believe, had some appointments, and General Washington took with him Mr. Reed of Philadelphia, a lawyer of some eminence, for his private secretary; and the gentlemen all set off for the camp. They had not proceeded twenty miles from Philadelphia, before they met a courier with the news of the battle of Bunker Hill, the death of General [Joseph] Warren, the slaughter among the British officers and men, as well as among ours, and the burning of Charlestown.

NEWS OF BUNKER Hill alerted everyone—the newly determined Congress and the newly assigned Commander in Chief alike—that the war had a momentum of its own. At least Congress made a good start toward taking control: in addition to naming Washington as general, it issued paper currency to finance the military, voted to raise special rifle companies from the backwoodsmen of Pennsylvania, Maryland, and Virginia, and set up numerous committees to work on the question of armaments and supplies. But before these decisions could take effect, the ragged army surrounding Boston carried out an operation that culminated in the battle of Bunker Hill.

The chain of events leading to the famous fight began on May 25, when the British warship *Cerberus* sailed into beleaguered Boston Harbor, carrying the three major generals dispatched by the king to assist General Gage. They were some of the most distinguished combat veterans in the officer corps: William Howe, Henry Clinton, and John Burgoyne. Burgoyne referred to his companions and himself as a "triumvirate of reputation"; though "Gentleman Johnny," as he was called, was a bit of a boastful peacock, his phrase certainly fit.[36] All three generals knew they had been sent by the king to drive Gage into decisive action.

The triumvirate of reputation could hardly believe the situation they encountered. As they sailed across the Atlantic, they had been unaware of the events at Lexington and Concord; they arrived to discover not only a war, but a tragic defeat of the king's troops— troops who were now shut up on the narrow Boston peninsula. They had been led to believe that the Americans were merely a ragged rabble, acting without central direction; and when they peered

[36]Quoted in Middlekauff, p. 281.

through their glasses at the enemy lines, they saw little to change that opinion. They saw unkempt civilians, wearing clothing of all descriptions, carrying mismatched firearms that ranged from proper military muskets to common fowling pieces. How could such a force besiege the British army?

The source of their arrogance—and contempt for the American rebels—went deeper than the stunning red coats of the king's infantry or the tall, black, bearskin hats of the grenadiers. The British army had been honed into a truly effective fighting force by decades of experience with the realities of combat in the eighteenth century. Everything about the military—its organization, its formations, its order and discipline—had been established to make the most effective use of the army's primary weapon, the musket.[37]

The British musket of the 1770s had been developed in the 1690s; nicknamed the "Brown Bess," it weighed ten pounds and measured four and a half feet from butt to muzzle. The weapon was simplicity itself: a smoothbore metal tube that fired a three-quarter-ounce, .75 caliber lead ball. The barrel was slightly larger than the ball, for ease of loading; but that also meant the ball, when fired, would rattle down the tube, bouncing back and forth before it left the muzzle. The end result: a wildly inaccurate firearm. At 120 yards, the bullet would stray as much as *five feet* off the mark.[38]

With such a weapon, even the greatest marksman would be helpless to hit anything even close to 100 yards away. To turn this technology into something lethal, then, European armies packed their men together into dense lines, training them to fire in volleys—that is, all at once—which created the equivalent of a giant shotgun. At full strength, British infantry regiments had 477 men, divided into ten companies. When in battle, the men would fall into formations three lines deep (staggered so the men in each rank could fire between the men in front of them, with the front row kneeling); they

[37] Field artillery and cavalry were also important elements of the eighteenth-century army. In most battles of the American Revolution, however, infantry reigned supreme. Cannons were rarely present in large enough numbers to dominate the fighting; similarly, cavalry was completely absent from many battles, only becoming important in the later phase of the fighting, in the South.

[38] W. J. Wood, *Battles of the Revolutionary War, 1775–1781* (New York: Da Capo Press, 1995), pp. xxx–xxxi.

would march up to within fifty yards of the enemy, and then start firing volleys by company, so that some part of the regiment was blasting away while the others were reloading. The men never bothered to aim at a specific target; they would "present" their muskets, pointing them in the general direction of the enemy before squeezing the triggers on command.

The dense line formation, then, solved the problem of firepower—how to turn this inaccurate weapon into something deadly on the battlefield. The next problem was reloading. With so many men packed together, chaos would result if each soldier reloaded at his own pace: they would get in each other's way, and inevitably some would not be ready to fire when the next command came. To create uniformity, the British army had a strict set of orders to regulate all the motions of firing.

A simplified account goes something like this: the soldier would ground his musket (putting the butt on the earth), open his ammunition box and retrieve a cartridge (a paper pouch containing both gunpowder and lead ball), tear it open, pour a small amount of gunpowder into the firing pan, pour the rest down the barrel of the musket, dump the bullet itself in afterward (perhaps first shoving in the paper as wadding), pull the ramrod out from its slot under the barrel, ram the ball and powder down to the firing chamber, put the ramrod back, lift the musket, cock the spring-loaded flint, then present the musket (aim it at the enemy). On command, he would pull the trigger, causing the flint to snap, creating a spark that would light the powder in the firing pan, which in turn would cause the gunpowder inside the barrel to explode. The expanding gas from the erupting gunpowder would drive the bullet down the barrel. Except for the natural processes of explosions and expanding gases, each step was strictly controlled by orders given by the officers at the end of each company line.

Firing in volleys meant that speed of reloading mattered more than accuracy; in battle, the two sides would stand fifty yards or less apart, blazing away—and whoever fired fastest usually won. Since loading was a long and slow process, the troops were put through repeated drill until they could move rapidly *and* in unison; there could be no substitute for such extensive training.

It took nerve to stand in the open and shoot when facing another line of men blasting back. That fact points to another purpose of the tightly locked line formation: moral support. Under the stress of battle, soldiers have a natural tendency to crowd together; the eighteenth-century line formation took advantage of that fact, allowing the men to draw strength from their shoulder-to-shoulder proximity. The tight grouping created social pressure as well; even when men began to die from the hailstorm of bullets, no one wanted to be the first in the unit to turn and flee. Training, discipline, and these intense moral bonds kept the troops together as they stood in the killing zone.

On the other hand, once a unit did break and run, it would often cause a contagion of fear to spread to connecting units along the battlefront. Locked together, the troops drew strength from each other; but when the men on one side turned to flee, moral support became moral collapse. Once a unit disintegrated in this way, it was completely vulnerable; often most of an army's losses would be suffered at this point, as the enemy rounded up panicked prisoners or shot down fleeing individuals.

To cause such a collapse of the enemy line was the great goal of battle. One of the most effective instruments in pursuing that goal (on top of musket fire) was the bayonet. Before its invention, firearm-carrying troops were accompanied by other soldiers with pikes—essentially long spears. The socket bayonet, however, allowed each man to mount the equivalent of a spearhead on the end of his musket. The socket was a circular fitting, leaving the musket muzzle unobstructed for firing.

The bayonet was a critical part of the infantryman's arsenal. Given the short range of the musket, and the length of time needed to reload, the two sides could often run to stabbing range after only two or three volleys. Once again, the side with the best discipline usually won; it took great courage to charge straight at a line of men who were blazing away with increasing effectiveness; it also took great courage to stand and await such an attack, knowing that brutal, hand-to-hand combat would soon follow.

Training, discipline, unit cohesion: they were the roots of victory on the eighteenth-century battlefield, whether the weapon was the bullet or the bayonet. Even simple actions such as marching forward or back—let alone changing direction—took intensive training. A humble obstruction like a plowed field could instantly disorder a regiment in line of battle, making it vulnerable; wheeling to face an unexpected attack from the flank could turn the men into a jumbled crowd.

The British enlisted men hailed from the lowest fringes of society; they most likely did not fight out of heartfelt political convictions, as the Americans did. But on the battlefield, that fact was often irrelevant. Could they reload and fire quickly? Could they maintain an even step and even lines, executing maneuvers instantly on command? Could they hold together and fire disciplined volleys? Could they launch a bayonet charge in solid ranks, with irresistible force? The newly arrived generals, Burgoyne, Clinton, and Howe, knew the answer to these questions was an emphatic yes. The inexperienced Americans, on the other hand, no matter how much they loved liberty, looked likely to break in battle.

Those generals and their fellow officers had other reasons to feel arrogant. They were all from the land-owning classes of gentry and aristocracy—since most had paid for their commissions. The sale of military ranks seems shocking to modern sensibilities; indeed, it led to some incompetent men gaining command. The eighteenth-century British failed to see it that way, however; they were convinced that the wealthy and noble-born were intrinsically superior. Furthermore, those who spent great sums to purchase commissions were generally dedicated to the military profession; as a whole, they learned their business well. And they were motivated by a yearning for honor, for reputation, for the praise and prestige that comes with bravery on the field, and especially with victory.

As the triumvirate of reputation sat down to a council of war with General Gage, then, it trusted in the fact that the British had the superior army—a highly trained force, logically organized for the technology of the day, led by competent officers. It did not matter that they were outnumbered by two to one or more; in their eyes, each British company was worth a regiment of American militia. The defeat at Concord was an anomaly—merely a sign to Burgoyne, Clinton, and Howe that Gage himself had somehow failed. They would quickly remedy the situation.

"The tactical options," Benson Bobrick notes, "were fairly plain. Boston was dominated by high ground to the north and the southeast."[39] This high ground rose up from two peninsulas, on either side of the town's own peninsula. Above Boston, Charlestown sat on the end of a jut of land spiked by three hills: Bunker (the tallest), Breed's, and Moulton's (the smallest). To the southeast, Dorchester Heights loomed above the mouth of the harbor from a boot-shaped spit of land.

Feeling the pressure to act, Gage presented the trio of official second-guessers with a plan to seize Dorchester Heights (still unoccupied by the rebels). That would secure the entrance to the harbor and create a base for offensive operations (the neck of land connecting Boston to the mainland was so narrow, the Americans easily blocked it off). The major generals gave the operation their hearty approval. Unfortunately for them, the American command learned of it virtually the same day it was agreed upon in the British headquarters.

General Artemus Ward called his own council of war as soon as news came of the enemy plan. His officers pushed for a preemptive strike—not at Dorchester Heights, but on the other side of Boston, on the Charlestown peninsula. Unused to the burden of command, Ward viewed the proposal with some trepidation; but at last he agreed. After dark on June 16, 1775, Colonel William Prescott led a party of 1,200 men onto Breed's Hill—the mount closest to Charlestown, and Boston itself.[40] Working through the night, they built a redoubt. This square, enclosed fortification consisted of an earthen parapet, constructed out of dirt dug from a partial trench. Fearful of being surrounded, Prescott also raised a breastwork (a dirt wall the men could stand behind) extending out to the northeast, toward the Mystic River, to cover the most vulnerable flank of the redoubt.

General Gage discovered the new works the next morning, when the warship *Lively* began firing on the Americans. After a hurried

[39]Bobrick, p. 140.

[40]The original plan was to fortify Bunker Hill, which stood higher; when the troops arrived on the peninsula, however, it appears Prescott made a decision to occupy Breed's Hill, as it was closest to both Charlestown and Boston.

meeting with Burgoyne, Clinton, and Howe, he abandoned his plans for Dorchester Heights and decided to attack the Americans on Breed's Hill. He turned to Howe to command the actual landing party. More than 1,500 hastily assembled British troops (backed by another 700 in reserve) landed at two points on the southeastern coast of the peninsula around one o'clock in the afternoon.

Howe planned to launch a diversionary attack on the left, directly against the redoubt; but his main thrust would be to his right— against that northeastern flank that Prescott had worried about. Howe intended to come around the American left, surround the redoubt, and capture everyone inside.

When the British troops deployed on the fields above Charlestown, however, they discovered that newly arrived American militiamen were now protecting the area to the northeast of the redoubt. Two New Hampshire regiments, under the command of Colonels John Stark and James Reed, had marched down to join Prescott's men; they assisted a detachment under Captain Thomas Knowlton in manning the breastwork, along with a rail fence that extended even farther toward the northeast and a hastily erected wall of stones along the water's edge. The Americans now had their left flank completely covered by troops commanded by extremely capable officers.

Nevertheless, Howe pushed his attack ahead. He trusted in the high level of training of his infantrymen, their experience in battle and maneuver, and their aristocratic officers. He felt sure that the American rabble atop Breed's Hill and along the breastworks would break and run at the first shot. But Howe failed to reckon on one important fact: the moment a jumbled crowd of men jump into a trench or spread out along a wall, they instantly become an organized line. The American defensive works automatically aligned the inexperienced militiamen, and the protection of the dirt walls bolstered their courage. The hastily erected redoubt and breastworks made up for the lack of training, and promised to save lives as well.

Meanwhile the British, as soon as they got within killing range of the American muskets, encountered rail fences that disrupted and slowed down their advance. A few American sharpshooters within Charlestown itself distracted them also, leading the king's commanders to fire indiscriminately at the little community. For the British, the battle of Bunker Hill began as a fiasco.

Immediately after the clash, General Gage dispatched two letters to the ministry in London, briefly summarizing the events of the day. The first reduced the bloody catastrophe into a brief account of a glorious victory. The second, written the same day, portrays the battle in a more realistic—and far grimmer—light. The battle of Bunker Hill,[41] he wrote, demonstrated an uncomfortable fact: "The rebels are not the despicable rabble too many have supposed them to be."

―――――――――

The Battle of Bunker Hill
by Thomas Gage

TO DARTMOUTH   BOSTON, JUNE 25th, 1775

I am to acquaint your Lordship with an action that happened on the 17th instant, between his Majesty's troops and a large body of the rebel forces.

An alarm was given at break of day on the 17th instant, by a firing from the *Lively* ship of war, and advice was soon afterwards received that the rebels had broke ground, and were raising a battery on the heights of the peninsula of Charlestown, against the town of Boston. They were plainly seen at work, and in a few hours a battery of six guns played upon their works. Preparations were instantly made for landing a body of men to drive them off; and ten companies of the grenadiers, ten of light infantry, with the 5th, 28th, 43rd, and 52nd Battalions, with a proportion of field artillery under the command of Major General Howe, and a Brigadier General [Robert] Pigot, were embarked with great expedition, and landed on the peninsula without opposition, under the protection of some ships of war,

―――

[41]Even though the fighting took place on Breed's Hill, the battle has been named after the largest hill on the peninsula, which the Americans originally intended to fortify.

armed vessels, and boats, by whose fire the rebels were kept within their works.

The troops formed as soon as landed, with light infantry posted on the right, and the grenadiers upon their left. The 5th and 38th Battalions drew up in the rear of those corps, and the 43rd and 52nd Battalions made a third line. The rebels upon the heights were perceived to be in great force, and strongly posted; a redoubt thrown up on the 16th at night, with other works full of men, defended with cannon, and a large body posted in the houses of Charlestown covered their right flank, and their center and left was covered by a breastwork, part of it cannon-proof, which reached from the left of the redoubt to the Mystic or Medford River.

This appearance of the rebels' strength, and the large columns seen pouring in to their assistance, occasioned an application for the troops to be reinforced with some companies of light infantry, and grenadiers, the 47th Battalion, and the first Battalion of Marines, the whole when in conjunction making a body of something above 2,000 men.

These troops advanced, formed in two lines, and the attack began by a sharp cannonade from our field pieces and howitzers, the line advancing slowly, and frequently halting to give time for the artillery to fire. The light infantry was directed to force the left point of the breastwork to take the rebel line in flank,[42] and the grenadiers to attack in front, supported by the 5th and 52nd Battalions. These orders were executed with perseverence, under a heavy fire from the vast numbers of the rebels, and notwithstanding various impediments before the troops could reach the works, and tho' the left under Brigadier General Pigot was engaged also with the rebels at Charlestown, which at a critical moment was set on fire, the Brigadier pursued his point, and carried the redoubt.[43]

[42]The light infantry attacked Colonel Stark's men on the narrow beach, on the far left of the American line. A steep drop-off from the fields to the beach isolated the river's edge from the rest of the battlefield; the redcoats attacked in a dense column. The New Hampshire militiamen annihilated the attacking British, forcing the survivors to withdraw.

[43]This report radically simplifies the story of the attack, which required no less than three assaults before it succeeded, at heavy cost to the British. Howe was forced to abandon his attacks on the breastworks northeast of the redoubt, and concentrate

The rebels were then forced from other strongholds, and pursued till they were drove clear off the peninsula, leaving five pieces of cannon behind them. . . .

This action has shewn the superiority of the King's troops, who under every disadvantage attacked and defeated above three times their own number, strongly posted, and covered by breastworks. . . .

TO DARTMOUTH   BOSTON, JUNE 25th, 1775

The success . . . [in the battle] was very necessary in our situation, and I wish most sincerely that it had not cost us so dear. The number of the killed and wounded is greater than our force can afford to lose, the officers who were obliged to exert themselves have suffered very much, and we have lost some extraordinary good officers.

The trials we have had shew that the rebels are not the despicable rabble too many have supposed them to be, and I find it owing to a military spirit encouraged amongst them for a few years past, joined with an uncommon degree of zeal and enthusiasm that they are otherwise. Wherever they find cover they make a good stand, and the country, naturally strong, affords it them, and they are taught to assist its natural strength by art, for they entrench and raise batteries. They have engineers to instruct them, one by the name of Gridley who served at the two sieges of Louisbourg. . . . They have fortified all the passes and heights round this town, from Dorchester to Medford on Mystic, and it's not impossible for them to annoy the town.

Your Lordship will perceive that the conquest of this country is not easy and can be effected only by time and perseverence, and strong armies attacking it in various quarters; and dividing their forces. Confining your operations on this side [in New England] only is attacking in the strongest part, and you have to cope with vast numbers.

It might naturally be supposed that troops of the nature of the

---

everything on the fortification itself. Despite Gage's claims (later in this selection) that the British were outnumbered three to one, the Americans actually had fewer troops engaged in the battle.

rebel army would return home after such a check as they have got [at Bunker Hill, but] in all their wars against the French they never shewed so much conduct, attention, and perseverence as they do now.

———

THE BRITISH ARMY launched three attacks that day. Each time, the Americans coolly waited to fire until the dense lines of red-coated infantry were within fifty yards; then, at command, they blasted a horrific volley that tore apart the enemy ranks. As General Howe watched his men go down like so much harvested wheat, he experienced a "moment that I never felt before": it seemed that he would lose a battle, and most of his men in the bargain.[44]

On the third assault, General Howe abandoned all hope of surrounding the redoubt; his men now littered the ground in wet heaps in front of the rail fence and breastworks. His second in command, General Robert Pigot, had cleared the snipers out of Charlestown by setting the place on fire; then the king's regulars turned their sole attention to the little fortification on the hill. By the time the last wave crashed against the American parapet, the militiamen were almost out of ammunition; Howe, on the other hand, had more than 400 reinforcements to back up his attack. For the last time, the rebels fired from Breed's Hill; scores of British troops fell, including Major Pitcairn, the commander at Lexington. Then the Americans fled, under covering fire from Stark's and Knowlton's troops. Those who failed to escape were bayoneted by the infuriated grenadiers.

The capture of the Charlestown peninsula cost the outnumbered British 226 dead and 828 wounded, compared to 140 dead Americans and 271 wounded. In other words, General Gage lost more than one out of every five soldiers available to him, simply to capture a spit of land that did him almost no good. "I think we have little reason to complain," wrote American General Nathanael Greene. "I wish we could sell them another hill at the same price."[45] Perhaps more important to the American cause, the heavy British casualties

[44]Quoted in Middlekauff, p. 291.
[45]Quoted in Bobrick, p. 143.

brought a halt to any further attempts at offensive action around Boston; and the strategic Dorchester Heights continued to remain unoccupied.

General Gage's misery at the outcome drips from his second letter to Dartmouth; the battle proved what he had told the ministry many times: "The conquest of this country is not easy." London was not facing a confused insurrection, one easily quashed with a mere show of force; this was a real war, requiring real force and real strategy—a strategy Gage tried to provide. But neither the king nor Lord North wished to hear anything from this general; they were weary of his too-realistic naysaying and revolted at the fiasco at Bunker Hill. They recalled him to Britain, putting Howe in command of the land forces in North America.

Two weeks after the battle, the Americans received a new commander as well. He was George Washington, the man nominated by John Adams and chosen unanimously by the Continental Congress. As he rode into the army's headquarters in Cambridge, he instantly impressed those who greeted him with his physical appearance alone. Unlike the aged, gray-wigged, stationary figure seen in paintings, standing erect and immobile beside desks and papers, the real Washington of 1775 was a vigorous man near the peak of his strength and energy. Only forty-three years old, he was a tall, powerful figure, hardened by numerous journeys into the Appalachian wilderness—by an outdoor life of fighting, surveying, and managing a growing array of lands and businesses. He was at ease in the saddle, and he strode with vigor and purpose.

His imposing physical presence was matched by his reputation— and reputation meant a great deal to this son of Virginia. Historians Stanley Elkins and Eric McKitrick, those masters of the character sketch, deftly describe the Washington of the time: "We do not ordinarily recollect that Washington's achievements in the frontier warfare of the 1750s against the French were a matter of general knowledge throughout the colonies, or that his name was personally known to King George II when Washington was still in his early twenties. Distinction for bravery at Laurel Mountain and Fort Necessity, and gallant behavior as Braddock's aide-de-camp at Fort Duquesne, were already behind him by the time he had become, at twenty-three, commander-in-chief of Virginia troops with the rank of colonel."

Toward the end of the French and Indian War, the already famous Washington resigned from the Virginia militia, winning election to the colony's House of Burgesses, where he sat until he took command of the Continental Army in 1775. Even as he pursued a brilliantly successful career as a land speculator, large-scale planter, and entrepreneur, he built a second career in public service. "In addition to continuous service in the Virginia House of Burgesses, which should be reckoned as a key constant," Elkins and McKitrick write, "he served also as justice of the peace for Fairfax County, vestryman and later warden of Phock Church in Truro Parish, and chairman of the meeting which adopted the Fairfax County Resolves of 1774. Meanwhile, as master of Mount Vernon, he accepted a status in his neighborhood which was itself quasi-public in nature. . . . It was thus a man of both substance and experience, as well as the object of wide respect, who went as a delegate to the first Provincial Convention in Williamsburg in 1774. There he was elected to the First Continental Congress. He went . . . and impressed the other delegates by the unobtrusive soundness of his judgment when he chose to give it."[46]

When the Second Continental Congress assembled after the outbreak of war, he attended in his military uniform, having already volunteered to raise a unit at his own expense. The other delegates, far from thinking that his costume was mere showmanship, respected the determination it represented, for Washington was known as a man who spoke with his actions. Here was a gentleman of wealth and good family, in an age that respected property and breeding; here was one of the very few American officers to win a transatlantic reputation in the French and Indian War, sitting among men who distinctly lacked military experience. Small wonder that they gave him supreme command of the fledgling army.

So much for the outer man—the inner man was a different story entirely. Even as the French and Indian War transformed his reputation, it opened his eyes to profound new knowledge about himself and his fellow creatures. In his early battles in the wilderness, he

[46]Elkins and McKitrick, pp. 35–37.

learned what it meant to stand amid flying lead, to issue orders and see them followed, to rally a horde of panicked men and turn them about to face the enemy again. When still in his early twenties, he had both ambushed and been ambushed; he had both surrendered to the enemy and defied defeat; he had seen the reality of fear and bravery in actual combat. He *loved* to fight, and to lead others to fight; after his first engagement he famously wrote that he found something charming in the sound of whistling bullets.

In the years that followed his battlefield exploits, he learned something else about war, and his ability to conduct it. He assumed command of the Virginia militia, taking responsibility for the defense of hundreds of miles of exposed frontier. Rather than leading troops into action, he spent his time supplying, manning, and maintaining distant forts and outposts. Washington learned the truth in an old military adage: amateurs chatter about strategy and tactics, while professional soldiers worry about logistics. Or, as Napoleon would later put it, an army marches on its stomach. He spent endless hours on the unglamorous tasks of obtaining supplies, figuring out how to move them into the mountains, keeping units up to strength, and securing funding from the House of Burgesses.

Fortunately, Washington had a first-rate mind to match his bravery. As he assumed command of the patchwork army gathered around Boston, he applied both experience and his prodigious capacity for organization to straighten out its administration. Though he gradually surrounded himself with excellent junior officers, he never had a staff in the modern sense (a small-scale bureaucracy, that is, to attend to details); instead, he conducted an enormous amount of paperwork in person—making sure there were enough carts, horses, and mules, issuing orders governing such matters as how often the camps were swept and kitchens inspected, corresponding with spies and informers. He knew what to expect, and what needed to be done; though fifteen years had passed since he last held command, he had kept his mastery of detail in good condition by juggling a bewildering array of enterprises over the years. This was the Washington most often missed by history: the man who literally kept shirts on the soldiers' backs, food on their plates, muskets in their hands, and bullets and powder to go with them.

But the shining reputation that Washington carried was also his burden. He was the product of Virginia's cavalier society, a man of the hierarchical eighteenth century; words such as honor, glory, and reputation mattered the world to him. Very much a creature of action—sometimes of impulse—he painstakingly trained himself to present an air of weighty dignity. He had once fought very hard to win a commission as a British officer, back in the days of the French and Indian War; his failure helped rein in his youthful ambition, to direct it onto a more public-spirited path—but he still aspired to an aristocratic appearance and temperament.

When he arrived in Cambridge, he virtually snorted at the near-anarchic disorder of the New England militia. These humble democrats had no manners, no discipline, no *respectability*. These things mattered more to him, as a Virginian, a military professional, and a member of the American gentry, than they did to these militiamen of the North. But the remarkable thing is not that Washington looked down on the New Englanders—it was that he overcame his own prejudices. He sincerely believed in American liberty and independence; he put his mind to his duty, as he always had, and learned to work with these volunteers.

Concern for reputation, however, and his desire to hear the bullets whistle once more, led him to propose an assault on Boston in early 1776. Fortunately, he called a council of war, rather than issuing the orders directly; his officers argued against it. They had learned their own ability to fight at Bunker Hill—but they also had learned that the British could fight very well indeed. An attack on Boston would be costly, and unnecessary.

The passage that follows reveals Washington's thoughts about the siege of Boston, as the winter of 1775–1776 moved along. With his plan for an assault voted down, he moved ahead with a second plan. Dorchester Heights still remained unoccupied—and it still remained the key to control of the harbor. To seize it in the dead of winter seemed a desperate scheme, but he knew the British would not ignore it forever.

The Conquest of Boston
by George Washington

26 FEBY., 1776: About ten days ago the severe freezing weather formed some pretty strong ice from Dorchester to Boston Neck, and from Roxbury to the Common. This I thought (knowing ice could not last) a favorable opportunity to make an assault upon the troops in town. I proposed it in council, but behold! though we had been waiting all the year for this favorable event, the enterprise was thought too dangerous! Perhaps it was—perhaps the irksomeness of my situation led me to undertake more than could be warranted by prudence.

I did not think so, and am sure yet that the enterprise, if it had been undertaken with resolution, must have succeeded. Without it, any would fail, but it is now at an end, and I am preparing to take post on Dorchester to try if the enemy will be so kind as to come out to us. . . .

MARCH 3rd, 1776: I hope in a few nights to be in readiness to take post on Dorchester as we are using every means in our power to provide materials for this purpose, the ground being so hard froze yet that we cannot intrench, & therefore are obliging to depend entirely upon Chandaliers, fascines, & screwed hay[47] for our redoubts. It is expected that this work will bring on an action between the King's troops and ours. . . .

MARCH 7th, 1776: On Monday night, I took possession of the heights of Dorchester with two thousand men under the command of General Thomas. Previous to this, and in order to divert the enemy's attention from the real object & to harrass, we began on Saturday night a cannonade and bombardment which with intervals was continued through the night, the same on Sunday—and on Monday a continued roar from seven o'clock till daylight was kept up between the enemy and us. . . . The cannonade . . . answered our expectation fully; for though we had upwards of 300 teams in motion at the same

---

[47]Washington here refers to baskets of dirt, used to build hasty fortifications (much in the manner of sandbags), along with large bundles of sticks (fascines) and hay, which were all piled up on the ground, as the freezing temperatures prevented the Americans from digging trenches.

instant carrying on our fascines & other materials to the neck & the moon shining in its full luster, we were not discovered till daylight on Tuesday morning.

As soon as we were discovered everything seem'd to be preparing for an attack [by the British], but the tide failing before they were ready, about one thousand only were able to embark in six transports in the afternoon; and these falling down towards the castle were drove on shore by a violent storm which arose in the afternoon of that day & continued through the night. Since that they have been seen returning to Boston—and whether from an apprehension that our works are now too formidable to make any impression on, or from what other causes I know not, but their hostile appearances have subsided & they are removing their ammunition out of their magazine—whether with a view to move bag & baggage or not I cannot undertake to say—but if we had powder . . . I would, so soon as we were sufficiently strengthened on the heights, to take possession of the point just oppose to Boston Neck [and] give them a dose they would not well like.

We had prepared boats, a detachment of 4,000 men, &c., &c., for pushing in to the west part of Boston if they had made any formidable attack upon Dorchester. I will not lament or repine at any act of Providence because I am in a great measure convert[ed] to Mr. Pope's opinion that whatever is, is right, but I think everything had the appearance of a successful issue if we had come to an engagement on that day. It was the 5th of March which I recalled to their remembrance as a day never to be forgotten—an engagement was fully expected—& I never saw spirits higher, or more ardor prevailing.

———

WASHINGTON CARRIED OUT the operation flawlessly. With his characteristically careful preparations, he built a formidable redoubt on Dorchester Heights in one night. Down in the town of Boston, General Howe's naval counterpart informed him that the fleet would have to withdraw as soon as the Americans mounted heavy guns in the works. Preparations for an evacuation began immediately; on March 17, 1776, the last British troops left for good.

The long winter had seen little fighting around besieged Boston, but Washington had been furiously busy. Even as he attended to matters minor and major from his headquarters in Cambridge, he had directed a desperate invasion of Canada. Acting on the direction of Congress, he had organized two thrusts across the St. Lawrence River, under Generals Richard Montgomery and Benedict Arnold. They and their men endured grueling marches through the wilderness in the heart of winter. They succeeded in capturing Montreal, but a New Year's Eve assault on Quebec, in the midst of a howling blizzard, failed utterly, leaving General Montgomery among the dead. Worn down and out of supplies, the little army fell back with the warm weather, abandoning all hope of conquering Canada.

As Washington's troops paraded into newly liberated Boston, almost a year had passed since the war began. That year had changed everything the colonists ever knew. Despite the long run of bitter disputes over taxation and representation, the path backward had always been open—there had always been ways of restoring something of the colonies' relationship with the mother country. But now an impenetrable barrier had fallen into place: a line of spilled blood. It is possible, of course, that if the British had dispersed the militia at Concord, if they had broken out of the siege of Boston, that American resistance might have collapsed. But such things did not happen: the rebels had held firm and (apart from the losses in Canada) had won. There would be no stepping back.

Not everyone realized that yet, of course. There would be a great deal of arguing before the public was truly committed to independence. John Adams, Samuel Adams, and others already knew, however, that events had once again left debate behind. Thanks to Washington and his unruly men, they believed a declaration of independence could not be very far away.

III

CRISIS

6

INDEPENDENCE

One may wonder if the American Revolution was a revolution at all. After all, the Continental Congress was a collection of the most respectable men in the thirteen colonies—men who were already active in government. Before the rebellion against Britain, the colonies had largely run their own affairs for most of their history. It is true that the crown picked the governors for most (but not all) of the American provinces, and that Parliament regulated trade and manufacturing; but the colonies taxed themselves, legislated for themselves, administered justice for themselves, even defended themselves against the French and Indians. It might seem as if the whole point of the war of independence was simply to convince the government in London of the reality of the existing situation. Did shipping out the royal governors and tax collectors constitute a real revolution?

The answer would be no—if that was all the revolution accomplished. The truth is, in just one year of war the Americans came a tremendous distance in both their convictions—their theory of government—and their political reality. This distance marked not just twelve calendar months, but a vast gulf between one historical era and the next.

As 1776 began, the quintessential fact was that all existing governments in the colonies had fallen, or were falling fast. Massachusetts had led the way: when General Gage took over as governor, he dismissed the elected legislature—indeed, he dismissed many public officials—in an attempt to tighten the loyalty of the entire governmental machinery. The colony's response was to establish an entirely new government, the Provincial Congress; it set up a fresh judicial and financial structure. This new edifice abandoned the keystone of the colony's charter: the ultimate authority of the crown, represented by the royal governor.

This change was more than cosmetic: the highly public debate about liberty and civil rights in the decade since the Stamp Act had caused a deepening commitment to egalitarianism throughout society. Like dry kindling slowly piling up, it predictably erupted when struck by the spark of war. In the Connecticut valley of western Massachusetts, for example, the old establishment—a handful of enormously rich and powerful men known as the River Gods—found itself swept out of power by a popular uprising. Here and elsewhere, mobs closed down the official courts; ad hoc committees and county congresses took over local governments. To hundreds of thousands of Americans, a new spirit of republicanism held sway, and it manifested itself in scores of spontaneously created councils, ruling with wider participation than ever before.[48]

This spirit, set aflame by British troops, was fanned by the indignant actions of the king himself. He declared the colonies to be out of his protection; he turned American ships into open prey on the high seas; he loudly announced his determination to crush the rebellion by force. George III was never a flexible man; the armed resistance drove him to absolute, unbending fury, which alienated the colonists even more. Once it was started, their shift toward greater liberty and democracy only accelerated as the war progressed.

Samuel Adams (along with his cousin John) led the fight in the Continental Congress for a formal declaration of independence in the winter and spring of 1776. The selection that follows consists of two of his letters, written to Samuel Cooper of Boston in April; they accurately represent the vehemence of Adams's arguments and his assessment of the political facts of the day. The first letter argues in favor of independence in terms of British actions: first he offers a prophetic assessment of the enemy's strategy for the next two years, then he shows that the king's own actions had made independence a necessity—even an existing reality. "Can nations at war," he asks, "be said to be dependent upon the other?"

The second letter focuses on the situation within the colonies themselves. Samuel Adams knew what historian Pauline Maier has

[48]For a discussion of the revolt against the River Gods, see Middlekauff, pp. 252–257. Gordon S. Wood's *The Radicalism of the American Revolution.* (New York: Alfred A. Knopf, 1992) provides a now classic account of the Revolution as a social and cultural phenomenon.

recently argued: the real action was at the local level, where revolutionary governments were rising up through the grassroots actions of the people themselves (a process encouraged by the Continental Congress). Adams runs through the list of colonies, accurately assessing their fervor for the cause of nationhood.

Despite the general momentum, there were still many, even in Congress, who refused to accept independence as the goal. Adams's response is telling: though he was known for his ideological commitment to republicanism, democracy, and liberty, here he flatly states that the tide of events will wash back arguments against independence. "We cannot make events," he writes. "Our business is wisely to improve them."

Is Not America Already Independent?
by Samuel Adams

TO SAMUEL COOPER   PHILADA., APRIL 3, 1776

I lately rec'd. a very obliging letter from you for which I now return you my hearty thanks. I wish your leisure would admit of your frequently favoring me with your thoughts of our public affairs. I do assure you I shall make use of them, as far as my ability shall extend, to the advantages of our country. If you please, I will employ a few minutes in giving you my own ideas, grounded on the best intelligence I have been able to obtain.

Notwithstanding the shame and loss [that] attended the measures of the British Court the last summer and fall, yet by the latest accounts rec'd. from our friends in that country, it appears that they are determin'd to persevere. . . . It is probable then that the Ministry have not quitted the plan which they agreed upon above a twelve-month ago; which was, to take possession of New York—make themselves masters of the Hudson's River & the Lakes, thereby securing Canada and the Indians—cut off all communication between the colonies northward & southward of the Hudson's River, and thus to subdue the former in hopes of instigating the negroes to make the others an easy prey. . . .

The King's troops have now abandon'd Boston, on which I sincerely congratulate you. We have not heard what course they have steer'd. I judge for Halifax. They may return if they hear that you are off your guard. . . .

France is attentive to this struggle and wishes for a separation of the two countries. I am in no doubt that she would with cheerfulness openly lend her aid to promote it, if America would declare herself free and independent; for I think it is easy to see what great though different effects it would have in both those nations. Britain would no longer have it in her power to oppress.

Is not America already independent? Why then not declare it? Upon whom was she ever supposed to be dependent, but upon that nation whose most barbarous usage of her, & that in multiplied instances and for a long time has render'd it absurd ever to put confidence in it, & with which she is at this time in open war. Can nations at war be said to be dependent upon the other?

I ask then again, why not declare for independence? Because, say some, it will forever shut the door of reconciliation. Upon what terms will Britain be reconciled with America? If we may take the confiscating Act of Parliamt. or the King's last proclamation for our rule to judge by, who will be reconciled upon our abjectly submitting to tyranny, and asking and receiving pardon for resisting it? Will this redound to the honor or the safety of America? Surely no. By such a reconciliation she would not only in the most shameful manner acknowledge the tyranny, but most wickedly, as far as would be in her power, prevent her posterity from ever hereafter resisting it. . . .

TO SAMUEL COOPER   PHILADA., APRIL 30, 1776

The ideas of independence [have] spread far and wide among the colonies. Many of the leading men see the absurdity of supposing that allegiance is due to a sovereign who has already thrown us out of his protection.

South Carolina has lately assumed a new government. The convention of North Carolina have unanimously agreed to do the same & appointed a committee to prepare & lay before them a proper form. They have also revok'd certain instructions which tied the hands of their delegates here. Virginia, whose convention is to meet on the third of next month, will follow the lead. The body of the people of Maryland are firm. Some of the principal members of their convention, I am inclined to believe, are timid or lukewarm, but an occurrence has lately fallen out in that colony which will probably give an agreeable turn to their affairs. Of this I will inform you at a future time. . . .

The lower counties on the Delaware are a small people but well affected to the common cause. In this populous and wealthy colony [Pennsylvannia] political parties run high. The newspapers are full of the matter but I think I may assure you that common sense prevails among the people—a law has recently passed in the Assembly here for increasing the number of representatives, and tomorrow they are to come to a choice in this city & diverse of the counties; by this means, it is said, the representation of the colony will be more equal. I am told that a very popular gentleman who is a candidate for one of the back counties has been in danger of losing his election because it was reported among the electors that he had declared his mind in this city against independence. . . . I mention this anecdote to give you an idea of the jealousy of the people and their attention to this point.

The Jerseys[49] are agitating the great question. It is with them rather a matter of prudence whether to determine till some others have done it before them. . . . I forbear to say anything of New York, for I confess I am not able to form any opinion of them. I lately rec'd. a letter from a friend in that colony informing me that they would soon come to a question of the expediency of taking up government; but to me it is uncertain what they will do. I think they are at least as unenlighten'd in the nature & importance of our political disputes as any one of the united colonies. I have not mention'd our little sister Georgia; but I believe she is as warmly engag'd in the cause as any of us, & will do as much as can be reasonably expected of her.

[49]New Jersey was originally divided into two colonies, East and West; even in 1776, the colony had two capitals, Burlington and Perth Amboy: one for each Jersey.

I was very solicitous the last fall to have governments set up by the people in every colony. It appears to me to be necessary for many reasons. When this is done, and I am inclin'd to think it will be soon, the colonies will feel their independence—the way will be prepared for a Confederation, and one government may be form'd with the consent of the whole—a distinct state compos'd of all the colonies with a common legislature for great & general purposes.

This, I was in hopes, would have been the work of the last winter. I am disappointed but I bear it tolerably well. I am disposed to believe that everything is order'd for the best, and if I do not find myself chargeable with neglect I am not greatly chagrined when things do not go exactly according to my mind. . . .

We cannot make events. Our business is wisely to improve them. There has been much to do to confirm doubting friends & fortify the timid. It requires time to bring honest men to think & determine alike even in important matters. Mankind are governed more by their feelings than by reason. Events which excite those feelings will produce wonderful effects. The Boston Port bill suddenly wrought a union of the colonies, which could not be brought about by the industry of years in reasoning on the necessity of it for the common safety. Since the memorable 19th of April [the battle of Concord] one event has brought another on, till Boston sees her deliverance from those more than savage troops upon which the execrable Tyrant so much relied for the completion of his horrid conspiracies and America has furnish'd herself with more than seventy battalions for her defense. . . . One battle would do more towards a Declaration of Independency than a long chain of conclusive arguments in a provincial convention or the Continental Congress.

"FORTIFY THE TIMID": Sam Adams had faith that events themselves would move the wavering to accept independence. He trusted in Britain's own blustering pigheadedness, in the king's belligerence, to keep American outrage fresh—and he trusted to General Washington's skill to keep those potent battles from turning into disasters. A revolution was truly sweeping the continent; his job, he wrote, was to "wisely improve" the transactions of the day—to simply let the people see how "the execrable Tyrant" was carrying out "his horrid conspiracies."

But independence remained an awkward subject for public debate. The colonists had always claimed that they were defending their existing rights as British subjects; that they merely sought a return to the way things had always been; that they had taken up arms against an undeserved provocation. To proclaim independence would admit that conservatism had dissolved into radicalism. Even more, it would turn the rebellion into an attack on the king himself.

Despite all the hostile acts and speeches of George III, rebelling directly against the king remained extremely difficult for most Americans. To do so was to knock out the keystone of the eighteenth-century Anglo-American society, for the king was the peak of the hierarchical, class- and status-defined world. Though the monarch had lost much political power in the previous century, he still occupied an enormous place in the imaginations of all British subjects.

Traditionally, there were only two legitimate ways to rebel against an English king: to boot him out in favor of a pretender, or rival candidate for the throne; or to argue that he was held captive by corrupt and evil advisers. The colonists fell back on this second formulation. Of course, it was exactly the argument used by the Puritans who fought against Charles I in the English Civil War—and they beheaded the king in the end. George III would never be in the Americans' power in that way, but the example must have been on the minds of many—though in the mouths of few. But the king's own actions and words made more and more colonists willing to abandon any trace of a connection to the crown.

Independence—with all its antimonarchical implications—erupted into the public debate in January 1776 with the publication of *Common Sense*, a pamphlet by a thirty-nine-year-old failed corset-maker named Thomas Paine. Paine had only resided in the colonies for a year before he wrote his famous tract; but his passion, his wit, and his ability to write clearly and powerfully commanded the attention of Americans everywhere. He wrote a blistering attack on the very idea of a king, conjuring up a vision of a society based purely upon popular consent, rather than a hereditary monarchy. *Common*

Sense sold more than 100,000 copies, and in so doing focused the public's attention on the question of independence or reconciliation.

Many historians, notably Pauline Maier in *American Scripture*, have argued that the influence of *Common Sense* has been exaggerated (especially by Thomas Paine himself). Scores of spontaneously organized associations, from town committees to brotherhoods of artisans and workers, were pushing the trend toward independence with their own discussions, debates, and resolutions. And many prominent thinkers recoiled at the anarchic implications of Paine's writing (he referred to government itself as a necessary evil). Some, such as John Adams, felt that the case was best rested on *necessity* rather than reason; like Samuel Adams, he felt that independence was being forced upon Americans, and that all the philosophizing in the world would not accomplish it.

All of these complaints may well be true. *Common Sense*, however, provided a focus for the debate. Whether Americans were in favor of Paine's arguments or against them, they talked about them, and so talked about independence. What's more, Paine broke ground in the attempt to build a new philosophical foundation for an American republic. Before the outbreak of war, the colonists' arguments were based on their rights under the British constitution, which they greatly revered. Now they faced a complete abandonment of that constitution. Paine reassured them that all would be well without it—that there were other sources of rights, of protections for their liberty and property, than the power of a king. In the end, if he accomplished little more than raising the volume of the debate, he accomplished a great deal.

The selection that follows offers only a brief excerpt of this long essay. It focuses not on Paine's arguments against monarchy, but on his attempts to convince his countrymen of the importance of this moment. Critics would attack *Common Sense* as "utopian" and "visionary," but the passage below shows Paine directly confronting the necessity of independence and the impossibility of reconciliation. This was probably the most effective part of his argument: the least abstract, the most direct, the most specific application of his thinking to the present situation. It retains its power to this day.

Common Sense
by Thomas Paine

In the following pages I offer nothing more than simple facts, plain arguments, and common sense; and have no other preliminaries to settle with the reader, than that he will divest himself of prejudice and prepossession, and suffer his reason and his feelings to determine for themselves; that he will put *on*, or rather that he will not put *off*, the true character of a man, and generously enlarge his views beyond the present day.

Volumes have been written on the subject of the struggle between England and America. Men of all ranks have embarked in the controversy, from different motives, and with various designs; but all have been ineffectual, and the period of debate is closed. Arms, as the last resource, decide the contest; the appeal was the choice of the king, and the continent hath accepted the challenge. . . .

The sun never shined on a cause of greater worth. 'Tis not the affair of a city, a country, a province, or a kingdom, but of a continent—of at least one eighth part of the habitable globe. 'Tis not the concern of a day, a year, or an age; posterity are virtually involved in the contest, and will be more or less affected, even to the end of time, by the proceedings now. Now is the seed time of continental union, faith, and honor. The least fracture now will be like a name engraved with the point of a pin on the tender rind of a young oak; the wound will enlarge with the tree, and posterity read it in full grown characters.

By referring the matter from argument to arms, a new era for politics is struck; a new method of thinking hath arisen. All plans, proposals, &c. prior to the nineteenth of April, i.e. to the commencement of hostilities, are like the almanacs of the last year; which, though proper then, are superseded and useless now. Whatever was advanced by the advocates on either side of the question then, terminated in one and the same point, viz. a union with Great Britain;

the only difference between the parties was the method of effecting it; the one proposing force, the other friendship; but it hath so far happened that the first hath failed, and the second hath withdrawn her influence.

As much hath been said of the advantages of reconciliation, which, like an agreeable dream, hath passed away and left us as we were; it is but right that we should examine the contrary side of the argument, and inquire into some of the many material injuries which these colonies sustain, and always will sustain, by being connected with, and dependent on Great Britain. To examine that connection and dependence, on the principles of nature and common sense, to see what we have to trust to, if separated, and what we are to expect, if dependent.

I have heard it asserted by some, that as America hath flourished under her former connection with Great Britain, that the same connection is necessary towards her future happiness, and will always have the same effect. Nothing can be more fallacious than this kind of argument. We may as well assert, that because a child has thrived upon milk, that it is never to have meat; or that the first twenty years of our lives is to become a precedent for the next twenty. But even this is admitting more than is true, for I answer roundly, that America would have flourished as much, and probably much more, had no European power had anything to do with her. The commerce by which she hath enriched herself are the necessaries of life, and will always have a market while eating is the custom of Europe.

But she has protected us, say some. That she hath engrossed us is true, and defended the continent at our expense as well as her own is admitted, and she would have defended Turkey from the same motive, viz. the sake of trade and dominion.

Alas, we have been long led away by ancient prejudices, and made large sacrifices to superstition. We have boasted the protection of Great Britain, without considering that her motive was *interest*, not *attachment*; that she did not protect us from *our enemies* on *our account*, but from *her enemies* on *her own account*, from those who had no quarrel with us on any *other account*, and who will always be our enemies on the *same account*. Let Britain wave her pretensions to the continent, or the continent throw off the dependence, and we should be at peace with France and Spain were they at war with Britain. The miseries of Hanover last war ought to warn us against connections.[50]

It hath lately been asserted in parliament, that the colonies have no relation to each other but through the mother parent country, i.e. that Pennsylvania and the Jerseys, and so on for the rest, are sister colonies by the way of England. This is certainly a very round-about away of proving relationship, but it is the nearest and only true way of proving enemyship, if I may so call it. France and Spain never were, nor perhaps ever will be, our enemies as *Americans*, but as our being the *subjects of Great Britain*.

But Britain is the parent country, say some. Then the more shame upon her conduct. Even brutes do not devour their young, nor savages make war upon their families; wherefore the assertion, if true, turns to her reproach; but it happens not to be true, or only partly so, and the phrase *parent* or *mother country* hath been jesuitically adopted by the [king] and his parasites, with a low papistical design of gaining an unfair bias on the credulous weakness of our minds. Europe, and not England, is the parent country of America. This new world hath been the asylum for the persecuted lovers of civil and religious liberty from *every part* of Europe. Hither have they fled, not from the tender embraces of the mother, but from the cruelty of the monster; and it is so far true of England, that the same tyranny which drove the first emigrants from home, pursues their descendants still. . . .

By admitting that we were all of English descent, what does it amount to? Nothing. Britain, being now an open enemy, extinguishes every other name and title. And to say that reconciliation is our duty, is truly farcical. The first king of England, of the present line (William the Conqueror) was a Frenchman, and half the peers of England are descendants from the same country; wherefore by the same method of reasoning, England ought to be governed by France.

Much hath been said of the united strength of Britain and the colonies, that in conjunction they might bid defiance to the world.

---

[50]Britain's royal family had come to England from Germany, where it had ruled (and continued to rule) the principality of Hanover. As a result, Hanover was a battleground in Britain's fight against France during the Seven Years War.

But this is mere presumption; the fate of war is uncertain, neither do the expressions mean anything; for this continent would never suffer itself to be drained of inhabitants to support the British arms in either Asia, Africa, or Europe.

Besides, what have we to do with setting the world at defiance? Our plan is commerce, and that, well attended to, will secure the peace and friendship of all Europe; because it is the interest of all Europe to have America a *free port*. Her trade will always be a protection, and her barrenness of gold and silver secure her from invaders.

I challenge the warmest advocate for reconciliation, to shew a single advantage that this continent can reap, by being connected with Great Britain. I repeat the challenge, not a single advantage is derived. Our corn will fetch its price in any market in Europe, and our imported goods must be paid for, buy them where we will.

But the injuries and disadvantages we sustain by that connection are without number; and our duty to mankind at large, as well as to ourselves, instruct us to renounce the alliance. Because any submission to, or dependence on, Great Britain tends directly to involve this continent in European wars and quarrels; and sets us at variance with nations who would otherwise seek our friendship. . . .

Europe is too thickly planted with kingdoms to be long at peace, and whenever a war breaks out between England and any foreign power, the trade of America goes to ruin *because of her connection with Britain*. The next war may not turn out like the last, and should it not, the advocates for reconciliation now will be wishing for separation then, because, neutrality in that case would be a safer convoy than a man of war.

Everything that is right or natural pleads for separation. The blood of the slain, the weeping voice of nature cries, 'TIS TIME TO PART. Even the distance at which the Almighty hath placed England and America is a strong and natural proof that the authority of the one over the other was never the design of Heaven. The time likewise at which the continent was discovered, adds weight to the argument, and the manner in which it was peopled increases the force of it. The Reformation was preceded by the discovery of America, as if the Almighty graciously meant to open a sanctuary to the persecuted in future years, when home should afford neither friendship nor safety.

The authority of Great Britain over this continent is a form of government which sooner or later must have an end. And a serious mind can draw no true pleasure by looking forward, under the painful and positive conviction that what he calls "the present constitution" is merely temporary. As parents, we can have no joy, knowing that *this government* is not sufficiently lasting to ensure anything which we may bequeath to posterity. . . .

Every quiet method for peace hath been ineffectual. Our prayers have been rejected with disdain; and only tended to convince us that nothing flatters vanity or confirms obstinacy in Kings more than repeated petitioning—and nothing hath contributed more than that very measure to make the Kings of Europe absolute. . . .

To say, they will never attempt it again is idle and visionary [delusional]; we thought so at the repeal of the Stamp Act, yet a year or two undeceived us; as well we may suppose that nations, which have been once defeated, will never renew the quarrel. . . .

I am not induced by motives of pride, party, or resentment to espouse the doctrine of separation and independence; I am clearly, positively, and conscientiously persuaded that it is the true interest of this continent to be so; that everything short of *that* is mere patchwork, that it can afford no lasting felicity—that it is leaving the sword to our children, and shrinking back at a time when a little more, a little farther, would have rendered this continent the glory of the earth.

As Britain hath not manifested the least inclination towards a compromise, we may be assured that no terms can be obtained worthy [of] the acceptance of the continent, or any ways equal to the expense of blood and treasure we have already been put to. . . . No man was a warmer wisher for reconciliation than myself, before the fatal nineteenth of April, 1775 [the date of Lexington and Concord], but the moment the event of that day was made known, I rejected the hardened, sullen-tempered Pharoah of [George III] forever; and disdain the wretch, that with the pretended title of FATHER OF HIS PEOPLE can unfeelingly hear of their slaughter, and composedly sleep with their blood upon his soul. . . .

The colonies have manifested such a spirit of good order and obedience to continental government, as is sufficient to make every reasonable person easy and happy on that head. No man can assign the least pretense to his fears, on any other grounds, that such as are truly childish and ridiculous, that one colony will be striving for superiority over another.

Where there are no distinctions there can be superiority; perfect equality affords no temptation. The republics of Europe are all (and we may say always) in peace. Holland and Switzerland are without wars, foreign or domestic. Monarchical governments, it is true, are never long at rest; the crown itself is a temptation to enterprising ruffians at *home*; and that degree of pride and insolence ever attendant on regal authority, swells into a rupture with foreign powers, in instances where a republican government, by being formed on more natural principles, would negotiate the mistake.

But where, says some, is the King of America? I'll tell you Friend, he reigns above, and doth not make havoc of mankind like the Royal — of Britain. Yet that we may not appear to be defective even in earthly honors, let a day be solemnly set apart for proclaiming a charter; let it be brought forth placed on the divine law, the word of God; let a crown be placed thereon, by which the world may know, that so far as we approve of monarchy, that in America THE LAW IS KING. For as in absolute governments the King is law, so in free countries the law *ought* to be King, and there ought to be no other. But lest any ill use should afterwards arise, let the crown at the conclusion of the ceremony be demolished, and scattered among the people whose right it is.

ALL ACROSS AMERICA in April, May, and June of 1776, dozens of local groups issued their own declarations of independence. County commissions, provincial congresses, committees of tradesmen argued, discussed, voted, and published their feelings about the making of a republic. On May 27, the Virginia delegates to the Continental Congress received new instructions from their legislature, directing them to vote for independence and the creation of a formal confederation of the colonies. When Pennsylvania's legislature balked at endorsing separation from Britain, mobs gathered to intimidate (successfully) the recalcitrant officeholders. The radicals in Congress—led by John and Samuel Adams, among others—gained strength as all these waves of public feeling washed against the chamber in Philadelphia.

Then came a stroke that sealed the decision. After *Common Sense*, after Concord and the siege of Boston, after the local resolves and legislative instructions, the king himself lent the radicals a hand: Congress learned that the ministry had contracted for German mercenaries to fight the Americans. The outrage was universal: now almost no one believed that reconciliation was even remotely possible.

On June 7, Richard Henry Lee of Virginia prepared the following motion: "That these United Colonies are, and of right ought to be, free and independent States, that they are absolved from all allegiance to the British Crown, and that all political connection between them and the State of Great Britain is, and ought to be, totally dissolved."[51] After a few days of debate, Congress voted to create a committee to prepare a formal declaration of independence.

John Adams, Benjamin Franklin, Roger Sherman, Robert R. Livingston, and that somewhat awkward man from Virginia, Thomas Jefferson, served on that committee. They had their hands full: each of them served on other committees as well, which met virtually around the clock to handle endless tasks relating to the war. Though our knowledge of the committee's actions is somewhat blurred (it kept scant records), it seems that John Adams nominated Jefferson to write the first draft of the declaration. He knew about Jefferson's skill with a pen (*A Summary View of the Rights of British North America* had circulated widely), and he rather liked the thirty-three-year-old patrician—a planter aristocrat so unlike the farmer-lawyer from Braintree.

Jefferson worked rapidly. He began with a now-famous preamble, asserting that all men are created equal, and that their rights stem from nature itself. This assertion marked the culmination of all previous arguments of the colonists, stepping away from the British constitution and traditional English liberties as the basis for their freedom

[51]Quoted in Middlekauff, p. 325.

and equality. It was a critical step for a people announcing their independence.

Next, he proceeded to attack George III as the source of the Americans' grievances. This section of the document can strike the modern ear as somewhat false. After all, the heart of the American complaint was with Parliament, not the crown. But two reasons (among others) drove Jefferson to single out the king. First, he and the rest of America were mad at him. George III personally directed the military, and had ordered the armed suppression of dissent in the thirteen colonies. More important, however, the king remained the foundation of British government. Despite all the powers accumulated by the elected Parliament, the monarchy remained the government's central institution; all official acts were carried out in the king's name. As discussed earlier, the crown was the keystone of British society itself. By leveling the charges against George III, Jefferson abandoned any chance of reconciliation: he was declaring that this rebellion was indeed a revolution.

The committee made few changes to Jefferson's draft. The members liked the way it combined broad statements of principle with a list of specific grievances—couched in the general language of previous documents in the English tradition. When it was presented to the Continental Congress as a whole, however, the editing pens came out in full force. Jefferson virtually cried in anguish as dozens of men pored over his draft, marking out claims here (such as the assertion that the king had forced the institution of slavery upon Americans), inserting language there. He felt convinced that the delegates had ruined his masterpiece. In fact, as Pauline Maier writes, they conducted one of the greatest acts of group editing in history.

A Declaration
by Thomas Jefferson and the Continental Congress

When in the course of human events it becomes necessary for one people to dissolve the political bands which have connected them with another, and to assume among the powers of the earth the separate and equal station to which the laws of nature and of nature's god entitle them, a decent respect to the opinions of mankind requires that they should declare the causes which impel them to the separation.

We hold these truths to be self-evident; that all men are created equal; that they are endowed by their Creator with certain unalienable rights; that among these are life, liberty, and the pursuit of happiness; that to secure these rights, governments are instituted among men, deriving their just powers from the consent of the governed; that whenever any form of government becomes destructive of these ends, it is the right of the people to alter or to abolish it, and to institute a new government, laying its foundation on such principles, and organizing its powers in such form as to them shall seem most likely to effect their safety and happiness. Prudence indeed will dictate that governments long established should not be changed for light & transient causes, and accordingly all experience hath shewn that mankind are more disposed to suffer, while evils are sufferable, than to right themselves by abolishing the forms to which they are accustomed. But when a long train of abuses and usurpations, pursuing invariably the same object, evinces a design to reduce them under absolute despotism, it is their right, it is their duty, to throw off such government, & to provide new guards for their future security. Such has been the patient sufferance of these colonies; & such is now the necessity which constrains them to alter their former systems of government. The history of the present king of Great Britain, is a history of repeated injuries and usurpations, all having in direct object the establishment of an absolute tyranny over these states. To prove this let facts be submitted to a candid world.

He has refused his assent to laws the most wholesome and necessary for the public good.

He has forbidden his governors to pass laws of immediate & pressing importance, unless suspended in their operation till his assent should be obtained; and when so suspended, he has utterly neglected to attend to them.

He has refused to pass other laws for the accommodation of large districts of people, unless those people would relinquish the right of representation in the legislature; a right inestimable to them, & formidable to tyrants only.

He has called together legislative bodies at places unusual, uncomfortable, & distant from the depository of their public records, for the sole purpose of fatiguing them into compliance with his measures.

He has dissolved Representative houses repeatedly for opposing with manly firmness his invasions on the rights of the people.

He has refused for a long time after such dissolutions to cause others to be elected whereby the legislative powers, incapable of annihilation, have returned to the people at large for their exercise, the state remaining in the mean time exposed to all the dangers of invasion from without, & convulsions within.

He has endeavored to prevent the population of these states; for that purpose obstructing the laws for naturalization of foreigners; refusing to pass others to encourage their migration hither; & raising the conditions of new appropriations of lands.

He has obstructed the administration of justice by refusing his assent to laws for establishing judiciary powers.

He has made judges dependent on his will alone, for the tenure of their offices, and the amount & payment of their salaries.

He has erected a multitude of new offices & sent hither swarms of officers to harrass our people, and eat out their substance.

He has kept among us, in time of peace, standing armies without the consent of our legislatures.

He has affected to render the military independent of, & superior to, the civil power.

He has combined with others [Parliament] to subject us to a jurisdiction foreign to our constitution and unacknowledged by our laws; giving his assent to their acts of pretended legislation

for quartering large bodies of armed troops among us;

for protecting them by a mock-trial from punishment for any murders which they should commit on the inhabitants of these states;

for cutting off our trade with all parts of the world;

for imposing taxes on us without our consent;

for depriving us in many cases of the benefits of trial by jury;

for transporting us beyond seas to be tried for pretended offenses;

for abolishing the free system of English laws in a neighboring province, establishing therein an arbitrary government and enlarging its boundaries so as to render it at once an example & fit instrument for introducing the same absolute rule into these colonies;[52]

for taking away our charters abolishing our most valuable laws, and altering fundamentally the forms of our governments;

for suspending our own legislatures, & declaring themselves invested with power to legislate for us in all cases whatsoever.

He has abdicated government here by declaring us out of his protection and waging war against us.

He has plundered our seas, ravaged our coasts, burnt our towns, & destroyed the lives of our people.

He is at this time transporting large armies of foreign mercenaries, to complete the works of death, desolation, & tyranny, already begun with circumstances of cruelty & perfidy scarcely paralleled in the most barbarous ages and totally unworthy the head of a civilized nation.

He has constrained our fellow citizens taking captive on the high seas to bear arms against their country, to become the executioners of their friends & brethren, or to fall themselves by their hands.

He has excited domestic insurrections amongst us and has endeavored to bring on the inhabitants of our frontiers the merciless Indian savages, whose known rule of warfare is an undistinguished destruction of all ages, sexes & conditions.

In every stage of these oppressions, we have petitioned for redress in the most humble terms; our repeated petitions have been answered only by repeated injury. A prince whose character is thus marked by every act which may define a tyrant, is unfit to be the ruler of a free people.

Nor have we been wanting in attention to our British brethren. We have warned them from time to time of attempts by their legislature to extend an unwarrantable jurisidiction over us. We have reminded them of the circumstances of our emigration and settlement here. We have appealed to their native justice & magnanimity, and

[52]A reference to the Quebec Act, one of the five Intolerable Acts passed by Parliament in 1774. It provided for royal rule of Canada, and established formal toleration of the Roman Catholic church there—something that had deeply alarmed the overwhelmingly Protestant Americans.

we have conjured them by the ties of our common kindred, to disavow these usurpations, which would inevitably interrupt our connections & correspondence. They too have been deaf to the voice of justice and consanguinity. We must therefore acquiesce in the necessity which denounces [announces] our separation and hold them, as we hold the rest of mankind, enemies in war, in peace friends.

We therefore the Representatives of the United States of America, in General Congress assembled, appealing to the supreme judge of the world for the rectitude of our intentions, do, in the name and by authority of the good people of these colonies, solemnly publish and declare, that these united colonies are and of right ought to be free and independent states; that they are absolved from all allegiance to the British Crown, and that all political connection between them and the state of Great Britain is & ought to be totally dissolved; & that as free & independent states, they have full power to levy war, conclude peace, contract alliances, establish commerce, & to do all other acts and things which independent states may of right do. And for the support of this declaration, with a firm reliance on the protection of divine providence, we mutually pledge to each other our lives, our fortunes, and our sacred honor.

ON JULY 4, 1776, the Continental Congress adopted the amended Declaration of Independence. It was ordered published, and distributed throughout the colonies—now *states.* Everywhere celebrations erupted, as the Declaration was read to cheering crowds. Meanwhile, another committee hurried along its work on the Articles of Confederation, establishing the formal structure of the central government of the new United States of America.

In July 1776, Americans could rest content. They had chased invading British troops back into Boston, then captured the city. They had waged a brave invasion of Canada; that effort had failed, but no honor was lost in the attempt. They had embarked on the complete rebuilding of their government, from the ground up. They had just declared their independence, and it seemed as if they had already won it in fact. But a few looked across the water, waiting for the next wave of British ships; Samuel Adams, for one, was convinced that "they are determin'd to persevere." They would indeed persevere, bringing on the greatest force yet seen in America—and with it, the darkest days of the fledgling republic.

7
TO THE BRINK

Washington was worried. It was April 1776; the army and all New England were celebrating the liberation of Boston; but still he fretted. Though General William Howe had just evacuated 10,000 British troops out of the Massachusetts port, Washington knew they would return. But where? How could he protect the entire American coastline with his handful of undisciplined militia? From his first days in command until his last, he remained acutely conscious of the enemy's control of the sea, which brought the freedom to descend anywhere a landing might be made; but the American general never felt it more keenly than he did now.

Fortunately, Washington was able to make an informed guess as to where the British would strike, thanks to the latest news from London. Dartmouth had been replaced as secretary for America by Lord George Germain—who heartily agreed with the king that the situation demanded a military solution. He was a man of determination but limited imagination; his idea of victory centered on a conquest of the rebellious provinces—rather like the British conquest of Canada in the French and Indian War—through a systematic occupation of cities, fortifications, and settled areas. The key, he believed, was the capture of the city of New York: it controlled the mouth of the Hudson River, which formed the natural barrier between New England and the rest of the colonies. In the north, the Hudson reached to within a short distance of the chain of rivers and lakes (principally Champlain and George) that formed a natural passage for troops moving down from Canada.

The Americans were well aware of Germain's fixation on New York and the Hudson. Samuel Adams accurately summed up the plan (in a selection in the previous chapter): "to take possession of New York—make themselves masters of the Hudson's River & the Lakes, thereby securing Canada and the Indians—cut off all communication between the colonies northward & southward of the Hudson's River, and thus to subdue the former in hopes of instigating the negroes to make the others an easy prey." The phrase "instigating the negroes" referred to a raid carried out in January by Lord Dunmore, former royal governor of Virginia, who promised to free all slaves who joined his forces. It was a perfectly logical (and reasonable) offer, but it struck at the core of white Southerners' fears of their enslaved labor force.

Germain's plan had severe flaws. Britain could only make a limited number of troops available for its campaigns in America—and a systematic conquest and occupation of the countryside, even of a river line like the Hudson, would require enormous manpower. But no one else in the ministry came up with a competing plan. Other options were available, of course, such as a pure combat strategy: to strike hard and repeatedly at the main American fighting force, break it up or destroy it, then move against the Continental Congress itself. The British faced grave difficulties in controlling millions of angry civilians; a focused attack on their central institutions and leadership might have been their best option. As Washington himself stressed repeatedly to Congress, his first goal was to preserve the army; as long as it was intact, the Revolution carried on.

Perhaps the imaginations of the men in London, however, were restrained by their political convictions. They refused to accept the rebellious colonies as a single unit, let alone a single republic; they looked across the Atlantic and saw thirteen rebellious provinces, to be suppressed one by one. They had trouble believing that the Americans *could*, let alone *should*, act with any central direction; to focus on Washington's army and the Continental Congress would raise their importance, even to accept (at some level) their legitimacy. So the secretary put in motion a daunting continental conquest.

Unfortunately for Germain, the men assigned to carry out his strategic vision feared the consequences of a pitched battle almost as much as Washington did. In overall command was Lord Richard Howe, a widely admired admiral who liked the Americans a great deal. His older brother had died fighting alongside the colonists in the French and Indian War, and the people of Massachusetts had paid for a monument to him in Westminster Abbey. Admiral Howe's younger brother William was the general in command of the land forces, and he shared some of his sibling's sentiments.

William had also seen firsthand how the Americans fought at Bunker Hill. Before that battle, he had felt certain that a hard blow by the king's regulars would disperse the inexperienced militia; but the horror of watching the supposed rabble throw back two determined assaults by the king's regulars had changed his mind. Like General Gage and Lord Percy after the battle of Concord, he developed a new respect for the determination of the rebels—and he learned how costly even a victory could be.

Despite any misgivings the Howe brothers may have had, they pushed ahead with Germain's scheme. In June 1776, the two men demonstrated to the awestruck Americans the power at Britain's disposal. Starting on June 11, they began to bring ships to the waters just outside New York Harbor: first a handful, then more, then dozens more. By the sixteenth, 130 vessels rolled and creaked in the waves beyond Staten Island, their great wooden hulls straining against heavy anchor chains. More ships arrived, creating a vast flotilla: looming ships of the line, their sides bristling with scores of heavy cannons; sleek, fast frigates; squat transports, laden with soldiers, bedding, food, water casks, gunpowder, lead, cookware, and all the necessities of a great army. In the jungle of rigging and masts above, hundreds of sailors scrambled along spars and into lofty lookouts. The fleet would eventually total 52 warships and 427 transports, bearing 35,000 soldiers—including 8,397 German mercenaries, who were known to the Americans as Hessians.

Inside the harbor, Washington waited with his men. In April he had acted on his guess that New York was the next British target, and he had marched his army south. Along the way, militiamen had dispersed to their homes and new militiamen had gathered; a constant struggle went on from day to day to train the raw recruits, provide them with weapons and ammunition, and prevent (as far as possible) the outbreaks of disease that so plagued army camps. Uniforms were out of the question: it was all the commander could do to ensure that his men had muskets. Instead, he issued orders detailing the insignia that officers should wear on their hats and clothing, so that all could recognize them. This ragged army totaled perhaps 17,000 men—roughly half the size of the enemy force.

Upon arriving in the city, Washington had carefully reviewed the tactical situation. The harbor was vast and deep, protected by the great mass of Staten Island to the south. New Jersey stood off to the west, and Long Island to the east. At the northern end of the harbor was Manhattan Island, more than a dozen miles long and only two across at its widest point. New York sat at the southern tip of the island, a prosperous town resting on a foundation of bedrock, separated from New Jersey by the North River (also called the Hudson) and from Long Island by the East River. Manhattan stretched off to the north, fairly flat up to its far end, where a plateau known as Harlem Heights rose steeply from the plains below.

The key, Washington believed, was Brooklyn Heights—a high bluff across the East River from New York. Gazing over the water from the town's wharves, he could see that cannons mounted on the heights could virtually close the harbor to enemy shipping. Not entirely—these waters were far more spacious than Boston's—but enough to protect New York itself. The general quickly set his men to work, throwing up defensive works on that strategic location, while he arranged for various other forts, trenches, and breastworks to be constructed around Manhattan.

On July 3, Howe landed 9,000 troops on Staten Island, establishing his main base for his operations against New York. The British general surveyed the harbor, much as Washington had, and came to similar conclusions. If he was to take the town and control its surroundings, he had to capture Brooklyn Heights—now defended by 9,000 strongly entrenched American soldiers under General Nathanael Greene (though Greene soon fell ill, leaving command to General Israel Putnam). A direct assault would be unnecessarily costly: even before the men landed below the bluffs, they would have to sail into a crossfire from the artillery on the heights and in New York itself. Therefore, he would capture it from the landward side, moving in from the interior of Long Island.

On August 22, Howe's operation began with a landing on the southern shore of Long Island by 22,000 British troops, under the command of General Henry Clinton. The Americans were outnumbered by more than two to one—and the redcoats had far greater training, discipline, and experience. Clinton refused to launch a hasty, head-on assault, however; like Howe, his respect for entrenched militia had grown, and he feared excessive casualties.[53] He took his time, feeling out the American position until he found a weakness. On August 27, he struck.

When the British attacked, the Americans had extended their lines well beyond Brooklyn Heights. Their right was anchored on a thick marsh surrounding Gowanus Creek; the center and left stretched along a fairly steep, heavily forested ridge called the Heights of Guan. Four passes penetrated the Heights; unfortunately, the Americans left Jamaica Pass, the most northern one, almost unguarded. Clinton moved his army through it with tremendous speed and secrecy, passing around the far left of the rebel line while diversionary forces attacked in front to distract them. The plan worked perfectly: the Americans suddenly found redcoats on all sides. The rebel army scrambled back to Brooklyn Heights, leaving behind more than a thousand men—most of them prisoners of the enemy.

Washington quickly brought thousands of reinforcements across the East River to bolster the beaten army now cowering in the defensive works on Brooklyn Heights. Howe's men pleaded with him to unleash an assault, but the general was still wary of attacking a fortified enemy. He also hated to shed any more blood in what was, in his eyes, a civil war, an unholy fight between countrymen. So he began a regular siege, digging trenches and building bastions for artillery batteries.

The American commander realized that he was beaten. With his men demoralized, with the enemy preparing for a heavy bombardment and possible assault, he had to abandon Brooklyn Heights. On the night of August 29, under the cover of a dense fog, Washington brought his entire force across the river to Manhattan, leaving behind a few cannons that got stuck in the mud.

Washington made preparations to defend the city; his weary

[53]At the end of June, just before joining the campaign against New York, Clinton had led an attack against Charleston, South Carolina, the principal seaport for the South. It had failed miserably, and the force was recalled to aid Howe in the North.

troops dug ditches and threw up barricades. In the early days of September, he discussed the situation with his senior officers in a council of war. The prevailing sentiment was to abandon the town, as important as it was; the American army was too vulnerable to being cut off from the interior. The commander agreed, and he began an orderly evacuation of essential supplies and equipment. Washington planned to move his army to Harlem Heights, the high plateau that dominated the northern end of Manhattan, where the island sharply narrowed.[54]

Suddenly he discovered that he hadn't a moment to lose: the British were landing troops at Kip's Bay, on the eastern shore of Manhattan between the city and Harlem Heights. Washington had to move fast to escape with the bulk of his army.

On September 22, Washington found a few moments to write to his brother and to Congress about the events of the previous few weeks—the disaster on Long Island, the evacuation of the city, and a smaller battle that followed. These were dark days for the American commander: his men were demoralized and depressed; he had done little but lead them on frantic retreats. But even in this grim situation, Washington looked for a chance to strike back. Others suffered emotional collapse, but the general kept alert, remaining in command of himself and his men as he searched for a way to turn the tide.

[54]This feature is now known as Washington Heights (though the New York City neighborhood also called Washington Heights only occupies a portion of the plateau). It rises just north of 125th Street. Benson Bobrick mistakenly calls this ridge Morningside Heights; the author of this volume, who lived for a number of years on 136th Street, would like to note that Morningside Heights lies south of 125th Street; a small valley cuts across the island, following the path of modern-day 125th Street, dividing the two heights. General Washington occupied the feature to the north, where his flanks were protected by rivers on either side.

The Defense of New York
by George Washington

TO

JOHN AUGUSTINE WASHINGTON   HEIGHTS OF HARLEM
SEPT. 22ND, 1776

With respect to the attack and retreat from Long Island . . . I shall only add, that in the former we lost about 800 men, more than three-fourths of which were taken prisoners. This misfortune happened in a great measure by two detachments of our people who were posted in two roads leading thro' a wood in order to intercept the enemy in their march, suffering a surprise, and making a precipitate retreat, which enabled the enemy to lead a great part of their force against the troops commanded by Lord Stirling [also known as William Alexander], which formed a third detachment—who behaved with great bravery and resolution.

As to the retreat from the Island, under circumstances we then were, it became absolutely necessary, and was effected without loss of men, and with but very little baggage [lost]. A few heavy cannon were left, not being movable, on account of the grounds being soft and miry thro' the heavy & incessant rains which had fallen. . . . Our retreat from thence . . . was absolutely necessary, the enemy having landed the main body of their army to attack us in front while their ships of war were to cut off all communication with the city, from whence resources of men, provisions, &c., were to be drawn.

Having made this retreat, not long after we discovered by the movements of the enemy and the information we received from deserters and others, that they declin'd attacking our lines in the city, and were forming a plan to get in our rear with their land army, by crossing the sound above us, and thereby cut off all intercourse with the country and every necessary supply. The ships of war were to cooperate, possess the North [Hudson] River, and prevent succors from the Jerseys, &c. . . .

I caused a removal of a part of our stores, troops, &c., from the city, and a council of general officers determined on Thursday the 12th that it must be entirely abandoned, as we had, with an army weaker than theirs, a line of sixteen or 18 miles to defend, to keep open our communication with the country, besides the defense of the city. We held up however every show and appearance of defense till our sick and all our stores could be brought away.

The evacuation being resolved on, every exertion in our power was made to baffle their designs, and effect our own. The sick were numerous (amounting to more than the fourth of our whole army) and an object of great importance; happily we got them away; but before we could bring off all our stores, on Sunday morning six or seven ships of war, which had gone up the East River some few days before, began a most severe and heavy cannonade to scour the ground and effect a landing of their troops. Three ships of war also ran up the North River that morning above the city, to prevent our boats and small craft carrying away our baggage, &c.

I had gone the evening before to the main body of our army which was posted about these heights & the plains of Harlem, where it seemed probable from the movements and disposition of the enemy [that] they meant to land & make an attack the next morning. However the event did not happen. Immediately on hearing the cannonade I rode with all possible expedition towards the place of landing [at Kip's Bay, on the eastern shore], and where breastworks had been thrown up to secure our men, & found the troops that had been posted there to my great surprise & mortification, and those ordered to their support (consisting of eight regiments), notwithstanding the exertions of their generals to form them, running away in the most shameful and disgraceful manner. I used every possible effort to rally them but to no purpose, & on the appearance of a small part of the enemy (not more than 60 or 70) they ran off without firing a single gun. . . . This scandalous conduct occasioned a loss of many tents, baggage, & camp equipage, which would have been easily secured had they made the least opposition.

The retreat was made with the loss of a few men only—well encamped, and still are on, the heights of Harlem which are well calculated for defense against all their approaches. . . .

The dependence which the Congress has placed upon the militia has already greatly injured & I fear will totally ruin our cause. Being subject to no control themselves they introduce disorder among the troops you have attempted to discipline while the change in their living brings on sickness. This makes them impatient to get home, which spreads universally & introduces abominable desertions. . . .

TO JOHN HANCOCK   HEIGHTS OF HARLEM
                                   SEPT. 22ND, 1776

The enemy appeared in several large bodies upon the plains about two & a half miles from thence. I rode down to our advanced posts to put matters in a proper situation if they should attempt to come on. When I arrived there, I heard a firing which I was informed was between a party of our Rangers under the command of Lieut. Col. Knowlton, and an advanced party of the enemy. Our men came in & told me that the body of the enemy, who kept themselves concealed, consisted of about three hundred as near as they could guess. I immediately ordered three companies of Col. Weedon's regiment from Virginia under command of Major Leitch & Col. Knowlton with his Rangers, composed of volunteers from different New England regiments, to try to get in their rear, while a disposition was making as if to attack them in front, and thereby draw their whole attention that way.

This took effect as I wished on the part of the enemy. On the appearance of our party in front, they immediately ran down the hill, and took possession of some fences & bushes and a smart firing began, but at too great a distance to do much execution on either side. The parties under Col. Knowlton & Major Leitch unluckily began their attack too soon, as it was rather in the flank than in the rear. In a little time Major Leitch was brought off wounded, having received three balls thro' his side, and in a short time after Col. Knowlton got a wound which proved mortal.

Their men, however, persevered & continued the engagement with the greatest resolution. Finding that they wanted a support, I advanced part of Col. Griffith's and Col. Richardson's Maryland regiments with some detachments from the Eastern regiments who were nearest the place of action. These troops charged the enemy with great intrepidity and drove them from the wood into the plain, and were pushing them from thence (having silenced their fire in a great measure) when I judged it prudent to order a retreat, fearing the enemy (as I have since found was really the case) were sending a large body to support their party. Major Leitch, I am in hopes, will recover, but Col. Knowlton's fall is much to be regretted, as that of a brave & good officer.

We had about forty wounded, the number of slain is not yet ascertained, but it is very inconsiderable. By a sergeant who deserted from the enemy & came in this morning, I find that their party was greater than I imagined—it consisted of the 2nd Battalion of light infantry, a battalion of the Royal Highlanders, & three companies of the Hessian riflemen, under the command of Brigadier Genl. Leslie. The deserter reports that their loss in wounded & missing was eighty-nine, and eight killed. In the latter his account is too small, as our people discovered and buried about double that number. This affair I am in hopes will be attended with many salutary consequences, as it seems to have greatly inspirited the whole of our troops.

———

THE AMERICANS WON. It was a small fight, to be sure, against advance units of Howe's army that were pushing a bit too eagerly after the retreating Americans. But it played an outsized role in Washington's imagination, and in the morale of the rebel troops.

On Long Island, they had been smashed—outgeneraled and, in large part, outfought. On Brooklyn Heights, they had felt doomed—a sentiment shared by Washington, who worked a near miracle in getting them over to Manhattan safely. At Kip's Bay, they had turned and run away, without so much as firing a shot. A lesser commander than Washington would have simply retreated as far from the enemy as possible, until his soldiers were back in fighting condition. But the Virginian never lost heart: he looked for every opportunity to hit back (or "baffle their designs," as he put it). At Harlem Heights, the beleaguered troops had the tremendous pleasure of seeing the backs of the vaunted Highlanders, who fled from the American onslaught. And Washington reassured himself that his tactical skills were as sharp as ever—that he could read the enemy, plan an impromptu trap, and get his men to move the way he wanted.

The rebel victory at Harlem Heights accomplished no strategic objectives, but it slowed the British juggernaut and gave the tired American army a moral and physical respite. Washington still had plenty to worry about. He still bitterly regretted the lack of a disciplined, professional fighting force, and resented the chaotic indifference of the militia.

His feelings against these citizen soldiers should not be viewed as antidemocratic—he simply needed the tools to fight an eighteenth-century war, and well-regimented regiments were at the top of his list. It was a matter of victory or defeat, of life or death, to get his men to march in even steps, to maintain a tight column or line, to wheel left or right on command, and to send off disciplined volleys. The heavy toll of disease in the camps could be cut instantly, if only the men followed his orders about how they maintained their quarters.

Shortly after the disastrous battle of Long Island, Congress finally acted to give Washington the army he needed. It voted to raise eighty-eight infantry battalions (two battalions made up each regiment, which had a maximum strength of 700 men), along with dragoons (musket-armed cavalrymen), artillery units, and engineers. These battalions became the Continentals—the republic's professional fighting force—who would in time rival the best of the British army. But not yet: recruitment was left up to each state, which delayed the creation of the Continental regiments. Washington would have to make do with short-term volunteers.

On October 12, the British struck again. This time Howe used the cover of fog to move his troops up the East River, landing them on the peninsula of Throgs Neck on the mainland. Once again, the Americans were in danger of being cut off. Washington left a few thousand men in Fort Washington in upper Manhattan, and took the rest north to White Plains. The slow-moving Howe followed, fighting a brief but bitter battle for a hill on the western end of the American line. Heavy British losses reduced Howe's already negligible taste for combat; when Washington pulled back to an even stronger position, the British general turned around and marched back to Manhattan, where he besieged Fort Washington.

Washington responded by dividing his forces. He had placed 3,000 in Fort Washington; now he left 7,000 in his current position, under General Charles Lee, and he crossed the Hudson with another

5,000, camping near Fort Lee in New Jersey. Then disaster struck: on November 16, Howe attacked and captured Fort Washington, taking its entire garrison along with critical arms and supplies. Two days later, General Charles Cornwallis crossed the Hudson with 6,000 British troops, threatening Fort Lee with a similar fate.

The little victory at Harlem Heights, it seems, was to be the only burst of light in the autumn of darkness for Washington and the American cause. Again and again, he was defeated, forced to fall back, forced to give up prisoners and fortifications. Leaving General Lee to protect upstate New York, he had crossed to New Jersey, where he was to be hounded without mercy by Cornwallis's force.

One of Washington's soldiers was the combative author of *Common Sense*. Thomas Paine proved as good with his actions as he was with his words, volunteering for the hazardous duty of fighting the conquering British. In this grim hour, he began publication of a commentary on current events called *The Crisis*. In it, he offered an often accurate but always opinionated account of the developments of the day, urging his newfound countrymen to hone their determination. The republic indeed faced a crisis; rather than shrink from it, Paine used it to evoke greatness in the making. They were much-needed words at the time; but they also offer a glimpse of the widespread panic of the moment, the sense that all might soon be lost. This was the breaking point of the American Revolution—the cause seemed as if it had bent as far as it possibly could.

The Crisis
by Thomas Paine

These are the times that try men's souls: The summer soldier and sunshine patriot will, in this crisis, shrink from the service of his country; but he that stands it NOW, deserves the love and thanks of man and woman. Tyranny, like hell, is not easily conquered; yet we have this consolation with us, that the harder the conflict, the more glorious the triumph. What we obtain too cheap, we esteem too lightly: 'Tis dear-ness only that gives everything its value. Heaven would seem strange indeed, if so celestial an article as FREEDOM should not be highly rated. Britain, with an army to enforce her tyranny, has declared that she has a right (*not only to* TAX) but "to BIND us in ALL CASES WHATSOEVER," and if being bound in that manner is not slavery, then is there not such a thing as slavery upon earth. Even expression is impious, for so unlimited a power can be only to GOD.

Whether the independence of the continent was declared too soon, or delayed too long, I will not now enter into as an argument; my own simple opinion is, that had it been eight months earlier, it would have been much better. We did not make a proper use of last winter, neither could we, while we were in a dependant state. However, the fault, if it were one, was all our own; we have none to blame but ourselves. But no great deal is lost yet; all that Howe has been doing for this month past is rather a ravage than a conquest, which the spirit of the Jerseys a year ago would have quickly repulsed, and which time and a little resolution will soon recover. . . .

'Tis surprising to see how rapidly a panic will sometimes run through a country. . . . Yet panics, in some cases, have their uses; they produce as much good as hurt. Their duration is always short; the mind soon grows through them, and acquires a firmer habit than before. But their peculiar advantage is, that they are the touchstones of sincerity and hypocrisy, and bring things and men to light, which might otherwise have lain forever undiscovered. In fact, they have the same effect on secret traitors, which an imaginary apparition would have upon a private murderer. They sift out the hidden thoughts of man, and hold them up in public to the world. Many a disguised tory has lately shewn his head, that shall penitentially solemnize with curses the day on which Howe arrived upon the Delaware.

As I was with the troops at Fort Lee, and marched with them to the edge of Pennsylvania, I am well acquainted with many circumstances, which those who lived at a distance know but little or nothing of. Our situation was exceedingly cramped, the place being on a narrow neck of land between the North [Hudson] River and the Hackensack. Our force was inconsiderable, being not one fourth so great as Howe could bring against us. We had no army at hand to have relieved the garrison, had we shut ourselves up and stood on the defense. Our ammunition, light artillery, and the best part of our stores had been removed upon the apprehension that Howe would endeavor to penetrate the Jerseys, in which case Fort Lee could be of no use to us; for it must occur to every thinking man, whether in the army or not, that these kind of field forts are only for temporary purposes, and last in use no longer than the enemy directs his force against the particular object, which such forts are raised to defend.

Such was our situation and condition at Fort Lee the morning of the 20th of November, when an officer arrived with information that the enemy with 200 boats had landed about seven or eight miles above. Major General Greene, who commanded the garrison, immediately ordered them under arms, and sent express to his Excellency General Washington at the town of Hackensack, distant by way of the ferry six miles. Our first object was to secure the bridge over the Hackensack, which laid up the river between the enemy and us, about six miles from us, and three from them.

General Washington arrived in about three quarters of an hour, and marched at the head of the troops towards the bridge, [at] which place I expected we should have a brush for; however, they did not choose to dispute it with us, and the greatest part of our troops went over the bridge, the rest over the ferry, except some which passed at a mill on a small creek, between the bridge and the ferry, and made their way through some marshy grounds up to the town of Hackensack, and there passed the river. We brought off as much baggage as the wagons could contain; the rest was lost. The simple object was to bring off the garrison, and to march them on till they could be strengthened by the Jersey or Pennsylvania militia, so as to be enabled to make a stand.

We stayed four days at Newark, collected in our outposts with some of the Jersey militia, and marched out twice to meet the enemy on information of their being advancing, though our numbers were greatly inferior to theirs. Howe, in my little opinion, committed a great error in generalship by not throwing a body of forces off from Staten Island through Amboy, by which means he might have seized all our stores at Brunswick, and intercepted our march into Pennsylvania. But if we believe the power of hell to be limited, we must likewise believe that their agents are under some providential control.

I shall not now attempt to give all the particulars of our retreat to the Delaware; suffice it for the present to say, that both officers and men, though greatly harrassed and fatigued, frequently without rest, covering, or provision, the inevitable consequences of a long retreat, bore it with a manly and a martial spirit.[55] All their wishes were one, which was, that the country would turn out and help them to drive the enemy back.

Voltaire has remarked that King William never appeared to full advantage but in difficulties and in action; the same remark may be made on General Washington, for the character fits him. There is a natural firmness in some minds which cannot be unlocked by trifles, but which, when unlocked, discovers a cabinet of fortitude; and I reckon it among those kind of public blessings, which we do not immediately see, that GOD hath blessed him with uninterrupted health, and given him a mind that can even flourish upon care. . . .

America did not, nor does not, want [lack] force; but she wanted a proper application of that force. Wisdom is not the purchase of a day, and it is no wonder that we should err at first setting off. From an excess of tenderness, we were unwilling to raise an army, and trusted our cause to the temporary defense of a well-meaning militia. A summer's experience has now taught us better; yet with those troops, while they were collected, we were able to set bounds to the progress of the enemy, and, thank GOD! they are again assembling. I always considered a militia as the best troops in the world for a sudden exertion, but they will not do for a long campaign.

Howe, it is possible, will make an attempt on this city [Philadelphia]; should he fail on this side of the Delaware, he is ruined. He stakes all on his side against a part on ours; admitting he succeeds, the consequences will be, that armies from both ends of the continent will march to assist their suffering friends in the middle states; for he cannot go everywhere; it is impossible. I consider Howe as the greatest enemy the tories have; he is bringing a war into their country

---

[55]Washington barely made it across the Delaware with his army before Cornwallis reached him. The American general took the wise precaution of collecting all the boats for dozens of miles along the riverbank, and taking them with him to the other side. When the British reached the water's edge, they had no way of striking the battered rebel force on the other side.

which, had it not been for him and partly for themselves, they had been clear of. . . .

I see no real cause for fear. I know our situation well, and can see the way out of it. While our army was collected, Howe dared not risk a battle, and it is no credit to him that he decamped from the White Plains, and waited a mean opportunity to ravage the defenseless Jerseys; but it is great credit to us, that, with a handful of men, we sustained an orderly retreat for near an hundred miles, brought off our ammunition, all our field pieces, the greatest part of our stores, and had four rivers to pass. None can say that our retreat was precipitate, for we were near three weeks in performing it, that the country might have time to come in. Twice we marched back to meet the enemy and remained out till dark. The sign of fear was not seen in our camp. . . .

Once more we are again collected and collecting; our new army at both ends of the continent is recruiting fast, and we shall be able to open the next campaign with sixty thousand men, well armed and clothed. This is our situation, and who will may know it. By perseverence and fortitude we have the prospect of a glorious issue.

———

PAINE'S BRAVE WORDS could not conceal the harrowing atmosphere of defeat that hung over the ragged American army as it shivered on the Pennsylvania side of the Delaware River. The rout in Long Island, the loss of New York, the loss of Fort Washington, the abandonment of Fort Lee and New Jersey: disaster had trailed in Washington's footsteps, clinging to his every movement like a shadow. Everyone feared that the enemy would simply march on to Philadelphia; in a panic, the Continental Congress hastily moved south to Baltimore.

It seemed as if Germain's strategy for conquering the young United States was working perfectly—and it seemed as if Washington was not the man to lead the rebel forces. Muttering against his leadership began to rise in some quarters; the malcontents looked instead to General Charles Lee, who still hovered in the highlands above New York with a strong detachment of the army. Lee encouraged such talk—indeed, the vain and ambitious officer made a perfect villain in this tale. Overrated by others, he naturally overrated himself, and he actually began to look forward to Washington's defeat as a means of advancing his own career.

During and after the retreat to the Delaware, Washington repeatedly ordered Lee to come to his assistance with his force; Lee simply ignored him. Indeed, his visions of power and glory led him to make wild, even dangerous statements. At the end of November 1776, he wrote a letter to James Bowdoin, president of the Massachusetts Committee of Public Safety, declaring, "Affairs appear in so important a crisis that I think the resolves of the Congress must no longer too nicely weigh with us. . . . There are times when we must commit treason against the laws of the State, for the salvation of the State. The present crisis demands this brave, virtuous kind of treason."[56]

Clearly the American cause had more against it than the British army; Charles Lee represented a threat to Washington personally, and to the army's chain of command. Fortunately, that problem suddenly disappeared. During the first two weeks of December, Lee finally began to march his men across New Jersey to join Washington; as he dawdled near Morristown, staying at a tavern away from camp, a detachment of British dragoons captured him in his dressing gown. It was an extraordinary stroke of good fortune—though no one realized it at the time, as his inflated reputation had yet to be pricked.

Washington received more good news in the fall of 1776—and everyone recognized it as good news at the time. Germain's plan called for a second offensive, down from Canada, through Lakes Champlain and George and the Hudson. Opposing this attack was General Benedict Arnold and the tattered remnants of the invasion force that had fallen back from Canada in the spring and summer. The key to forestalling a southward advance, Arnold realized, would be control of Lake Champlain: nestled between the Adirondack and Green mountains, the long waterway offered the only practical way south. In August, he began to construct a makeshift fleet to match the British boats gathering at the northern end of the lake. On October 11, the two naval forces met in battle; Arnold's outnumbered force was nearly destroyed—but in the process, it inflicted such heavy

---

[56]Quoted in Bobrick, p. 224.

losses that the British had no choice but to fall back. There would be no invasion from Canada in 1776.

On December 13, General Howe called the campaign to a halt. European armies rarely fought during the winter; the difficulties of moving and maintaining troops in cold weather were serious indeed, and custom called for a seasonal cease-fire. The tradition made more sense now than ever, for the winter promised to be a harsh one. Howe dispersed his troops in garrisons around the state of New Jersey; on Cornwallis's recommendation, he stationed strong detachments in Pennington, Trenton, and Bordentown, close to the American army. Even the cautious British commander found no reason to worry about this scattered deployment: Washington had fewer than 5,000 worn-out men, many of whom would leave for home when their enlistments expired on January 1, 1777. And Howe put some of his best troops in these forward positions—Hessians, highly professional German soldiers who had proved their worth at White Plains and Fort Washington. Indeed, the British general could rest contentedly on his accomplishments: he had captured the most strategic seaport on the American coast, smashed and dispersed the American army, and occupied the state of New Jersey.

Washington was anything but content. His tiny, tired army would soon shrink even further. The cause he believed in so much had suffered one heavy blow after another, until it seemed doomed. And this proud man deeply felt the wounds that repeated defeat had inflicted on his reputation; he cherished his honor, and he felt now that he had precious little left.

But Washington was as strong-minded as he was proud. In the battle of Harlem Heights, he had demonstrated a fundamental aspect of his personality: in the darkest moments, he refused to accept defeat, looking instead for the smallest opportunity to strike back. It was a faculty easily overlooked or underestimated; in fact, it was quite rare in commanding generals, who in all ages have felt the burden of their responsibilities, the fear of losing what little they have left.

Now, as heavy snows began to descend on his tiny army, he conceived a bold gamble. As he pored over his maps, as he listened to reports by British deserters, as he read letters from his scouts, spies, and informers, he created a plan to take advantage of Howe's winter inertia and his forces' wide dispersion. Washington decided to attack the most exposed British outpost: Trenton, a town on the New Jersey side of the Delaware, garrisoned by 1,500 crack Hessian troops commanded by Colonel Johann Rahl. But the Americans had to act fast: reinforcements had temporarily swelled the rebel army to 6,000 men, but New Year's Day—the date of so many expiring enlistments—was fast approaching.

Washington did what he could to secure as many advantages as possible. He planned to attack early on the day after Christmas, knowing that the Hessians would have been up late the night before, celebrating the holiday. He planned to bring an unusually large number of artillery pieces, since he knew that the heavy snow would dampen the firing pans of the muskets, rendering them useless after one or two shots. And he moved his men with extraordinary secrecy—the enemy scarcely expected a winter attack across the ice-clogged Delaware River, but Washington left nothing to chance.

His soldiers may have seen little but defeat in the preceding weeks, but at least they were now combat veterans. As they collected for the attack on Christmas Day, they moved with energy and a fair amount of discipline. Not everything went perfectly as the troops marched to a crossing point a few miles above Trenton, yet Washington was pleased at the conduct of the troops. But a night crossing of the great river was enormously risky; it inevitably led to delays, and the general began to fear that all would be lost. Two days later, Washington was able to report to Congress that things had turned out all right after all.

Trenton
by George Washington

TO JOHN HANCOCK   HEADQUARTERS NEWTON,
27TH DECEMBER, 1776

I have the pleasure of congratulating you upon the success of an enterprise which I had formed against a detachment of the enemy lying in Trenton, and which was executed yesterday morning.

The evening of the 25th I ordered the troops intended for this service to parade back of McKonkey's Ferry, that they might begin to pass as soon as it grew dark, imagining we should be able to throw them all over, with the necessary artillery, by 12 o'clock, and that we might easily arrive at Trenton by five in the morning, the distance being about nine miles. But the quantity of ice made that night, impeded the passage of boats so much, that it was three o'clock before the artillery could all be got over, and near four, before the troops took up their line of march.

This made me despair of surprising the town, as I well knew we could not reach it before the day was fairly broke, but as I was certain there was no making a retreat without being discovered, and [the army would be] harassed on repassing the river, I determined to push on at all events. I formed my detachment into two divisions, one to march by the lower or River road, the other, by the upper or Pennington Road. As the divisions had nearly the same distance to march, I ordered each of them, immediately upon forcing the out guards, to push directly into the town, that they might charge the enemy before they had time to form. The upper division arrived at the enemy's advanced post exactly at eight o'clock, and in three minutes after, I found from the fire on the lower road that that division had also got up. The out guards made but small opposition, tho' for their numbers they behaved very well, keeping up a constant retreating fire from behind houses.

We presently saw their main body formed, but from their motions, they seem'd undetermined how to act. Being hard pressed by our troops, who had already got possession of part of their artillery, they attempted to file off by a road on their right leading to Princeton, but perceiving their intention, I threw a body of troops in their way, which immediately checked them. Finding from our disposition that they were surrounded, and that they must inevitably be cut to pieces if they made any further resistance, they agreed to lay down their arms. The number that submitted in this manner was 23 officers and 886 men. Col. Rahl, the commanding officer, and seven others were found wounded in the town. I don't know exactly how many they had killed, but I fancy not above twenty or thirty, as they never made any regular stand. Our loss is very trifling indeed, only two officers and one or two privates wounded. . . .

In justice to the officers and men, I must add that their behavior upon this occasion reflects the highest honor upon them. The difficulty of passing the river in a very severe night, and their march thro' a violent storm of snow and hail, did not in the least abate their ardor. But when they came to the charge, each seemed to vie with the other in pressing forward, and were I to give a preference to any particular corps, I should do great injustice to the others.

———

WASHINGTON'S DARING PLAN worked to perfection. He routed the famed Hessians, capturing the bulk of the enemy troops. His own men fought bravely and well; such officers as Nathanael Greene, Henry Knox, and Alexander Hamilton kept their cool at all levels of command, as the swirling snow forced many units to take the initiative during the fight. Congress—and the entire republic— cheered. The battle of Trenton was simply a superb achievement.

News of the battle alarmed Howe beyond measure. Frantically he sent for Cornwallis, who was preparing to ship out for England; Howe told him to assume command of the king's forces in New Jersey, while he forwarded all possible reinforcements to the Delaware River. If Howe and Cornwallis could reach the American army, they were determined to smash it.

Washington, meanwhile, led his little force back across the Delaware. He had just won a glorious victory, sending the British command into a panic, but still he worried. He pleaded with the men due to leave the army on New Year's Day to stay on for just two weeks more, promising a $10 bounty for doing so. He wrote to Robert Morris, the wealthy merchant who virtually financed the Revolution, pleading for money. Morris responded with $50,000 in paper currency, along with all the gold and silver he could collect. Militiamen from Pennsylvania suddenly marched into camp; together with the extended enlistments, Washington managed to maintain a force of 5,000 men. Once again, he crossed the Delaware, taking his army back into Trenton, combining it with another detachment under General John Cadwalader.

As Washington collected his men at the scene of his recent victory, Earl Cornwallis marched toward him with 8,000 well-equipped, highly trained soldiers. Cornwallis found his advance slowed by a delaying force sent toward him by Washington; again and again, the little American detachment forced the British to deploy to fight—and once they did, the Americans scrambled back out of reach. Finally, on January 2, 1777, the British marched into Trenton, driving Washington's army back behind Assunpink Creek, just south of town. After some skirmishing and cannonading, the two sides settled down for the night. Cornwallis told his officers, "We've got the old fox safe now. We'll go over and bag him in the morning.[57]

If he was there in the morning, Cornwallis might have added. Once again, Washington conceived a risky move in the face of superior forces. He was in a desperate situation: he had a larger enemy force in front, and a wide, fast-moving, ice-clogged river at his back. He had placed himself within striking distance of the British army— he risked losing everything. A typical general would have been satisfied with his success at Trenton and not recrossed the Delaware. But Washington had already shown that he was not a typical general. When Cornwallis awoke that next morning, he was stunned to see that the American army had slipped away in the night; and he would soon discover that it had *not* retreated.

Princeton
by George Washington

TO JOHN HANCOCK   PLUCKEMIN [N.J.]
                                   JANUARY 5TH, 1777

I have the honor to inform you, that since the date of my last from Trenton, I have removed with the army under my command to this place. The difficulty of crossing the Delaware [the second time], on account of the ice, made our passage over it tedious, and gave the enemy an opportunity of drawing in their several cantonments and

[57]Quoted in W. J. Wood, p. 79.

assembling their whole force at Princeton. Their large pickets advanced towards Trenton, their great preparations & some intelligence I had received, added to their knowledge that the first of January brought on a dissolution of the best part of our army, gave me the strongest reasons to conclude that an attack on us was meditating.

Our situation was most critical and our force small. To remove immediately was again destroying every dawn of hope which had begun to revive in the breasts of the Jersey militia, and to bring those troops which had first crossed the Delaware, and were laying at Croswix's under Genl. Cadwalader & those under Genl. Mifflin at Bordentown (amounting in the whole to about 3,600) to Trenton, was to bring them to an exposed place. One or the other, however, was unavoidable. The latter was preferred & they were ordered to join us at Trenton, which they did by a night march on the 1st instant.

On the 2nd, according to my expectation, the enemy began to advance upon us, and after some skirmishing the head of their column reached Trenton about 4 o'clock, whilst their rear was as far back as Maidenhead. They attempted to pass Assunpink Creek, which runs through Trenton at different places, but finding the fords guarded, halted & kindled their fires. We were drawn up on the other side of the creek. In this situation we remained till dark, cannonading the enemy & receiving the fire of their field pieces, which did us but little damage.

Having by this time discovered that the enemy were greatly superior in number and that their design was to surround us, I ordered all our baggage to be removed silently to Burlington soon after dark, and at twelve o'clock, after renewing our fires & leaving guards at the bridge in Trenton and other passes on the same stream above, marched by a roundabout road to Princeton, where I knew they could not have much force left and might have stores.[58] One thing I was certain of, that it would avoid the appearance of a retreat (which was of course to run the hazard of the whole army being cut off), whilst we might by a fortunate stroke withdraw Genl. Howe from Trenton and give some reputation to our arms.

[58]Princeton was deeper into New Jersey, far behind Cornwallis's position. Rather than retreating, Washington had circled around into the British rear.

Happily we succeeded. We found Princeton about sunrise with only three regiments and three troops of light horse in it, two of which were on their march to Trenton. These three regiments, especially the two first, made a gallant resistance, and in killed, wounded, and prisoners must have lost 500 men, upwards of one hundred of them left dead in the field; and with what I have with me & what were taken in the pursuit & carried across the Delaware, there are near 300 prisoners, 14 of which are officers—all British. . . .

The rear of the enemy's army laying at Maidenhead (not more than five or six miles from Princeton), was up with us before our pursuit was over, but as I had the precaution to destroy the bridge over Stony Brook (about half a mile from the field of action), they were so long retarded there as to give us time to move off in good order for this place. . . .

My original plan when I set out from Trenton was to have pushed on to Brunswick [the main British supply base], but the harrassed state of our own troops (many of them having had no rest for two nights & a day) and the danger of losing the advantage we had gained by aiming at too much, induced me by the advice of my officers to relinquish the attempt. . . . The enemy, from the best intelligence I have been able to get, were so much alarmed at the apprehension of this, that they marched immediately to Brunswick without halting. . . .

From the best information I have received, Genl. Howe has left no men either at Trenton or Princeton. The truth of this I am endeavoring to ascertain that I may regulate my movements accordingly. The militia are taking spirit and I am told are coming in fast from this state, but I fear those from Philadelphia will scarcely submit to the hardships of a winter campaign much longer, especially as they very unluckily sent their blankets with their baggage to Burlington. I must do them justice, however, to add that they have undergone more fatigue and hardship than I expected militia (especially citizens) would have done at this inclement season.

━━━━━━━━━

AT THE BLEAKEST moment of the Revolution, General Washington carried out one of the finest military campaigns of the eighteenth century. Blasted out of New York, hustled out of New Jersey, left with a tired, half-trained army that would soon disperse, he chose to attack. At Trenton, he executed a tactical triumph, surprising and capturing a large Hessian detachment—a sizeable proportion of the British force in New Jersey. Then, instead of resting on his achievement, he led his men back into the lion's mouth, drawing Cornwallis down to Trenton, deceiving him long enough to circle around his army and shatter his rear guard at Princeton. Washington himself had shown outstanding skill and personal bravery on the Princeton battlefield, rallying his troops after his advance units suffered an initial reverse, then sweeping the enemy away. In the end, General Howe pulled in most of his outposts as the American army settled in at Morristown. King Frederick the Great of Prussia, the foremost military leader of the day, hailed Washington's operation as a stroke of genius.

The "glorious cause," as Washington called it, had been pushed to the brink in the fall of 1776; the general's daring leadership had pulled it back. The first year of war had spoiled the Americans, in a way, as they won a string of victories against the unprepared British forces. Then came Howe's carefully planned invasion of New York, startling the republic with the power of the aroused and angry empire. At that moment, when Howe stood victorious, the American public truly feared that all would be lost; then Washington won his victories, changing everything.

The battles of Trenton and Princeton did not win back all the lost ground, of course, but they accomplished something essential at this dark hour. They reassured the rebels that they could absorb defeats and still fight back; that the Revolution would not be lost with one city, or one state, or even a succession of heavy blows. The Americans learned through experience what Thomas Paine had argued in print: "By perseverance and fortitude we have the prospect of a glorious issue."

8
PHILADELPHIA

As the state of New Jersey began to thaw out of the cold winter of 1776–1777, George Washington had good reason to anticipate a bright summer. Though he had lost New York to General Howe's forces the year before, his victories at Trenton and Princeton had won international respect. During the winter months, he had kept small detachments constantly in the field, preventing British foraging parties from gathering supplies in the countryside. Earl Cornwallis (Howe's field commander) was forced to abandon one outpost after another. The American general could be satisfied that he had locked the British inside New York, while he dominated the landscape beyond.[59]

Within his Morristown camp, Washington could count other advantages that he had gained during the cold season. For long weeks, he had cajoled and threatened state governments into recruiting men for the professional Continental regiments, rather than their own militias; slowly the new, long-term recruits began to filter in. "By early May, as the hills around Morristown turned green," writes historian Robert Middlekauff, "the battalions Congress had authorized began to take form. Before the end of the month the army had reached almost 9,000 effectives—forty-three battalions—and they could be armed, for muskets, powder, and clothing had arrived from a France still cautiously watching the struggle and surreptitiously giving aid to the Americans."[60]

In the enemy headquarters, Generals Howe and Cornwallis felt as disgruntled as Washington was hopeful. The American victories during the winter had left a sour taste in their mouths, spoiling the

[59]Howe also held Newport, Rhode Island, which he had captured the year before to serve as a naval station.
[60]Middlekauff, p. 365.

plate of delicious successes they had tasted from Long Island to Fort Lee. Washington, they believed, deserved to be humbled. To that end, they engaged in a series of maneuvers in early summer, designed to trap the rebel army. Their antagonist, however, refused to be drawn into a pitched battle, preferring to give his raw soldiers time to train and gain a little experience.

Howe may not have put much faith in the efforts to catch Washington; his mind had already turned to a new plan for 1777. The year before, he had captured two important American seaports, New York and Newport; now another beckoned—the largest city in the United States, and the capital of the young republic. He was going to attack Philadelphia.

The English commander believed that the conquest of major towns allowed him to stifle the American economy by cutting off trade and manufacturing, and to exert influence into the surrounding countryside. But Philadelphia held out another prospect as well, one that would dominate British strategic planning for the rest of the war. He believed he could rouse Pennsylvania's many Tories—loyalists to the crown. The name "Tory" came from the nickname for England's own conservatives; the rebels in America often called themselves Whigs, after Britain's liberal party. Howe could hardly care less about nicknames, however; if he was to conquer the rebellious colonies, he had to rally the support of the loyal population.

How many Americans remained true to George III will never be determined for certain; certainly there was a substantial number, perhaps as much as 15 to 20 percent of the population, but they were spread unevenly throughout the country. In some areas, such as the city of New York, the Mohawk River valley of the same state, and parts of Pennsylvania, they amounted to a strong force. But often they were terrorized into silence or flight by their Whig neighbors—the Revolutionaries had seized control of most local governments, clamping down on known Tories. But whether they were many or few, the loyalists gave the British army hope of maintaining some civilian support for its operations.

Howe wrote to Lord Germain on April 2, 1777, informing him of his plans against Philadelphia. The secretary for America wrote back, warmly approving the general's proposed operation. What Germain failed to mention directly, however, was that a completely different strategy—perhaps even a contradictory one—was in the works for that same year. General John Burgoyne had proposed a renewed effort to invade New York from Canada, and Germain and the king had agreed to it. As a key part of this operation, Burgoyne had stressed that Howe should drive north along the Hudson from New York, to meet his column as he advanced southward; Germain, however, never instructed Howe to cooperate with Burgoyne. As a result, each of the two generals began his attack under the illusion that his was the principal campaign of the year.

It is impossible to know why Germain failed to make the obviously necessary choice between the two strategies. At first glance, his indecision seems especially puzzling: he was known, as Robert Middlekauff writes, as "one of the tough men in the ministry"—the hardest of the hard-line advocates of suppressing the Revolution by force. Yet he was enormously insecure as well. In the Seven Years War, he had been court-martialed and convicted for refusing to lead an attack; though he was eventually brought into the government, "the stink of cowardice" (in Middlekauff's words) still stayed with him. Stewing in his own self-hatred, he could not bring himself to overrule the plans of a decorated general from the illustrious Howe family—or those of "Gentleman Johnny" Burgoyne, a high-society favorite who had won a reputation for valor in the same war that had stained Germain with shame.[61]

Back across the Atlantic, Howe proceeded with his campaign. On July 8, he began to load 18,000 troops onto transports in New York Harbor; on the 24th, he took his fleet out to sea. Washington strongly suspected that his destination was Philadelphia; on the 31st, his guess was confirmed by reports of scores of ships off the Delaware Capes. The British commander took his time in feeling out the American defenses along Chesapeake Bay and the Delaware River, giving Washington an opportunity to concentrate his army near Philadelphia. To reassure the population, he marched his 16,000 men through the city streets. John Adams watched the parade and came away worried. "Our soldiers," he wrote, "have not yet quite the air of soldiers."[62]

---

[61]Middlekauff, pp. 369–370.
[62]Quoted in Bobrick, p. 264, and Middlekauff, p. 385.

On August 25, Howe landed his men along the Elk River in Maryland and prepared for an offensive against Philadelphia. As he marched north, his troops ravaged the countryside, raiding farmhouses for food and loot. The general put a stop to the depredations with severe punishments, but he had already begun to lose what little support he had. In early September, he came up against Washington's lines, located across the deep Brandywine Creek. On the 11th, he attacked.

The battle of the Brandywine proved to be the low point of Washington's career. In general, he was at his best when he was on the spot, able to survey the battlefield with his surveyor-trained eyes, snapping out orders with his customary decisiveness and rallying the troops with his remarkable charisma. But at the Brandywine, he was forced to stretch out his regiments for miles along the stream, guarding the fords where the British army might cross. Howe found a weak spot—an unguarded ford seventeen miles above Washington's headquarters. He pushed up his Hessians to threaten Washington's front, while he sent the bulk of his army on a long, winding march across that distant ford.

The result was a repeat of the battle of Long Island, with the flanks reversed. Washington soon learned that the redcoats were pouring down on his right; the American line bent back, then finally broke. General Nathanael Greene conducted a skillful rearguard action, giving the rebel army time to escape the field.

Howe had won a splendid victory, but it had not been without a price. The inexperienced Continentals had fought hard, inflicting significant casualties on the redcoats. Washington, unlike Howe, was able to replace his losses by calling in militia and additional Continental battalions from outlying areas. Nevertheless, the Americans had suffered a serious reverse, soon made worse by an additional disaster. After retreating from the Brandywine, Washington had detached General Anthony Wayne to "hang on" Howe's army (harassing it by ambushing foraging parties, felling trees across the roads, etc.). At Paoli, a British detachment attacked Wayne's sleeping men at one o'clock in the morning, bayoneting more than 300 in their tents and capturing another hundred.

Fear, demoralization, and outright panic burned through the

states as Howe grasped for Philadelphia. Washington—the "old fox" who had dazzled the world at Trenton and Princeton—found himself outsmarted; he had to face the fact that he probably could not protect the American capital.

The sensations of the day can best be expressed by two prominent participants: Thomas Paine and John Adams. The first selection below comes from an issue of Paine's *The Crisis*, written immediately after the battle of the Brandywine. Once again, he found himself pleading with his adopted countrymen to buck up in the hour of defeat—to remain resilient to the end. Paine's assessment of the situation was quite intelligent, but he *was* a propagandist. For a less guarded view of the day, we turn to John Adams's diary, in the selection immediately following Paine's words. This leading member of the Continental Congress describes the panic and anguish felt in Philadelphia as Howe hovered just beyond the Schuylkill River, the last line of defense. Adams struggled with it himself, but what he found most damning was not his fear, but his reason: he knew the odds were against the republic.

The Brandywine
by Thomas Paine

Those who expect to reap the blessing of freedom must, like men, undergo the fatigues of supporting it. The event of yesterday is one of those kind alarms which is just sufficient to rouse us to duty, without being of consequence enough to depress our fortitude. It is not a field of a few acres of ground, but a cause that we are defending, and whether we defeat the enemy in one battle, or by degrees, the consequence will be the same.

Look back at the events of last winter and the present year, there you will find that the enemy's successes have always contributed to reduce them. What they have gained in ground, they paid so dearly for in numbers, that their victories have in the end amounted to defeats. We have always been masters at the last push, and always shall while we do our duty. Howe has once been on the banks of the Delaware, and from thence driven back with loss and disgrace; and why not be again driven from the Schuylkill? His condition and ours are very different. He has everybody to fight; we have only his *one* army to cope with, and which wastes away at every engagement; we can not only reinforce, but can redouble our numbers; he is cut off from all supplies, and must sooner or later inevitably fall into our hands.

Shall a band of ten or twelve thousand robbers, who are this day fifteen hundred or two thousand men less in strength than they were yesterday, conquer America, or subdue even a single state? The thing cannot be, unless we sit down and suffer them to do it. Another such a brush, notwithstanding we lost the ground, would, by still reducing the enemy, put them in a condition to be afterwards totally defeated.

Could our whole army have come up to the attack at one time, the consequences had probably been otherwise; but our having different parts of the Brandywine Creek to guard, and the uncertainty which road to Philadelphia the enemy would attempt to take, naturally afforded them an opportunity of passing with their main body at a place where only a part of ours could be posted; for it must strike every thinking man with conviction, that it takes a much greater force to oppose an enemy in several places, than is sufficient to defeat in any one place. . . .

There are many men who will do their duty when it is not wanted; but a genuine public spirit always appears most when there is most occasion for it. Thank God! our army though fatigued, is yet entire. The attack made by us yesterday, was under many disadvantages, naturally arising from the uncertainty of knowing which route the enemy would take; and from that circumstance, the whole of our force could not be brought up together time enough to engage all at once. Our force is yet reserved; and it is evident that Howe does not think himself a gainer by the affair, otherwise he would this morning have moved down and attacked General Washington. . . .

Our army must undoubtedly feel fatigue, and want a reinforcement of rest, though not of valor. Our own interest and happiness call upon us to give them every support in our power, and make the burden of the day, on which the safety of this city [Philadelphia] depends, light as possible. Remember, gentlemen, that we have forces both to the northward and southward of Philadelphia, and if the enemy be but stopped till those can arrive, this city will be saved, and the enemy finally routed.

Flight from Philadelphia
by John Adams

SEPTEMBER 15, 1777. MONDAY. Friday, the 12th, I removed from Captain Duncan's, in Walnut Street, to the Rev. Mr. Sprout's in Third Street, a few doors from his meeting-house. Mr. Marchant, from Rhode Island, boards here with me.

Mr. Sprout is sick of a fever. Mrs. Sprout and the four young ladies, her daughters, are in great distress, on account of his sickness and the approach of Mr. Howe's army; but they bear their affliction with Christian patience and philosophic fortitude. The young ladies are Miss Hannah, Olive, Sally, and Nancy. The only son is an officer in the army; he was the first clerk in the American war-office.

We live in critical moments! Mr. Howe's army is at Middleton and Concord. Mr. Washington's, upon the banks of the Schuylkill, a few miles from him. . . . This city is the stake for which the game is played. I think there is a chance of saving it, although the probability is against us. Mr. Howe, I conjecture, is waiting for his ships to come into the Delaware. Will Washington attack him? I hope so; and God grant him success.

SEPTEMBER 16. TUESDAY. No newspaper this morning. Mr. Dunlap has moved or packed up his types. A note from General Dickinson, that the enemy in New Jersey are four thousand strong. Howe is about fifteen miles from us, the other way. The city seems to be asleep, or dead, and the whole state scarce alive. Maryland and Delaware the same. The prospect is chilling on every side; gloomy, dark, melancholy, and dispiriting. When and where will the light spring up? Shall we have good news from Europe? Shall we hear of a blow struck by Gates? Is there a possibility that McDougall and Dickinson should destroy the detachment in the Jerseys? From whence is our deliverance to come? or is it not to come? Is Philadelphia to be lost? If lost, is the cause lost?

No; the cause is not lost, but it may be hurt. I seldom regard reports, but it is said that Howe has marked his course from Elk [River] with depredation. His troops have plundered hen-roosts, dairy-rooms, the furniture of houses, and all the cattle in the country. The inhabitants, most of them are Quakers, are angry and disappointed, because they were promised the security of their property. It is reported, too, that Mr. Howe lost great numbers in the battle of the Brandywine.

SEPTEMBER 18. THURSDAY. The violent north-east storm, which began the day before yesterday, continues. We are yet in Philadelphia, that mass of cowardice and Toryism. . . .

SEPTEMBER 19. FRIDAY. At three, this morning, was waked by Mr. Lovel, and told that the members of Congress were gone, some of them, a little after midnight; that there was a letter from Mr. [Alexander] Hamilton, aide-de-camp to the General, informing that the enemy were in possession of the ford and the boats, and had it in their power to be in Philadelphia before morning, and that, if Congress was not removed, they had not a moment to lose.

Mr. Marchant and myself arose, sent for our horses, and, after collecting our things, rode off after the others. Breakfasted at Bristol, where many members determined to go the Newtown road to Reading. We rode to Trenton, where we dined. . . .

SEPTEMBER 21. SUNDAY. It was a false alarm which occasioned our flight from Philadelphia. Not a soldier of Howe's has crossed the Schuylkill. Washington has again crossed it, which I think is a very injudicious maneuver. I think his army would have been best disposed on the west side of the Schuylkill. If he had sent one brigade of his regular troops to have headed the militia, it would have been enough. With such a disposition, he might have cut to pieces Howe's army, in attempting to cross any of the fords. Howe will not attempt it. He will wait for his fleet in Delaware River; he will keep open his line of communication with Brunswick, and at last, by some deception or other, will slip unhurt into the city.

Burgoyne has crossed Hudson's River, by which General Gates thinks he is determined at all hazards to push for Albany, which General Gates says he will do all in his power to prevent him from reaching. But I confess I am anxious for the event, for I fear he will deceive

Gates, who seems to be acting the same timorous, defensive part, which has involved us in so many disasters.

O, Heaven! Grant us one great soul! One leading mind would extricate the best cause from that ruin which seems to await it for the want of it. We have as good a cause as ever was fought for; we have great resources; the people are well tempered. One active, masterly capacity would bring order out of this confusion, and save this country.

HOWE CAPTURED PHILADELPHIA. He did it in much the manner John Adams anticipated when he guessed that the British general, "by some deception or other, will slip unhurt into the city." Howe skillfully took advantage of the impression left by the battle of the Brandywine: he marched far up the Schuylkill, making Washington fear that he would be outflanked again. The American general followed with all his men, moving up the other side of the river; then the British quickly marched back down again, crossed the river unopposed, and captured the town. Fortunately for the Revolution, the members of the Continental Congress had already fled for their lives.

As John Adams wrote, there were other campaigns raging at the same moment—especially between General Burgoyne and American General Horatio Gates, north of Albany. But those events deserve a chapter of their own. Washington and the Continental Congress had serious problems here in Philadelphia.

The American Commander in Chief must have been battered by emotion as Howe outmaneuvered and outfought him. It seemed that every time Washington tried to defend an important objective—first New York, now Philadelphia—there was nothing he could do to stop the British from capturing it. And yet he never surrendered to depression, or even to anger at the stain on his beloved reputation. As always, adversity brought out the best in the Virginian; he immediately began to look for ways to strike back.

Washington's next operation clearly revealed his strategic outlook, which remained consistent throughout the war. He knew that he rarely had as many troops, overall, as the army he was opposing; nor were they as well trained or as well equipped. For those reasons, he always sought to avoid a pitched battle between the two main armies—and the disastrous defeat on the Brandywine reinforced his conviction. But he had to keep hitting back, for a number of reasons: first, to maintain the morale of his troops and the American people; second, to wear down the British army by attrition, since the enemy's losses could not be easily replaced; and third, to score politically important victories to pressure the government in London to acknowledge American independence.

Washington knew there was only one way to take battle to the British: to concentrate all of his army against only a segment of the enemy. In other words, he would compensate for strategic inferiority with temporary, tactical superiority.[63] His first such operation was the fight at Harlem Heights, followed by the far more important battles of Trenton and Princeton. It should also be said that Washington liked to attack—it suited his personality. And now, with Philadelphia lost, the general gave full rein both to his rational analysis and his combative streak.

Howe, it appeared, had dispersed his troops in and around the city. This created an opportunity for the Americans, not unlike that of the winter before, when the isolation of the Hessians at Trenton had made them vulnerable. Washington decided to march his entire force against a large British detachment at Germantown, a small village five miles northwest of Philadelphia. To ensure surprise, he made a night march from his camp, starting on the afternoon of October 3 and ending at two in the morning the next day, stopping his troops just shy of the enemy outposts.

Washington planned a complex attack: he called for four separate columns to converge on Howe's camp, starting at five in the morning on October 4. Unfortunately, the actual assault ran into unforeseen difficulties. A dense fog initially helped the Americans by allowing them to surprise the unsuspecting enemy; unfortunately, it also caused confusion among the patriots themselves, causing some units

[63]The reader should be aware of the difference between strategy and tactics: the first refers to large-scale issues of military operations—the management of an entire theater or campaign; the second deals with the individual battlefield—the maneuvers and combat in a specific skirmish or battle. In other words, the strategic is large-scale, the tactical small-scale.

to fire on each other. When a British detachment took refuge in a stone house, the Americans stopped to drive them out, rather than simply bottling them up with a few men and marching on with the main attack.

The assault succeeded in throwing the redcoats back in a panic; Anthony Wayne's men were particularly savage, seeking revenge for the massacre at Paoli. But the various problems on the American side gave Howe time to rally his troops. The British general was tired: he was fond of carousing, and he had been up all night playing faro. But in this crisis he proved his worth, as he shook his soldiers into formation and sent them forward in a rolling counterattack. Now it was the rebels' turn to give way, but without the fear or disorder that had marked the end of the Brandywine. The plan had just been a little too complex for the inexperienced soldiers—though without the fog, they might have pulled it off.

The battle of Germantown was hardly an American victory, but it was not considered much of a win for the British, either. Once again, Washington had shown his resilience, his skill in finding vulnerable points in the enemy army. Once again, the American citizen soldiers had proven themselves tough fighters, able to take a defeat like the Brandywine and Paoli, and battle back with fierce determination. The clash resonated across the Atlantic, as governments in Paris and Madrid noted how the United States recovered from so serious a loss as the capture of its capital.

One of the best assessments was made by a soldier who fought at Germantown—Thomas Paine, the sharp-tongued, self-appointed spokesman for the Revolution. The passage that follows comes from another issue of *The Crisis*; in it, Paine predictably argues that everything had turned out to the Americans' advantage. But it should be noted that he makes several good points in these paragraphs; he may have been partisan, but he offers a remarkably accurate assessment of the results of the fighting around Philadelphia. Interestingly, he addressed the first part of his message directly to Howe, and the second to his countrymen—but the British general probably reserved his own judgment.

Germantown
by Thomas Paine

TO GENERAL HOWE

Your progress from the Chesapeake was marked by no capital stroke of policy or heroism. Your principal aim was to get General Washington between the Delaware and the Schuylkill and between Philadelphia and your army. In that situation, with a river on each of his flanks, which united about five miles below the city, and your army above him, you could have intercepted his reinforcements and supplies, cut off all his communication with the country, and, if necessary, have dispatched assistance to open a passage for General Burgoyne. This scheme was too visible to succeed. . . .

There has been something unmilitarily passive in you from the time of your passing the Schuylkill and getting possession of Philadelphia to the close of the campaign. You mistook a trap for a conquest, the probability of which had been made known to Europe, and the edge of your triumph taken off by our own information long before.

Having got you into this situation, a scheme for a general attack up on you at Germantown was carried into execution on the fourth of October, and though the success was not equal to the excellence of the plan, yet the attempting it proved the genius of America to be on the rise and her power approaching to superiority. The obscurity of the morning was your best friend, for a fog is always favorable to a hunted enemy. Some weeks after this, you, likewise, planned an attack on General Washington while at Whitemarsh. Marched out with infinite parade, but on finding him preparing to attack you the next morning, you prudently cut about and retreated to Philadelphia with all the precipitation of a man conquered in imagination.

Immediately after the battle of Germantown, the probability of Burgoyne's defeat gave a new policy to affairs in Pennsylvania, and it was judged most consistent with the general safety of America to wait the issue of the Northern campaign. Slow but sure is sound work. . . . You resolved upon a retreat, and the next day, that is, on the 19th, withdrew your drooping army into Philadelphia. This movement was evidently dictated by fear; and carried with it a positive confession that you dreaded a second attack. It was hiding yourself among the women and children, and sleeping away the choicest part of a campaign in expensive inactivity. An army in a city can never be a conquering army. The situation admits only of defense. It is a mere shelter; and every military power in Europe will conclude you to be eventually defeated. . . .

TO THE INHABITANTS OF AMERICA

With all the pleasure with which a man exchanges bad company for good, I take my leave of Sir William and return to you. It is now nearly three years since the tyranny of Britain received its first repulse by the arms of America. A period, which has given birth to a new world and erected a monument to the folly of the old. . . .

I confess myself one of those who believe the loss of Philadelphia to be attended with more advantages than injuries. The case stood thus. The enemy imagined Philadelphia to be of more importance to us than it really was; for we all know that it had long ceased to be a port; not a cargo of goods had been brought into it for near a twelve month, nor any fixed manufactories, nor even ship-building carried on in it. Yet as the enemy believed the conquest of it to be practicable, and to that belief added the absurd idea that the soul of America was centered there, and would be conquered there, it naturally follows, that their possession of it, by not answering the end proposed, must break up the plans they had so foolishly gone upon, and either oblige them to form a new one, or to give over the attempt. . . .

Howe, likewise, cannot conquer where we have no army to oppose. . . . If he retreats from Philadelphia, he will be despised; if he stays, he may be shut up and starved out. . . . He has his choice of evils and we of opportunities. If he moves early, it is not only a sign but a proof that he expects no reinforcement, and his delays will prove that he either waits for the arrival of a plan to go upon, or force to execute it, or both; in which case, our strength will increase more than his, therefore in any case we cannot be wrong if we do but proceed.

"WE CANNOT BE wrong if we do but proceed," Paine wrote. Indeed, in the weeks following Howe's capture of the capital, John Adams and the other members of the Continental Congress shook themselves out of their depression and came to the same conclusion. The British had one army sitting in New York, another in Philadelphia; and the rebels controlled all else. Paine was quite right to note, "An army in a city can never be a conquering army"—at least not with the limited number of troops available to General Howe.

In the fighting of 1777, of course, there was one other British army operating in America: General Burgoyne's force, marching toward Albany from Canada. The result of that campaign, fought simultaneously with that around Philadelphia, would have a rather different result. For if Washington's attack on Germantown gave the Americans a dose of grim determination, the fighting against Burgoyne gave them simple, straightforward joy.

9

SARATOGA

"I look upon America as our child, which we have already spoilt by too much indulgence." These words expressed a paternal sentiment that was clear enough—but the man who spoke them bore little resemblance to a father. As he stood in the House of Commons in 1774, he was already past fifty, and his face showed the hard life of a dandy, a gambler, a playwright, and a politician—a life of too many parties, too many late nights, too much alcohol. He had been nicknamed "Gentleman Johnny," but not from any of the avocations just named; soldiers called him that, for John Burgoyne was a distinguished officer of the British army.[64]

Burgoyne was a full decade older than George Washington, but he lagged behind the Virginian in maturity. As Washington aged, he strove to attain a classical Roman dignity; he yearned to be an American Stoic in gravity and severity. He came as close as perhaps any man could. But Gentleman Johnny yearned for the applause of the crowd—the smart crowd, the aristocratic crowd—as he snapped off quips, penned amusing little farces, wagered at the card table, and condescended from his seat in Parliament. He received quite a lot of applause, too, because he was good at almost everything he did. When he led a cavalry brigade in Portugal during the Seven Years War, he earned a well-deserved reputation for bravery and dash.

But when he arrived in America during the siege of Boston, he found it a terrific bore. As the junior member of the trio of major generals sent by the king to assist Thomas Gage, he had little to do. Howe led the attack on Bunker Hill, Clinton did whatever Clinton did, and Burgoyne did nothing. In 1776, he was ordered to Canada, where he swept away the last remaining American troops. That, too, was a distinctly uninteresting duty; the remnants of the rebel invasion

[64]The quotes are in Bobrick, pp. 244–247.

force were so bedraggled, so thoroughly beaten, a crowd of small children might have driven them back. Then he served as Guy Carleton's second in command during the abortive offensive south through Lake Champlain. Burgoyne learned that to be second in command of everything is to be first in nothing. His impatience only grew when Carleton turned back after the bitter naval battle with Benedict Arnold's fleet. Thoroughly disgusted, he returned to London with the onset of cold weather.

While Washington outsmarted and outfought Howe and Cornwallis in cold New Jersey, Burgoyne penned an influential essay in warm, safe London. Titled *Thoughts on Conducting the War from the Side of Canada*, it essentially restated Lord Germain's existing plan for conquering the United States (or rebellious colonies, as the British considered them). He did, however, elaborate further, offering ideas for making it work in 1777. The main invasion force, traveling down Lake Champlain to the Hudson River, should have no less than 8,000 regular troops, he argued; a second column should leave Fort Oswego, on New York's Lake Ontario coastline, and drive toward Fort Stanwix, a strongpoint on the Mohawk River (which extended due west from the Hudson). This second force would distract the rebels on Lake Champlain and pick up support in an area known to be strongly loyalist. Finally, a third column should ascend from New York, driving up the Hudson to meet the forces coming down from Canada. Having severed New England from the rest of the colonies, the British could simply mop up the remaining resistance.

As mentioned, this was essentially Germain's existing plan; even Samuel Adams had summed up the same strategy a year before. But the brittle, insecure Germain thought that the gentleman-playwright general had written it up so nicely, it deserved the king's personal attention. George III found it to be a splendid plan; the monarch and his secretary for America adopted it as the main strategy for 1777, assigning Burgoyne himself to command the main column that would attack from Canada. Burgoyne could not have been more pleased: his *Thoughts on Conducting the War* had earned the best review of his literary career—an independent military command.

There was a small problem, of course: General William Howe was still supreme land commander in North America, and he had a completely different plan of operations for the year. As the previous chapter has already shown, he intended to attack Philadelphia. Germain simply fudged the question. He could not bring himself to order Howe to cooperate with Burgoyne; he never even formally notified him of Burgoyne's plan. All he did was send off a copy of a letter he had written to General Guy Carleton in Canada, ordering that officer to place the attack force under Burgoyne's command. To make matters worse, he left Burgoyne under the impression that Howe was at his disposal. And so Germain sweetly waved goodbye as Gentleman Johnny departed London for Canada on March 27, 1777, letting him go in blissful ignorance of the thorough mess in strategic planning for the year.

It is difficult to know how much damage Germain's indecision really inflicted on the British cause. If Howe had remained in New York, preparatory to a move north, Washington also would have lingered in the area; the American general might even have united his army with the rebel forces in the north, leading to a tremendous victory over one of the three columns envisioned in Burgoyne's plan. But when Howe went to Philadelphia he pulled Washington with him, far from Burgoyne's invading army. The conflicting plans might have been a hidden blessing.

On the other hand, if Burgoyne and Howe had truly moved toward each other at the same time, they would have forced the Americans to divide their forces to stop both invading armies. By concentrating their attack in time as well as space, the British could have denied the Americans the use of interior lines—the ability to shift forces from one threat to another by virtue of being in the center. If Burgoyne's plan worked correctly, it could have been decisive. Of course, no one will ever know what might have happened if Howe had cooperated.

There was, in fact, an air of fantasy about the whole idea of slicing the American republic in half. The War of Independence was fought by very few troops in a very large space; no army ever established solid control over a large territory, unless it had the support of the civilian population. If all the soldiers in the British army were stationed along the Hudson River—if every outpost in the sprawling empire was emptied, if all the German mercenaries were thrown in as well—Burgoyne still could not have walled off New England from the rest of the republic. His strategy looked marvelous on a map, but in reality there always would have been unguarded passes in the mountains, unwatched stretches of the river. It was rather like trying to cut the Atlantic in two by sailing a ship from London to Boston.

However, such observations can only put his strategy in perspective; his plan still represented a grave threat to the American cause. No one in the states wanted another British army marching through the countryside; no one wanted to lose the forts that dotted Lake Champlain, Lake George, and the Hudson River; no one was willing to let Burgoyne advance unimpeded. A risky battle would *have* to be fought somewhere along his path. The rebels knew Burgoyne could not erect a barrier between the states, but they feared his attack nonetheless.

And they knew very well the attack was coming. The expedition was a very poorly guarded secret: specific details of Burgoyne's plans could be heard in conversation in taverns, military tents, and government chambers. Unfortunately, the American army in the north was deeply troubled. The commander, General Philip Schuyler, was a formal, somewhat aristocratic, extremely wealthy Dutch-American officer; his democratically minded New England troops never took much of a liking to him. Even worse, his highly popular and highly capable subordinate, Benedict Arnold, departed in a huff when Congress refused to elevate him to major general in the spring, when it announced a batch of promotions.

Schuyler did his best to prepare the northern defenses. He lived in the area, so he knew that only one route was possible for the attack from Montreal: Lake Champlain, the spectacular, 110-mile-long waterway that split the natural barrier of the Adirondack and Green mountains. Perhaps four-fifths of the way down the lake, a short portage separated it from Lake George, another major body of water that came to within fifteen miles of the Hudson River; beyond the portage, a slender extension of Champlain called the South Bay continued to the southeast, turning into Wood Creek. All of these waters passed through extremely rugged wilderness.

The first major stronghold on Lake Champlain was Crown Point, shortly above the connection to Lake George; but the keystone of the American defenses was Fort Ticonderoga, located at the portage itself. A stone fortress constructed by the French, it had won a reputation for invincibility during the French and Indian War, when General Montcalm successfully defended it against a much larger British army (William Howe's older brother died in the preliminary skirmishing before that battle). It was now held by American General Arthur St. Clair, with about 2,000 men; across Lake Champlain (which was quite narrow at that point) was another important fortification on Mount Independence. A floating boom spanned the waters there to prevent any British ships from passing.

If Burgoyne conquered Ticonderoga and then crossed over into Lake George, he would face Fort George at the south end. If he were to continue down the South Bay, he would run into Fort Anne. Beyond both these strongholds was Fort Edward on the eastern bank of the Hudson River, where Schuyler had his headquarters. The American commander might not have been popular, but he had plenty of obstacles to slow the British advance.

On May 6, 1777, General Burgoyne sailed into Quebec on H.M.S. *Apollo*, invigorated by his success at persuading Germain and the king to support his proposed offensive. In short order, he took command of the men designated for the attack, leaving General Guy Carleton behind in Canada. The troops did not amount to the number he had wanted, but that was an old story for generals, and Burgoyne remained extremely confident. His redcoats included some of the finest professional infantry in the world; the same could be said for his large contingent of German troops (mostly from Brunswick). Hundreds of Indians flocked to his camp from the Catholic missions where they lived, eager for the scalps, prisoners, and glory that they and their fathers had won in previous wars against the Americans. And two units of rangers—Canadians and American loyalists—added another essential scouting force for this wilderness campaign.

Perhaps Burgoyne's greatest strength was in his list of subordinates. He formally divided his force into Left and Right Wings. The Right Wing, consisting of most of the British troops, came under the command of Major General William Phillips, a respected strategist and an expert artillery specialist. The Left, composed of the German regiments, was led by General Baron Friedrich Adolph von Riedesel, a particularly energetic and capable officer. Rounding out this impressive senior leadership was Brigadier General Simon Fraser, whom Burgoyne relied on to lead the advanced corps of light troops.

At the end of June, Burgoyne got all his men into canoes, boats, and ships, and began to sail down Lake Champlain. This year, unlike the year before, there was no Benedict Arnold to stop him with an improvised fleet. Down the British force came, mile after mile, until it reached Crown Point. In the first selection that follows, Burgoyne describes the start of his expedition; immediately after that comes a much more vivid account from Lieutenant Thomas Anburey, a junior officer in General Fraser's strike force. Anburey offers a highly detailed, highly personal narrative of the campaign, as the army came up against Ticonderoga; met the Americans in the confused wilderness battle at Hubbardton; and drove on into the woods between Lake Champlain and Fort Edward on the Hudson.

The Expedition from Canada
by John Burgoyne

I left London on the 27th of March, and upon my departure from Plymouth, finding the *Albion* man-of-war ready to sail for New York, I wrote to Sir W. Howe by that conveyance, upon the subject of my expedition, and the nature of my orders. I arrived at Quebec the 6th of May. Sir Guy Carleton immediately put under my command the troops destined for the expedition, and committed to my management the preparatory arrangements. From thence I wrote a second letter to Sir William Howe, wherein I repeated that I was entrusted with the command of the army destined to march from Canada, and that my orders were to force a junction with his excellency. . . . I proceeded to Montreal on the 12th. . . .

Certain parts of the expected force . . . fell short. The Canadian troops, stated in the plan at 2,000, consisted only of three companies, intended to be of 100 men each, but in reality not amounting to more than 150 upon the whole; nor could they be augmented. The corvées, which are detachments of provincials without arms, to repair roads, convey provisions, or any other temporary employment for the king's service, could not be obtained in sufficient number, nor kept to their employments. . . . Notwithstanding all impediments, the army assembled between the 17th and 20th of June at Cumberland Point, upon Lake Champlain.

On the 21st I held a conference with the Iroquois, Algonquins, Abenakis, and Ottawas Indians, in all about four hundred. . . . The priest to whom they seemed devoted, and the British officers employed to conduct them, and to whose control they engaged to submit, gained advantages and spread terror without barbarity. The first party sent out made several of the enemy prisoners in the heat of action, and treated them with European humanity.

During the movement of the different corps to this general rendezvous, I wrote a third letter to Sir William Howe. The chief purport of it was to give him "intelligence of my situation at the time, and of my expectations of being before Ticonderoga between the 20th and 25th instant; that I did not apprehend the effective strength of the army would amount to above 6,500 men. . . ."

I beg leave to state an extract from my orders to the army at Crown Point June 30. The words were these: "The army embarks tomorrow to approach the enemy. The services required of this particular expedition are critical and conspicuous. During our progress occasions may occur, in which no difficulty, nor labor, nor life are to be regarded. This army must not retreat." . . . The idea of forcing a way to Albany by vigorous exertions against any opposition we might meet, was general and fixed through the whole army. . . .

All therefore that is necessary before I quit this first period of the campaign, is to give a precise state of the effective strength of the army, at the time it assembled.

On the 1st of July, the day we encamped before Ticonderoga, the troops consisted of[65]

British rank and file	3,724
German ditto	3,016
	6,740 regulars, exlusive of artillerymen
Canadians and Provincials, about	250
Indians about	400
	650

A Fortress and a Battle
by Thomas Anburey

CAMP AT CROWN POINT   JUNE 30, 1777

Let me just relate in what manner the army passed the lake, which was by brigades, generally advancing from seventeen to twenty miles a day, and regulated in such a manner that the second brigade should take the encampment of the first, and so on successively, for each brigade to fill the ground the other quitted; the time for departure was always at daybreak. . . .

I cannot forbear picturing to your imagination one of the most pleasing spectacles I ever beheld. When we were in the wildest part of the lake, whose beauty and extent I have already described, it was remarkably fine and clear, not a breeze stirring, when the whole army appeared in one view in such perfect regularity, as to form the most complete and splendid regatta you can possibly conceive. A sight so novel and pleasing, could not fail of fixing the admiration and attention of everyone present.

[65]The numbers listed below understate somewhat Burgoyne's forces. He also had 600 artillerymen (and 138 field pieces), along with some 500 American loyalists, serving in the Queen's Loyal Rangers and the King's Loyal Americans. His total force exceeded 8,000 men.

In the front, the Indians went with their birch bark canoes, containing twenty or thirty in each, then the advanced corps in such a regular line, with the gunboats, then followed the [frigates] *Royal George* and *Inflexible,* towing large booms, which are to be thrown across two points of land, with the other brigs and sloops following; after them the first brigade in a regular line, then the Generals Burgoyne, Phillips, and Riedesel in their pinnaces; next to them were the second brigade, followed by the German brigades, and the rear was brought up with the sutlers and followers of the army.

Upon the appearance of so formidable a fleet, you may imagine they were not a little dismayed at Ticonderoga, for they were apprised of our advance, as we every day could see their watch-boats. We had, it is certain, a very strong naval force, but yet it might have been greatly in the power of the Americans to have prevented our passing the lake so rapidly as we have done, especially as there are certain parts of it where a few armed vessels might have stopped us for some time; but it is an invariable maxim with the Americans, of which there are numberless instances in the last campaign, never to face an enemy but with very superior advantages, and the most evident signs and prospects of success. . . .

CAMP AT SKENESBORO   JULY 12, 1777

No doubt, after so much as I have repeatedly mentioned to you in my former letters relative to Ticonderoga, and the vigorous defense it was universally supposed the enemy would make, you will be greatly surprised to receive a letter from me, at so great a distance beyond that important post. . . .

After we had gained possession of Sugar Hill,[66] on the 5th instant, that very evening we observed the enemy making great fires; it was then generally thought they were meditating an attack, or that they were retreating, which latter circumstance really was the case, for

[66]Sugar Loaf Hill was a very high mount that towered over Ticonderoga. It was so rugged that the Americans were certain the British could not get artillery pieces up its slopes—but Burgoyne's men managed to do exactly that, leaving the fort completely vulnerable.

about daybreak intelligence was brought to General Fraser, that the enemy were retiring, when the pickets were ordered to advance, which the brigades, as soon as they were accoutered, were to follow.

They were soon ready, and marched down to the works; when we came to the bridge of communication, we were obliged to halt till it was sufficiently repaired for the troops to pass, as the enemy, in their abandoning the works, had destroyed it. . . . In a short time after the bridge was rendered passable, our brigade crossed, and we advanced up to the picketed fort, where the British colors were instantly hoisted. . . . After we had remained some little time in the fort, orders came for the advanced corps to march in pursuit of the enemy, who, we were informed, had gone [east] to Hubbardton, in order to harrass their rear. . . . At three in the morning our march was renewed, and about five [in the morning] we came up with the enemy. . . .

This war is very different from the last in Germany; in this the life of an individual is sought with as much avidity as the obtaining a victory over an army of thousands. . . . [67]

In this action [at Hubbardton] I found all manual exercise [the formal technique for loading and firing in massed volleys] is but an ornament, and the only object of importance it can boast of was that of loading, firing, and charging with bayonets; as to the former, the soldiers should be instructed in the best and most expeditious method. Here I cannot help observing to you, whether it proceeded from an idea of self-preservation, or natural instinct, but the soldiers greatly improved the mode they were taught in, as to expedition, for as soon as they had primed their pieces, and put the cartridge in the barrel, instead of ramming it down with their rods, they struck the butt end of their piece upon the ground, and bringing it to the *present*, fired it off. The confusion of a man's ideas during the time of action, brave as he may be, is undoubtedly great; several of the men, upon examining their muskets, after all was over, found five or six cartridges, which they were positive to the having discharged.

[67]At Hubbardton, General Fraser's strike force, 850 strong, attacked the 1,000 men of the American rear guard as they were eating breakfast. The Americans were rallied by Colonel Turbott Francis, and they put up a heroic defense. In the thick woods and steep hills, formal lines were useless; units became disorganized and divided, turning the fight into what is often called a soldier's battle between isolated clusters of men.

CAMP AT SKENESBORO   JULY 14, 1777

The advantages of the ground [in the battle of Hubbardton] was wholly on the side of the Americans, added to which the woods were so thick that little or no order could be observed in advancing upon the enemy, it being totally impossible to form a regular line; personal courage and intrepidity was therefore to supply the place of military skill and discipline. The native bravery of our countrymen could not be more resolutely displayed than in this action, nor more effectually exerted.

It was a trial of the activity, strength, and valor of every man that fought. At the commencement of the action the enemy were everywhere thrown into the greatest confusion, but being rallied by that brave officer, Colonel Francis, whose death, though an enemy, will ever be regretted by those who can feel for the loss of a gallant and brave man, the fight was renewed with the greatest degree of fierceness and obstinacy. Both parties engaged in separate detachments unconnected with each other, and the numbers of the enemy empowered them to front, flank, and rear. Some of these detachments, notwithstanding an inferiority, most resolutely defended themselves, and the fate of the day was undecided till the arrival of the Germans, who, though late, came in for a share of the glory in dispersing the enemy in all quarters. . . .

That soldiers have many hair-breadth escapes, I am sure was never more fully verified, than in regard to Lord Balcarres, who commands the light infantry; he had near thirty balls shot through his jacket and trousers, and yet only received a small graze on the hip. Others were equally as unfortunate, for upon the very first attack of the light infantry, Lieutenant Haggit received a ball in each of his eyes. . . .

We are still encamped at this place [Skenesboro, north of Fort Anne], waiting for the arrival of provisions, bateaux [boats], and many other incumbrances [that] armies in general are but very seldom troubled with. . . . I mention this, that you may not be surprised at our not making such rapid marches, and over-running the country, as they in all probability will.

The army are all assembled at this place, and in a few days the advanced corps [will] march to Fort Edward. You would like to learn the movements of the other part of the army, after we got possession of Ticonderoga; I was not with them, but you shall know what I have been able to collect.

After a passage had been made . . . the main body of the army pursued the enemy by South Bay, within three miles of this place, where they were posted in a stockaded fort, with armed galleys. The first brigade was disembarked with an intention of cutting off the enemy's retreat, but their hasty flight rendered that maneuver useless. The gunboats and frigates pursued the armed vessels, and when the enemy arrived at the falls of this place, they made a defense for some time, after which they blew up three of their vessels, and the other two struck.

On the enemy's retreat they set fire to the fort, dwelling house, sawmill, iron works, and all the buildings on this plantation, destroyed the bateaux, and retired to Fort Edward. . . .

We are obliged to wait some time in our present position, till the roads are cleared of the trees which the Americans felled after their retreat. You would think it almost impossible, but every ten or twelve yards great trees are laid across the road, exclusive of smaller ones, especially when it is considered what a hasty retreat they made of it. Repairing the bridges is a work of some labor, added to which, a stock of provisions must be brought up previous to our marching on Fort Edward. We lie under many disadvantages in prosecuting this war, from the impediments I have stated, and we cannot follow this great military maxim, "in good success push the advantage as far as you can."

While this part of the army is thus employed, the remainder are conveying the gunboats, bateaux, and provision vessels into Lake George, to scout that lake, and secure the future route of our magazines; when that force is ready to move down the lake, the army will proceed to possess Fort Edward, by which means the enemy, if they do not abandon Fort George [on the south end of Lake George], must inevitably be caught, as they will be enclosed by the two armies. During these movements General Riedesel is to make a diversion into Connecticut, and reconnoiter the country, and by that feint to draw the attention of the Americans to almost every quarter.

LIEUTENANT ANBUREY PARTICIPATED in some of the most glorious British victories in the entire War of Independence. The bloodless capture of Ticonderoga—a reputedly invincible fortress—was seen as a marvel. When George III heard the news, he ran about, shouting, "I have beat them! Beat all the Americans!" On the spot he pledged to make Burgoyne a lieutenant general.

The ensuing battle of Hubbardton—when General Fraser's advanced corps struck the American rear guard—should have added a note of caution. The rebels fought extremely hard, throwing back a determined attack in terrain that favored militia, who preferred to fight under cover, in loose formation. Only the last-minute arrival of the Germans turned the tide, as Riedesel sent his men charging into an assault, singing a chilling battle hymn at the top of their voices, with a band playing behind them. But a victory, Burgoyne thought, was a victory, and so he continued down the South Bay to Skenesboro without fear.

On the American side, these same events caused consternation. "The evacuation of Ticonderoga and Mount Independence is an event of chagrin and surprise not apprehended, nor within the compass of my reasoning," Washington wrote.[68] Many suspected cowardice, or even outright treason. How could this invulnerable fortress fall without a fight? Of course, these observers from a distance could not know what General St. Clair knew, when he looked up that morning and saw British cannons high on Sugar Loaf Hill; he preferred to slip out with all his men than to let most of them be massacred by the guns on that mountain.

General Schuyler faced a crisis. Every day, his militia slipped away; they had no desire to linger with a losing army when they could be defending their homes against the far-ranging Indians in Burgoyne's army. By July 14, the day that Lieutenant Anburey wrote the last letter in the selection above, Schuyler's Northern Department could count only 2,600 Continentals and less than 2,000 militiamen. So he did what he could. He begged for assistance from Washington, who sent Benedict Arnold (now recovered from his earlier sulk over the promotions) and 500 frontier riflemen under Colonel Daniel Mor-

[68]Quoted in Bobrick, p. 253.

gan; the two commanders were probably the best combat leaders in the American army. And Schuyler began a scorched-earth policy against Burgoyne's advance, destroying any possible supplies in the countryside surrounding the enemy; his wife set fire to his own crops as the British approached.

Burgoyne's thinking mirrored Schuyler's. For the British commander, supplies—not battles—dictated the next course of action. As his army moved through the wilderness, it relied on an enormous logistical tail—hundreds of boats and carts, dozens of magazines, scores of horses, and men to handle it all. If the general did not plan correctly at each step, he knew his army could literally begin to starve before it ever arrived at Albany. Schuyler's destruction of food, forage, and supplies prevented the British from collecting what they needed in the countryside—so everything had to come down from Canada.

Preposterously enough, this heavily burdened army dragged with it far more than necessary weapons and matériel—it carried all the accoutrements of aristocratic high life. For the gentleman officer, going on campaign was partially a matter of recreation, and he left none of the comforts of life behind. Musicians, servants, cooks, mistresses, furniture, dinnerware, fine wine—Burgoyne and his senior staff brought all the luxuries. General von Riedesel even had his wife and children along for the fun, and many other officers brought wives as well. One of Burgoyne's lieutenants wrote, "We have frequent dinees [sic] and constantly music; for my part . . . this campaigning is a favorite portion of life: and none but stupid mortals can dislike a lively camp, good weather, good claret, good music, and the enemy near."[69]

Moving all this—and the men too—through the wilderness was not easy. With the Americans fleeing before his victorious advance, Burgoyne spent most of his time worrying about two things: time and boats. His ability to feed his army was strictly dependent upon the number of boats available; that would change, of course, once he broke out of the wilderness by capturing Albany. So he had to reach Albany quickly.

As he looked at the map, he thought he saw an answer to all his worries. In his original plan, he intended to cross the army from Lake

---

[69]Quoted in Bobrick, p. 273.

Champlain to Lake George, sail to the southern end and capture Fort George, and then cross a mere fifteen miles of woods to Fort Edward on the Hudson. It is important to note that those fifteen miles were already traversed by a military road, constructed twenty years before. All in all, Burgoyne's original analysis correctly identified the fastest means of getting his army to Albany. But now he noticed that Lake Champlain's South Bay continued farther south, turning into Wood Creek, which ran close to Fort Edward. Instead of taking his troops north again, all the way back to the portage to Lake George, he could keep going south, down Wood Creek to the Hudson. This would save time *and* boats (which otherwise would be tied up in moving troops, not supplies).

Burgoyne's decision to march through the woods from Lake Champlain to Fort Edward, rather than going back for the easier Lake George route, had a tremendous impact on the campaign. It would take him weeks to march twenty miles through the wilderness, giving the Americans time to collect troops and supplies, as well as generals Arnold and Morgan. Would it have been faster if the British had gone the other way? In all likelihood, yes, though we can never know for sure.

In the first selection below, however, Burgoyne indignantly defends his decision; though historians have often mocked his arguments, his reasons deserve consideration. The second selection, immediately following, offers evidence that cuts in both directions. Lieutenant Anburey argues that Burgoyne was right (especially with regard to the effect of the march on Fort George); but he also mentions the incredible difficulties the troops suffered as they creeped through the dense wilderness of Wood Creek, day after demoralizing day. Schuyler employed hundreds of men in cutting down trees across the likely path of the British army; as Anburey wrote in the selection above, "You would think it almost impossible, but every ten or twelve yards great trees are laid across the road." In the wilderness between Fort Anne and Fort Edward, there was no road—just trees, swamps, and man-made obstacles. Anburey also offers an interesting anecdote about this unusual wilderness campaign, offering rare insight into American determination.

Wood Service
by John Burgoyne

I come now to the second period of the campaign, comprehending the transactions of the time the pursuit of the enemy from Ticonderoga created, and the corps of Brigadier-General Fraser and the 9th Regiment rejoined the army, after the respective actions of Hubbardton and Fort Anne, to the time when the army passed the Hudson's River to attack the enemy near Stillwater.

It had proved impossible immediately to follow the quick retreat of the enemy farther, from the nature of the country, and the necessity of waiting a fresh supply of provisions. But it appeared evident to me, that could a rapid progress towards Albany be effected, during their dispersion and panic, it would be decisive on the success of the expedition.

Question has been made by those who began at this period to arraign my military conduct, whether it would not have been more expedient for the purpose of rapidity to have fallen back to Ticonderoga, in order to take the convenient route of Lake George, rather than to have persevered in the laborious and difficult route by land to Fort Edward. My motives for preferring the latter were these: I considered not only the general imprecisions which a retrograde motion is apt to make upon the minds of both enemies and friends, but also, that the natural conduct of the enemy in that case would be to remain at Fort George, as their retreat could not then be cut off, in order to oblige me to open trenches, and consequently to delay me, and in the meantime they would have destroyed the road from Fort George to Fort Edward. On the other hand, by persisting to penetrate by the short cut from Fort Anne, of which I was then master, to Fort Edward, though it was attended with great labor, and many alert situations, the troops were improved in the very essential point of wood service. I effectually dislodged the enemy from Fort George without a blow; and seeing me master of one communication, they did not think it worth while to destroy the other.

The great number of boats, also, which must necessarily have been employed for the transport of the troops over Lake George, were by this course spared for the transport of provision, artillery, and ammunition.

The success answered this reasoning in every point; for by the vigilance of General Phillips, to whom I had committed the important part of forwarding all the necessaries from Ticonderoga, a great embarkation arrived at Fort George on July 29th. I took possession of the country near Fort Edward on the same day, and independently of other advantages, I found myself much more forward in point of time than I could possibly have been by the other route.[70]

Another material motive . . . was that during the time my army was employed in clearing Wood Creek and cutting roads, and the corps under Major-General Phillips was working to pass the transports over Lake George, I was enabled to detach a large corps to my left, under Major-General Riedesel, and thereby assist my purpose of giving jealousy to Connecticut, and keeping in check the whole country called the Hampshire Grants.

Down Wood Creek
by Thomas Anburey

CAMP AT FORT EDWARD   AUGUST 6, 1777

We are arrived at this place, in which it was thought the enemy would have made a stand, but upon intelligence of our advancing, they precipitately abandoned it, as did the garrison of Ticonderoga. Very fortunately for the garrison of Fort George, they had passed this place about an hour before our arrival; had they been that much later, they must have been inevitably cut off. . . . [71]

[70]Burgoyne depicts his march through the woods to Fort Edward as a stroke of genius, one that gained him time. But it undoubtedly slowed his progress to a crawl, granting the Americans a critical reprieve. In addition, his creep through the woods exhausted and disorganized his army as it marched in the summer heat. Despite the fierce criticism he has taken for it, however, he was indeed concerned about the shortage of boats, and his move did force the Americans to abandon Fort George.

[71]As Burgoyne predicted, the garrison at Fort George on Lake George abandoned their position when they learned that the British army had arrived in their rear. Thus Burgoyne was spared a lengthy siege of Fort George—but at the cost of weeks of creeping through the forest.

The distance from our late encampment to this place was small, but the many obstacles the enemy had thrown in our way made it a matter of astonishment, considering the laborious march we had undergone, that we should arrive so soon. . . .

At this encampment the expected Indians have joined us; they seem to possess more bravery, and much more humanity, than those who accompanied us across Lake Champlain, as the following little anecdote will convince you.

A few days since several of them fell in with a scouting party of Americans, and after a little skirmish, the enemy fled to their bateaux, and rowed across the river. The Indians fired at, but could not reach them, and being greatly exasperated at their making their escape, perceiving a hog-trough, they put their firearms into it, stripped, and swam across the river, pushing the hog-trough before them. The Indians gained the shore lower down than the Americans, surprised and took them prisoners, and brought them back in the bateaux across the river.

One of the Americans, a very brave fellow, was wounded in the skirmish, and unable to walk, when the Indians brought him upon their backs for near three miles, with as much care and attention as if he had been one of their own people.

As the Indians approached the camp, we were all apprised of their bringing in some prisoners by their setting up the war whoop; but everyone was astonished, and as equally pleased, at their humanity, in beholding an Indian bringing on his back the chief of the party. He was taken before General Fraser, but would give no answer to any question, and behaved in the most undaunted manner. The General, imagining that by shewing him attention he might gain some information from him, ordered him some refreshment; and when the surgeon had examined his wound, told him he must immediately undergo an amputation; which, being performed, he was requested to keep himself still and quiet, or a locked jaw would inevitably ensue. To this he replied with great firmness, "Then I shall have the pleasure of dying in a good cause, that of gaining the independence of the American colonies."

I mention this circumstance, to show how cheerfully some of them will sacrifice their lives in pursuit of this favorite idol. Such was the man's restless disposition, that he actually died the next morning. This death was generally regretted, as one among the very few who act from principle.

An Expedition to Bennington
by John Burgoyne

It was at this time that Major-General Riedesel conceived the purpose of mounting his dragoons [who had been marching without horses]. In the country he traversed during his detached command, he found the people frightened and submissive. He was industrious and expert in procuring intelligence in parts of the country more remote than Bennington, and entertained no doubt of success were an expedition formed under the command of Lieutenant-Colonel [Friederich] Baum.

On the arrival of the army at Fort Edward, the great object of attention was the transports from Fort George. The distance was about sixteen miles, the roads wanting great repair, the weather unfavorable, the cattle and carriages scarce. . . . It was soon found, that in the situation of the transport service at that time, the army could barely be victualled from day to day, and that there was no prospect of establishing a magazine in due time for pursuing present advantages. The idea of the expedition to Bennington originated upon this difficulty, combined with the intelligence reported by General Riedesel, and with all I had otherwise received.

I knew that Bennington was the great deposit of corn, flour, and store cattle; that it was guarded only by militia; and every day's account tended to confirm the persuasion of the loyalty of one description [part] of the inhabitants and the panic of the other. Those who knew the country were the most sanguine in this persuasion.

Had my intelligence been worse founded, I should not have hesitated to try this expedition with such troops, and under such instructions, as I gave to the commanding officer, for so great a purpose as that of a supply sufficient to enable the army to follow at the heels of a broken and disconcerted enemy. The German troops employed were of the best I had of that nation. The number of British was small; but it was the select light corps of the army, composed of chosen men from all the regiments, and commanded by Captain Fraser, one of the most distinguished officers in his line of service that ever I met with.

BURGOYNE TOOK THREE weeks to drive from Skenesboro to Fort Edward. What military experts call "friction" had rubbed his army raw: the sheer toil of trudging through the near-impenetrable woods had exhausted his men, disordered his units, worn out his animals, and consumed precious supplies.

One of his biggest problems involved the Native American warriors Lieutenant Anburey admired so. Impatient for action and eager for material rewards for their efforts, a group of Indians had raided a nearby farmhouse, killing and scalping a young woman named Jane McCrea. The incident became a rallying cry for the rebel cause—and it was all the worse for the fact that Jane McCrea was a Tory. Feelings between the colonists and the Native Americans had always run close to pure racial hatred; the Americans viewed most Indians as barbarians. Thanks to the McCrea killing, even loyalists now dreaded the force that Burgoyne had unleashed to "spread terror," as he himself described the Indian role.

But Burgoyne worried less about innocent civilians than about horses and oats. His bedraggled army was tattered, tired, and hungry after its "wood service," and there were precious few supplies to be had at Fort Edward. Schuyler's scorched-earth policy had seen to that. So he quickly grasped at Riedesel's suggestion that an expedition be sent east to Bennington, to capture an overstuffed rebel supply depot. As an added benefit, the German dragoons could find mounts in that district. Once on horseback, the dragoons could serve as scouts, or launch charges in combat—something certain to shock the American militia. On August 11, the expedition to Bennington set out from Fort Anne: 800 men, under the command of Lieutenant Colonel Friederich Baum.

Baum was a tough, professional soldier—but he spoke no English, and he had never fought a campaign like this one. His opponent, however, was a local man who knew this sort of fighting very well. Brigadier General John Stark had won a formidable reputation with his heroic leadership at Bunker Hill; now, as Baum approached, he called in detachments of militia and set a trap that won him even greater fame. On August 15, he utterly annihilated Baum's detachment, killing or capturing virtually all 800 men. When a British relief party approached Bennington, Stark brutalized it in turn.

Burgoyne's decision to send Baum to Bennington seemed logical at the time. First, he needed the supplies stockpiled there; second, he had nothing but contempt for the American forces. The campaign so far had been string of victories; when Burgoyne arrived at Fort Edward, he thought he faced "a broken and disconcerted enemy." In retrospect, however, it obviously proved to be a disaster. He allowed the Americans to concentrate against just one part of his army (much as Washington tried to do against Howe); and that detachment consisted of 15 percent of Burgoyne's combat force—small enough to be vulnerable, big enough to be a serious loss when it was destroyed.

What the English general failed to understand, most of all, was the nature of the American militia. When gathered in the camp of a formal, regular army, militiamen were frustrating for professional officers: they resented discipline, often ignored orders, and simply melted away when they tired of campaigning. British veterans of the French and Indian War (and Washington in the Revolution) complained endlessly about the American militia. But the battle of Bennington proved how valuable they could be when defending their home territory. As Baum advanced, they seemed to spring from the ground, collecting into a strong force in days. With their own neighborhood at stake, they fought with astonishing bravery, charging right into the enemy lines. Here and elsewhere, the militia truly made the Revolution a popular war—a mass uprising as well as a formal conflict.

In the British camp, Burgoyne barely had time to absorb the news when he heard from another important detachment—one far to the west of Fort Edward. In his original plan, he had called for three columns to spear toward Albany. The first had been thrown into doubt by Howe's departure for Philadelphia—though Howe left General Henry Clinton in the city of New York, with orders to assist Burgoyne if possible. The second was the main force, camped at Fort

Edward. The third column was the body now in question, consisting of British regulars, Tory rangers, Canadian militia, and Hessian light infantry (over 1,000 men, all told) and 1,000 Indians; it was led by Lieutenant Colonel Barry St. Leger, a twenty-year veteran who had served in the French and Indian War.

St. Leger's mission was to distract the main American army, and to rally the many loyalists in the Mohawk River valley west of Albany. To do so, he had taken his men from the St. Lawrence River in Canada, down the Lake Ontario shoreline to Oswego; from there he drove east to the Mohawk. In all this, he was greatly aided by Sir John Johnson, who served as British agent to the Six Nations of the Iroquois; his late father, Sir William Johnson, had built a close relationship with the Iroquois in preceding decades, and John Johnson had inherited those ties. He had persuaded the Six Nations to contribute a large contingent of warriors, headed by famed Mohawk chief Joseph Brant. The main obstacle in the path of this force was Fort Stanwix, manned by 750 New York militiamen. On August 3, St. Leger began a siege of the post, stationing his soldiers and Indian allies in a rough semicircle around it.

Once again, a British detachment faced American militia—not only in the fort, but in a relief force now marching west to rescue the besieged garrison. Some 800 men advanced along the Mohawk River under the command of General Nicholas Herkimer. Lieutenant Colonel St. Leger responded forcefully, sending a large number of Tory rangers and Indians to ambush Herkimer's force. As St. Leger himself reported to Burgoyne, it was virtually the last decision he made that would have any effect on the campaign.

Fort Stanwix
by Barry St. Leger

A minute detail of every operation since my leaving La Chine [Canada], with the detachment entrusted to my care, your Excellency [Burgoyne] will permit me to reserve to a time of less hurry and mortification than the present, while I enter into the interesting scene before Fort Stanwix, which I invested [laid siege to] the 3rd of August. . . .

On the 5th, in the evening, intelligence arrived by my discovering parties on the Mohawk River, that a reinforcement of eight hundred militia, conducted by General Herkimer, were on their march to relieve the garrison, and were actually at that instant at Oriskany,[72] an Indian settlement twelve miles from the fort [to the east]. The garrison being apprised of their march by four men, who were seen to enter the fort in the morning through what was thought an impenetrable swamp.

I did not think it prudent to wait for them, and thereby subject myself to be attacked by a sally from the garrison in the rear, while the reinforcement employed me in front. I therefore determined to attack them on the march, either openly or covertly, as circumstances should offer. At the time I had not two hundred and fifty of the King's troops in camp, the various and extensive operations I was under an absolute necessity of entering into having employed the rest, and therefore could not send above eighty white men, rangers and troops included, with the whole corps of Indians. Sir John Johnson put himself at the head of this party, and began his march that evening at five o'clock, and met the rebel corps at the same hour the next morning.

The impetuosity of the Indians is not to be described on the sight of the enemy (forgetting the judicious disposition formed by Sir John, and agreed to by themselves, which was to suffer the attack to being with the [British] troops in front, while they should be on both flanks and rear). They rushed in, hatchet in hand, and thereby gave the enemy's rear an opportunity to escape [while the main part of the American column rallied on higher ground]. In relation to the victory, it was equally complete as if the whole had fallen; nay more so, as the two hundred who escaped only served to spread the panic wider. But it was not so with the Indians: their loss was great (I must be understood [as using] Indian computation; being only about thirty killed, and the like number wounded, and in that number some of

[72]St. Leger actually wrote "Oriska."

their favorite chiefs and confidential warriors were slain). On the enemy's side, almost all their principal leaders were slain. General Herkimer has since died of his wounds.[73]

It is proper to mention, that the four men detached with the intelligence of the march of the reinforcement, set out the evening before the action, and consequently the enemy could have no account of the defeat, and were in possession only of the time appointed for their arrival; at which, as I suspected, they made a sally with two hundred and fifty men towards Lieutenant Bird's[74] post, to facilitate the entrance of the relieving corps, or bring on a general engagement with every advantage they could wish.

Captain Hoyes was immediately detached to cut in upon their rear, while they engaged the lieutenant. Immediately upon the departure of Captain Hoyes, [I,] having learned that Lieutenant Bird, misled by the information of a cowardly Indian that Sir John was pressed, had quitted his post to march to his assistance, I marched the detachment of the King's regiment in support of Captain Hoyes, by a road in sight of the garrison, which, with executive fire from his party, immediately drove the enemy into the fort, without any further advantage than frightening some squaws, and pilfering the packs of the warriors which they left behind them. . . . [75]

I found that our cannon had not the least effect upon the sodwork of the fort, and that our royals had only the power of teasing, as a six-inch plank was a sufficient security for their powder magazine, as we learnt from deserters. . . . There was nothing now to be done but to approach the town by sap [trench], to such a distance that the rampart might be brought within their portice, at the same time all materials were preparing to run a mine under their most formidable bastion.

[73]Though Herkimer's force was prevented from reaching Fort Stanwix, the battle of Oriskany is usually called an American victory. Herkimer foolishly allowed himself to be ambushed; but when the Indians attacked prematurely, he held together most of his men, rushed to high ground, and held his own in a bitter, hand-to-hand battle. After driving back the enemy force, Herkimer withdrew; the Iroquois suffered heavy losses in the close-quarters fighting.

[74]All of the men named in the rest of this selection, except for Arnold, were British officers.

[75]This "pilfering" was actually the calculated destruction of the Indian camp, which (together with the losses the warriors suffered at Oriskany) would seriously damage their morale.

In the midst of these operations, intelligence was brought in by our scouts of a second corps of 1,000 men being on the march. The same zeal no longer animated the Indians; they complained of our thinness of troops, and their former losses. I immediately called a council with the chiefs; encouraged them as much as I could; promised to lead them on myself, and bring into the field 300 of the best troops. They listened to this, and promised to follow me, and agreed that I should reconnoitre the ground properest for the field of battle the next morning, accompanied by some of their chief warriors, to settle the plan of operations.

When upon the ground appointed for the field of battle, scouts came in with the account of the first number, swelled to 2,000; immediately after, a third, that General Burgoyne's army was cut to pieces, and that Arnold was advancing, by rapid and forced marches, with 3,000 men. It was at this moment I began to suspect cowardice in some, and treason in others; however, I returned to camp, not without hopes, with the assistance of my gallant co-adjutor, Sir John Johnson, and the influence of the superintending colonels, Claus and Butler, of inducing them to meet the enemy. A council, according to their custom, was called, to know their resolutions; before the breaking up of which I learned that 200 had already decamped. In about an hour they insisted that I should retreat, or they would be obliged to abandon me. I had no other party to take (and a hard party it was, to troops who could do nothing without them, to yield to their resolves); and therefore proposed to retire at night, sending on before my sick, wounded, artillery, etc., down the Wood Creek [toward Oswego], covering them by our line of march.

———

BENEDICT ARNOLD RETURNED to action just in time. After he arrived in the American camp, General Schuyler quickly sent him west with another relief force to rescue Fort Stanwix. As he moved ahead, he spread the word that his detachment was far larger than it was. This was too much for the Iroquois, already jittery after the loss of their warriors and the destruction of their camp; they told St. Leger that the time had come to go home. Though Herkimer's New York militia retreated after the battle of Oriskany, they accomplished a great victory through their determined stand—a victory sealed by Arnold's march west.

After the twin triumphs of Bennington and Oriskany, thousands of militiamen poured into Schuyler's camp, now located at Stillwater, on the western banks of the Hudson River, a short distance north of Albany. Continentals came in, too, along with the crack riflemen of Colonel Morgan's detachment, and Arnold soon returned with reinforcements from the west. But Schuyler himself was soon to go. His delaying strategy had paid off, thanks in large part to the initiative of John Stark and the bravery of Nicholas Herkimer; but his prickly personality won him no admirers, in the army or in Congress. One general, however, had plenty of friends in Congress (particularly John Adams), and on August 4 those friends voted to make him commander of the Northern Department.

Schuyler's replacement was Horatio Gates, a fifty-year-old major general experienced in military affairs. He was the son of an English servant (humble origins that won him the affection of New Englanders) and a long-serving veteran of the British army (experience that earned him respect in Congress). After the French and Indian War, he had settled in North America, and now he fought for the Revolution. His technical expertise made him arrogant at times, dismissive of the instant officers all around him who previously had been merchants and farmers; and his arrogance fed his rising ambition. Unfortunately, his knowledge of how an army was run was not always matched by a knowledge of how it was used; when the time came for action, he often found himself at a loss.

Gates, however, began well enough: his men liked him, and he made the sound choice of moving the army to Bemis Heights, north of Stillwater. He had learned that Burgoyne was crossing the Hudson to the west bank; at Bemis Heights, where the uplands to the west came down to meet the river, Gates stood a good chance of stopping the British advance. Accordingly, he put the men to work, building fortifications on the hills that towered 200 feet over the Hudson. The construction was directed by Benedict Arnold and a Polish engineer, Colonel Thaddeus Kosciuszko. Colonel Morgan kept scouts out to the north, where the fields of Freeman's Farm marked the only break in the thick woods.

As General Burgoyne brought his army across the Hudson, he had little idea that he now faced an enemy perhaps 7,000 strong (including battle-hardened Continental infantry). He was resolved, however, to fight on rather than retreat. The year before, he had been disgusted by the withdrawal of General Carleton after the battle with Arnold's makeshift fleet; he was determined not to make the same mistake now, despite the destruction of Baum and the retreat of St. Leger. His force was still a powerful one; his men still the finest in the world. An exposed detachment might fall, he reasoned, but surely not his main army. Besides, he was certain that Clinton would soon attack north from New York, forcing the Americans to split their forces.

By September 16, Burgoyne had all his men on the west side of the Hudson, and he began his march south toward Bemis Heights. On the 18th, he ran into American scouts, alerting him to the presence of the enemy—though he still had precious little information about their numbers or disposition. The next day, he decided to attack. He went forward with 4,200 men, perhaps three quarters of his effective force, divided into three columns. The left wing consisted of the German regiments, 1,100 men under General Riedesel, which marched along the river road. The center column came under the command of General Hamilton, though Burgoyne himself marched with it; it was made up of four British regiments, with some artillery support. The right wing, farthest from the river, was led by General Fraser; he had with him the light infantry and grenadiers, along with some Indians and Tory rangers.

Fraser's force had to march much farther than the other two, to get into position; since Burgoyne could not see his own men in the thick woods, a signal gun was fired to announce the time of attack. But the Americans knew they were coming; Morgan's sharpshooting riflemen kept an eye on the British movements while the impetuous Arnold pleaded with Gates to launch an attack. If the Americans struck now, he argued, while the British were still in the thick woods, they would have a distinct advantage; if they let the redcoats assault the fortification itself, they would allow the enemy to fight on his own terms. After some indecision, Gates agreed—and Morgan began an assault on Fraser's right wing.

Burgoyne later offered a very accurate account of the events leading up to the battle of Freeman's Farm (sometimes called the first
battle of Saratoga, or the first battle of Bemis Heights). Once again,
logistics weighed heavily in his decision making, and he counted on
Clinton's advance from New York to distract the enemy. But mingled
with his rational analysis was a lingering contempt for the Americans
as soldiers. Immediately following Burgoyne's words, in the selections
that follow, comes the writing of Lieutenant Thomas Anburey, who
marched with the right wing, under General Fraser. As the battle
began, Anburey once again encountered a prisoner, who taught him
something General Burgoyne scarcely believed: the Americans meant
to fight.

Across the Hudson
by John Burgoyne

The only resource that remained for proceeding towards Albany after
the disappointment of this expedition [the one destroyed at Ben-
nington], viz. to press forward a necessary supply of provision, and
other indispensable articles, from Fort George. . . .

No possible exertion was omitted. It is not uncommon for gentlemen, unacquainted with the peculiarities of the country to which
I am alluding, to calculate the transport of magazines by measuring
the distance upon a map, then applying the resources of carriage, as
practiced in other countries. I request permission to shew their mistake. . . . It was necessary to bring forward to Fort Edward four score
or a hundred boats, as mere carriage-vessels for the provisions; each
boat made a hard day's work for six or more horses, including the
return of the horses. At the next carrying-place . . . it was necessary
to place a considerable relay of horses to draw over, first, a portion
of carriage-boats, and afterwards the provision, as it arrived. I have
not mentioned the great number of other boats necessary to be
brought forward to form bridges, to carry baggage and ammunition,

and the number of carriages framed to transport the boats themselves at the ensuing carrying-places, as we should proceed to Albany. . . .

On the 13th of September, the store of provision, amounting to about thirty days' consumption, was completed. . . . And it is now time to enter upon consideration of that object, which is held by some to be conclusive upon the executive part of the campaign, the passage of the Hudson's River.

Two errors, respecting this passage, though of opposite and incompatible natures, are supposed to have contributed to the ill success that ensued; the one, the error of delay, the other, that of precipitation. In defense against the first, I refer to my effort at Bennington to procure supplies, and to the impediments I have just now stated after that effort failed. . . . The state of things at this important crisis, and my reasoning upon it . . . I will now only touch them shortly. On the one hand, my communications were at an end; my retreat was insecure; the enemy was collected in force, they were strongly posted; Colonel St. Leger was retiring from Fort Stanwix. These were difficulties, but none of them insurmountable. On the other hand, I had dislodged the enemy repeatedly, when in force, and more strongly posted; my army was conscious of having the superiority, and eager to advance.

I expected cooperation [from Howe]; no letters from Sir William Howe removed that expectation. . . . The letter of 17th of July mentioned that General's return to my assistance, should Washington turn his force towards me; indicated, as I thought, an expectation of my arrival at Albany; and informed me that Sir Henry Clinton was left at New York, and would act as occurences might direct. I did *not* know Sir Henry Clinton's force. I *did* know, that considerable reinforcement might be then expected at New York from England. . . .

And I am still convinced, that no proof that could have been brought from appearances, intelligence, or reasoning, could have justified me to my country, have saved me from the condemnation of my profession, or produced pardon within my own breast, had I not advanced, and tried a battle with the enemy. . . .

Provisions for about thirty days having been brought forward, the other necessary stores prepared, and the bridge of boats completed, the army passed the Hudson's River on the 13th and 14th of September, and encamped on the heights and in the plain of Saratoga, the enemy being then in the neighborhood of Stillwater.

The whole army made a movement forward, and encamped in a good position in a place called Dovacote. It being found that there were several bridges to repair, that work was begun under cover of strong detachments, and the same opportunity was taken to reconnoitre the country. The army renewed their march, repaired other bridges, and encamped upon advantageous ground about four miles from the enemy.

The enemy appeared in considerable force, to obstruct the further repair of bridges, and with a view, as it was conceived, to draw on an action where artillery could not be employed. A small loss was sustained in skirmishing; but the work of the bridges was effected. The passage of a great ravine, and other roads towards the enemy, having been reconnoitted [sic], the army advanced in the following order.

Brigadier-General Fraser's corps, sustained by Lieutenant-Colonel [Francis] Breymann's corps, made a circuit, in order to pass the ravine commodiously, without quitting the heights, and afterwards to cover the march of the line to the right. These corps moved in three columns, and had the Indians, Canadians, and Provincials upon their fronts and flanks. The British line, led by me in person, passed the ravine in a direct line south, and formed in order of battle as fast as they gained the summit, where they waited to give time to Fraser's corps to make the circuit, and to enable the left wing and artillery (which, under the commands of Major-General Phillips and Major-General Riedesel, kept the great road and meadows near the river in two columns, and had bridges to repair) to be equally ready to proceed. The 47th Regiment guarded the bateaux.

The signal guns, which had been previously settled to give notice to all the columns being ready to advance, having been fired between one and two o'clock, the march continued. The scouts and flankers of the column of the British line were soon fired upon from small parties, but with no effect. After about an hour's march, the pickets, which made the advance guard of that column, were attacked in force, and obliged to give ground; but they soon rallied and were sustained.

On the first opening of the wood I formed the troops. A few

cannon shot dislodged the enemy, at a house from whence the pickets had been attacked; and Brigadier-General Fraser's corps had arrived with such precision, in point of time, as to be found upon a very advantageous height on the right of the British.

In the meantime, the enemy, not acquainted with the combination of the march, had moved in great force out of their intrenchments, with a view of turning the line upon the right; and, being checked by the disposition of Brigadier-General Fraser, countermarched, in order to direct their great effort to the left of the British. From the nature of the country, movements of this sort, however near, may be effected without a possibility of being discovered [due to the thick woods].

About three o'clock, the action began by a very vigorous attack on the British line [in the center], and contined with great obstinancy till after sunset.

With a Prisoner on the British Right
by Thomas Anburey

The signal guns for all the columns to advance were fired between one and two o'clock, and after an hour's march, the advanced party, consisting of the pickets of the center column, under the command of Major Forbes, fell in with a considerable body of the enemy, posted in a house and behind fences, which they attacked. . . .

In this skirmish, a bat-man of General Fraser's rescued from the Indians an officer of the Americans, one Captain Van Swearingham, of Colonel Morgan's Virginia riflemen. . . . The bat-man brought him up to General Fraser (who now had come up to the two companies he had detached), who interrogated him concerning the enemy, but could obtain no other answer, than that their army was commanded by Generals Gates and Arnold. General Fraser, exceedingly provoked that he could gain no intelligence, told him if he did not immediately inform him as to the exact situation of the enemy, he would hang him up directly. The officer, with the most undaunted firmness, replied, "You may, if you please." The General, perceiving he could make nothing of him, rode off, leaving him in the custody of Lieutenant Dunbar of the artillery.

My servant, just at this period, arrived with my canteen, which was rather fortunate, as we stood in need of some refreshment after our march through the woods, and this little skirmish. I requested Dunbar, with his prisoner, to partake of it, and sitting down upon a tree, we asked this Captain a variety of questions, to which he always gave evasive answers, and we both observed he was in great spirits.

At last I said to him, "Captain, do you think we shall have any more work upon our hands today?" To which he replied, "Yes, yes, you'll have business enough, for there are many hundreds all round you now." He had hardly spoke the words, than from a wood a little way in our front there came an excessive heavy fire. . . . I then hastened to my company, on joining of which I met a number of men who were retiring wounded.

———

GENERAL BURGOYNE COMMITTED a terrible error at Freeman's Farm: he dispersed his men in three widely separated columns. The three divisions were so far apart that they could not adequately support one another; and the woods were so thick, Burgoyne could not keep track of what was happening on the battlefield.

The Americans quickly took advantage of this critical mistake— rather, Morgan and Arnold took advantage of it, using only part of the total force. Gates remained behind with the rest, indecisive and inert. The battle began with an attack by Morgan's riflemen. The thick forest suited the type of weapon they carried: the rifle was far more accurate than the smoothbore musket, allowing Morgan's men to pick off the officers and artillerymen in the British force. On a clear battlefield, they would have been vulnerable: the bullet of a rifle fit the barrel so tightly, a soldier had to use a mallet with the ramrod to drive it home; as a result, a rifle took far longer to load than a musket. In addition, American rifles could not be fitted with bayonets—at close quarters, the men used hatchets instead, or simply swung the firearms like clubs. But at Freeman's Farm, the heavy woods gave them cover, allowing them to duck out of sight and reload, then pick their targets when they fired.

Morgan struck the far right of the British force—Fraser's wing—in an attack that was soon thrown back; then they returned, fighting a seesaw action. Meanwhile, General Benedict Arnold arrived on the scene with the Continental infantry. Like Morgan, Arnold was one of those rare commanders who had an instinctive grasp of what was happening in the confusion of the battlefield. Even now, as dense clouds of smoke from the gunpowder drifted through the forest, Arnold realized that Burgoyne had divided his force. He decided to attack the *center* column, while Morgan tied up the enemy's right wing. If he could destroy or disperse Burgoyne's center, he could easily swing around and roll up Fraser's corps.

Lieutenant James Hadden commanded a battery of artillery pieces in Burgoyne's center force, under the overall command of Captain Jones. In the selection below, he picks up shortly after the start of the fighting, then moves on to the desperate hours that followed General Arnold's attack. Hadden was in the thick of the fight in the British center, serving beside the 62nd Regiment as Arnold led his men across the clearing of Freeman's Farm, bringing the battle to its moment of crisis.

On the Line in the Center
by James Hadden

Nearly a quarter of an hour before we [in the center column] resumed our march the pickets of the British line (100 rank & file) advanced under Major [Gordon] Forbes (9th Regt.) and were repulsed with loss by a corps of riflemen commanded by the rebel Colonel Morgan. Major Forbes was wounded and the retreat of his detachment was secured by the battalion of light infantry sent from the column on the right commanded by Brig'r General Fraser.

The British troops halted & formed till the whole of Major Forbes's party came in—and having commenced a fire without orders (by which many of our own people were killed in retreating) Major Kingston proposed the firing a gun to check it, which had the desired

effect and by that accident I fired the first shot from the main body
of this army.

About 2 o'clock in the afternoon the British regiments arrived
opposite to Freeman's House thro. which I was order'd to fire a shot;
and it not taking effect Capt. Jones laid the second himself with success, but there being no enemy in it (tho. it was from hence Major
Forbes was first attacked) the troops passed a small bridge (over a
hollow way and large gutter apparently made by heavy falls of rain)
and took post at the skirt of a wood a little beyond it. . . .

The enemy being in possession of the wood almost immediately
attacked the corps which took post beyond [the] two log huts on
Freeman's Farm. Capt. Jones's brigade was hasten'd to their support,
I was advanced with two guns to the left of the 62nd Regt. and, the
two left companies being formed *en potence* [at a sharp angle to the
main line] I took post in the angle. Lieut. Reid who remain'd with
Capt. Jones and the other two was posted between the 9th & 21st
Regts.

In this situation we sustained a heavy tho. intermitting fire for
near three hours, and Gen'l Fraser's corps being also attacked, tho.
partially, five companies of the 24th Regt. were advanced into the
wood in their front, and being repulsed a second attempt was made
with [the] whole regiment, in which they succeeded with the loss of
about fifty men.

The enemy continuing the heat of their attack on the flank (and
occasionally the rear) of the 62nd Regt. that corps suffered very
much; and having lost in killed or wounded nineteen out [of] twenty-
two artillery[men] attached to my two guns posted in the angle, I
applied to Brig'r Gen'l Hamilton for a supply of infantry; and (while
speaking to him my cap was shot thro. in the front) not being able
to obtain relief was referr'd to Gen'l Phillips who was with Gen'l
Burgoyne just beyond one of the two log huts.

On making known my situation Capt. Jones was ordered to let
me have all the men from one of Lt. Reid's guns with a view I believe
to retire mine a little; Capt. Jones was ordered to accompany me
himself.

The enemy being reinforced and advancing closer, since the fire
of the flank guns were silenced, I found on my return that the 62nd

Regiment had made an unsuccessful effort to reinforce them, by which that Regt. lost 25 prisoners, and being worn down had begun to get into confusion, in which situation I found them. Capt. Jones immediately began firing, but being himself very soon wounded as were also the whole of the men we brought up, I was desired to endeavor to effect the retreat of my guns; but before I could accomplish it, the 62nd Regt., having lost 187 killed or wounded and 25 prisoners (out of between 3 & 4 hundred of which the effectives of the battalion consisted), were forced to abandon the hill & on it my guns.

Having supported Capt. Jones in my arms for some time, I carried him into one of the huts which was filled with wounded and being some time before I could find a place to lay him in, the whole of the troops had quitted the height and it was with difficulty I got within our own line which was advancing under Gen'l Phillips, and at that time not more than a hundred yards from the enemy, who were following the retreating troops.

During this attack the 20th Regt. was thrown into the wood on the left of the corn field and repulsed the enemy, which saved the rear of the 62nd Regt. from being galled by them.

As the attack was so much on the left, the 9th Regt., not being useful in their original situation, was retired across the bridge and continued as a corps of reserve . . . when Gen'l Phillips, arriving with some more guns under Col. Williams, advanced at the head of the British line (with two German regiments on their left) and repossessed the height and my guns. The grenadiers under Gen'l Fraser moving forward on the right at the same time a very heavy fire commenced, [and] the rebels thus pressed retreated on all sides, and being driven across the field made the best of their way to their works. By this time it being nearly dark no further pursuit was attempted.

No Fruits
by John Burgoyne

Major-General Phillips, upon first hearing the firing, found his way through a difficult part of the wood to the scene of action, and brought up with him Major Williams and four pieces of artillery; and from that moment I stood indebted to that gallant and judicious second for incessant and most material services; particularly for restoring the action in a point which was critically pressed by a great superiority of fire, and to which he led up the 20th Regiment at the utmost personal hazard. Major-General Riedesel exerted himself to bring up a part of the left wing, and arrived in time to charge the enemy with regularity and bravery.

Just as the light closed, the enemy gave ground on all sides, and left us completely masters of the field of battle, with the loss of about five hundred men on their side, and, as supposed, thrice that number wounded. The darkness preventing a pursuit, the prisoners were few.

The behavior of the officers and men in general was exemplary. . . . The artillery in general was distinguished, and the brigade under Captain Jones, who was killed in the action, was conspicuously so.

The army lay upon their arms the night of the 19th, and the next day took a position nearly within cannon-shot of the enemy, fortifying their right, and extending their left to the brow of the heights, so as to cover the meadows through which the great river runs, and where their bateaux and hospitals were placed. . . .

It was soon found that no fruits, honor excepted, were attained by the preceding victory, the enemy working with redoubled ardor to strengthen their left, their right was already unattackable.

──────────

THE BATTLE OF Freeman's Farm was an unmitigated disaster for Burgoyne. The bravery and tactical skill of Daniel Morgan and Benedict Arnold stopped the British army literally in its tracks. Only the quick action of General Phillips, in command of the reserve, and General Riedesel, with the left wing, had saved the British army from complete disaster. The hardened German commander heard the firing, saw that his own front was clear, and led his men into the attack as fast as they could come up. The Americans retreated, but they had inflicted 600 casualties—almost twice their own losses. Burgoyne pulled back, entrenched, and sent desperate messages to Clinton in New York, begging for an attack to divert the rebels.

Clinton actually did launch a thrust north, capturing a string of forts along the Hudson. When he had advanced for what he felt was a reasonable distance, he turned around and went home. General Gates never bothered to send as much as a single man to oppose him. But Burgoyne remained ignorant of this limited stroke—the messenger Clinton sent with news of his attack (and retreat) was captured by the Americans.

Meanwhile, Gates and Arnold very nearly came to blows. Arnold was infuriated with his commander, who had sat passively in camp during the entire battle—then wrote to Congress of the victory without mentioning Arnold's valor. Few men were as proud as the Connecticut general who had fought so hard at Freeman's Farm; but few commanders were as insecure as General Gates. Gates confined Arnold to his tent, then dismissed him, replacing him with General Benjamin Lincoln. Bitter, angry, but still desperate for more fighting, Arnold lingered on in the American camp, much to Gates's irritation.

Meanwhile, the usually indecisive Gates engaged in some actual generalship. He extended the American fortifications, and prepared for another battle. He felt certain Burgoyne would attack again. On October 4, the same day as the battle of the Brandywine, he wrote to Washington, "Perhaps his despair may dictate to him to risque all on one throw; he is an old gamester and has seen all chances in his time."[76] Two days later, on October 6, Burgoyne led a picked force of 1,500 men on a reconnaissance in force toward the left of the American lines. When Gates learned of it, he ordered Morgan to lead a counterattack, beginning the battle of Bemis Heights.

Once again, Burgoyne's own words offer insight into the decisions and events within the British lines. His account below reaches from the immediate aftermath of the battle of Freeman's Farm to that moment on October 6 when Morgan's men crashed into his second thrust south.

———

[76]Quoted in Bobrick, p. 276.

A Reconnaissance in Force
by John Burgoyne

On our side it became expedient to erect strong redoubts for the protection of the magazines and hospital, not only against a sudden attack but also for their security in case of a march to turn the enemy's flank.

A messenger arrived from Sir Harry Clinton with a letter in cipher, informing me of his intention to attack Fort Montgomery [on the Hudson above New York] in about ten days from the date of his letter, which was the 12th instant. . . . He [the messenger] was sent back the same night to inform Sir Harry of my situation, and of the necessity of a diversion to oblige General Gates to detach from his army, and my intention to wait favorable events in that position, if possible, to the 12th of October. . . .

In this situation things continued till the 7th [of October], when no intelligence having been received of the expected cooperation, and four or five days for our limited stay in the camp only remained, it was judged advisable to make a movement to the enemy's left, not only to discover whether there were any possible means of forcing a passage, should it be necessary to advance, or of dislodging him for the convenience of the army, which was in the greatest distress on account of the scarcity.

A detachment of fifteen hundred regular troops, with two twelve-pounders, two howitzers, and six six-pounders, were ordered to move, and were commanded by myself, having with me Major-General Phillips, Major-General Riedesel, and Brigadier-General Fraser. The guard of the camp upon the heights was left to Brigadier-General Hamilton and Specht; the redoubts and the plain to Brigadier-General Gall; and, as the force of the enemy immediately in their front consisted of more than double their numbers, it was not possible to augment the corps that marched beyond the numbers above stated.

I formed the troops within three-quarters of a mile of the enemy's left; and Captain Fraser's rangers, with Indians and Provincials, had orders to go by secret paths in the woods to gain the enemy's rear, and by shewing themselves there to keep them in check.

The further operations were prevented by a very sudden and rapid attack of the enemy on our left, where the British grenadiers were posted to support the left wing of the line. Major Acland, at the head of them, sustained the attack with great resolution; but the enemy's great numbers enabling them in a few minutes to extend the attack along the front of the Germans, which were immediately to the right of the grenadiers, no part of that body could be removed to make a second line to the flank, where the stress of the fire lay.

The right was at this time engaged, but it was soon observed that the enemy were marching a large corps round their flank, to endeavor cutting off their retreat. The light infantry and part of the 24th Regiment, which were at that post, were therefore ordered to form a second line, and to secure the return of the troops into camp. While this movement was proceeding, the enemy pushed a fresh and strong reinforcement to renew the action upon the left; which, overpowered by a great superiority, gave way, and the light infantry and 24th Regiment were obliged to make a quick movement to save that point from being entirely carried; in doing which, Brigadier-General Fraser was mortally wounded.[77]

The danger to which the lines were exposed, becoming at this moment of the most serious nature, orders were given to Major-General Phillips and Riedesel to cover the retreat, while such troops as were most ready for the purpose returned to the defense of them. The troops retreated, hard pressed, but in good order; they were obliged to leave six pieces of cannon, all the horses having been killed; and most of the artillery-men, who had behaved as usual with the utmost bravery under the command of Major Williams, being either killed or wounded.

AT THE CRITICAL moment, Arnold returned to the battlefield. He nearly went insane with impatience after the fighting began, cursing, drinking, and galloping about the American camp; more than

---

[77]General Fraser was bravely rallying his troops in the face of the American attack when Colonel Morgan called for his best marksman to shoot him down. The first two shots grazed the general and his horse; the third sent him tumbling to the earth, mortally wounded.

anything else, he seems to have been driven by a pure adrenaline-loaded lust for battle itself. Ignoring Gates's orders to stay clear, he finally rushed to the front and led the final assaults himself.

Thomas Anburey was stationed in the British works as Arnold's attack rolled in against the redoubts; his account vividly describes his emotions as he realized that he was watching a crushing defeat in the making. Immediately following his words come those of General Burgoyne, who frantically tried to lead his men out of a desperate situation.

In the Redoubts
by Thomas Anburey

In camp, and not in personal danger, as the mind is left to reflection, it is impossible to describe how much it is affected in beholding the wounded continually coming in, amid incessant roar of cannon and musketry, where perhaps many brave fellows are dying for their country—perhaps too in an unsuccessful battle! I can never consent to be left in camp again.

After many hours [of] impatient anxiety, towards the close of evening the grand stroke came. I had little hope to become a partaker in the action; but about that time the troops came pouring into the camp as fast as they could, and shortly after Generals Burgoyne, Phillips, and Ricdesel. It is impossible to describe the anxiousness depicted in the countenance of General Burgoyne, who immediately rode up to the quarter guards, and when he came to that of our regiment, I was across a ravine, posting a sergeant's guard. Upon inquiring eagerly for the officer, I came to him. "Sir," said the General, "you must defend this post to the very last man."

You may easily conceive, upon receiving those orders, I judged everything to be in a dangerous situation. There was not a moment for thought, for the Americans stormed with great fury the post of the light infantry, under the command of Lord Balcarres, rushing close to the lines, under a severe fire of grapeshot and small arms.

This post was defended with great spirit, and the enemy, led on by General Arnold, as gallantly assaulted the works; but on the General's being wounded, the enemy were repulsed, which was not till after dark.

In this attack, I was but an observer, as our quarter guard was some distance from the lines, but not sufficiently as to be out of danger, as the balls were continually dropping down amongst us. In order that you may form some idea with what obstinacy the enemy assaulted the lines, from the commencement, at which time it was dark, till they were repulsed, there was a continual sheet of fire along the lines, and in this attack we were fully convinced of what essential service our artillery was.

During the time the enemy were so vigorously attacking our lines, a party assaulted those of the Germans, commanded by Colonel Breymann, but either for want of courage, or presence of mind, they, upon the first attack of the enemy, were struck with such a terror, that instead of gallantly sustaining their lines, they looked on all as lost, and after firing one volley, hastily abandoned them. That brave officer, Colonel Breymann, in endeavoring to rally his soldiers, was unfortunately killed. By the enemy's obtaining possession of the German lines, they gained an opening upon our right and rear. . . .

The courage and obstinacy with which the Americans fought were the astonishment of everyone, and we now become fully convinced that they are not that contemptible enemy we had hitherto imagined them, incapable of standing a regular engagement, and that they would only fight behind strong and powerful works.[78]

Saratoga
by John Burgoyne

Under the disadvantages, thus apparent in our situation, the army was ordered to quit the present position during the night, and take post upon the heights above the hospital. . . . Intelligence was now

[78]This last paragraph has been moved for narrative continuity.

received that the enemy were marching to turn the right; and no means could prevent that measure but retiring towards Saratoga. . . .

At our arrival near Saratoga, a corps of the enemy, between five and six hundred, were discovered throwing up intrenchments on the heights, but retired over a ford of the Hudson's River at our approach, and joined a body posted to oppose our passage there. . . . The attacks upon the bateaux were continued; several were taken and retaken, but their situation being much nearer to the main force of the enemy than to ours, it was found impossible to secure the provisions any otherwise than by landing them and carrying them upon the hill. This was effected under fire, and with great difficulty.

The possible means of farther retreat were now considered in councils of war, composed of the general officers. . . . The only one that seemed at all practicable was, by a night-march to gain Fort Edward, with the troops carrying their provisions upon their backs; the impossibility of repairing bridges putting a conveyance of artillery and carriages out of the question, it was proposed to force the ford at Fort Edward, or the ford above it. Before this attempt could be made, scouts returned, with intelligence that the enemy were intrenched opposite these fords, and possessed a camp in force on the high ground, between Fort Edward and Fort George, with cannon. They had also parties down the whole shore, to watch our motions, and posts so near to us, upon our own side of the water, as must prevent the army moving a single mile undiscovered.

The bulk of the enemy's army was hourly joined by new corps of militia and volunteers, and their numbers together amounted to upwards of 16,000 men. Their position, which extended three parts in four of a circle around us, was, from the nature of the ground, unattackable in all parts. . . . During this time, the men lay continually upon their arms, and were cannonaded in every part; even rifle-shot and grapeshot came into all parts of the line. . . .

The council of war was extended to all in the field-officers and captains commanding the corps of the army, and the event ensued which I am sure was inevitable, and which, I trust, in that situation was honorable, but which it would be superfluous and melancholy to repeat.

IN THE END, Burgoyne had only 5,800 wounded, tired, demoralized men left; every day, the American army grew, as militiamen poured in to share in the victory. Trapped at Saratoga, battered by artillery and rifle fire, he surrendered.

Gates had won a stunning victory—but the real glory belonged to Daniel Morgan and Benedict Arnold, and, of course, their very brave and hard-fighting men. These commanders had taken full advantage of the wilderness terrain, of the power of the American rifle, of Burgoyne's own mistakes in battle; and they had led their assaults with conspicuous valor. Again Arnold's thin skin erupted with a rash of bitterness, as Gates kept to himself the credit for this astonishing accomplishment.

Even worse, Gates issued remarkably generous terms to his trapped, defeated enemy. Every man was to be paroled, allowed to return to England on the promise that he would not fight again in America. Of course, the returned men would simply free up redcoats stationed elsewhere to fight in the war. Congress wisely abrogated this Convention of Saratoga; it allowed the officers to go, but kept the thousands of enlisted men as prisoners of war. Burgoyne returned to England, disgraced and driven from the service.

Americans immediately realized that the victory at Saratoga would change the course of the war. It had been a dark year for the republic—New York and Newport under occupation, Philadelphia fallen, Washington beaten back. Then came the news from the north: an entire British army had been destroyed—the professional soldiers of Britain and Brunswick had been outfought by Continentals, militia, and frontier riflemen. "The news of Burgoyne's surrender," wrote John Adams, "lifted us up to the stars." Celebrations erupted across the country.

There was one more result from Saratoga. When word of the triumph crossed the Atlantic, the courts of France and Spain took notice; they began to seriously negotiate with representatives of the Continental Congress. The Americans, they suddenly realized, might actually *win* this war of independence. The "children," as Burgoyne once called them, were coming into their inheritance.

10
WINTER

Victory at Saratoga did not dislodge Howe from Philadelphia. So there Washington stayed, hovering outside the city with his lean but battle-hardened army. As October 1777 passed away, he had yet to benefit from the great triumph in the north; reinforcements and captured weapons would not be available for some time, as Gates used them to retake the lost forts on Lake Champlain. So the American Commander in Chief had little choice but to spend the winter doing what he liked least: nothing.

Howe had finally learned his lesson, after the disasters at Trenton and Princeton, and the recent battle of Germantown. He pulled in his detachments and concentrated his army within a tightly defended perimeter in the city itself. Washington could find no weaknesses to attack, so he waited and watched.

Early in November Howe marched toward the American camp at Whitemarsh, deciding at the last moment to avoid a battle. Howe came out once more in early December, engaged in some light skirmishing, then withdrew. So in late December Washington pulled his men back eighteen miles northwest of Philadelphia, to where the Valley Creek joined the Schuylkill River. The spot was out of easy reach of the redcoats; it had plenty of fresh water, and the terrain made it easy to defend. It was called Valley Forge.

Valley Forge has been a synonym for misery ever since the killing winter of 1777–1778. One of the men who shivered the season away there was Albigence Waldo, a surgeon of a Continental infantry regiment from Connecticut. In the pages that follow, his diary traces the life of the American army from early November—the tense days following Germantown, as the rebels kept close to the redcoats outside Philadelphia—through January, when the pathetic emcampment at Valley Forge finally began to shape up. His words capture the bitter skirmishing between small detachments of the two armies, the petty theft that plagued this patriot force, and the uncertainty and rumor that dogged virtually every day—as Howe marched out and then retreated, leaving the men to wonder when another great battle might erupt. Finally, Waldo describes the pain of the infamous winter camp, as disease and malnutrition wracked the soldiers who stayed on, loyal to the cause, day after miserable day. Hundreds died at Valley Forge; yet somehow the army carried on.

Valley Forge
by Albigence Waldo

November 10, 1777—Captain [Henry] Lee, of the Light Dragoons, brought in Capt. Nichols of the English packet whom he took prisoner at New Castle. I heard Capt. Nichols observe that one hour before he was taken he had the following reflections: "His Majesty has made me commander of a fine ship—a packet, too; I need not ever fight. I have nothing to do but transport gentlemen and ladies of the first rank. I have a fine stock of provisions aboard, hens, turkeys, geese, pigs, ducks, wine, and cider. I have a good interest at home, and what is above all, an agreeable family. I am not troubled in my mind. In short, I've nothing to make me uneasy, and believe I am the happiest man in the world."

Capt. Nichols was now the unhappiest man in the world. His reflections were turned upon the vicissitudes of life, the sudden changes of fortune and variety of events that may happen to a man in the course of a few hours. . . .

An incessant cannonading at or near Red Bank this day. No salt to eat dinner with. . . .

November 25—In the evening we march for Haddonfield (not far from Red Bank) where we arrived in the morning of

November 26—Lay in the forest of Haddonfield, cold and uncomfortable. Two Hessian deserters came in who declar'd our little parties had kill'd a number of the enemy—15 prisoners were brought in, 2 women.

November 27—Return'd to Mount Holly. Same day Greene's division and Glover's brigade (who had arriv'd from the Northward 2 days before) march to Burlington. Morgan with his riflemen were left with the militia to harrass the enemy as they were recrossing the river from Red Bank to the city.[79]

November 28—The remainder of us marched to Burlington. P.M. the rear of the army crossed over to Bristol. A storm prevented the baggage going over this night, which prevented Dr. L. [Samuel Lee] & myself also crossing with our horses.

November 29—Storm increas'd. About one p.m. an alarm was made by a report that the enemy were within 15 minutes march of the town to take the baggage. Those of us who had horses rode up to Burdentown. The baggage and the sick were all hurried out of town the same way, but had not got 2 miles before they were turn'd back on its being a false alarm. For the sake of good living however Dr. L., Parson E. [Ellis], & myself went to Burdentown up the river, liv'd well, & crossed over to Windsor next day, and arrived at Bristol in the evening when I had my shoes and silver buckles stole. Dr. L. had a valuable great coat stole the day before at Burlington.

December 1—We marched to head quarters [Whitemarsh] and our division (McDougal's) encamped on the left of the second line. Our former station was in the center of the front line. Here huts of sticks & leaves shelter'd us from the inclemency of the weather and we lay pretty quiet until

December 5—At 3 o'clock a.m. the alarm guns were fired and troops immediately paraded at their several alarm posts. The enemy were approaching with their whole strength to give us battle. Nothing further remarkable ensued this day—at night our troops lay on their arms, the baggage being all sent away except what a man might run or fight with.

December 6—The enemy forming a line from towards our right to the extremity of our left upon an opposite height to ours in a wood. Our men were under arms all day and this night also, as our wise general was determined not to be attack'd napping.

December 7—Alarm given. Troops on their several posts. Towards noon Col. Ch. Webb's Regt. [the 2nd Connecticut] were partly sur-

[79]Daniel Morgan had already returned from the north, after the victory at Saratoga.

rounded and attacked on the right of the army. They being overpowered by numbers, retreated with loss—Lieut. [John] Harris kill'd. A scattering fire through to the left soon began & continued a few minutes, till our pickets ran in. The firing soon ceased on the right & continued on the left, as tho' a general attack was meant to being there. On this supposition the left were reinforced. But a scattering fire was kept up by Morgan's battalion, at intervals all day, and concluded with a little skirmish at sunset. Our troops lay on their arms this night also. Some firing among the pickets in the night. . . .

December 9—We came from within the breastworks, where we had been coop'd up four tedious days, with clothes & boots on night and day, and resumed our old huts east of the breastwork. The rest of the army chiefly had their huts within the lines. We are insensible what we are capable of enduring till we are put to the test. To endure hardships with good grace we must always think of the following maxim: "Pain succeeds pleasure, & pleasure succeeds pain."

December 10—Lay still.

December 11—At four o'clock the whole army were order'd to march to Swedes Ford on the River Schuylkill, about 9 miles N.W. of Chestnut Hill, and 6 from White Marsh, our present encampment. At sun an hour high the whole were mov'd from the lines and on their march with baggage. This night encamped in a semicircle nigh the ford. The enemy had march'd up the west side of Schuylkill—Potter's brigade of Pennsylvania militia were already there, & had several skirmishes with them with some losses on his side and considerable on the enemy's. . . .

I am prodigious sick & cannot get anything comfortable—what in the name of Providence am I to do with a fit of sickness in this place where nothing appears pleasing to the sicken'd eye & nauseating stomach. But I doubt not Providence will find out a way for my relief. But I cannot eat beef if I starve, for my stomach positively refuses to entertain such company, and how can I help that?

December 12—A bridge of wagons made across the Schuylkill last night consisting of 36 wagons, with a bridge of rails between each. Some skirmishing over the river. Militia and dragoons brought into camp several prisoners. Sunset—We are order'd to march over the river—it snows—I'm sick—eat nothing—no whiskey—no forage—

Lord—Lord—Lord. The army were till sunrise crossing the river—some at the wagon bridge & some at the raft bridge below. Cold & uncomfortable.

December 13—The army march'd three miles from the west side of the river and encamp'd near a place call'd the Gulph and not an improper name neither, for this Gulph seems well adapted by its situation to keep us from the pleasures & enjoyments of this world, or being conversant with anybody in it. . . .

It is upon consideration for many good purposes [that] we are to winter here—1st There is plenty of wood & water. 2nd There are but few families for the soldiery to steal from—tho' far be it from a soldier to steal. 4th *[sic]* There are warm sides of hills to erect huts on. 5th They will be heavenly minded like Jonah when in the belly of a Great Fish. 6th They will not become homesick as is sometimes the case when men live in the open world—since the reflections which will naturally arise from their present habitation, will lead them to the more noble thoughts of employing their leisure hours in filling their knapsacks with such materials as may be necessary on the journey to another Home.

December 14—Prisoners & deserters are continually coming in. The army which has been surprisingly healthy hitherto, now begins to grow sickly from the continued fatigues they have suffered this campaign. Yet they still show a spirit of alacrity & contentment not to be expected from so young troops. I am sick—discontented—and out of humor. Poor food—hard lodging—cold weather—fatigue—nasty clothes—nasty cookery—vomit half my time—smoked out of my senses—the Devil's isn't—I can't endure it—Why are we sent here to starve and freeze—What sweet felicities have I left at home: A charming wife—pretty children—good beds—good food—good cookery—all agreeable—all harmonious. Here all confusion—smoke & cold—hunger & filthiness—a pox on my bad luck. There comes a bowl of beef soup—full of burnt leaves and dirt, sickish enough to make a hector spew—Away with it boys, I'll live like the chameleon upon air.

Poh! Poh! cries Patience within me—you talk like a fool. Your being sick covers your mind with a melancholy gloom, which makes everything about you appear gloomy. See the poor soldier, when in health—with what cheerfulness he meets his foes and encounters every hardship—if barefoot, he labors thro' the mud & cold with a song in his mouth extolling war & Washington—if his food be bad, he eats it notwithstanding with seeming content—blesses God for a good stomach and whistles it into digestion.

But harkee Patience, a moment—There comes a soldier, his bare feet are seen thro' his worn-out shoes, his legs nearly naked from the tatter'd remains of an only pair of stockings, his breeches not sufficient to cover his nakedness, his shirt hanging in strings, his hair dishevell'd, his face meager; his whole appearance pictures a person forsaken & discouraged. He comes, and cries with an air of wretchedness & despair, I am sick, my feet lame, my legs are sore, my body covered with this tormenting itch—my clothes are worn out, my constitution is broken, my former activity is exhausted by fatigue, hunger, & cold, I fail fast, I shall soon be no more! And all the reward I get will be—"Poor Will is dead."

People who live at home in luxury and ease, quietly possessing their habitations, enjoying their wives & families in peace, have but a very faint idea of the unpleasing sensations, and continual anxiety the man endures who is in a camp, and is the husband and parent of an agreeable family. These same people are willing we should suffer everything for their benefit & advantage, and yet are the first to condemn us for not doing more!!

December 14—Quiet. Eat parsimmons, found myself better for their lenient operation. Went to a house, poor & small, but good food within—eat too much from being so long abstemious, thro' want of palatables. . . .

December 16—Cold rainy day, baggage ordered over the Gulph of our division, which were to march at ten, but the baggage was order'd back and for the first time since we have been here the tents were pitch'd, to keep the men more comfortable. Good morning Brother Soldier (says one to another) how are you? All wet I thank'e, hope you are so (says the other). The enemy have been at Chestnut Hill opposite to us near our last encampment the other side of Schuylkill, made some ravages, kill'd two of our horsemen, taken some prisoners. We have done the like by them. . . .

December 18—Universal thanksgiving—a roasted pig at night.

God be thanked for my health which I have pretty well recovered. How much better I should feel, were I assured my family were in health. . . .

Rank & precedence make a good deal of disturbance & confusion in the American army. The army are poorly supplied with provision, occasioned it is said by the neglect of the commissary of purchases. Much talk among officers about discharges. Money has become of too little consequence. The Congress have not made their commissions valuable enough. Heaven avert the bad consequences of these things!! . . .

December 21—[Valley Forge] Preparations made for huts. Provisions scarce. Mr. Ellis went homeward—sent a letter to my wife. Heartily wish myself at home, my skin & eyes are almost spoil'd with continual smoke. A general cry thro' the camp this evening among the soldiers, "No meat! No meat!" The distant vales echo'd back the melancholy sound—"No meat! No meat!" Imitating the noise of crows & owls, also, made a part of the confused music.

What have you for dinners, boys? "Nothing but fire cake & water, sir."[80] At night, "Gentlemen, the supper is ready." What is your supper, lads? "Fire cake & water, sir." Very poor beef has been drawn in our camp the greater part of this season. A butcher bringing a quarter of this kind of beef into camp one day who had white buttons on the knees of his breeches, a soldier cries out—"There, there is some more of your fat beef, by my soul I can see the butcher's breeches's buttons through it."

December 22—Lay excessive cold & uncomfortable last night— my eyes are started out from their orbits like a rabbit's eyes, occasion'd by a great cold & smoke.

What have you got for breakfast, lads? "Fire cake & water, sir." The Lord send that our Commissary of Purchases may live [on] fire cake & water, till their glutted guts are turned to pasteboard.

Our division are under marching orders this morning. I am ashamed to say it, but I am tempted to steal fowls if I could find them, or even a whole hog, for I feel as if I could eat one. But the

---

[80]Fire cake was a "thin bread made of flour and water and baked over the campfire" (Middlekauff, p. 413).

impoverish'd country about us affords but little matter to employ a thief, or keep a clever fellow in good humor. But why do I talk of hunger & hard usage, when so many in the world have not even fire cake & water to eat? . . .

December 23—The party that went out last evening not return'd today. This evening an excellent player on the violin in that soft kind of music, which is so finely adapted to sir up the tender passions, while he was playing in the next tent to mine, these kind of soft airs it immediately called up in remembrance all the endearing expressions, the tender sentiments, the sympathetic friendship that has given so much satisfaction and sensible pleasure to me from the first time I gained the heart & affections of the tenderest of the fair. . . . I wish'd to have the music cease, and yet dreaded its ceasing, least I should lose sight of these dear ideas, which gave me pain and pleasure at the same time. . . .

December 25, Christmas—We are still in tents, when we ought to be in huts—the poor sick suffer much in this cold weather. But we now treat them differently from what they used to be at home, under the inspection of old women and Doctor Bolus Linctus. We give them mutton & grogg and a capital medicine once in a while, to start the disease from its foundations at once. We avoid piddling pills, powders, Bolus's Linctus's cordials and all such insignificant matters. . . .

December 28—Yesterday upwards of fifty officers in Gen. Greene's division resigned their commissions—six or seven of our regiment are doing the like today. All this is occasion'd by officers' families being so much neglected at home on account of provisions. Their wages will not by considerable [amount] purchase a few trifling comfortables here in camp, & maintain their families at home, while such extravagant prices are demanded for the common necessaries of life. . . .

The present circumstances of the soldier is better by far than the officers, for the family of the soldier is provided for at the public expense if the articles they want are above the common price—but the officer's family are obliged not only to beg in the most humble manner for the necessaries of life, but also to pay for them at the most exorbitant rates. . . . When the officer has been fatiguing thro' wet & cold and returns to his tent where he finds a letter directed to him from his wife, fill'd with the most heart-aching tender complaints a woman is capable of writing—acquainting him with the incredible difficulty with which she procures a little bread for herself & children—and finally concluding with expressions bordering on despair, of procuring a sufficiency of food to keep soul & body together through the winter. . . . When such, I say, is the tidings they constantly hear from their families—What man is there, who has not the least regard for his family, whose soul would not shrink within him? Who would not be disheartened from persevering in the best of causes—the cause of his country—when such discouragements as these lie in his way, which his country might remedy if they would?

December 28—Building our huts.

December 29—Continued the work. Snowed all day pretty briskly. The party of the 22nd, return'd—lost 18 men, who were taken prisoners by being decoyed by the enemy's light horse. . . .

So much talk about discharges among the officers—& so many are discharged—his Excellency [Washington] lately expressed his fears of being left alone with the soldiers only. . . .

All Hell couldn't prevail against us, if Heaven continues no more than its former blessings—and if we keep up the credit of our money which has now become of the last consequence. If its credit sinks but a few degrees more, we shall then repent when tis too late—& cry out for help when no one will appear to deliver. We who are in camp, and depend on our money entirely to procure the comforts of life, feel the importance of this matter. He who is hoarding it up in his chest, thinks little more of it than how he shall procure more.

December 30—Eleven deserters came in today—some Hessians & some English. One of the Hessians took an axe in his hand & cut away the ice of the Schuylkill which was 1½ inches thick & 40 rods wide and waded through to our camp—he was ½ an hour in the water. They had a promise when they engag'd that the war would be ended in one year—they were now tired of the service. . . .

December 31—Apply'd . . . for a furlow. . . . I concluded to stay—& immediately set about fixing accommodations for the sick, &c., &c.

We got some spirits and finish'd the year with a good drink &

thankful hearts in our new hut, which stands on an eminence that overlooks the brigade, & in sight of the front line. The Major and Commissary Little are to live with us which makes our hut Head Quarters.

In the evening I joyfully received a letter from my good and loving wife. The pleasure and satisfaction a man enjoys upon hearing of the health & peace of a friend, and more especially of a wife, on whose affections & peace his own happiness depends, is a greater pleasure than . . .

1778, January 1. New Year.—I am alive. I am well. Huts go on briskly, and our camp begins to appear like a spacious city. . . .

Nothing tends to the establishment of the firmest friendship like mutual sufferings which produces mutual intentions and endeavors for mutual relief which in such cases are equally shar'd with pleasure and satisfaction—in the course of this, each heart is laid open to full view—the similar passions in each, approximate themselves by a certain impulsive sympathy, which terminates in lasting esteem. . . .

January 3—Our hut, or rather our hermit's cell, goes on briskly, having a short allowance of bread this morning we divided it with great precision, eat our breakfast with thankful hearts for the little we had, took care of the sick, according to our daily practice, and went to work on our little humble cottage. . . .

Today his Excellency in orders acquainted the troops of the Congress's high approbation of their spirited perseverence and good conduct this campaign, that rations should be raised monthly in proportion to the rise of the articles of life, that the Congress were exerting themselves to supply the Commissary and Clothiers Departments, with a greater quantity of better stores than hitherto . . . and that a month's wages extraordinary shall be given to every officer & soldier who shall live in huts this winter.

Good encouragement this, and we think ourselves deserving of it, for the hunger, thirst, cold, & fatigue we have suffer'd this campaign, altho' we have not fought much, yet the oldest soldiers among us have called the campaign a very severe & hard one. . . .

Sunday, January 4—I was call'd to relieve a soldier thought to be dying—he expir'd before I reach'd the hut. He was an Indian— an excellent soldier—and an obedient good natur'd fellow. He engaged for money doubtless as others do; but he has serv'd his country faithfully—he has fought for those very people who disinherited his forefathers. Having finished his pilgrimage, he was discharged from the War of Life & Death. His memory ought to be respected, more than those rich ones who supply the world with nothing better than money and vice.

FAR TO THE north, Native and white Americans had spent the year killing each other with hateful fury; but here in this miserable camp, Waldo met an Indian who had made the "glorious cause" his own. He recognized the death of this man for what it was: a startling reminder that the bond between these citizen soldiers, forged by their mutual suffering, transcended all their former divisions—that the mere act of hanging together in the face of death had given them a shared national identity. The very idea of America as a common country scarcely existed twelve years before; but perseverance against adversity had made them all Americans, above all else.

As Valley Forge began to emerge as a livable camp, in January and February of 1778, another change swept over the army. It came with a confident, middle-aged Prussian who announced himself as Frederick Wilhelm Ludolf Gerhard Augustin, Baron von Steuben. He claimed to have been a lieutenant general under Frederick the Great; the truth was, he had indeed been an officer in the Prussian army, but his noble title and his claimed rank were pure fiction. Nevertheless, Steuben stood out from the dozens of European officers who came looking for work with the rebel army; unlike so many others, he asked for no fat salary, nor even for a prestigious rank. He simply wanted to help.

Steuben could speak no English, but he hit it off with Washington nonetheless. The Prussian was, after all, a professional soldier—that much was clear from his conversation and his military bearing. And he volunteered to help with the one thing that the American army needed most: training. The Continentals had proven themselves tough, determined fighters at Germantown—even in their defeat at the Brandywine—but they remained only half trained. They needed the drill, the practice, the physical technique needed to make the most out of their weapons and formations, to be able to maneuver smoothly over uneven ground. Steuben took up the task with vigor.

The Prussian officer executed his assignment with flair. He established a model company of one hundred men, drilling it until it could demonstrate for the rest of the army. But he soon encountered greater difficulties than his lack of English. Americans had long enjoyed a greater degree of equality, of participation in public affairs, than any people in Europe; with the Revolution in full swing, they were fast discarding the vestiges of the old hierarchical order. The citizen volunteers whom Steuben encountered were a far cry from the peasant foot soldiers of Prussia, so he had to abandon the bullying and intimidation that held European armies together. "In the first place," he wrote to an old fellow soldier in Europe, "the genius of this nation is not in the least to be compared with that of the Prussians, Austrians, or French. You say to your soldier, 'Do this,' and he doeth it, but I am obliged to say, 'This is the reason why you ought to do that,' and he does it."[81]

By the end of the winter, the Continental army had emerged not only as a body of determined veterans, but as a highly trained, professional force. Steuben had introduced important innovations, along with a standard manual of drill: when the Americans formed a line formation for battle, they now stood in two ranks, rather than three like the British. His experience had shown that the third rank was often crowded out by the first two; the two-line formation actually increased a unit's firepower, and allowed it to extend itself farther to each side. Furthermore, the Continentals began to receive actual uniforms,[82] along with French Charleville muskets, which were superior to the British model.

The American army had suffered greatly during the long winter, but it emerged stronger than ever. Men who had never seen the inside of a military tent one or two years before were now professional

[81]Quoted in Middlekauff, p. 419.

[82]Uniforms were enormously important in combat. Consistent clothing allowed generals to identify their own units on the battlefield, which became increasingly confused in combat, with great clouds of smoke from the primitive gunpowder drifting across the lines. For details of the Continentals' formations and weapons, see the introduction to W. J. Wood, *Battles of the Revolutionary War*.

soldiers. Washington's own abilities and confidence had grown, as he absorbed the lessons of his victories, defeats, and near misses. And the outcome of the campaign in the north had washed across the continent, reassuring everyone that victory was possible—perhaps even near at hand.

No one captured the newfound confidence of 1778 better than Thomas Paine, the master propagandist. In the selection that follows, Paine once again addresses General Howe, with a fairly sound review of the events of the previous year. His words were broadcast throughout the colonies, as a part of *The Crisis* series of pamphlets; only this time, Paine no longer needed to buck up the failing spirits of his countrymen. It was clear to everyone that America had been snatched from destruction, and now had a chance for victory.

Snatched from Destruction
by Thomas Paine

TO GENERAL HOWE

When I look back on the gloomy days of last winter and see America suspended by a thread, I feel a triumph of joy at the recollection of her delivery, and a reverence for the characters which snatched her from destruction. To doubt *now* would be a species of infidelity, and to forget the instruments which saved us *then* would be ingratitude.

The close of that campaign left us with the spirits of conquerors. The northern districts were relieved by the retreat of General Carleton over the lakes. The army under your command were hunted back and had their bounds prescribed. The Continent began to feel its military importance, and the winter passed pleasantly away in preparations for the next campaign.

However confident you might be on your first arrival, the course of the year seventy-six gave you some idea of the difficulty, if not impossibility, of conquest. To this reason I ascribe your delay in opening the campaign in seventy-seven. The face of matters, on the close of the former year, gave you no encouragement to pursue a discretionary war as soon as the spring admitted the taking the field: for though conquest, in that case, would have given you a double portion of fame, yet the experiment proved too hazardous. The ministry, had you failed, would have shifted the whole blame upon you, charged you with having acted without orders, and condemned at once both your plan and your execution.

To avoid those misfortunes, which might have involved you and your money accounts in perplexity and suspicion, you prudently waited the arrival of a plan of operations from England, which was, that you should proceed for Philadelphia by way of the Chesapeake, and that Burgoyne, after reducing Ticonderoga, should take his route by Albany, and, if necessary, join you.[83]

The splendid laurels of the last campaign have flourished in the north. In that quarter America hath surprised the world, and laid the foundation of her this year's glory. The conquest of Ticonderoga (if it may be called a conquest) has, like all your other victories, led on to ruin. Even the provisions taken in that fortress (which by General Burgoyne's return was sufficient in bread and flour for nearly 5,000 men for ten weeks, and in beef and pork for the same number of men for one month) served only to hasten his overthrow, by enabling him to proceed to Saratoga, the place of his destruction. A short review of the operations of the last campaign will shew the condition of affairs on both sides.

You have taken Ticonderoga and marched into Philadelphia. These are all the events which the year hath produced on your part. A trifling campaign indeed, compared with the expenses of England and the conquest of the continent. On the other side, a considerable part of your northern force has been routed by the New York militia under General Herkimer. Fort Stanwix hath bravely survived a compounded attack of soldiers and savages, and the besiegers have fled. The battle of Bennington has put a thousand prisoners into our hands, with all their arms, stores, artillery, and baggage. General Burgoyne in two engagements has been defeated; himself, his army, and all that were his and theirs are now ours. Ticonderoga and Indepen-

[83]Paine, of course, has it wrong here: Howe attacked Philadelphia on his own initiative.

dence are retaken, and not the shadow of an enemy remains in all the northern districts. At this instant we have upwards of eleven thousand prisoners, between sixty and seventy pieces of brass ordnance, besides small arms, tents, stores, &c., &c.

In order to know the real value of those advantages we must reverse the scene, and suppose General Gates and the force he commanded to be at your mercy as prisoners, and General Burgoyne with his army of soldiers and savages to be already joined to you in Pennsylvania. So dismal a picture can scarcely be looked at. It hath all the traces and colorings of horror and despair; and excites the most swelling emotions of gratitude by exhibiting the miseries we are so graciously preserved from. . . .

Let me ask, sir, what great exploits have you performed? Through all the variety of changes and opportunities which the war hath produced, I know no one action of yours that cannot be styled masterly. You have moved in and out, backward and forward, round and round, as if valor consisted in a military jig. The history and figure of your movements would be truly ridiculous could they be justly delineated. They resemble the labors of a puppy pursuing its tail; the end is still at the same distance, and all the turnings round must be done over again.

The first appearance of affairs at Ticonderoga wore such an unpromising aspect, that it was necessary, in July, to detach a part of the forces to the support of that quarter, which were otherwise destined or intended to act against you, and this, perhaps, has been the means of postponing your downfall to another campaign. The destruction of one army at a time is work enough. We know, sir, what we are about, what we have to do, and how to do it.

———

THE AMERICANS KNEW what they were about, Paine wrote— but the British themselves were increasingly unsteady. In May 1778, Lord North's ministry replaced Howe with General Henry Clinton as commander in chief in America, sending orders to evacuate Philadelphia and consolidate the troops in New York. Clinton rejoiced at the change. He hated Howe, and probably agreed with Paine's judgment that Howe had performed no "great exploits," nothing "masterly" in the course of his campaigns.

In June, Clinton prepared his troops for departure from Philadelphia, sending the sick and his heavy supplies by ship. The rest of his army—roughly 10,000 men—would march overland to New York, along with an immense supply train of 1,500 wagons. "Besides the soldiers' possessions and the officers' baggage," writes Robert Middlekauff, "there were the laundries, bakeries, blacksmiths' shops, all vital to the life of an eighteenth-century army, and almost equally important the bat horses, private carriages, hospital supplies, and inevitably the camp followers," including wives, children, mistresses, and servants.[84]

Washington kept his army close to Clinton's force as it slowly crawled out of Philadelphia; he longed for a chance to strike with his reinvigorated regiments. The vulnerability of the British column was stressed by one of the newest members of his staff, a young Frenchman named Marie Joseph Paul Yves Roch Gilbert du Motier, Marquis de Lafayette—better known simply as Lafayette. As this French nobleman pointed out, Clinton's supply train alone stretched out for twelve miles behind the main force. Washington agreed that it was ripe for an assault, choosing to attack the British rear on June 28, 1778.

Unfortunately, leadership of the strike force fell to Charles Lee, the treacherous officer who had been captured by the British back before the battle of Trenton. He had been freed in a prisoner exchange, and welcomed back by the Americans, who valued his experience as a professional officer. Lee behaved erratically, first refusing and then demanding command of the attacking element.

On the morning of June 28, Lee's force of 5,000 men approached the 2,000 troops of the British rear guard near Monmouth Court House, New Jersey. It was a day of intense heat, causing many soldiers on both sides to collapse from the temperature alone. But it would be Charles Lee, not the weather, that ruined the American assault. Lee simply fell apart, pulling some of his men back after making contact, leaving others to their own devices. Meanwhile, the redcoats collected for a counterattack.

[84]Middlekauff, p. 420.

Washington arrived on the scene and beheld mass confusion—confusion caused not by the British, but by Lee. The infuriated general dismissed the babbling Lee and restored the American line. By now, Clinton and his subordinate Charles Cornwallis were throwing regiments into the attack as fast as they could come up. Once again, Washington demonstrated his coolness in his face of disaster; he quickly concentrated his artillery on a nearby hill and got his men back into formation. As the redcoats came on, his troops cut them to pieces. Clinton gave up his counterattack, withdrawing from the field under the cover of darkness.

The battle of Monmouth Court House was not a glorious assault on the British rear, as Washington intended; rather, it was a well-conducted defense against a blundering counterattack. As a result, it did not turn out to be the decisive victory that he hoped for—but it was a victory nonetheless. He had shown his resilience and tactical prowess; his men had proved their bravery once again and—even more important—had demonstrated how well they had absorbed the training of the previous winter. As Clinton pulled back into New York, Washington could take satisfaction in what he had accomplished.

More significant than the British withdrawal from Philadelphia was the reason behind it. London now had a new enemy: France had recognized the United States, and had entered the war in an alliance with the new republic.

American ambassadors had been striving for a compact with the court in Versailles for some months when news arrived of the victory at Saratoga. That triumph convinced the French foreign minister, Charles Gravier de Vergennes, that the Americans might win—that France now had a chance to get revenge for the losses of the Seven Years War. With Benjamin Franklin leading the negotiations, the two sides signed a treaty of alliance in February 1778. Shortly before Washington met Clinton at Monmouth Court House, Britain and France went to war.

The French entry into the war changed the strategic situation drastically for the British. They worried less about French troops arriving in North America than they did about French attacks on English colonies in the West Indies. These sugar-producing isles were considered almost as valuable as the thirteen provinces of America. And war against France was a traditional sort of venture, something the king and the ministry could easily understand (as opposed to the intractable problem of conquering more than three million angry Americans). So orders had gone out for Clinton to withdraw from Philadelphia, consolidate in New York, and free up troops for attacks on French possessions in the Caribbean.

But another idea lingered in the mind of Lord Germain, as he pondered the map of America in his London office. To win the war, the British had to rally the support of civilians—they had to draw on the population of loyalists scattered around the colonies. Germain was certain that large numbers of Tories lived in the South, a region largely ignored in the first three years of war. He took a first step toward a campaign there in late 1778, when he dispatched a small force that took control of Georgia, the youngest and least populated of the thirteen states. Perhaps, Germain thought, Clinton should direct all his efforts to the South—and Britain just might crush the Revolution after all.

IV

VICTORY

11

WAR COMES TO THE SOUTH

Lieutenant Colonel Banastre Tarleton was a horseman. The son of a prominent English merchant, he had progressed from his birth in Liverpool to an Oxford education to a commission in the King's Dragoon Guards in just twenty-one years. He was a dashing fellow, as a cavalry officer ought to be (at least in the minds of the British), and he exuded nothing but confidence and competence. After he arrived in New York in 1776, he organized a special unit of loyalists; he trained his men hard, forming them into a mixed force of cavalry and infantry called Tarleton's Legion (or the British Legion, or the Loyalist Legion). General Henry Clinton liked the hard-driving Tarleton; so when he prepared for an invasion of South Carolina in late 1779, he decided to bring along the twenty-five-year-old cavalryman—and his legion.

Clinton chose to attack the South because he had few other options. Operations around New York had been frustrating, thanks to General Washington and his increasingly capable army. While a British fleet had thwarted a French and American attack on Newport, Washington continued to threaten Clinton's outposts in the highlands along the Hudson River, north of New York. On July 15, 1779, General Anthony Wayne had led a stunningly successful surprise attack against Stony Point, a riverside fortress that seemed impregnable. After that humiliating loss, Clinton realized that he could gain little in the North—and as Commander in Chief in America, he had no desire to go the way of Thomas Gage or William Howe.

Back in London, meanwhile, Howe busied himself with a furious attack on the ministry. Insulted at being recalled, he demanded a parliamentary investigation of his conduct. He offered a number of witnesses who described the incredible difficulties of the war in America.

Lord Germain fought back. Though the secretary for the Amer-

ican colonies had shrunk from confronting the general the year before, now he lashed back, offering his own witness to counter Howe's
defense. Major General James Robertson swore that two-thirds of
Americans were loyal to the king, desperate to be freed from "Congress's tyranny."[85] Though the debate went on, Germain could feel
a certain amount of pressure building to end the war—at least, to put
it on hold while fighting continued against the French. To resist that
pressure, he needed victories, preferably victories that would tap the
well of loyalists that he had so publicly insisted was hiding beneath
the surface.

Both Clinton and Germain believed that the South was largely
loyal to the king. Culturally and religiously, it differed markedly from
the rest of the America: the Church of England held sway through
much of the region; it had a plantation economy, run by wealthy men
who resembled the landowners in the British Parliament; and even
the backcountry settlers were thought to be loyal, as they were in
large part recent immigrants from Ulster, Scotland, and northern England. Furthermore, the British had overrun underpopulated Georgia
in 1778, capturing Savannah and Augusta. So the general and secretary agreed that the primary target of the 1780 campaign would be
Charleston, South Carolina, a town of 12,000 people and the leading
Southern seaport.

In December 1779, Clinton loaded his expeditionary force onto
transports in New York Harbor; the day after Christmas he set sail
for the South. He brought with him some of the finest soldiers and
officers in the army, including General Charles Cornwallis (veteran of
so many battles in the North), and that confident cavalryman Lieutenant Colonel Tarleton.

Just a few years after that campaign, Tarleton wrote a memoir of
his experiences in America. In his Oxford-trained, formal style, the
young officer referred to himself in the third person—but his insights
and observations were distinctly first-person. And his experiences
were remarkable indeed: a formal siege of an American city (one of
the few real sieges of the war), followed by a wide-ranging campaign
of fast marches and cavalry raids. As Tarleton's account reveals, the

[85]Quoted in Middlekauff, p. 437.

purpose of the entire endeavor was as much political as military—and before it was over, the British would have reason to consider it a success on both counts.

Invasion
by Banastre Tarleton

Sir Henry Clinton ordered a number of transports to be fitted up for the reception of a corps of about eight thousand, five hundred men; likewise, horse, ordnance, and victualling vessels requisite for such an army. South Carolina suggested itself as the grand object of the enterprise; the mildness of the climate, the richness of the country, its vicinity to Georgia, and its distance from General Washington, pointed out the advantage and facility of its conquest.

As soon as the commander in chief had certain intelligence of the return of the French fleet to the West Indies,[86] he arranged the public business of New York, committed the command of the King's troops during his absence to Lieutenant-General Knyphausen, and embarked with four flank battalions, twelve regiments and corps, British, Hessian, and Provincial, a powerful detachment of artillery, two hundred and fifty cavalry, and ample supplies of military stores and provisions.

Vice-Admiral [Marriot] Arbuthnot, with a naval force competent to the purpose, and which was superior to anything in the American seas, prepared to convoy this expedition to the place of its destination. On the 26th of December, 1779, the whole fleet got underway, and without difficulty cleared the ice in New York harbor. . . . On the 10th of February, 1780, the transports, with [a] great part of the army on board, convoyed by a proper force, sailed from Savannah [Georgia] to North Edisto [South Carolina], the place of debarkation, which had been previously appointed. . . .

The transports all entered the harbor the next day, and the army

[86]Charles Hector Théodat, Comte d'Estaing, had led a French fleet from the Mediterranean to North America when war erupted between France and Britain. He had operated around Rhode Island for a time, until a fleet under Admiral Howe induced him to sail for the West Indies.

immediately took possession of John's Island and Stono ferry; James's island, Perreneau's landing, Wappo cut, and other adjacent places, were soon afterwards obtained; and by a bridge thrown over the canal, the necessary communications were secured, and the advanced part of the King's army occupied the bank of Ashley river, opposite to Charlestown [Charleston].[87] This position, for the present, was the most eligible that could be established; the air was healthful, and provisions were plentiful; its situation equally covered the Wappo cut, through which the boats and galleys were to pass for the crossing the troops over Ashley river, and protected the corps which was to march under the command of Brigadier-General Patterson from Savannah.

When the commander in chief quitted that place, to proceed to the neighborhood of Charlestown, many of the transports were not arrived from the voyage; the loss of men and stores made it necessary to dispatch an order to New York for reinforcements of both, from that garrison. . . .

The general and his engineers having fixed upon the point and mode of attack, a large working party broke ground, under cover of an advanced detachment, on the night of the 1st of April [1780]. Two large redoubts were thrown up within eight hundred yards of the American lines, and were not discovered before daybreak, when the fire from the town had very inconsiderable effect. The next evening, another redoubt was added, and for five successive days and nights, the labor of artificers and soldiers was directed to the construction of batteries, which on the eighth were completed with artillery.

In the meantime, Admiral Arbuthnot had been fully occupied in accomplishing the general's wishes. Heavy cannon were collected from the line-of-battle ships, and conveyed to the magazines; detachments of seamen were furnished to act on shore, under the commands of Captains Elphinstone and Evans; and preparations were made for passing Charlestown bar. . . . The bar was passed on the 20th of March without any accident, notwithstanding the enemy's

[87]Tarleton consistently wrote "Charlestown" instead of "Charleston." It has been left unchanged, as it reflects contemporary usage. The reader should not confuse the place with Charlestown, Mass.

galleys attempted to prevent the boats from sounding the channel. . . .

At this period of the siege, and before the batteries opened, Sir Henry Clinton and Admiral Arbuthnot thought it advisable to send a summons to Major-General [Benjamin] Lincoln, who commanded in Charlestown, representing the dangerous consequences of a cannonade and storm, stating the present as the only favorable opportunity for preserving the lives and properties of the inhabitants, and warning the commander that he should be responsible for all the calamities which might be the result of his temerity and obstinancy. General Lincoln answered, that the same duty and inclination which prevented him from abandoning Charlestown, during sixty days' knowledge of their hostile intentions, operated now with equal force in prompting him to defend it to the last extremity.

The defenses of Charlestown, on the land side, consisted of a chain of redoubts, lines, and batteries, extending from one river to the other, and furnished with eighty cannon and mortars. The front works of each flank were strengthened by swamps, originating from the neighboring rivers, and tending towards the center, through which they were connected by a canal passing from one to the other. Between these outward impediments and the redoubts were two strong rows of abatis,[88] the trees being buried slanting in the earth, with their branches facing outwards, formed a fraize work against the assailants; and these were farther secured by a ditch double picketed [with wooden walls on each side]. In the center, the natural defenses were inferior to those on the flanks; to remedy this defect, and to cover the principal gate, a horn work of masonry had been constructed, which being closed during the siege, formed a kind of citadel.

The fortifications facing the two rivers and the harbor had been erected with uncommon labor and expense. Ships with chevaux de fraise,[89] connected by spars and booms, were employed to block up

[88]Abatis was a primitive ancestor of barbed wire: it was a tangle of felled trees and sharpened branches, spread before a defensive position to slow an attacking force down.

[89]Chevaux-de-frise were logs punched through with crisscrossing sharpened stakes.

the channels, in order to hinder a near approach of the King's frigates; and piles and pickets were fixed in the ground, at all landing places, to prevent any debarkation from boats. The whole extent was likewise covered by batteries, formed of earth and palmetto wood, judiciously placed, and mounted with heavy cannon.

The garrison, under the orders of Major-General Lincoln, was composed of ten weak Continental and state regiments; of militia, drawn from the Carolinas and Virginia; and of inhabitants of the town; amounting in the whole to near six thousand men, exclusive of sailors. The body of regular troops destined for this service, although assisted by the militia and the inhabitants, was scarcely adequate to the defense of such extensive fortifications, and could have been more usefully employed in the field; where judicious operations, assisted by the resources to be found in the country, and by the approaching heat of the season, would have protected the greatest part of the fertile province of South Carolina, would have soon overbalanced the present superiority of the British forces. . . . General Washington adopted this line of action, when he abandoned New York island for the Jerseys, when he yielded Philadelphia to the English arms, and in many other instances where a contrary conduct, to all human appearance, would have unavoidably established the sovereignty of Great Britain.[90]

On the rejection of the summons, the batteries were opened, and soon obtained a superiority over those of the town. . . . The attacks were planned with judgment, and the works were pushed with industry. Soon after the middle of April, the second parallel[91] was carried within four hundred and fifty yards of the enemy's main works, new batteries were constructed, and all the communications were secured. . . . Charlestown became completely invested. . . .

The besieging army finished their third parallel, which they had carried close to the canal, and by a sap pushed to the dam which

---

[90]Coincidentally, this analysis was shared by Thomas Paine, who argued in *The Crisis* that Washington had lost nothing by abandoning the cities of New York and Philadelphia.

[91]A parallel was a trench dug by the besieging forces parallel to the enemy's lines. A sap (mentioned in the next paragraph) was a projecting trench extended toward the defender.

supplied it with water on the right, drained it in several parts to the bottom. On the 6th and 7th of May, the artillery was mounted in the batteries of this parallel, and the traverses and communications were perfecty completed. Thus enclosed on every side, and driven to its last defenses, Sir Henry Clinton wishing to preserve Charlestown from destruction, and to prevent that effusion of blood which must be the inevitable consequence of a storm, opened a correspondence on the 8th with General Lincoln, for the purpose of a surrender. But the conditions demanded by the American commander being deemed higher than he had a right to expect from his present situation, they were rejected, and hostilities renewed.

The batteries on the third parallel were then opened, and by the superiority of fire, both of artillery and small arms, the British troops were able to gain the counterscarp [inner wall] of the outwork which flanked the canal, which they likewise passed, and then pushed on their approaches directly towards the ditch of the place. The present state of danger now urged the citizens and militia, who had formed the objections to the late conditions, to acquiesce in their being relinquished. General Lincoln accordingly proposed to surrender on the terms lately offered.

The commander in chief and the admiral, besides their dislike to the cruel extremity of a storm, were not disposed to press to unconditional submission an enemy whom they wished to conciliate with clemency. They now granted the same conditions which they had before prescribed as the foundation for treaty. The capitulation was signed the 11th of May, and on the 12th, Major-General [Alexander] Leslie, by the order of Sir Henry Clinton, took possesion of Charlestown. . . .

By the articles of capitulation, the garrison were allowed some of the honors of war; they were to march out of the town, at an hour appointed for that purpose, to the ground between the works of the place and the canal, where they were to deposit their arms. But the drums were not to beat a British march, or the colors to be uncased. The Continental troops and seamen were to keep their baggage, and to remain prisoners of war until they were exchanged. The militia were to be permitted to return to their respective homes as prisoners on parole; and while they adhered to this parole, were not to be molested by the British troops in person or property. . . .

Seven general officers, ten Continental regiments, and three battalions of artillery became prisoners upon this occasion. The whole number of men in arms who surrendered, including town and country militia, and French, amounted to five thousand, six hundred and eighteen, exclusive of near a thousand seamen. . . .

After the surrender of the town, the commander in chief, without loss of time, adopted measures which appeared both judicious and necessary. . . . He circulated proclamations amongst the inhabitants of South Carolina, well calculated to induce them to return their allegiance, and to manifest their loyalty by joining the King's troops. . . . The proclamations issued by the general produced great effect in South Carolina. In most of the districts adjoining to Charlestown, great numbers offered to stand forth in the defense of the British government, and many did voluntarily take up arms, and place themselves under the direction of Major [Patrick] Ferguson, who was appointed to receive and command them. A general revolution of sentiment seemed to take place, and the cause of Great Britain appeared to triumph over that of the American Congress. . . .

The commander in chief having established order in Charlestown, and having marked the line of conduct to be observed throughout Carolina towards the friends and enemies of Great Britain, began to make arrangement for his return with part of the army to New York, which had been particularly exposed by the attempts of General Washington, owing to an uncommonly severe winter. Previous to his embarkation, he planned several expeditions to march into the interior parts of the country. One, to move up the Savannah river into Georgia; another, to pass the Saluda to Ninety-Six; and a third, under the command of Earl Cornwallis, to cross the Santee river, and by marching up the northeast bank, to endeavor to strike at Colonel [Abraham] Buford's corps, which was retreating to North Carolina with artillery and a number of wagons, containing arms, ammunition, and clothing.

Earl Cornwallis left his ground near Huger's bridge on the 18th of May, and directed his march to Lenew's ferry, with five pieces of cannon, and upwards of two thousand, five hundred men. Boats were collected with some difficulty to pass the troops, the Americans having concealed or destroyed all within their reach to retard the progress of the royal army. By the information of negroes, who discovered where some were secreted, and by the assistance of carpenters, who repaired others that were damaged, the light troops were not long prevented from crossing the river. . . .

On the 22nd, the army moved forwards upon the same road by which Colonel Buford had retreated ten days before. The infantry marched to Nelson's ferry with as much expedition as the climate would allow. From this place, Earl Cornwallis thought proper to detach a corps, consisting of forty of the 17th Dragoons, and one hundred and thirty of the Legion, with one hundred mounted infantry of the same regiment and a three pounder [cannon], to pursue the Americans, who were now so much advanced as to render any approach of the main body impracticable. Lieutenant-Colonel Tarleton [the writer], on this occasion, was desired to consult his own judgment as to the distance of the pursuit, or the mode of attack. To defeat Colonel Buford, and to take his cannon, would undoubtedly, in the present state of the Carolinas, have considerable effect. . . .

[After hard marching,] Lieutenant-Colonel Tarleton found himself not far distant from the enemy, and, though not in a suitable condition for action, he determined as soon as possible to attack, there being no other expedient to stop their progress, and prevent their being reinforced the next morning. . . .

Colonel Buford's force consisted of three hundred and eighty Continental infantry of the Virginia line, a detachment of [Colonel William] Washington's cavalry, and two six pounders. He chose his post in an open wood, to the right of the road; he formed his infantry in one line, with a small reserve. He placed his colors in the center, and he ordered his cannon, baggage, and wagons to continue their march.

Lieutenant-Colonel Tarleton made his arrangement for the attack with all possible expedition. He confided his right wing, which was composed of sixty dragoons, and nearly as many mounted infantry, to Major Cochrane, desiring him to dismount the latter, to gall the enemy's flank before he moved against their front with his cavalry. Captains Corbet and Kinlock were directed, with the 17th Dragoons and part of the Legion, to charge the center of the Americans; whilst Lieutenant-Colonel Tarleton, with thirty chosen horse and some infantry, assaulted their right flank and reserve. This particular situation the commanding officer selected for himself, that he might discover the effect of the other attacks. . . .

The disposition being completed without any fire from the enemy, though within three hundred yards of their front, the cavalry advanced to the charge. On their arrival at fifty paces, the Continental infantry presented [their muskets], when Tarleton was surprised to hear their officers command them to retain their fire till the British cavalry was nearer. This forbearance in not firing before the dragoons were within ten yards of the object of their attack prevented their falling into confusion on the charge, and likewise deprived the Americans of the further use of their ammunition. Some officers, men, and horses, suffered by this fire; but the [American] battalion was totally broken, and slaughter commenced before Lieutenant-Colonel Tarleton could remount another horse, the one with which he led his dragoons being overturned by the volley. Thus in a few minutes ended an affair which might have had a very different termination.[92]

The British troops had two officers killed, one wounded; three privates killed, thirteen wounded; and thirty-one horses killed and wounded. The loss of officers and men was great on the part of the Americans, owing to the dragoons so effectually breaking the infantry, and to a report amongst the cavalry, that they had lost their commanding officer, which stimulated the soldiers to a vindictive asperity not easily restrained. Upwards of one hundred officers and men were killed on the spot.

WHEN TARLETON CHARGED the American line, the patriot officers scarcely knew how to respond. They were used to fighting other regiments of infantry, not rampaging horsemen: in the fighting

---

[92]The Americans betrayed their unfamiliarity with a cavalry charge. When facing an infantry attack, most officers worried that their men would fire too soon. Cavalry, however, was vulnerable when charging at a line of men, as it had no way of firing back; an early volley could disorder the charge by wounding and frightening horses. The Americans waited until it was too late to fire a second time.

around Philadelphia, New York, and Saratoga, there had been precious few cavalry charges. At first, Tarleton's dragoons trotted easily toward the patriot line, and the Americans decided to wait before unleashing a volley. But in the last few dozen yards, the loyalists kicked their horses into a full gallop; when the Continentals finally fired, it was too late to stop the charge. The Legion cavalrymen broke through, slashing left and right with their sabers. When Tarleton himself fell from his mount, they believed he had died—and so they cut down the American infantry, even after the beaten soldiers tried to surrender.

Tarleton's victory over Buford did indeed produce the "considerable effect" he had been looking for: it eliminated organized resistance within South Carolina. As Clinton guessed, many local residents were still loyal to the crown, and they flocked by the hundreds to the royal army recruiters. But this vicious fight also stirred the patriots to new determination; they coined the bitter phrase "Tarleton's quarter" as a synonym for British brutality.

Even as the king's forces dispersed or destroyed the last remnants of the Continental army in South Carolina, hundreds of local men spontaneously gathered in partisan units. A ferocious guerrilla conflict erupted in the South, as skillful local leaders such as Francis Marion and Thomas Sumter led hit-and-run attacks on enemy outposts. To fight this new threat, the British relied heavily on the newly organized loyalist militia.[93] As a result, the campaign in the South took on the character of a civil war, as Tory and patriot neighbors battled each other in private vendettas, isolated skirmishes, and full-blown battles.

The Continental army had not given up the fight, of course. Off to the north lingered a small force under General Johann de Kalb, a capable French officer serving with the Americans. His men were exhausted, demoralized, and poorly equipped, but he kept them within striking distance of South Carolina. Unfortunately for de Kalb, the politically popular General Horatio Gates was pressing Congress for an appointment as head of the Southern Department. Many looked

---

[93]In addition to locally raised units, the British employed Tarleton's Legion; it was composed of American loyalists also, but most of the men were from New York, another state with numerous Tories. The Legion had high-quality training and equipment, making it the equivalent of a regular army unit.

to the victor of Saratoga to duplicate his previous feat in the Carolinas.

But none of this information was known to the British command as General Henry Clinton prepared to return to New York. It seemed clear enough that a great victory had been won: the city of Charleston captured, a major American army destroyed, a second and smaller force crushed, and the interior pacified. Clinton decided his place was in the North, facing Washington; he left General Charles Cornwallis in charge, with orders to drive into North Carolina and Virginia.

Cornwallis was glad to see Clinton go. The Commander in Chief seemed to irritate everyone he worked with: Howe, Admiral Arbuthnot, and now Cornwallis. And like Burgoyne three years earlier, Cornwallis looked forward to an independent command. He, too, was a member of Parliament, and a true aristocrat—an earl, to be precise. In the hierarchical world of eighteenth-century England, this nobleman carried himself with self-assurance and a deeply ingrained sense of superiority. Cornwallis also had real talent as a soldier: a natural leader, he possessed bravery, professional skill, and exceptional tactical instincts. He could lead a cavalry charge or map out a plan for battle with equal ability.

But the war to date had frustrated this talented, aristocratic officer. In the beginning, things had gone well for him. After the victories of Long Island and Fort Washington, he had led the chase as the American army retreated across New Jersey and over the Delaware. When Washington struck back at Trenton, Cornwallis commanded the British counterstroke. Unfortunately, Washington outgeneraled him, marching around his army to break up his rear guard at Princeton. The next year had brought some satisfaction with the battle of the Brandywine and the occupation of Philadelphia. But then came the evacuation, ending in the battle of Monmouth Court House, where Washington had mauled the assaults that Cornwallis had led in person.

By now, Cornwallis was tired of indecisive battles and inglorious campaigns; he leaped at the chance to command a department, to achieve real victories, to show how the American war could be won. But first he had to cope with the messy problem of those patriot partisans, and the Continental army under General de Kalb. The earl could not have worried too greatly over either one: on one hand, he believed, South Carolina was rising for the king; on the other, he had the advantage of professional British soldiers—especially Lieutenant Colonel Banastre Tarleton.

Conquest
by Banastre Tarleton

Upon Sir Henry Clinton's departure, the command of the King's troops to the southward devolved to Lieutenant-General Earl Cornwallis. The submission of General Williamson in Ninety-Six, who formerly commanded the militia of that district, and the dispersion of a party of Americans who had assembled at an iron-work on the northwest border of the province, put a temporary period to all resistance in South Carolina.

The heat of the summer, the want of stores and provisions, and the unsettled state of Charlestown and the country, impeded the immediate invasion of North Carolina; Earl Cornwallis dispatched emissaries with instructions to the leading men in that province, to attend to the harvest, to prepare provisions, and to remain quiet, till the King's troops were ready to advance, which operation could not take place before the latter end of August or the beginning of September. . . .

In the beginning of June, Colonel Lord [Francis] Rawdon, with the volunteers of Ireland and a detachment of Legion infantry, made a short expedition into a settlement of Irish, situated on Waxhaws. The sentiments of the inhabitants did not correspond to his lordship's expectations. He there learned what experience confirmed, that the Irish were the most averse of all other settlers to the British government in America. During the stay of the volunteers of Ireland in the Waxhaws, many of the inhabitants gave their paroles; an obligation they readily violated, when called to arms by the American commanders. . . .

The news brought in by . . . loyalists created some astonishment in the military, and diffused universal consternation amongst the inhabitants of South Carolina: They reported that Major-General [Johann] de Kalb, a French officer in the American service, was advancing from Salisbury with a large body of Continentals; that Colonel Porterfield was bringing state troops from Virgina; that General [Richard] Caswell had raised a powerful force in North Carolina; and that Colonel [Thomas] Sumter had already entered the Catawba, a settlement contiguous to the Waxhaws. These accounts being propagated, and artfully exaggerated, by the enemies within the province, caused a wonderful fermentation in the minds of the Americans, which neither the lenity of the British government, the solemnity of their paroles, by which their persons and properties enjoyed protection, nor the memory of the undeserved pardon so lately extended to so many of them, had sufficient strength to retain [them] in a state of submission or neutrality. . . .

The state of the country, and the exaggerated reports of the Americans, occasioned frequent patrols of cavalry and mounted infantry from the advanced British posts; one of which experienced both disgrace and defeat. Lieutenant Colonel Turnbull, on some intelligence from Fishing Creek, sent Captain Huck of the Legion to investigate the truth. The detachment committed to his care consisted of thirty-five dragoons of the Legion, twenty mounted infantry of the New York volunteers, and about sixty militia. On his arrival at the crossroads, near the source of Fishing Creek, Captain Huck neglected his duty, placing his party carelessly at a plantation without advancing any pickets, or sending out patrols. Some Americans who were assembled in the neighborhood heard of his negligent situation, and with an inferior force surprised and destroyed him, and a great part of his command. . . .

[Now] Colonel Sumter [felt] a desire of signalizing himself, by attacking some of the British posts upon the frontier. Having gained the necessary information, he directed his efforts against the corps at Rocky Mount. . . . After three attacks, the last of which some of the forlorn hope [the most desperate] penetrated within the abatis, the American commander retreated with loss and precipitation. In the gallant defense of this post, Lieutenant-Colonel Turnbull had one officer killed, one wounded, and about ten men killed and wounded.

Colonel Sumter crossed Broad river, and retired to his former camp in the Catawba settlement; where, reinforcing the numbers he had lost at Rocky Mount, was soon in a condition to project other operations. This active partisan was thoroughly influenced by enterprise, and that to keep undisciplined people together, it is necessary to employ them. For this purpose, he again surveyed the state of the British posts upon the frontier and on minute examination he deemed Hanging Rock the most vulnerable. . . .

On the 6th of August, at seven o'clock in the morning, he approached the flank of the post, which was entrusted to the North Carolina [loyalist] refugees, under the orders of Colonel Bryan. This loyalist, with his undisciplined people, though opposed by troops equally undisciplined, soon retreated from his ground, and Colonel Sumter directed the weight of his attack against the Legion infantry, which resisted his efforts with great coolness and bravery. . . .

Colonel Sumter still persevered in his attack, and very probably would have succeeded, if a stratagem employed by Captains Stewart and McDonald, of the British Legion, had not disconcerted his operations. These officers, with forty mounted infantry, were returning the same morning from Rocky Mount, and on the route heard the cannon and musketry at Hanging Rock. On a nearer approach to their post, they judiciously left the Rocky Mount [road], and made a circuit to get into the main Camden road, to reinforce their companions. When they arrived in sight of the Americans, the bugle horn was directed to sound the charge, and the soldiers were ordered to extend their files, in order to look like a formidable detachment. This unexpected appearance deranged the American commander, and threw his corps into a state of confusion, which produced a general retreat. . . .

Colonel Sumter rallied his men not far from Hanging Rock, and again fell back to the Catawba settlement, to collect more men from the Waxhaws, and to receive refugees, who flocked from all parts of South Carolina. The repulses he had sustained did not discourage him, or injure his cause. The loss of men was easily supplied, and his reputation for activity and courage was fully established by his late enterprising conduct. . . .

As soon as General Washington obtained accounts of the critical situation of Major-General Lincoln to the southward, owing to the great addition of force carried to that quarter under the immediate direction of the British commander in chief, he judiciously determined to send a considerable detachment of Continentals from the American army in the Jerseys, to stop the progress of the royalists. This powerful reinforcement was committed to Major-General de Kalb, an officer of reputation, who pressed forwards the troops with indefatigable attention. By long and repeated marches they now approached the frontier of South Carolina. . . . But another commander in chief was soon afterwards appointed, and sent to the southward.

On the 24th of July [1780], Major-General Gates arrived in the American camp. His name and former good fortune reanimated the exertions of the country. Provisions were more amply supplied by the inhabitants, and the Continental troops soon reached the frontier of South Carolina. . . .

The approach of General Gates with an army of six thousand men induced Lord Rawdon gradually to contract the posts upon the frontier, in order to assemble his forces. . . . In less than two days the militia [drafted for service with the British] mutinied, and securing their own officers and the sick, conducted them prisoners to General Gates, in North Carolina. This instance of treachery in the east of the province followed the perfidious conduct of Lieutenant-Colonel Lisle on the western border, and strongly proved the mistake of the British in placing confidence in the inhabitants of the country when acting apart from the army. . . .

Lord Rawdon sent regular information of every material incident, or movement, made by the Americans, and by the King's troops on the frontier, to Earl Cornwallis at Charlestown; where the public business, relative to claims, commercial arrangements, and other civil regulations, required great time to reduce it to order. The appearance of a formidable army in the province prevented a methodical completion of the system of government, and called the attentions of Earl Cornwallis to objects of more immediate importance. His lordship, therefore, prepared to leave Charlestown, after some of the most necessary and essential points were adjusted. . . .

[Meanwhile,] the situation of the British hospital and magazine, and the present distance of the army, pointed out to Lord Rawdon the propriety of falling back from Lynches creek, and concentrating his force near Camden. The move was accordingly made, without any molestation from the enemy, and an encampment was chosen at Log town, the most eligible place to be found in the neighborhood of Camden, which did not afford any naturally advantageous position for defensive consideration. . . .

Lord Cornwallis, on his arrival with the army, adopted the most likely measures to obtain intelligence of the enemy's force and position; he likewise directed his attention to strengthen the British regiments and provincial corps, by mustering the ablest convalescents; and he was not unmindful of his cavalry. Upon application from Lieutenant-Colonel Tarleton, he ordered all the horses of the army, belonging both to regiments and departments, to be assembled. The best were selected for the service of the cavalry, and, upon the proprietors receiving payment, were delivered up to the British Legion. These active preparations diffused animation and vigor throughout the army.

On the 15th the principal parts of the King's troops had orders to be in readiness to march. In the afternoon Earl Cornwallis desired Lieutenant-Colonel Tarleton to gain circumstantial intelligence, by intercepting a patrol, or carrying off some prisoners from an American picket. About ten miles from Camden, on the road to Rugeley's mills, the advanced guard of the Legion, in the evening, secured three American soldiers. The prisoners reported that they came from Lynches creek, where they had been left in a convalescent state, and that they were directed to join the American army, on the high road, that night, as General Gates had given orders for his troops to move from Rugeley's mills to attack the British camp next morning near Camden.

The information received from these men induced Tarleton to countermarch before he was discovered by any patrol of the enemy's outpost. The three prisoners were mounted behind dragoons, and conveyed with speed to the British army. When examined by Earl Cornwallis, their story appeared credible, and confirmed all other intelligence of the day. Orders were immediately circulated for the regiments and corps designed for a forward move, to stand to their arms. . . .

About ten o'clock the King's troops moved from their ground, and formed their order of march on the main road to Rugeley's mills . . . The royal army proceeded in a compact state with most profound silence. A little after two the advanced guard of the British charged the head of the American columns. The weight of the enemy's fire made the detachment of the Legion give way after their officer was wounded, and occasioned the light infantry, the 23rd and 33rd Regiments, to form across the road. Musketry continued on both sides near a quarter of an hour, when the two armies, finding themselves opposed to each other, as if actuated by the same present feelings and future intentions, ceased firing.

On examining the guides, and the people of the country, Earl Cornwallis discovered that the ground the British army now occupied was remarkably favorable to abide the event of a general action against the superior numbers of the enemy. The fortunate situation of two swamps, which narrowed the position, so that the English army could not be outflanked, instantly determined the British general to halt the troops upon this ground, and order them to lie down to wait the approach of day. These commands were executed as soon as a few small pickets were placed in the front. . . .

When the day broke, General Gates, not approving of the situation of Caswell's and [Edward] Stevens's brigades, was proceeding to alter their position. The circumstance, being observed by the British, was reported to Earl Cornwallis, who instantly, in person, commanded [Lieutenant Colonel James] Webster's division to advance, and dispatched the same order by an aide-de-camp, to Lord Rawdon on the left. The action became immediately general along the front, and was contested on the left and in the center with great firmness and bravery. . . .

The morning being hazy, the smoke hung over, and involved both armies in such a cloud, that it was difficult to see or estimate the destruction on either side. Notwithstanding the resistance, it was evident the British moved forwards; the light infantry and the 23rd Regiment being opposed only by militia, who were somewhat deranged by General Gates's intended alteration, first broke the enemy's front line, which advantage they judiciously followed, not by pursuing the fugitives, but by wheeling on the left flank of the Continentals, who were abandoned by their militia.

The contest was yet supported by the Maryland brigades and the Delaware regiment, when a part of the British cavalry, under Major Hanger, was ordered to charge their flank, whilst Lieutenant-Colonel Tarleton, with the remainder of his regiment, completed their confusion. Baron de Kalb, on the right of the Americans, being still ignorant of the flight of their left wing and center, owing to the thickness of the air, made a vigorous charge with a regiment of Continental infantry through the left division of the British, and when wounded and taken, would scarcely believe that Gates was defeated.

After this last effort of the Continentals, rout and slaughter ensued in every quarter. . . . The Continentals, the state troops, and the militia abandoned their arms, their colors, and their cannon, to seek protection in flight, or to obtain it from the clemency of the conquerors. . . .

In the action near Camden, the killed, wounded, and missing of the King's troops, amounted to three hundred and twenty-four, officers included. The destruction fell principally upon the center, owing to the well-directed fire of the Continentals, and the execution done by the American artillery. The Americans lost seventy officers, two thousand men (killed, wounded, and prisoners), eight pieces of cannon, several colors, and all their carriages and wagons.

———

AN UNMITIGATED DISASTER had befallen the American army at Camden. Once again, Gates had demonstrated his complete inability to actually *lead* an army in battle. At Freeman's Farm and Bemis Heights, his rightful role had been taken up by Daniel Morgan and Benedict Arnold, who had directed the actual fighting; their success concealed Gates's own failings. But at Camden, when he once again lapsed into inertia, no one could take his place. De Kalb did a fine job with the American right wing, but he was isolated from the other half of the army as it collapsed before the British attack. Gates fled the field, gathering the pathetic remnants in Hillsboro several days later.

Gates suffered a thoroughly deserved disgrace as a result of Camden. Congress conducted an investigation of his actions, though it waited until October to replace him with Nathanael Greene, the Rhode Islander who had proven himself time and time again under General Washington. Gates then resigned from the army.

Cornwallis, on the other hand, reveled in his triumph. This was no Germantown or Monmouth Court House—it was a truly decisive victory, over the fabled conqueror of Saratoga. The battle cleared the way for an invasion of North Carolina (and damped down his worries about the patriot guerrillas who were terrorizing the countryside). Already he could see himself as the general who won the war in America.

The "glorious cause" suffered another heavy blow that year. In September 1780, word came that the most valiant of American generals, Benedict Arnold, had defected to the enemy. Arnold's British contact, John André, was captured with papers that revealed how he had conspired to deliver the Hudson River fortress of West Point to the British. Arnold had always been driven more by pride than patriotism; and in the days before his treason, money had emerged as his greatest concern. He had even been court-martialed for embezzling army funds. André was hanged, but Arnold escaped to General Clinton; thus the British lost a brave officer in return for a traitor, who brought no fortress with him. Arnold earned 6,000 guineas, an appointment as a British brigadier general, a unit of deserters called the American Legion, and an eternity of infamy.

With Arnold's defection complete, all eyes turned once more to the South. There, it seemed, nothing could stop Cornwallis from conquering North Carolina, invading Virginia, and combining with Clinton to overthrow the new republic. It looked as if the United States had been plunged into darkness once more.

12

GREENE'S WAR

By the autumn of 1780, General Charles Cornwallis had accomplished more than any other British commander in the war so far. He had conquered an entire state, South Carolina, and now he stood ready to take over its sister to the north. He had virtually destroyed a major American army under Horatio Gates, the hero of Saratoga, and now no enemy forces stood between his redcoats and Charlotte, North Carolina. And yet, his troubles were only beginning.

In describing Cornwallis's invasion of the Carolina backcountry, a string of cliches comes to mind: he knocked over a beehive, stirred up a hornets' nest, stepped in a colony of fire ants. Perhaps the most apt metaphor is one not found in nature: he set loose a pack of mountain lions. Of course, mountain lions are solitary creatures who hunt without assistance, staking out isolated territories of their own. But the description fits the men who now hunted Cornwallis and his Tory allies—for they, too, were remote, independent, and dangerous. And they gathered in an unprecedented pack to battle the British army.

These people were the borderers, the over-the-mountain men— usually misnamed the Scotch-Irish. Of the four main culture groups that settled colonial America, they were the last to arrive—hailing from Northern Ireland, Scotland, and the border counties of northern England. Starting in the early years of the 1700s, they had shipped themselves across the Atlantic in great numbers (especially in the last few decades before the Revolution), and they banded together as recent immigrants were apt to do. As Samuel Johnson wrote in 1773, "Whole neighborhoods formed parties for removal; so that departure from their native country is no longer exile. . . . They carry with them their language, their opinions, their popular songs, and hereditary merriment: they change nothing but the place of their abode."[94]

They came late to the colonies, when much of the best coastal land was already claimed. But they were accustomed to a hard life, and they knew ways of turning steep valley slopes into farms, so they quickly moved into the Appalachian backcountry—especially in the South. There, in the rugged hills and mountains beyond the rice and tobacco plantations of the plains, they carried on the distinctive way of life that set them apart. They were called crackers, rednecks, and hoosiers—but these were nicknames they had brought with them from north Britain.

That distinctive way of life posed serious problems for the British as they attempted to pacify the Carolinas. "The backsettlers, no less than other colonists in every part of British America," writes historian David Hackett Fischer, "brought with them a special way of thinking about power and freedom, and a strong attachment to their liberties. . . . In 1768, the people of Mecklenberg County, North Carolina, declared, 'We shall ever be more ready to support the government under which we can find the most liberty.' "[95] The remoteness of their valley homes, both in Britain and in America, only reinforced this fierce attachment to freedom.

Along with freedom came independence—and belligerence. A distinctive strain of violence ran through the backcountry, not just by accident but as a way of life. The borderers' system of justice, Fischer writes, "captured the two vital principles of backcountry order ways—the idea that order was a system of retributive violence and that each individual was the guardian of his own interests in that respect. Even sheriffs in the backcountry shared the same ideal of retributive violence, and often took the law into their own hands."[96]

This is not to say that the hill counties were the scene of unending bloodshed; but a willingness to resort to force defined both social behavior and the sense of self. Nor was it all individual violence: in the backcountry, these settlers from Ulster, Scotland, and northern England fought bitter wars against powerful Native American tribes.

[94]Quoted in David Hackett Fischer, *Albion's Seed: Four British Folkways in America* (New York: Oxford University Press, 1989), p. 605. Fischer's work is a monumental account of the British culture groups who created colonial America.

[95]Fischer, *Albion's Seed*, p. 777.

[96]*Ibid.*, p. 767.

They maintained their own militia companies, relying on the highly accurate rifle, the weapon of choice on the Appalachian frontier. As in the British Isles, they were held together by a strong sense of inherited community, of clan and kinship ties, and by the leadership of certain elite families; the wave of immigration included some substantial residents of north Britain, who quickly emerged as strong leaders in the isolated valleys of the New World.

As Cornwallis pushed into the back parts of South Carolina, he stirred those leaders to action. Over the mountains, in the remote parts of the Appalachians, men began to gather, carrying their rifles, their powder, their well-worn hatchets. They were determined to deal out personal justice to this invading army that threatened their property, their families, and their liberty.

The British officer assigned to flush out those riflemen was also a Scotsman, and a rifleman as well. He was Major Patrick Ferguson, a thirty-six-year-old man with both remarkable skills and a remarkable mind. He was renowned as the best marksman in the Royal Army—a master with the rifle. Of course, the rifle remained impractical on the European battlefield, due to its dangerously slow rate of reloading, so Ferguson began to search for a solution. The result was a revolutionary breech-loading weapon; it eliminated the need to ram cartridges down the muzzle, allowing Ferguson to squeeze off six rounds a minute. It had all the accuracy of a standard rifle, and it could be reloaded *faster* than a smoothbore musket. It was so advanced, in fact, that no one could see its potential. Only 200 were ever produced.

Ferguson might have been frustrated by the fate of his invention, but he never lost his enthusiasm for service as a British officer. As the campaign in the South developed, this energetic major took on the chore of organizing units out of the loyalist recruits who flocked to the king's flag in the low country. Arming them with standard-issue muskets and bayonets, he soon led them on a sweep of the frontier, searching for those rifle-carrying mountaineers, while Cornwallis took the main army toward Charlotte, North Carolina.

Once again, Lieutenant Colonel Banastre Tarleton's account offers first-person insight into those triumphant days following the British victory at Camden. With the main Continental army out of the way, the entire South seemed ripe for conquest. But Cornwallis soon began to realize that as soon as he destroyed one force, another sprang out of nowhere to take its place.

King's Mountain
by Banastre Tarleton

The immediate advance of the King's troops into North Carolina would undoubtedly, at this critical period, have been productive of various and important advantages. The appearance of the royal forces after such a brilliant success would have animated their friends, discouraged their enemies, and continued the confusion and dispersion of the American army. But, however useful and beneficial such an expedition might have proved, many material requisites and necessary arrangements were not in convenient state or sufficient forwardness to warrant the undertaking. The number of the sick in the hospital, the late addition of the wounded, the want of troops, and the deficiency of forces upon the frontier, operated with the present heat of the climate and the scarcity of provisions in North Carolina. . . .

In order to keep alive the British interest in North Carolina, Major [Patrick] Ferguson's corps of rangers, and about one thousand loyal militia, were advanced to the western borders, to hold communication with the inhabitants of Tryon County till the King's troops under Earl Cornwallis were in condition to advance. . . .

Before the middle of September, part of the forces being arrived, with a reinforcement from Charlestown [Charleston] consisting of the 7th Regiment and some recruits for the provincials, the intended movement into North Carolina was immediately undertaken. . . . On the 22nd, Earl Cornwallis directed the British Legion and light infantry to cross the Catawba at Blair's ford, in order to form the advanced guard, for the immediate possession of Charlotte town. . . .

Earl Cornwallis moved forwards as soon as the Legion under Major Hanger joined him. A party of the militia fired at the advanced dragoons and light infantry as they entered the town, and a more considerable body appeared drawn up near the court house. The conduct of the Americans created suspicion in the British. An ambuscade was apprehended by the light troops, who moved forwards for some time with great circumspection. A charge of light cavalry, under Major Hanger, dissipated this ill-grounded jealousy, and totally dispersed the militia. . . .

Charlotte town afforded some conveniences, blended with great disadvantages. . . . The aptness of its intermediate situation between Camden and Salisbury, and the quantity of its mills, did not counterbalance its defects. The town and environs abounded with inveterate enemies; the plantations in the neighborhood were small and uncultivated; the roads narrow, and crossed in every direction; and the whole face of the country covered with close and thick woods.

In addition to these disadvantages, no estimation could be made of the sentiments of half of the inhabitants of North Carolina, whilst the royal army remained at Charlotte town. It was evident, and it had been frequently mentioned to the King's officers, that the counties of Mecklenburg and Rohan were more hostile to England than any other in America. The vigilance and animosity of these surrounding districts checked the exertions of the well affected, and totally destroyed all communication between the King's troops and the loyalists in the other parts of the province. No British commander could obtain any information in that position, which would facilitate his designs, or guide his future conduct. . . .

The foraging parties were every day harrassed by the inhabitants, who did not remain at home to receive payment for the produce of their plantations, but generally fired from covert places to annoy the British detachments. Ineffectual attempts were made upon convoys coming from Camden, and the intermediate post at Blair's mill; but individuals with expresses were frequently murdered. . . .

It is here necessary to take a retrospective view of the western frontier of Georgia and South Carolina. A Colonel [Elijah] Clarke had assembled a corps of back woodsmen about the beginning of September, with which he marched to attack the British post at Augusta. . . . Although this expedition was baffled, the cloud which hung over was not dispersed. Many parties from the back settlements had taken the field to reinforce Clarke, and overwhelm some post or detachment on the frontier. The distance of the country from whence the mountaineers marched, together with the rapidity of their movements on horseback, equally prevented intelligence of their approach, or preparation for their reception.

The failure of Colonel Clarke before Augusta inspired Lieutenant-Colonel [John] Cruger with an idea of cutting off his retreat to the mountains. He gave notice of his design to Major Ferguson, then employed upon the frontier, who willingly concurred in the project. Cruger, after gaining some advantage, found the pursuit was carrying him too far from Ninety-Six, to which he judiciously returned. Ferguson, unfortunately, adhered to the plan of striking at Clarke, and thought the direction which he had taken towards Gilbert town perfectly consonant to his purpose.

The object Clarke aimed at was to form a communication with many detachments of his friends who were approaching; or, if the superiority or advanced situation of Ferguson prevented that intention, to join Colonel Sumter on the borders of South Carolina. Near the end of September, Major Ferguson had intelligence of Clarke's having joined Sumter, and that a swarm of backwoodsmen, by an unexpected and rapid approach to Gilbert town, now threatened his destruction. He dispatched information to Earl Cornwallis of the superior numbers to which he was opposed, and directly commenced his march to the Catawba. . . .

Colonels [William] Campbell, [Benjamin] Cleveland, [Isaac] Shelby, [John] Sevier, [James] Williams, Brandon, and [Edward] Lacey, being informed at Gilbert town of the retreat of Ferguson by the Cherokee road, towards King's Mountain, selected sixteen hundred chosen men on horseback for a vigorous pursuit. The rapid march of this corps soon rendered an action inevitable. Major Ferguson heard of the enemy's approach at King's Mountain; he occupied the most favourable position he could find, and waited the attack.

The action commenced at four o'clock in the afternoon, on the 7th of October, and was disputed with great bravery for near an hour, when the death of the gallant Ferguson threw his whole corps into total confusion. No effort was made after this event to resist the enemy's barbarity, or revenge the fall of their leader. By American accounts, one hundred and fifty officers and men of the provincials were wounded, and eight hundred were made prisoners. The mountaineers, it is reported, used every insult and indignity, after the action, toward the body of Major Ferguson, and exercised horrid cruelties on the prisoners that fell into their possession. . . .

On the 10th, Earl Cornwallis gave orders to Lieutenant-Colonel Tarleton to march with the light infantry, the British Legion, and a three-pounder to assist Major Ferguson, no certain intelligence having arrived of his defeat. It was rumored with great confidence by the Americans in the neighborhood of Charlotte town, and the probability of the circumstance gave weight to the report. . . .

Accordingly, Tarleton marched to Smith's ford, below the forks of the Catawba, where he received certain information of the melancholy fate of Major Ferguson. This mortifying intelligence was forwarded to Charlotte town, and the light troops crossed the river to give protection to the fugitives, and to attend the operations of the enemy.

The destruction of Ferguson and his corps marked the period and the extent of the first expedition into North Carolina. Added to the depression and fear it communicated to the loyalists upon the borders, and to the southward, the effect of such an important event was sensibly felt by Earl Cornwallis at Charlotte town. The weakness of his army, the extent and poverty of North Carolina, the want of knowledge of his enemy's designs, and the total ruin of his militia, presented a gloomy prospect at the commencement of the campaign. A farther progress by the route which he had undertaken could not possibly remove, but would undoubtedly increase, his difficulties; he therefore formed a sudden determination to quit Charlotte town, and pass the Catawba river. . . . The King's troops left Charlotte town on the evening of the 14th. . . .

The success of the Americans at King's Mountain, and the distance of Earl Cornwallis's army, prompted many of the disaffected inhabitants of South Carolina to again violate their paroles, and to unite under a leader in the eastern part of the province. Mr. [Francis] Marion, by his zeal and abilities, shewed himself capable of the trust committed to his charge. He collected his adherents at the shortest notice in the neighborhood of the Black river, and, after making incursions into the friendly [loyalist] districts, or threatening the communications, to avoid pursuit he disbanded his followers. The alarms occasioned by these insurrections frequently retarded supplies on their way to the army; and a late report of Marion's strength delayed the junction of the recruits who had arrived from New York for the corps in the country. . . .

Directions were given to Lieutenant-Colonel Tarleton to pass the Wateree to awe the insurgents. . . . Whilst the British Legion and the light infantry were employed in watching the security of Camden and afterwards engaged in the expedition against General Marion, Earl Cornwallis received intelligence of the approach of General Sumter [from the west]. In a few days the information became particular, in respect to the number of Americans and their position. These necessary points being ascertained, the noble Earl communicated his design of striking at General Sumter to Major Wemyss, of the 63rd Foot. . . .

This body of mounted infantry, with an officer and forty men, who were left at the headquarters from the Legion cavalry, composed strength sufficient for the expedition, and the execution of it was committed to Major Wemyss.

On the 8th, being furnished with guides, he left the army in the evening, and moved towards Fish Dam, the camp of General Sumter. The rapidity of the march, or the shortness of the distance, brought him to the American post sooner than he expected. A delay till daybreak, which was the time intended for the attack, he thought would discover [reveal] his design, and afford the enemy an opportunity to decamp. Actuated by these considerations, he determine to attempt General Sumter's detachments without loss of time, and before any discovery had been made by the patrols.

At one o'clock in the morning, Major Wemyss, at the head of his corps, charged the picket, when, out of five shots which were fired, two took place in the arms and knee of the British commanding officer. This event rendered the surprise useless, and General Sumter owed, perhaps, his own and the safety of his people to the personal misfortune of Major Wemyss. The second in command, not being fully acquainted with the plan previous to the accident of his superior officer, was at a loss how to proceed; which state of uncertainty gave Sumter time to recover his people from confusion, and make a handsome retreat. The British had near twenty officers and men killed and wounded. . . .

About this time, the American force in North Carolina assumed a tolerable appearance. General Gates had advanced from Hillsboro in the middle of November to reinforce the detachments on the Yadkin; and on the 25th, he again moved forwards with the Continentals and militia to Six-Mile run, where he was joined by Colonels White, [William] Washington, and Armand, with two hundred cavalry and two pieces of cannon. . . .

In the beginning of December, General [Daniel] Morgan and Colonel [William] Washington, with some Continental light infantry and cavalry, advanced through the Waxhaws to Hanging Rock; from which place they detached a threatening summons to Colonel Rugeley, who commanded the [loyalist] militia of the Camden district, and was posted with one hundred men at his own house, where some defences had been erected. Rugeley, being intimidated by the summons and the appearance of the Americans, who placed the resemblance of a cannon opposite his house, surrendered to the light dragoons without firing a shot. The Continental infantry had not advanced within three miles of the post, when this irresolute commander laid down his arms.

General Morgan retreated with his prisoners to the main army, which about this time changed its leader; General Gates being recalled upon the appointment of Major General Greene to succeed him in the Southern department.

———

CORNWALLIS COULD SCARCELY accept the reports of Ferguson's destruction at King's Mountain. The major had been a highly capable, innovative officer—better qualified than anyone else to operate in the rugged hill country. And his Tory infantry units consisted of well-trained men, making up an important part of the British force in the Carolinas. The defeat was almost unbelievable. Even worse, it set South Carolina aflame, causing guerrilla activity to erupt across the state.

Though Cornwallis struggled to understand King's Mountain, it was in fact one of the few battles where American frontiersmanship overwhelmed the traditional, formal methods of the British army. The two key factors were terrain and weaponry. Ferguson's men occupied a mountaintop, seemingly a strong defensive position; when the fighting erupted, however, the Tories fired over the heads of the attacking patriots (a common occurrence when troops shoot downhill). In addition, the slopes were heavily wooded, which suited the attackers' preference for moving as individuals, dodging from tree to tree for cover. The forest, and this creeping assault, allowed the attackers to use their rifles to advantage. While Ferguson's men fired in volleys, the mountain men picked off the defenders one by one; when the loyalists counterattacked down the hill, the backsettlers scampered away, only to return to the offensive soon after. The heavy, accurate fire simply overwhelmed the British forces.

As the miserable Cornwallis retreated from North Carolina, he soon had more to deal with than Marion, Sumter, and the other guerrilla commanders. The main American army in the South was coming back to life. Its renewed energy came less from increased manpower than from the arrival of extremely capable officers: Brigadier General Daniel Morgan and General Nathanael Greene, the army's new commander.

In the previous selection, Tarleton revealed how Morgan reinvigorated the demoralized army, as he snatched up isolated British detachments. Greene, too, dramatically boosted the army's confidence. Like Morgan, he had proven himself in battle, playing a critical role in the New York, New Jersey, and Philadelphia campaigns; always cool-headed, he had skillfully protected Washington's retreat from the Brandywine and Germantown. Now he had a chance to show what he could do on his own (with the assistance, of course, of Morgan's considerable talents).

Greene's strategy and his impact on the army are best described in the account of Henry Lee—renowned as Light-Horse Harry, the future father of Confederate general Robert E. Lee. In 1780, however, he was a recent graduate of Princeton, not yet twenty-five years old. Despite his youth, Lee quickly emerged as an American counterpart to Banastre Tarleton; he even commanded his own Legion, which (like Tarleton's) combined well-trained infantry with well-mounted cavalry. This enterprising, often hot-headed young officer was already a veteran, experienced in the scouting, foraging, and independent operations that fell to light forces such as his. And, like

Tarleton, Lee wrote a thorough and fairly accurate memoir after the war (referring to himself in the third person throughout).

Lee was not actually present for many of the events outlined in the selection below; he was off to the southeast, cooperating with Francis Marion's partisans. Instead, it fell to General Morgan to lead the first confrontation between the reenergized American force and Cornwallis's army. But Lee's account is invaluable, because he was privy to the smallest details of Morgan's operations; Lee was close friends with the general, and he undoubtedly heard Morgan's personal story of his activities. And they were desperate activities indeed: Greene now embarked on an risky strategy in the face of a fine enemy commander with a well-trained army—a strategy that rested squarely on the shoulders of Daniel Morgan.

Cowpens
by Henry Lee

General Greene directed his whole attention to the high duties of his command. On reviewing his army, he found its total not more than two thousand, of which the major part was militia. Notwithstanding the exertions of his predecessor to establish magazines, he found three days' provision only on hand, and the country around him exhausted. His supply of ammunition was very scanty; and Virginia was the nearest point from which a replenishment could be obtained.

Such means and resources badly comported with the grand design of arresting the progress of the conqueror, and restoring the two lost states to the Union. Capable of doing much with little, Greene was not discouraged by this unfavorable prospect. His vivid plastic genius soon operated on the latent elements of martial capacity in his army, invigorated its weakness, turned its confusion to order, and its despondency into ardor. . . . He collected around his person able and respectable officers; and selected, for the several departments, those who were best qualified to fill them. His operations then commenced with a boldness of design well calculated to raise the drooping hopes of his country, and to excite the respect of his enemy.

This illustrious man had now reached his thirty-eighth year. In person he was rather corpulent, and above the common size. His complexion was fair and florid; his countenance serene and mild, indicating a goodness which seemed to shade and soften the fire and greatness of its expression. His health was delicate, but preserved by temperance and regularity.

The British army still remained at Winnsboro. General Greene determined to draw in the detachment under Smallwood, which was advanced some distance in his front, and to risk the division of his force by taking two positions on each flank of the British army. . . .

The return of Smallwood's detachment to camp was followed by the immediate departure of the army from Charlotte. The division intended for operations in the western quarter was composed of four hundred Continental infantry under Lieutenant Colonel [John] Howard, of the Maryland line, two companies of the Virginia militia under captains Triplett and Tate, and remnants of the First and Third regiments of dragoons, one hundred in number, under Lieutenant Colonel [William] Washington. It was placed under the care of Brigadier General Morgan, who was to be strengthened on his march by bodies of mountain militia from Carolina and Georgia.

He was ordered to pass the Catawba, and take post in the country between the Broad and Pacolet rivers. By this disposition, General Greene secured an abundance of wholesome provisions for his troops; afforded safe rendezvous for the militia in the East and West, on whose aid he necessarily relied; re-excited by his proximity the spirit of revolt, which preceding events had repressed; menaced the various posts of the enemy, and their intermediate communications; and compelled Lord Cornwallis to postpone his advance into North Carolina, until he should have cleared the country to the west of his enemy. During Brigadier Morgan's march, he received a part of the expected succor, amounting to nearly five hundred militia under General [Andrew] Pickens; and passing Broad river, he established himself near the point of its confluence with the Pacolet. . . .

Lord Cornwallis learned the disposition of the hostile army, and about the end of December became acquainted with the progress of

Morgan. Greene was seventy miles to his right, and Morgan fifty on his left. Lord Cornwallis began to apprehend a design on Ninety-Six; and determined to direct his first steps against Morgan, lest the junction of numerous bodies of mountain militia with that enterprising officer should enable him to destroy all communication with Augusta, and finally to carry that post, if not Ninety-Six.

The [British] Legion horse and foot, the light infantry attached to it, the Seventh Regiment and first battalion of the Seventy-First Regiment, with two field pieces, were put in motion under Lieutenant Colonel Tarleton. The first object was to protect Ninety-Six; and the next, to bring Morgan to battle, or repel him into North Carolina. . . .

Lieutenant Colonel Tarleton lost no time in approaching his enemy. Morgan was duly apprised of the advance, and of the movement of the British army. At the head of troops able and willing to fight, he was rather disposed to meet than to avoid his foe; and would probably have resolved on immediate action had he not felt the danger of delay in consequence of Cornwallis's advance up the Catawba. Nevertheless he indicated a desire to dispute the passage of the Pacolet, to which Tarleton was fast approaching; but he relinquished this plan, in consequence of the enemy's having passed the river on his left, and retired with a degree of precipitation which proved how judiciously the British commander had taken his first steps.

Tarleton passed through the ground on which Morgan had been encamped, a few hours after the latter had abandoned it; and, leaving his baggage under a guard with orders to follow with convenient expedition, he pressed forward throughout the night in pursuit of the retiring foe. After a severe march through rugged country, he came in sight of his enemy about eight o'clock in the morning (January 17, 1781); and having taken two of our videts [pickets or outlying sentries], he learned that Morgan had halted at the Cowpens, not far in front, and some distance from the Broad river. Presuming that Morgan would not risk an action unless driven to it, Tarleton determined, fatigued as his troops were, instantly to advance on his enemy, lest he might throw his corps safe over the Broad river.

Morgan, having been accustomed to fight and to conquer, did not relish the eager and interrupting pursuit of his adversary; and sat down at the Cowpens to give rest and refreshment to his harassed troops, with a resolution no longer to avoid action, should his enemy persist in pressing it. Being apprised at the dawn of day of Tarleton's advance, he instantly prepared for battle. This decision grew out of irritation of temper, which appears to have overruled the suggestions of his sound and discriminating judgment.

The ground about Cowpens was covered with open wood, admitting the operation of cavalry with facility, in which the enemy trebled Morgan. His flanks had no resting place, but were exposed to be readily turned; and the Broad river ran parallel to his rear, forbidding the hope of a safe retreat in the event of disaster. Had Morgan crossed this river, and approached the mountain, he would have gained a position disadvantageous to the cavalry, but convenient for riflemen; and would have secured a less dangerous retreat. But these cogent reasons, rendered more forcible by his inferiority in numbers, could not prevail. Confiding in his long-tried fortune, conscious of his personal superiority in soldiership, and relying on the skill and courage of his troops, he adhered to his resolution. Erroneous as was the decision to fight in this position when a better might easily have been gained, the disposition for battle was masterly.[97]

Two light parties of [rifle-armed] militia, under Major [Joseph] McDowell of North Carolina, and Major [John] Cunningham of Georgia, were advanced in front, with orders to feel the enemy as he approached; and, preserving a desultory, well-aimed fire as they fell back to the front line, to range with it and renew the conflict. The main body of the militia composed this line, with General [Andrew] Pickens at its head. At a suitable distance in the rear of the first line a second was stationed, composed of the Continental infantry and two companies of Virginia militia, under captains Triplett and Tate,[98] commanded by Lieutenant Colonel Howard. Washington's cavalry, reinforced with a company of mounted militia armed with sabres, was

[97]Morgan later said that he chose this dangerous battlefield because it would force his militiamen to fight; like other experienced commanders, he knew that militia were far more likely to break and run than professional infantry. With a river behind them, they had nowhere to go.

[98][Original author's footnote] These two companies of militia were general Continental soldiers who, having served the time of their enlistment, had returned home, regularly discharged.

held in reserve; convenient to support the infantry, and protect the horses of the rifle militia, which were tied agreeably to usage in the rear.

On the verge of battle, Morgan availed himself of the short and awful interim to exhort his troops. First addressing himself, with his characteristic pith, to the line of militia, he extolled the zeal and bravery so often displayed by them when unsupported with the bayonet or sword; and declared his confidence that they could not fail in maintaining their reputation, when supported by chosen bodies of horse and foot, and conducted by himself. Nor did he forget to glance at his unvarying fortune, and superior experience; or to mention how often, with his corps of riflemen, he had brought British troops equal to those before him to submission. He described the deep regret he had already experienced in being obliged, from prudential considerations, to retire before an enemy always in his power; exhorted the line to be firm and steady; to fire with good aim; and if they would pour in but two volleys at killing distance, he would take upon himself to secure victory.

To the Continentals, he was very brief. He reminded them of the confidence he had always reposed in their skill and courage; assured them that victory was certain if they acted well their part; and desired them not to be discouraged by the sudden retreat of the militia, *that* being part of his plan and orders. Then taking post with this line, he waited in stern silence for the enemy.

The British Lieutenant-Colonel, urging forward, was at length gratified with the certainty of battle; and being prone to presume on victory, he hurried the formation of his troops. The light and Legion infantry, with the Seventh Regiment, composed the line of battle, in the center of which was posted the artillery, consisting of two grasshoppers [light pieces mounted on legs, not wheels]; and a troop of dragoons was placed on each flank. The battalion of the Seventy-First Regiment, under Major [Archibald] McArthur, with the remainder of the cavalry, formed the reserve.

Tarleton placed himself with the line, having under him Major Newmarsh, who commanded the Seventh Regiment. The disposition was not completed, when he directed the line to advance, and the reserves to wait further orders. The American light parties quickly yielded, fell back, and arrayed with Pickens. The enemy, shouting, rushed forward upon the front line, which retained its station, and poured in a close fire; but [as the British were] continuing to advance with the bayonet on our militia, they retired and gained with haste the second line. Here, with part of the corps, Pickens took post on Howard's right, and the rest fled to their horses; probably with orders to remove them to a further distance.

Tarleton pushed forward, and was received by his adversary with unshakable firmness. The contest became obstinate; and each party, animated by the example of its leader, nobly contended for victory. Our line maintained itself so firmly, as to oblige the enemy to order up his reserve. The advance of McArthur reanimated the British line, which again moved forward; and, outstretching our front, endangered Howard's right. This officer instantly took measures to defend this flank by directing his right company to change its front [to face right]; but, mistaking this order, the company fell back; upon which the line began to retire, and General Morgan directed it to retreat to the cavalry. This maneuver being performed with precision, our flank became relieved, and the new position was assumed with promptitude.

Considering this retrograde movement the precursor of flight, the British line rushed on with impetuosity and disorder; but as it drew near, Howard faced about, and gave it a close and murderous fire. Stunned by this unexpected shock, the most advanced of the enemy recoiled in confusion. Howard seized this happy moment, and followed his advantage with the bayonet. This decisive step gave us the day. The reserve having been brought near the line, shared in the destruction of our fire, and presented no rallying point to the fugitives.

A part of the enemy's cavalry, having gained our rear, fell on that portion of the militia who had retired to their horses. Washington struck at them with his dragoons, and drove them before him. Thus, by simultaneous efforts, the infantry and cavalry of the enemy were routed. Morgan pressed home his success, and the pursuit became vigorous and general. The British cavalry, having taken no part in the action, except the two troops attached to the line, were in force to cover the retreat. This, however, was not done.

The zeal of Lieutenant Colonel Washington in pursuit having carried him far before his squadron, Tarleton turned upon him with the troop of the Seventh Regiment of dragoons, seconded by many of his officers. The American Lieutenant Colonel was first rescued from this critical contest by one of his sergeants, and afterwards by a fortune shot from his bugler's pistol.[99]

This check concluded resistance on the part of the British officer, who drew off with the remains of his cavalry, collected his stragglers, and hastened to Lord Cornwallis. The baggage guard, learning the issue of the battle, moved instantly toward the [main] British army. A part of the horse, who had shamefully avoided action, and refused to charge when Tarleton wheeled on the impetuous Washington, reached the camp of Cornwallis on Fisher's creek, about twenty-five miles from Cowpens, in the evening. The remainder arrived with Lieutenant Colonel Tarleton on the morning following.

In this decisive battle we lost about seventy men, of whom twelve only were killed. The British infantry, with the exception of the baggage guard, were nearly all killed or taken: one hundred, including ten officers, were killed; twenty-three officers and five hundred privates were taken. The artillery, eight hundred muskets, two standards, thirty-five baggage wagons, and one hundred dragoon horses, fell into our possession.

The victory of the Cowpens was to the South what that of Bennington had been to the North. General Morgan, whose former services had placed him high in public estimation, was now deservedly ranked among the most illustrious defenders of his country.

———————

THE AMERICAN VICTORY at Cowpens staggered General Cornwallis. Until news of the battle arrived, the situation had seemed ripe for a British victory, one that would make up for the terrible defeat at King's Mountain. First, Greene's army was smaller than Cornwallis's and it had a lower proportion of regular troops. Second, Greene

———

[99]It is believed that Washington and Tarleton personally engaged in a brief but intense sword fight on horseback during this chaotic pursuit of the fleeing British force.

had foolishly divided his inferior force, sending Morgan west while he marched east, offering the British a chance to devour the American army in two easy bites. Cornwallis had seized the opportunity by sending one of his best officers after Morgan. Then came word of Cowpens, and Greene's strategy no longer seemed so foolish after all.

The battle of Cowpens was not a large battle—a little over a thousand men fought on each side. But it had enormous consequences, in both military and political terms. Cornwallis's army was already stretched thin; and every day it was pulled tighter, with the defeat at King's Mountain and the constant guerrilla attacks that forced him to protect every post and supply train. So when Morgan annihilated Tarleton's detachment at Cowpens, he sliced off an irreplaceable chunk of the king's army in the South. Now Cornwallis would barely have the manpower to hold on to South Carolina, let alone conquer North Carolina and Virginia.

The moral effect of the battle, however might have been its most significant result. This was the first American victory in the South in a fight between the regular forces of the two sides—and it was a crushing victory indeed. Morgan's plan of action is still considered a tactical gem, one of the most masterly battles of the eighteenth century. His hard-earned experience, skill, and familiarity with the conduct of men in combat all came together, producing exhilaration among patriots and despair among the British and loyalists. And Americans believed the humiliation of Banastre Tarleton—whose name was now a synonym for brutality—was perhaps the greatest benefit of all.

Devastating as the defeat might have been, Cornwallis responded with courage and resilience. Without a moment's pause, he put his army on the road to catch Daniel Morgan. He miscalculated Morgan's movements, however, and spent a day headed in the wrong direction, giving his gritty opponent a chance to escape.

After Morgan slipped from his grasp, Cornwallis decided to take drastic action. In his eyes, it was pointless to march around South Carolina, chasing after guerrillas. The easiest way to pacify the country was to win a crushing victory over Greene's army, one that would demoralize the patriots in the South. So he stripped his army down to make it faster, ordering the burning of all nonessential equipment. Such a step would be drastic for any military force; but an eighteenth-century army marched with an enormous quantity of extraneous material. Officers' luxuries now joined the private soldiers' loot in the flames; even tents and other items normally considered absolute necessities were tossed in the bonfires. Perhaps no other measure better demonstrated Cornwallis's ruthlessness and determination. Marching in the dead of winter, he would catch and crush General Greene, or suffer the consequences.

In the American camp, Greene soon learned of Cornwallis's actions. At this point, he had a few options to choose from. He could stand and fight; he could slip away from the advancing British, but remain in the Carolinas; or he could retreat across the Dan River into Virginia. He seriously considered all three, but in the end he chose to retreat. Like Washington, he knew he had to preserve his army at all costs; in particular, he had to save his small corps of professional Continental infantry. He expected reinforcements, but they had not yet arrived, and Cornwallis's men still outnumbered Greene's.

But Greene also saw direct benefits in an escape over the Dan. With every step back, he came closer to his supplies and reinforcements. Cornwallis, on the other hand, moved farther away from his—and almost every mile traversed by his supply wagons was infested by patriot guerrillas. But the retreat was an extremely dangerous operation, one that required fierce, unrelenting effort and great skill in command.

One of the key American officers in the effort to foil Cornwallis on this desperate escape was Henry Lee—the famed Light-Horse Harry, leader of the Legion. Lee and his men covered the rear of the main American force, remaining almost within gunshot of the relentlessly advancing British all the way to the Dan. In the passage below, he recounts his exhausting race, and his independent operations in the days that followed. Whether fighting redcoats or loyalists, Lee never asked for mercy—and he rarely gave it.

The Race to the Dan
by Henry Lee

Lord Cornwallis received the unexpected, doleful tidings of Tarleton's defeat with serenity, but deep regret. He had been baffled in his first expedition into North Carolina by the fall of Ferguson; and this late disaster seemed to forbid perseverance in his second. With a view to retrieve, by the celerity of his movements, the severe loss he had sustained, he formed the wise resolution of converting his army into light troops by the destruction of his baggage.

Commanding this sacrifice without respect to persons, he set the example himself, by committing to flames the baggage of headquarters. With zeal and alacrity his faithful army obeyed the mandate. Everything was destroyed, save a small supply of clothing, and a sufficient number of wagons for the conveyance of hospital stores, of salt, of ammunition, and for the accommodation of the sick and wounded. . . .

This arrangement being finished, Lord Cornwallis moved from Fisher's creek, determined on unceasing efforts to destroy Morgan, and recover his lost troops; to keep separate the two divisions of Greene's army; and, should he fail in these attempts, to bring Greene to action before he could reach Virginia.

Morgan, always attentive to duty, took measures for retreat the moment victory had declared in his favor. In the evening of the same day he crossed the Broad river, and moved by forced marches to the Catawba, before Lord Cornwallis could reach its banks.

General Greene was quickly advised of the advance of the British army from Winnsboro and Camden through the upper country; and accordingly issued his preparatory orders for movement. On the subsequent day he received the gratifying intelligence of the victory at the Cowpens. Foreseeing the enemy's objects, he hastened his march in conformity with his previous disposition, and despatched a courier to Marion and Lee [the author himself], apprising them of his decampment and ordering the latter to rejoin with all possible celerity. . . .

Morgan redoubled his exertions to reach it [Greene's army]; but with all his activity, so keen and persevering had been Cornwallis's pursuit, that he had just crossed the river on the evening of the 29th of January, [1781,] when the British van appeared on the opposite banks. A heavy fall of rain, during the night, rendered the Catawba unfordable. . . . The waters continued high for two days, and gave the Brigadier time to place his prisoners in safety. . . .

Greene was neither less active, nor less diligent. Continuing on the direct road to Guilford court-house, he reached that place on the 7th of February. . . . The united force of Greene, including five hundred militia, exceeded two thousand three hundred; of which, two hundred and seventy were cavalry of the best quality. The army of Cornwallis was estimated at two thousand five hundred; but his cavalry, although more numerous than that of his adversary, was far inferior in regard to the size, condition, and activity of the horses. Taking into view his comparative weakness, General Greene determined to continue his retreat to Virginia.

The British general was twenty-five miles from Guilford court-house; equally near with Greene to Dix's Ferry on the Dan, and nearer to the upper shallows or points of that river which were supposed to be fordable, notwithstanding the late swell of water. Lieutenant Colonel [Edward] Carrington, quartermaster-general, suggested [to Greene] the propriety of passing Irwin's Ferry, seventy miles from Guilford court-house, and twenty below Dix's. Boyd's Ferry was four miles below Irwin's; and the boats might easily [be] brought down from Dix's to assist in transporting the army at these near and lower ferries. The plan of Lieutenant Colonel Carrington was adopted and that officer was charged with the requisite preparations.

The route of retreat being determined, the place of crossing designated, and measures taken for the collection of boats, General Greene formed a light corps, consisting of some of the best infantry under Lieutenant Colonel Howard of Washington's cavalry, the Legion of Lee, and a few militia riflemen, making in all seven hundred. These troops were to take post between the retreating and advancing army, to hover round the skirts of the latter, to seize every opportunity of striking in detail, and to retard the enemy by vigilance and judicious positions, while Greene with the main body hastened towards the Dan, the boundary of his present toils and dangers.

The command of the light corps was offered to Brigadier Morgan, whose fitness for such service was universally acknowledged, and whose splendid success had commanded the high confidence of the general and army. Morgan declined the arduous task; and being at that time afflicted, as he occasionally was, with rheumatism, intimated a resolution of retiring from the army. Greene listened with reluctance to the excuse, and endeavored to prevail on him to recede from his determination. Lieutenant Colonel Lee [the author], being in habits of intimacy with Morgan, was individually deputed to persuade him to obey the universal wish. . . . For a moment he paused; then discovered a faint inclination to go through the impending conflict; but finally returned to his original decision. His refusal of the proffered command was followed by a request to retire; which was granted.

Colonel Otho Williams of Maryland, an accomplished gentleman and experienced soldier, being called to the station . . . accepted it with cheerfulness and diffidence. This last arrangement being finished, Greene put his army in motion, leaving Williams on the ground.

The greater the distance between the main army and the light troops, the surer would be Greene's retreat. Williams, therefore, soon after breaking up from Guilford court-house on the 10th, inclined to the left, for the purpose of throwing himself in front of Lord Cornwallis.[100] This movement was judicious, and had an immediate effect. His Lordship, finding a corps of horse and foot close in front, whose strength and object were not immediately ascertainable, checked the rapidity of his march to give time for his long extended line to condense. . . .

The enemy persevering in his rapid advance, our rear guard (composed of the Legion of Lee) and the British van under Brigadier O'Hara, were in sight [of each other] during the day. Throughout the night, the corps of Williams held a respectful distance, to thwart, as far as was practicable, nocturnal assault. . . .

[100]Williams acted not merely to shield the rear of the main force, but to deceive the British as to Greene's movements. He skillfully misled Cornwallis, leading him away from the point where Greene was to cross the Dan.

Cornwallis, at length in Greene's rear, urged his march with re-doubled zeal, confident of overtaking his adversary before he could reach the Dan. Adverse efforts to accelerate and to retard were un-ceasingly exhibited during the evening; the enemy's van being some-times so close as to indicate a determination to force the light troops to prepare for defense. Avoiding a measure replete with peril, Wil-liams persevered in his desultory retreat.

More than once were the Legion of Lee and the van of O'Hara within musket shot; which presented so acceptable an invitation to the marksmen flanking the Legion, that they were restrained with difficulty from delivering their fire.. This disposition being effectually checked, the demeanour of the hostile troops became so pacific in appearance that a spectator would have been led to consider them members of the same army. Only when a defile or a water course crossed our route did the enemy exhibit any indication to cut off our rear; in which essays, being always disappointed, their useless efforts were gradually discontinued.

The fall of night excited pleasure, as it promised respite from toil. But illusory was the expectation! For the British general was so eager to fall on Greene, whom he believed within his grasp, that the pursuit was not intermitted. The night was dark, the roads deep, the weather cold, the air humid. Williams, throwing his horse in front, and the infantry of the Legion in the rear, continued his retreat. . . .

About noon Colonel Williams received a letter from General Greene, communicating the delightful tidings of his passage over the Dan on the preceding day. The whole corps became renovated in strength and agility; so powerful was the influence of the mind over the body. The great object of their long and faithful labors being so nearly accomplished, a general emulation pervaded all ranks to hasten to the boundary of their cares and perils. The hopes of the enemy were still high, and he rivalled our increased celerity; the van of O'Hara following close on the rear of Lee.

About three in the evening we arrived within fourteen miles of the river; and Colonel Williams, leaving the Legion of Lee to wait on the enemy, took the nearest course to Boyd's Ferry. Before sunset he gained the river, and was soon transported to the opposite shore. Lee, at the assigned period, directed his infantry to follow on the route of Williams; and about dark withdrew with his cavalry, the enemy being still in motion. Between the hours of eight and nine, the cavalry reached the river, just as the boats had returned from landing the Legion infantry. . . .

The horses were turned into the stream, while the dragoons, with their arms and equipments, embarked in the boats. Unluckily some of the horses turned back, and gaining the shore, fled into the woods; and for some time apprehensions were entertained that they might be lost. They were, however, recovered; and being forced into the river, followed those preceding them. In the last boat, the quartermaster-general, attended by Lieutenant Colonel Lee and the rear troops, reached the friendly shore.

In the evening Lord Cornwallis had received the unwelcome news of Greene's safe passage over the Dan, and now relinquished his expectation of annihilating a second army. . . .

No operation during the war attracted the public attention more than did this: not only the toils and dangers encountered by a brave general and his brave army interested the sympathy of the nation, but the safety of the South, hanging in on its issue, excited universal concern. The danger of this contingency alarmed the hearts of all, especially the more reflecting, who deemed the integrity of the Union essential to American liberty and happiness, and indispensable for our future safety and strength.

Destroy the army of Greene, and the Carolinas with Georgia inevitably become members of the British Empire. Virginia, the bulwark of the South, would be converted first into a frontier, then into the theater of war. . . . Happily for these states, a soldier of consummate talents guided the destiny of the South. . . .

Cornwallis, baffled in every expectation, much as he deserved success (for certainly no man could have done more than he did), now turned his attention to produce solid advantage out of the eclat he had acquired in forcing Greene to abandon the state. Selecting Hillsboro as headquarters, one of the principal towns of North Carolina,[101]

---

[101][Original author's footnote] Newbern and Hillsboro were the alternate seats of royal government in North Carolina; as were Burlington and Perth Amboy in the province of New Jersey.

he, after one day's repose of his army, proceeded hither by easy marches. Here he erected the King's standard, and invited, by his proclamation, judiciously prepared and opportunely promulgated, all liege subjects to prove their fidelity by contributing their aid in restoring the blessings of peace and order to their convulsed country. . . .

In the camp of Greene, joy beamed in every face; and, as if every man was conscious of having done his duty, the subsequent days to the reunion of the army on the north of the Dan were spent in mutual [con]gratulations; with the rehearsal of the hopes and fears which agitated every breast during the retreat; interspersed with the many simple but interesting anecdotes with which every tongue was strung.

Meanwhile, the indefatigable Greene gave his mind and time to the hastening of his long-pressed and much-wanted reinforcements; devising within himself, in the same moment, plans to augment his forces through his personal weight, and the influence of those ready to co-operate with him. . . .

Availing himself of Greene's abandonment of North Carolina, of his undisturbed occupation of Hillsboro, and of his quiet possession of Wilmington on the Cape Fear river by a detachment from Charleston under the orders of a Major Craig, Lord Cornwallis began to realize the expectations he had so long and so sanguinely indulged. The royalists everywhere were preparing to rise, while the well-affected to the cause of America, despairing of protection, began to look for safety in submission.

Greene, persevering in his determination to risk his army again in North Carolina—to rouse the drooping spirits of his friends, and to check the audacity of his foes—the Legion of Lee, strengthened by two companies of the veterans of Maryland under Captain Oldham, with the corps of South Carolina militia under Brigadier Pickens, was ordered, in the morning of the 18th, to repass the Dan. . . . Pickens and Lee were commanded to gain the front of Cornwallis, to place themselves as close to him as safety would permit to interrupt his communication with the country, to repress the meditated rising of the loyalists, and, at all events, to intercept any party of them which might attempt to join the enemy.

These officers lost no time in advancing to the theater of operations; and having [been] in the course of the march provided [with] capable guides, sat down that evening in a covert position, short of the great road leading from the Haw river to Hillsboro, and detached exploring parties of cavalry on the roads towards Hillsboro and towards the Haw. . . .

[Lee then discovered the location of Tarleton's camp, the rendezvous for loyalist recruits in the area. In an attempt to trap Tarleton or the unsuspecting Tories, Lee decided to pass off his own Legion as a force of British soldiers on their way to Tarleton's camp as reinforcements.] The stratagem could not fail in imposing on the country people, however well acquainted they might be with the appearance of British troops, so far as respected the Legion, inasmuch as both cavalry and infantry were dressed in short green coats, with other distinctions exactly resembling the enemy's light corps.

Lee's van officer, preceding him a few hundred yards only, was met by two well-mounted young countrymen, who being accosted in the assumed character, promptly answered that they were rejoiced in meeting us, having been sent forward by Colonel [John] Pyle for the purpose of ascertaining Tarleton's camp, to whom the colonel was repairing with four hundred loyalists. These youths were immediately sent to Lieutenant Colonel Lee, but were preceded by a dragoon, with the information imparted. Immediately upon the arrival of the dragoon, Lee despatched his adjutant with the intelligence to Brigadier Pickens, requesting him to place his riflemen (easily distinguished by the green twigs in their hats, the customary emblem of our militia in the South) on the left flank, out of sight; which was readily to be done, as we were then in a thick wood; at the same time to assure him that Lee was determined, in conformity with the concerted plan, to make an attempt with the Legion, of turning the occurrence to advantage. . . .

This communication was scarcely finished, before the two dragoons rode up with the two countrymen, who were received with much apparent cordiality; Lee attentively listening with seeming satisfaction to their annunciation of the laudable spirit which had actuated Colonel Pyle and his associates, and which they asserted was rapidly spreading through the country. Finding them completely deceived (for they not only believed the troops they saw to be British,

but overlooking what had been told them, took them to be Tarleton's, addressing the commandant [Lee] as that officer); Lee sent one
of them back with the two dragoons to his van, thence to proceed
to Colonel Pyle with Lieutenant Colonel Tarleton's congratulations,
and his request that they would be so good as to draw out on the
margin of the road, so as to give convenient room for his much-
fatigued troops to pass without delay to their night position, while
the other was detained to accompany the supposed Tarleton. Orders
were at the same time despatched to the van officer to halt as soon
as he got in sight of the loyalists. . . .

The column of horse now became complete in union with the
van, and Colonel Pyle was in sight on the right of the road, drawn
up as suggested, with his left to the advancing column. This last
circumstance was fortunate, as Lieutenant Colonel Lee had concluded
to make known to the Colonel his real character as soon as he should
confront him, with a solemn assurance of his and his associates' perfect exemption from injury, with the choice of returning to their
homes, or of taking a more generous part by uniting with the defenders of their common country against the common foe. By Pyle's
lucky occupation of the right side of the road, it became necessary
for Lee to pass the whole line of the loyalists before he could reach
their colonel, and thus to place his column of horse in the most
eligible situation for any vicissitude.

They were mounted like our militia, fitted like them to move on
horseback and to fight dismounted. Their guns (rifles and fowling
pieces) were on their shoulders, the muzzles consequently in an opposite direction to the cavalry. In the event of discovery, they must
have changed the direction before they could fire—a motion not to
be performed, with a body of dragoons close in with their horses'
heads and their swords drawn.

The danger of this rare expedient was by no means so great as it
appears to be on first view.

Lee passed along the line at the head of the column with a smiling
countenance, dropping, occasionally, expressions complimentary to
the good looks and commendable conduct of his loyal friends. At
length he reached Colonel Pyle, when the customary civilities were
promptly interchanged. Grasping Pyle by the hand, Lee was in the

act of consummating his plan, when the enemy's left, discovering Pickens's militia, not sufficiently concealed, began to fire upon the rear of the cavalry commanded by Captain Eggleston. This officer instantly turned upon the foe, as did immediately after the whole column.

The conflict was quickly concluded, and bloody on one side only. Ninety of the royalists were killed, and most of the survivors wounded. Dispersing in every direction, not being pursued, they escaped. . . . Pyle, falling under many wounds, was left on the field as dying, and yet he survived. We lost not a man, and only one horse. . . .

General Greene . . . passed the Dan on the 23rd, strengthened in a small degree by the corps of militia under Stevens, and took a direction towards the headwaters of the Haw river. He was highly gratified by the success of his advanced troops, officially communicated to him after he had entered North Carolina; and was pleased to estimate the destruction of Pyle and his loyalists as more advantageous than would have been a victory over Lieutenant Colonel Tarleton.

Soon after Tarleton returned to Hillsboro, the British general quitted his position—moving with his whole force to the country from which Tarleton had just been chased, for the purpose of giving complete protection to his numerous friends inhabiting the district between the Haw and Deep rivers, whose danger in attempting to join him while so distantly situated had lately been fatally exemplified. As soon as this movement on the part of his Lordship was known to General Greene, he again resorted to his former expedient of placing a strong light corps between him and the enemy. . . .

The return of Greene to North Carolina, and the destruction of Colonel Pyle's loyalists, baffled the hopes so long entertained by the British general, and [which were] fast realizing after his possession of Hillsboro; where, in the course of one day, seven independent companies of loyalists were raised. . . .

Greene [on the other hand], penetrating Cornwallis's views [that is, his plans to recruit an army of loyalists], foresaw their certain success if he remained long out of the state, waiting for reinforcements himself. He discerned the probability that his enemy would acquire a greater proportionate strength: with the essential difference, that what we obtained would be mostly militia, a fluctuating force, whereas that gained by the enemy would stand to him throughout the contest.

To arrest the progress of this scheme, pursued with pertinacity by the British general, it was necessary to again risk himself, his army, and the South. He therefore passed the Dan as soon as it was in his power, depending on the resources of his fertile mind, and the tried skill and courage of his faithful, though inferior, army.

CORNWALLIS WAS GROWING irritated, frustrated, and tired. This combination of regular, guerrilla, and civil war strained his talents to the breaking point. Every victory he won seemed to do him little good; every battle or skirmish he lost seemed magnified beyond proportion among the people of the Carolinas. Wherever he went, resistance seemed to flare up, rather than die down. Even when he gathered his loyalist supporters into militia units, it only offered the patriots a chance to wipe them out.

Cornwallis was a confident, even arrogant man—but he harbored no illusions about Nathanael Greene. He recognized him as a worthy opponent, careful and cunning, able to take advantage of this peculiar kind of warfare in the South. Greene himself had described his force as a "fugitive army," exerting influence in the countryside rather than smashing into the British in climactic battles. The race to the Dan showed Greene's skills at their best: he lured Cornwallis hundreds of miles away from his base in Charleston, always keeping one step ahead as he fooled the British commander about where he would go next. When he escaped over the Dan into Virginia, and Cornwallis turned to gathering supporters around Hillsboro, he detached Light-Horse Harry Lee to break up the loyalist militia—which he did with great flair in the massacre known as Pyle's Defeat.

Lee's brutal destruction of Pyle's loyalist militia terrified the Tories in the South, virtually eliminating the flow of reinforcements to Cornwallis's army. However, the skirmish may have convinced Greene that there was more local support for the British than there actually was: part of the point of the retreat to the Dan was to pull

Cornwallis away from his base, so it was a matter of concern if the British could now collect supplies and men in North Carolina. Bolstered by his own reinforcements, eager to damp down the Tories, Greene crossed the Dan in the other direction, offering Cornwallis the chance for battle.

Cornwallis wanted nothing else. Since the glorious victory at Camden, the war in the South had been nothing but frustration for him. Thanks to King's Mountain, Cowpens, and Pyle's Defeat, he could put no more than 2,000 men in the field, after providing garrisons for forts and escorts for supply trains. He lacked the manpower to control the countryside, so he needed a big victory to swing the momentum of the war in his direction—and to terrorize the unfriendly population. Cornwallis's army was now outnumbered by Greene's, thanks to American reinforcements—but almost every man in the British force was a highly trained professional soldier, while most of the American troops were half-drilled militiamen. And his men had suffered severely, especially with the destruction of their baggage; they wanted a chance to strike back at their tormentors.

So when Greene reappeared in North Carolina, Cornwallis moved swiftly to meet him in battle. After some maneuvering, the two armies collided in the heavily wooded countryside around a tiny cluster of buildings called Guilford Court House. As Greene deployed his men, he borrowed some ideas from Daniel Morgan—offering a defense in depth, with militia in the first two lines and the Continentals in the third. But this terrain was a far cry from that of Cowpens: in the thick forest, the three lines could not directly support one another, nor could Greene see all that was happening on the battlefield. Instead, he had to trust to the bravery and initiative of his subordinates, and of the men themselves. As Lieutenant Colonel Henry Lee would later write, most were worthy of that trust—but some were not.

Guilford Court House
by Henry Lee

Crossing the Haw near its source, the American general established himself between Troublesome creek and Reedy fork. And changing his position every day, sometimes approaching Colonel Williams [who led the light corps], sometimes falling back upon the Troublesome, he held Cornwallis in perfect ignorance of his position, and stopped the possibility of a sudden interruption. Showing himself in so many quarters, he considerably augmented the fears of the loyalists. . . .

At the iron works on Troublesome creek, General Greene received the pleasing intelligence that his reinforcements and supplies were approaching; and hearing at the same time from Colonel Williams that Lord Cornwallis had retired from the contest of skill, determined to give repose to his troops and wait for his long expected succor. . . .

Our force was now estimated at four thousand five hundred, horse, foot, and artillery, of which, the Continental portion did not amount to quite one thousand six hundred.[102] To acquaint himself with the character of his late accession of troops, and to make ready the many requisite preparations for service, the general continued in his position at the iron works, having drawn in most of the light corps. The Legion of Lee, and the Virginia militia attached to it under the colonels Preston and Clarke, still hovered around the enemy under the direction of Lieutenant Colonel Lee.

The American dragoons, far superior in the ability of their horses, struck so close to the British camp as to render their intercourse with the country [their foraging] very difficult, and subjected the British general to many inconveniences, besides interrupting his acquirement of intelligence. . . . Feeling his privations daily, Lord Cornwallis, leaving his baggage train to follow, made a sudden movement late in the evening. . . .

Lieutenant Heard, of the Legion cavalry, was detached in the evening with a party of dragoons to place himself near the British

---

[102]Cornwallis's force numbered some 1,900, though it consisted of veteran, professional troops.

camp, and to report from time to time such occurrences as might happen. About two in the morning this officer communicated that a large body of horse were approaching the meeting house, which was not more than six miles from our headquarters. . . . The enemy continued, though slowly, to approach; and at length he [Heard] communicated that his various attempts to pass down the flank as directed had proved abortive, having been uniformly interrupted by patrols ranging far from the line of march; yet that he was persuaded that he heard the rumbling of wheels, which indicated a general movement.

This being made known to the general, Lee was directed to advance with his cavalry, to bear down these interruptions, and to ascertain the truth. . . . Lee being convinced, from the appearance of the guards, that Cornwallis was not far in the rear, drew off his infantry; and covering them from any attempt of the British horse, retired towards the American army. General Greene, being immediately advised of what had passed, prepared for battle; not doubting that the long-avoided, now wished-for, hour was at hand.

Guilford court-house, erected near the great state road, is situated on the brow of a declivity, which descends gradually with an undulating slope for about a half mile. It terminates in a small vale, intersected by a rivulet. On the right of the road is open ground with some few copses of wood, until you gain the last step of the descent, where you see thick glades of brushy wood reaching across the rivulet. On the left of the road from the court-house, a deep forest of lofty trees, which terminates nearly in a line with the termination of the field on the opposite side of the road. Below this forest is a small piece of open ground, which appeared to have been cultivated in corn the preceding summer. This small field was long but narrow, reaching close to the swamp bordering upon the rivulet.

In the road Captain [Anthony] Singleton was posted, in a line with the termination of the large field and the commencement of the small one, with two six-pounders within close shot of the rivulet, where the enemy, keeping the road, would pass.[103] Across the road

[103]In this and succeeding paragraphs, Lee details the American deployment. It can be summarized quickly: the third, or rear, line consisted of the Continental infantry, positioned on a ridge; the second line consisted of the Virginia militia, positioned in the heavy woods below the ridge; the first line had Lee's Legion and some

on his left, some few yards in his rear, the North Carolina militia were ranged under generals [John] Butler and [Pinketham] Eaton. At some distance behind this line, the Virginia militia, led by the generals [Edward] Stevens and [Robert] Lawson, were formed in a deep wood; the right flank of Stevens and the left flank of Lawson resting on the great road.

The Continental infantry, consisting of four regiments, were drawn up in the rear of the Virginia militia, in the field to the right of the road; the two regiments of Virginia, conducted by Colonel Green and Lieutenant Colonel Hawes, under the order of Brigadier [Isaac] Huger, composing the right; and the two of Maryland, led by Colonel [John] Gunby and Lieutenant Colonel Ford, under the orders of Colonel [Otho] Williams, composing the left. Of these, only the regiment of Gunby was veteran; the three others were composed of new soldiers, among whom were mingled a few who had served from the beginning of the war; but all the officers were experienced and approved.

Greene, well informed of his enemy's inferiority in number, knew he could present but one line, and had no reserve; considering it injudicious to weaken either of his lines by forming one. On the right, Lieutenant Colonel Washington with his cavalry, the old Delaware company under the brave Captain Kirkwood, and Colonel Lynch with a battalion of the Virginia militia, was posted with orders to hold safe that flank. For the same purpose, and with the same orders, Lieutenant Colonel Lee was stationed on the left flank with his Legion and the Virginia riflemen commanded by Colonel [Richard] Campbell.

In our rear line our small [artillery] park was placed, with the exception of two sixes under Captain Singleton—who was now with the front line, but directed to repair to the rear as soon as the enemy should enter into battle, and there take his assigned station.

As soon as the British van appeared Singleton opened a cannonade upon it—convincing Lord Cornwallis of his proximity to the American army. Lieutenant McLeod, commanding the royal artillery,

---

riflemen on the far left, the North Carolina militia in the center, and Washington's cavalry with some riflemen on the far right. The first line stood on the edge of the woods, facing two open fields. The first two lines straddled the road.

hastened up with two pieces, and, stationing himself in the road near the rivulet, returned our fire. Thus the action commenced: the British general in the meantime arranging his army in order of battle. Although he could form but one full line, he took the resolution of attacking an able general advantageously posted, with a force more than double, a portion whereof he knew to be excellent, supported by a cavalry of the first character. Yet such was his condition, that Lord Cornwallis was highly gratified with having it in his power, even on such terms, to appeal to the sword. The Seventy-First [Regiment], with the Regiment of Bose,[104] formed his right under the order of Major General [Alexander] Leslie; his left was composed of the Twenty-Third and Thirty-Third Regiments, led by Lieutenant Colonel [James] Webster.

The royal artillery, directed by Lieutenant MacLeod, and supported by the light infantry of the guards and Jaegers, moved along the road in the center. The first battalion of guards, under Lieutenant Colonel Norton, gave support to the right, while Brigadier [Charles] O'Hara, with the grenadiers and second battalion of guards, maintained the left. Lieutenant Colonel Tarleton, with the cavalry in column, formed the reserve on the road, in the rear of the artillery.

The moment the head of the British column passed the rivulet, the different corps, in quick step, deployed to the right and left, and soon were ranged in line of battle.

Leslie instantly advanced upon the North Carolina militia. These troops were most advantageously posted under cover of a rail fence, along the margin of the woods; and Campbell's riflemen and the Legion infantry connected in line with the North Carolina militia, turning with the fence as it approached the rivulet; [they] raked by their fire the right of the British wing, entirely uncovered—the Legion cavalry, in the woods, in a column pointing to the angular corner of the fence ready to support the militia on its right, or the infantry of the Legion to its left. The appearance in this quarter was so favorable that sanguine hopes were entertained by many of the officers, from the manifest advantage possessed, of breaking down the enemy's right before he approached the fence; and the troops exhibited great zeal and alacrity.

[104]The Regiment of Bose was a Hessian unit, composed of German mercenaries.

Lieutenant Colonel Webster took his part with his usual ability—moving upon the . . . militia. . . . When the enemy came within long shot, the American line, by order, began to fire. Undismayed, the British continued to advance, and having reached the proper distance, discharged their pieces and rent the air with their shouts. To our infinite distress and mortification, the North Carolina militia took to flight, a few only of Eaton's brigade excepted, who clung to the militia under Clarke; which, with the Legion, manfully maintained their ground.

Every effort was made by the generals Butler and Eaton, assisted by Colonel Davie, commissary general, with many of the officers of every grade, to stop this unaccountable panic; for not a man of the corps had been killed, or even wounded.[105] Lieutenant Colonel Lee joined in the attempt to rally the fugitives, threatening to fall upon them with his cavalry. All was vain—so thoroughly confounded were these unhappy men, that, throwing away arms, knapsacks, and even canteens, they rushed like a torrent headlong through the woods.

In the meantime the British right became so injured by the keen and advantageous contest still upheld by Clarke and the Legion, as to render it necessary for Leslie to order into line his support under Lieutenant Colonel Norton, a decided proof of the difficult condition to which he must have been reduced, had the North Carolina militia done their duty. The chasm in our order of battle produced by this base desertion, was extremely detrimental in its consequences; for being seized by Leslie, it threw the corps of Lee out of combination with the army, and also exposed it to destruction.

General Leslie,[106] turning the Regiment of Bose, with the battal-

---

[105]Lee apparently did not know that Greene, following Morgan's example at Cowpens, had told the North Carolina militia that they had to deliver just two volleys, then they could retreat. In addition, British witnesses claimed that there was considerable carnage from the exchange of fire not only among the attacking redcoats, but also among the American militia.

[106]To recapitulate the commanders on each side: *British*: Leslie, commanding the British right wing; Webster, commanding the British left wing; O'Hara, commanding some of the British Guards and Grenadiers. *American*: Lee and Campbell, commanding the far left of the American first line; Stevens and Lawson, commanding the Virginia militia of the second line; Washington, commanding the far right of the American first line, which fell back to support the second; Lynch, commanding riflemen under Washington.

ion of Guards, upon Lee, pressed forward himself with the Seventy-
First to cover the right of Webster—now keenly engaged with the
Virginia militia [of the second line]; and seized the most advantageous position, which he preserved throughout the battle. Noble was
the stand of the Virginia militia; Stevens and Lawson, with their faithful brigades, contending for victory against the best officer in the
British army, at the head of two regiments distinguished for intrepidity and discipline. So firm did they maintain the battle (secured on
their flank by the position taken by Washington, who, anxious to
contribute to the aid of his brave countrymen, introduced Lynch's
battalion of riflemen upon the flank of Webster, already fully engaged
in front) that Brigadier O'Hara, with grenadiers and second battalion
of the guards, were brought into the line in support of Webster.

As soon as this assistance was felt, Lieutenant Colonel Webster,
turning the Thirty-Third [Regiment] upon Lynch, relieved his flank
of all annoyance; and instantly O'Hara, advancing with the remainder
of the left wing with fixed bayonets, aided by the Seventy-First under
Leslie, compelled first Lawson's brigade and then Stevens's to abandon the contest. Unhappily the latter general received a ball through
his thigh, which accelerated not a little the retreat of his brigade. The
militia no longer presented even the show of resistance; nevertheless,
such had been the resolution with which the corps under Lee, sustaining itself on the left against the first battalion of Guards and the
Regiment of Bose, and so bravely did the Virginia militia support the
action on the right, that . . . every corps of the British army, excepting
the cavalry still in reserve, had been necessarily brought into battle,
and many of them had suffered severely. . . .

Persevering in his determination to die or to conquer, the British
general did not stop to concentrate his force, but pressed forward to
break our second line. The action, never intermitting on his right,
was still sternly maintained by Colonel Norton's battalion of Guards
and the Regiment of Bose with the [American] rifle militia and the
Legion infantry; so that this portion of the British force could not be
brought to bear upon the [American] third line, [now] supported by
Colonel Washington at the head of the horse, and Kirkwood's Delaware company [of Continental regulars]. General Greene was well
pleased with the present prospect, and flattering himself with a happy

conclusion, passed along the line, exhorting his troops to give the finishing blow.

Webster, hastening over the ground occupied by the Virginia militia, sought with zeal the Continental line, and presently approached its right wing. Here was posted the First Regiment of Maryland, commanded by Colonel Gunby, having under him Lieutenant Colonel Howard. The enemy rushed into close fire; but so firmly was he received by this body of veterans, supported by Hawes's regiment of Virginia and Kirkwood's company of Delawares ([Webster] being weakened in his contest with Stevens's brigade, and as yet unsupported, as the troops to his right not having advanced from inequality of ground or other impediments) that with equal rapidity he was compelled to recoil from the shock [of an American bayonet charge].

Recrossing a ravine in his rear, Webster occupied an advantageous height, waiting for the approach of the rest of the line. Very soon [British] Lieutenant Colonel [James] Stuart, with the first battalion of Guards, appeared in the open field, followed successively by the remaining corps, all anxious to unite in this last effort. Stuart, discovering Ford's regiment of Maryland on the left of the First Regiment, and a small copse of woods concealing Gunby, pushed forward upon Ford, who was strengthened by Captain Finley with two six-pounders. Colonel Williams, commanding the Maryland line, charmed with the late demeanor of the First Regiment, hastened towards the Second, expecting a similar display, and prepared to combine his whole force with all practicable celerity; when, unaccountably, the Second Regiment gave way, abandoning to the enemy the two field pieces.[107]

Gunby being left free by Webster's recession, wheeled to his left upon Stuart, who was pursuing the flying Second Regiment. Here the action was well fought; each corps manfully struggled for victory; when Lieutenant Colonel Washington, who had, upon the discomfiture of the Virginia militia, placed himself upon the flank of the Continentals, agreeably to the order of battle, pressed forward with his cavalry.

---

[107]The Second Regiment was composed of new recruits, whereas the other Continentals were veterans. The retreat of this unit created a hole in the American line, which the British charged into.

Stuart beginning to give ground, Washington fell upon him sword in hand, followed by Howard with fixed bayonets, now commanding the regiment in consequence of Gunby being dismounted. This combined operation was irresistible. Stuart fell by the sword of Captain Smith, of the First Regiment; the two field pieces were recovered; his battalion driven back with slaughter—its remains being saved by the British artillery, which, to stop the ardent pursuit of Washington and Howard, opened upon friends as well as foes; for Cornwallis, seeing the vigorous advance of these two officers, determined to arrest their progress, though every ball levelled at them must pass through the flying Guards. Checked by this cannonade, and discovering one regiment passing from the woods on the enemy's right, across the road, and another advancing in front, Howard, believing himself to be out of support, retired, followed by Washington.

To these two [British] regiments (which were the Seventy-First, which General Leslie had so judiciously conducted after the ignominious flight of the North Carolina militia, and the Twenty-Third, the right of Webster), Brigadier O'Hara, though grievously wounded, brought the remnant of the First Battalion of Guards, whom he in person rallied; and, with the grenadiers, filled up the interval between the left and right wing.

Webster, the moment Stuart appeared in the field, putting Ford to flight, recrossed the ravine and attacked Hawes's regiment of Virginia, supported by Kirkwood's company. The action was renewed in this quarter with vigor; the Seventy-First and Twenty-Third, connected in their center by the First Battalion and Grenadier Guards, having at the same time moved upon Howard.

Meanwhile, the long impending contest upon the enemy's right [involving Lee and Clarke] continued without intermission; each of the combatants getting gradually nearer to the flanks of their respective armies, to close with which was the desired object of both. At length Lieutenant Colonel Norton, with his battalion of Guards, believing the Regiment of Bose adequate to the contest, and close to the great road to which he had been constantly inclining, pressed forward to join the Seventy-First [in the main battle with the American third line]. Relieved from this portion of the enemy, Lieutenant Colonel Lee dispensed with his cavalry, heretofore held in the rear to cover retreat in case of disaster, ordering it to close with the left of the Continental line, and there to act until it should receive further orders.

Upon Bose the rifle and the Legion infantry now turned with increased animation and with confidence of success. Lieutenant Colonel Buisy, of the Regiment of Bose, continued to defend himself with obstinancy; but pressed as he was by superior force, he at length gave ground, and fell back into the rear of Norton. Still annoying him with the rifle corps under Clarke, Lee hastened with his infantry to rejoin his cavalry upon the flank of the Continentals, the point so long and vainly contended for. In this route he found the battalion of Guards under Norton in possession of the height first occupied by Lawson's brigade of Virginia militia. With this corps again the Legion infantry renewed action; and supported by the van company of the riflemen, its rear still waiting upon Lieutenant Colonel Buisy, drove it back upon the Regiment of Bose. Every obstacle now removed, Lee pressed foward, followed by Clarke, and joined his horse close by Guilford court-house.

Having seen the flight of the Second Regiment of Maryland, preceded by that of the North Carolina militia—the corps of Lee severed from the army . . . and in all probability not able to regain its station in the line—Greene, immutable in the resolution never to risk the annihilation of his force, and adverting to its scanty supply of ammunition, determined . . . to provide for retreat. Colonel Green, one of the bravest of brave soldiers, with his regiment of Virginia, was drawn off without having tasted of battle, and ordered to a given point in the rear for the security of this movement. Had General Greene known how severely his enemy was crippled, and that the corps under Lee had fought their way to his Continental line, he would certainly have continued the conflict; and in all probability would have made it a drawn day, if not have secured to himself the victory. Ignorant of these facts, and finding Webster returned to battle—O'Hara, with his rallied guards in line—and General Leslie, with the Seventy-First, connected with them on the right, and followed, as he well knew, by the remnant of his wing—he persevered in his resolution and directed a retreat, which was performed deliberately under the cover of Colonel Green. . . .

General Greene preferred leaving his artillery to risking the loss of lives in drawing them off by hand [the horses being dead]. Just after this had taken place, Lieutenant Colonel Lee joined his cavalry at the court-house; and unpursued, retired down the great Salisbury road, until a cross-road enabled him to pass over to the line of retreat. The Seventy-First and Twenty-Third Regiments, supported by the cavalry of Tarleton, followed our army with the show of falling upon it; but the British general soon recalled them, and General Greene, undisturbed, was left to pursue his retreat. He halted first three miles from the field of battle to collect stragglers and fugitives, and afterwards retired leisurely to his former position at the iron works. . . .

Thus the battle terminated. It was fought on the 15th of March, a day never to be forgotten in the Southern section of the United States. The atmosphere was calm and illumined with a cloudless sun; the season rather cold than cool; the body was braced, and the mind high toned by the state of the weather. Great was the stake, willing were the generals to put it to hazard, and their armies seemed to support with ardor the decision of their respective leaders.

The British general fought against two to one; but he had greatly the advantage in the quality of his soldiers. General Greene's veteran infantry being only the First Regiment of Maryland, the company of Delaware under Kirkwood (to whom none could be superior), and the Legion infantry; all together making on that day not more than five hundred rank and file. The Second Regiment of Maryland and the two regiments of Virginia were composed of raw troops; but their officers were veteran, and the soldier is soon made fit for battle by experienced commanders. . . . The North Carolina militia, as has been seen, abandoned us; and we had only the Virginia militia and the rifle corps under Colonel Campbell and Colonel Lynch to balance the enemy's superiority over our regular infantry. . . .

The slaughter was prodigious on the side of the enemy, making, in killed and wounded, nearly one third of his army. The official report states the loss to amount to five hundred and thirty-two men, of whom ninety-three were found dead on the field of battle [and another fifty died soon after, out of a total of 1,900 British troops]. Lieutenant Colonel Stuart of the Guards, and Lieutenant O'Hara of the Royal Artillery, brother to the general, with many other officers, were killed. The Brigadiers O'Hara and Howard, Lieutenant Colonels Webster and Tarleton, the Captains Stuart, Maynard, Goodryche, Maitland, Schulty, Peter, and Lord Dunglas, with several subalterns, were wounded; as were Captains Wilmonsky and Eichenbrodt, of the Regiment of Bose, with five subalterns.

Our loss was very disproportionate; only fourteen officers and three hundred and twelve, rank and file, of the Continental troops killed, wounded, and missing. . . .

General Greene, after reaching Troublesome creek, arrayed himself again for battle; so persuaded was he that the British general would follow up his blow, and so well satisfied with his own condition, though considerably reduced by the flight of the North Carolina militia, and by the voluntary and customary return of portions of that from Virginia. But the enemy was in no condition to advance. The name of victory was the sole enjoyment of the conqueror, the substance belonging to the vanquished. Truly did the eloquent Mr. Fox exclaim in the British House of Commons, "Another such victory would destroy the British army." . . .

Afflicting were the sensations of the British general when he looked into his own situation after the battle. Nearly a third of his force slaughtered; many of his best officers killed or wounded; and that victory for which he had so long toiled, and at length gained, bringing in its train not one solitary benefit. No body of loyalists crowding around his standards; no friendly convoys pouring in supplies; his wants pressing, and his resources distant. The night succeeding this day of blood was rainy, dark, and cold: the dead unburied, the wounded unsheltered, the groans of the dying, and the shrieks of the living, shed a deeper shade over the gloom of nature. The victorious troops, without tents and without food, participated in the sufferings which they could not relieve. . . . The retreat of the British general evinced, unequivocally, his crippled condition.

GUILFORD COURT HOUSE, writes one historian, "proved to be one of the bloodiest battles of the war, and most of the blood that was shed was British."[108] Cornwallis brought 1,900 men onto the field; at the end of the day, 532 were casualties—more than one quarter of his army. The Americans, on the other hand, suffered far less, both in terms of the percentage and absolute number of men killed, wounded, or captured. Out of 4,444 troops, Greene had 78 dead and 132 injured. He withdrew from the battlefield because of the great disorder of his men, as the shock of combat broke up formations and mingled units together—but it would be a mistake to say he was driven away.

Guilford Court House was called a British victory at the time, and in many books written since. The reason is simple: the Americans retreated, and Cornwallis held the battlefield. But this definition makes sense only in terms of the eighteenth-century preoccupation with honor; in every other way, it was a smashing American triumph. Greene's judicious tactics and the heroic determination of his troops chewed Cornwallis's army to pieces, leaving it a tattered rag. And what Cornwallis needed was a carpet, a powerful force to spread across the Carolinas.

Greene's conduct at Guilford Court House, however, has been criticized over the years. By choosing to fight in dense woods, he left his three lines relatively isolated, unable to support each other—nor could he personally control the battle, since he simply couldn't see where everyone was in the forest. In addition, he left himself no reserve; while Morgan at Cowpens had kept Washington's cavalry back, so it could strike the finishing blow, Greene had no such force in hand. As a result, when his third line was disordered by the heavy fighting with the Guards, he had no spare men to drive the British back while he reformed his troops for further battle.

But it is exceedingly easy to criticize after the result of a battle is known. General Greene faced grave difficulties as he tried to incorporate the militia—soldiers of very uneven quality—into an army based on the Continental regulars. And the woods gave a tremendous advantage to the Virginia militiamen of the second line; they were able to fight their part of the battle on their own terms, shooting from behind trees rather than in formal lines. The men of Lee's Le-

[108]W. J. Wood, p. 256.

gion conducted themselves valiantly, and the third line recovered quickly when the raw 2nd Regiment of Maryland broke and fled. It was a battle, after all, in keeping with Greene's campaign: not a fight to the death, not a contest of honor, but a gritty, realistic effort to wear the enemy down. In that, Greene succeeded brilliantly.

Cornwallis decided not to follow up his so-called victory; when Greene offered battle again, he declined. He had little choice: his army was a ruin, and another clash would probably destroy it completely. By now he was fed up with the Carolinas. With the bulk of the population in arms against him, with too few troops to fight even a conventional campaign, with an opponent who skillfully seized every advantage, Cornwallis literally could not win. So he decided to leave. He assigned Lord Rawdon to command the garrisons still in South Carolina, and he set off for Virginia, hoping that reinforcements and a change of venue might bring back the light to his once-shining fortunes.

Greene had won. He still had some hard fighting to do against the British forces left in South Carolina, but he was a fugitive no more. In a sense, his campaign was a triumph for George Washington's strategy: to preserve the main army, and wear down the enemy by smashing isolated detachments. Morgan's victory at Cowpens was a result of Greene's intelligent application of this thinking; and Guilford Court House, where he surrendered ineffable honor in favor of concrete attrition, brought the strategy to its zenith. And Greene grasped the importance of the guerrilla forces rampaging through South Carolina; by coordinating his activities with theirs, he had stretched Cornwallis's forces to the breaking point.

So Cornwallis marched north in a huff, and Greene happily let him go. The American general turned his attention to Lord Rawdon in South Carolina, and continued his brilliant campaign. By the end of September, Greene would reconquer all of the South, except for Savannah and Charleston. And except for the coast of Virginia, where Cornwallis was headed. But from now on, Cornwallis was George Washington's problem.

13
YORKTOWN

Who can measure the pressure of command? An eighteenth-century general had absolute responsibility for his army: it would not stir unless he required it; it did not eat unless he ordered it. A commander in that era often lacked an extensive staff to care for important details; and so his army would pollute itself, sicken, and starve unless he saw to its every need. When the army marched, he decided which roads it would take, and arranged for horses and wagons; when it camped, he selected the grounds; when near the enemy, he sent out the scouts and planned for battle. And when combat was joined, he made his personal presence felt in the fighting, as he watched the action, issued orders, and inspired the men by example. Even the simplest campaign required a commanding general with extraordinary energy, confidence, and endurance.

Charles Cornwallis was just such a general, a twenty-year veteran of training, campaigning, and combat. He had proved his personal bravery and professional skill time and again—but his greatest strength was his tough-minded resilience. At Guilford Court House, for instance, he ignored his recent losses and attacked an army twice the size of his own; when one of his regiments began to lose a hand-to-hand fight with the American line, he ordered his artillery to fire grapeshot into the struggling mass, killing friend and foe alike until the enemy pulled back.

But by April 1781, even Cornwallis began to succumb to the strain of command. He had crushed Gates at Camden and pacified South Carolina—only to find the state harder to control than ever. He had invaded North Carolina—only to have his loyalist recruits slaughtered at King's Mountain. He had seized a golden opportunity to crush Nathanael Greene, when the American general divided his little army in two—only to lose a major part of his own force at Cowpens. He had stripped his army bare and invaded North Carolina

294

a second time—only to see Greene escape across the Dan. He even drove the Americans off the field at Guilford Court House—only to be left with a shattered remnant of an army.

The campaign of 1780–1781 had been a nightmare—and Cornwallis's next action can be seen simply as an effort to wake up from it. Instead of retreating to South Carolina and starting over again (battling guerrillas and fencing with Greene), he just walked away. He sent a messenger to Lord Rawdon, telling him to take command of the forces still in the Carolinas, and then he led his battered little army north to Virginia. There he planned to join forces with one of his oldest friends, Major General William Phillips—a plan driven by Cornwallis's psychological state as much as his need for reinforcements. As historian Robert Middlekauff writes, "Phillips, a fat and comfortable man, might have steadied Cornwallis. And at this moment Cornwallis needed some ballast. He was tired from a long and depressing campaign, and he was looking for excuses for his abandonment of the Carolinas. He was also looking for direction."[109]

The unsteady earl should not be judged too harshly, for his task was nearly impossible. The size of his force was minuscule compared to the enormity of the terrain he had to control. He also faced one of the finest commanders in the American army: Greene lacked the refined tactical instincts of the veteran Cornwallis, but he was a master strategist—and his strategy more than made up for any shortcomings on the battlefield.

But Cornwallis's biggest problem was the nature of the American Revolution itself. As he discovered in the Carolinas, it differed sharply from anything the British army had encountered before: this was truly a people's war. Cornwallis, like all other royal officers, learned to fight in the formal wars between European states—and there wasn't a general in the king's service who knew how to battle a guerrilla insurrection, to stifle militia that rose up overnight, to defeat an army that had no fixed points to defend.

Psychologically wrecked, lacking the material or mental tools to break the resistance in the Carolinas, Cornwallis set out for Virginia, where his friend William Phillips awaited. But when he arrived in

[109]Middlekauff, p. 559.

Williamsburg on May 15, 1781, he discovered that Phillips had died
of a fever five days before. Cornwallis did gain more than 5,000
troops (bringing his army up to 7,000 men), but he would never get
that much-needed ballast that his old comrade might have provided.

The other thing Cornwallis needed was direction—and he got
precious little of it from his Commander in Chief, General Henry
Clinton. Clinton himself constantly struggled against the stress of
command; his solution was usually to do nothing. Since withdrawing
into New York, he had protected Newport against a combined
French-American attack, and dispatched 5,000 men to the West Indies to capture St. Lucia, but his efforts ended there. Like Lord
North's ministry in London, he felt torn by the conflicting priorities
of the war, now that France had joined in; but given a choice between
fighting in America and fighting in the West Indies, he did little of
either.

Clinton made up for his lack of initiative with an excess of irri-
tability. His relations with North's ministry were not good, and he
had long since alienated Cornwallis (an old comrade from the Seven
Years' War). Now he grew even more prickly when he learned that
the earl had walked away from his post in the Carolinas. His grum-
bling at Cornwallis's somewhat bizarre decision is understandable,
but Clinton offered no real plan of his own. Instead, he sent a succession of contradictory orders to his subordinate, infecting the weary
Cornwallis with his own confusion and uncertainty.

That exhaustion, that confusion and uncertainty, comes through
clearly in Cornwallis's own account of his decision to march to Virginia, and in Clinton's complaints about his aristocratic subordinate.
In the passages below, Cornwallis provides a rather pathetic chain of
reasoning for his departure from the region under his command.
Clinton, on the other hand, leaves the impression of an indecisive
commander, afraid to take responsibility for the officers nominally
under his supervision. These are the words of weary, petulant men,
willing to let the entire war collapse on points of personal pride. They
little realized that their pettiness would lead them into a monumental
trap.

March to Virginia
by Charles Cornwallis

It is foreign to the present purpose, and I shall therefore not endeavour to enumerate the many difficulties which I had to struggle with in my command of the Southern district, previous to the march into North Carolina in the beginning of the year 1781. This measure [the invasion of North Carolina] was thought expedient not only by me, but by the Commander in Chief [Clinton]. I was principally induced to decide in favor of its expediency from a clear conviction that the men and treasures of Britain would be lavished in vain upon the American war, without the most active exertions of the troops alloted for that service; and that while the enemy could draw their supplies from North Carolina and Virginia, the defence of the frontier of South Carolina, even against an inferior army, would be, from its extent, the nature of the climate, and the disposition of the inhabitants, utterly impracticable [while the Americans controlled North Carolina].

The many untoward circumstances which occurred during the four months succeeding the complete victory of Camden had entirely confirmed me in this opinion. Our hopes of success in offensive operations were not founded only upon the efforts of the corps under my immediate command, which did not much exceed three thousand men; but principally upon the most positive assurances given by apparently credible deputies and emissaries that, upon the appearance of a British army in North Carolina, a great body of the inhabitants were ready to join and co-operate with it, in endeavouring to restore his Majesty's Government.

The disaster of the 17th of January [the battle of Cowpens] cannot be imputed to any defect in my conduct, as the detachment was certainly superior to the force against which it was sent, and put under the command of an officer of experience and tried abilities [Tarleton]. This misfortune, however, did not appear irretrievable; and to have abandoned, without absolute necessity, the plan of the campaign would have been ruinous and disgraceful: ruinous, by engaging us in a defensive system, the impracticability of which I have already stated; and disgraceful, because the reasons for the undertaking still existed in their full strength, the public faith was pledged to our friends in North Carolina, and I believed my remaining force to be superior to that under the command of General Greene. . . .

The unexpected failure of our friends rendered the victory of Guilford of little value. I know that it has been asserted or insinuated that they were not sufficiently tried upon this occasion. But can any dispassionate person believe that I did not give every encouragement to people of all descriptions to join and assist us, when my own reputation, the safety of the army, and the interests of my country, were so deeply concerned in that junction and assistance? All inducements in my power were made use of without material effect; and every man in the army must have been convinced that the accounts of our emissaries had greatly exaggerated the number of those who professed friendship for us. . . .

This disappointment, and the wants and distresses of the army, compelled me to move to Cross creek; but meeting there with no material part of the promised assistance and supplies, I was obliged to continue my march to Wilmington, where hospitals and stores were ready for us. Of this move I sent information by several expresses to Lord Rawdon, but unfortunately they all failed.[110] My attention then was, as soon as I should have equipped my own corps, and received a part of the expected reinforcement from Ireland, to return to the upper country in hopes of giving some protection to South Carolina, and of preserving the health of the troops, until new measures could be concerted with the Commander in Chief.

The march of General Greene into South Carolina, and Lord Rawdon's danger, made my situation very critical. Having heard of the arrival of a packet [ship] from Europe, without any certain accounts of the sailing of the reinforcement, I thought it too hazardous to remain inactive; and, as it was impossible to receive in time any orders or opinions from Sir Henry Clinton to direct me, it became my duty to act from my own judgment and experience. I therefore, upon mature deliberation, decided to march into Virginia, as the safest and most effectual means of employing the small corps under my command, in contributing towards the general success of the war.

[110]That is, the messengers were killed by American partisans.

I came to this resolution principally for the following reasons: I could not remain at Wilmington, lest General Greene should succeed against Lord Rawdon, and, by returning to North Carolina, have it in his power to cut off every means of saving my small corps, except that disgraceful one of an embarkation, with the loss of the cavalry, and every horse in the army. From the shortness of Lord Rawdon's stock of provisions, and the great distance from Wilmington to Camden, it appeared impossible that any direct move of mine could afford him the least prospect of relief; in the attempt, in case of a misfortune to him, the safety of my own corps might have been endangered; or if he extricated himself, the force in South Carolina, when assembled, was, in my opinion, sufficient to secure what was valuable to us, and capable of defence in that province.[111]

I was likewise influenced by having just received an account from Charlestown [Charleston] of the arrival of a frigate with dispatches from the Commander in Chief, the substance of which . . . was that General Phillips had been detached to the Chesapeake, and put under my orders; which induced me to hope that solid operations might be adopted in that quarter. And I was most firmly persuaded that, until Virginia was reduced, we could not hold the more Southern provinces; and that, after its reduction, they would fall without much resistance, and be retained without much difficulty.

With these sentiments, I joined General Phillips's corps at Petersburg on the 20th of May, a few days after his death; but from his papers, and dispatches from the Commander in Chief directed to him, which I received at that place on the 24th of May, I found there were other projects in contemplation, which to me were entirely new. The Commander in Chief desired General Phillips to give his opinion concerning the scheme of operations in the upper Chesapeake, and the design upon Philadelphia. I thought it my duty, as I was then in his place, to offer mine: which was, that I could not see sufficient

[111]Cornwallis's defense of his abandonment of the Carolinas is both curious and contradictory. Previously he had always acted bravely and with great vigor, but here he admits, in essence, that he was scared—scared that he would be destroyed by Greene if he tried to save Rawdon in South Carolina (since Rawdon was likely to be annihilated before he could reach him). Then he claims that Rawdon could take care of himself. Overall, he reveals the distress and confusion he felt when he realized his so-called victory at Guilford had cost him control of North Carolina.

grounds for approving either of these schemes; nor indeed could I bring myself to think any other plan, but the attempt to reduce Virginia, at that time either expedient or important. But I informed Sir Henry Clinton that I should repair to Williamsburg about the time when I should probably receive his answer, in order to be in readiness to execute his commands; and that I should employ the intermediate space in destroying such of the enemy's stores and magazines as might be within my reach. . . .

Since Sir Henry Clinton had declared positively in his first and in several subsequent dispatches against the plan of reducing Virginia, no explicit alternative was left to me, between complying with the requisition (contained in his letters of the 11th and 15th of June) of such troops as I could spare from a healthy defensive station, or engaging in operations in the upper Chesapeake. . . . Accordingly, that I might comply with those orders of the 11th and 15th of June, I passed James river (my remaining force being insufficient to fortify and maintain a post on the Williamsburg neck) and embarked the troops required with all possible dispatch. And it will be seen by the correspondence, that the Commander in Chief's opinion of the indispensable necessity of an harbour for line-of-battle ships only appears in his letter of the 11th of July, after he had been acquainted [with the fact] that the troops intended for the expedition against Philadelphia would soon be ready to sail.

Hampton Road was recommended by that order [as the place to build a fortified naval base]; but, as it was, upon examination, found totally unfit for the purpose desired, every person can judge whether the order did not, in its spirit, become positive to occupy York [Yorktown] and Gloucester; the only harbour in the Chesapeake that I knew of then, or indeed that I have heard of since, in which line-of-battle ships can be received, and protected against a superior naval force; and, as the harbour was the indispensable object, I thought it unnecessary to enter into a description of the disadvantage of the ground against a land attack, since there remained no other choice.

A Naval Station
by Henry Clinton

The plan I had formed for the campaign of 1781 (upon the expectation of a reinforcement from Europe—from the West Indies—and from the Southward after operations should cease in that quarter—added to what I might be able to spare at the time from the small force under my immediate command at New York) was calculated to make a fair and solid effort in favour of our friends in a district[112] where I had some reason to believe they were numerous and hearty, and where I judged it might be made with little danger, even from a temporary naval superiority of the enemy.

This plan had been suggested to the Minister in the year 1780, and more particularly explained to him in 1781, notwithstanding which a preference was given to another, which seemed to be forced upon me by Lord Cornwallis's quitting the Carolinas, where I had left him in command, and marching into Virginia: a measure, I must say, determined upon without my approbation, and very contrary to my wishes and intentions. The Minister directed me to support Lord Cornwallis and [a] solid operation in Virginia; the danger of which, without a covering fleet, I had constantly represented to him. He repeatedly and positively promised me a covering fleet. . . .

Although I had every reason to disapprove of Earl Cornwallis's march into Virginia without consulting me (at the risk of engaging me in dangerous operations, for which I was not prepared), yet, as I supposed he acted with at least the approbation of the Minister, I left him as free as air when he arrived there, to plan and execute according to his discretion. . . .

And here, perhaps, it may be proper to give the reasons which induced me to recommend to Lord Cornwallis to secure a naval station for large ships, if one could be found that was capable of being fortified and maintained against a temporary superiority of the enemy at sea. . . . Although I ought not to have apprehended that the enemy could have had a superiority at sea, after the assurances I had received

[112][Original author's footnote] If reinforced as promised I intended to carry on operations on Delaware neck [at the head of Chesapeake Bay].

from the Minister, I yet always wished to guard against even a possibility of it. Finding, therefore, by Lord Cornwallis's letters, that on
his arrival in the Chesapeake, he had not a plan of his own to propose,
and that he did not incline to follow the one I had offered to his
consideration, I recommended the taking of a respectable defensive
station either at Williamsburg, or York [Yorktown] (the latter of
which his Lordship informed me in a letter, dated 26th of May, he
was inclined, from the reports which had been made to him, to think
well of as a naval station and place of arms) and left his Lordship at
liberty to keep all the troops he had in Virginia (amounting to about
seven thousand men).

His Lordship, misconceiving my intentions . . . and considering
my call for three thousand men as unconditional, tells me that he
could not with the remainder keep York and Gloucester; and that he
should repass James river and go to the station at Portsmouth. Which
resolution (I confess) surprised me, as he had a little before . . . represented that post as unhealthy, and requiring an army to defend it.
On receipt of his Lordship's letter, I immediately consulted the Admiral, who was of the opinion that a naval station for large ships was
absolutely necessary, and recommended Hampton Road. Therefore,
in my letter of the 11th of July, I directed his Lordship to examine
and fortify Old Point Comfort, which the Admiral and I thought
would cover that Road, and in which there had been a fort for that
purpose for fifty years. . . .

But his Lordship informing me in his letter of the 27th of July,
that it was the opinion of the captains of the navy, the engineers, and
himself, that any works erected on Old Point Comfort, "might be
easily destroyed by a fleet, and would not answer the purpose; and
that therefore, according to the spirit of my orders, should seize York
and Gloucester, as the only harbour in which he could hope to be
able to give effectual protection to line-of-battle ships." I supposed
his Lordship had entirely approved of these posts . . . and consequently I did not object to the choice he had made.

THE TWO GENERALS seemed to be in a competition to see who
could absolve himself of responsibility faster. Cornwallis had simply

given up his assigned task—to pacify the Carolinas—and yet he blamed Clinton for his troubles. He responded to Clinton's orders with passive-aggressive petulance, neglecting to tell him about the supposed weakness of Yorktown against a land attack. Clinton, on the other hand, refused to behave like a Commander in Chief, claiming that his own hands were tied by the ministry and Cornwallis's unexpected actions. The spat between the two generals had gone beyond quibbling to an active feud, turning British operations into an uncoordinated mess.

Before the bitter letters began to fly up and down the coast, it looked for a time as if Cornwallis had become his old self again. In late May and early June, he began to terrorize the Virginia countryside, sending his cavalry on hard-hitting raids into the interior. On June 4, Lieutenant Colonel Tarleton rode into Charlottesville, where the state government was meeting. Governor Thomas Jefferson scampered to safety with only ten minutes to spare, but Tarleton captured a thousand muskets, along with other invaluable supplies.

Cornwallis's opponent in this mobile warfare was Marie Joseph Paul Yves Roch Gilbert du Motier, the Marquis de Lafayette, at the head of 1,200 Continentals and 2,000 Virginia militiamen. The talented, idealistic young Frenchman had been fighting in America for almost four years; by now he knew better than to pit his small force against a larger army of professional soldiers. But when Washington sent him reinforcements under General Anthony Wayne, Lafayette decided to attack Cornwallis's rear guard on July 6. It was a trap: the British general was at his best in the battle, ambushing Wayne's force and inflicting heavy casualties. On July 20, Cornwallis received the orders to build a naval station, and his active operations drew to a close.

The war had changed a great deal over the previous six years. Washington was now an experienced commander—a veteran of more battles than many contemporary generals fought in their lifetimes. The American army still relied heavily on militia, but the Continentals now compared favorably with the best soldiers in the British army. And then there were the French. Lafayette had come to America as an individual volunteer, but he was followed by roughly 5,000 French troops. In July 1780, General Jean Baptiste Donatien de Vimeur,

Comte de Rochambeau, had arrived with these men—a small fraction
of France's army, but a formidable addition to Washington's slender
forces.

At first glance, Rochambeau might have seemed a poor choice
for service in the United States. He was a count, a veteran of the
wars in Europe, and seven years older than Washington; in addition,
he spoke no English. A typical Frenchman with these qualifications,
in this age of honor and aristocracy, might have condescended to the
American commander and his army. But the two generals quickly
learned to trust one another. Rochambeau, like Washington, was
forthright and diplomatic; perhaps most important, he readily agreed
to take orders from the tall Virginian.

The French had made their presence felt immediately, recapturing
Newport in Rhode Island, which they now used as a station of their
own. In May 1781, the Comte de Barras arrived to take command
of the small French fleet based there. As the summer wore on, Washington hoped to combine his regiments with the French army, co-
ordinate their activities with Barras, and attack Henry Clinton's
garrison in New York. Accordingly, the two forces united in the Hudson valley highlands above the city as Washington probed for weaknesses in the British defenses. Washington bolstered his numbers by
calling up the militia, creating a combined army of roughly 9,000
men—half of them French and half American. He knew about Cornwallis's move into Virginia, but he felt that the main theater was here
on the Hudson, against the enemy Commander in Chief.

As Washington and Rochambeau maneuvered around New York,
they little realized that the war would soon change drastically, thanks
to events on the far side of the Atlantic Ocean. In an unusual reversal
of naval roles, the French government embarked on an adventurous
policy at sea, while the British became increasingly timid. Specifically,
the French decided to send a fleet of twenty-four ships of the line,
under Admiral Comte de Grasse, to the West Indies; this squadron
arrived off the island of Martinique on April 28, 1781, decisively
shifting the balance of power in the western Atlantic.

De Grasse was a fit man for the mighty task of battling the British
at sea. Born in 1722, he first set sail at the age of sixteen, fighting in
numerous engagements between 1738 and 1763. He was familiar

with the details of manning and supplying ships of war, with the intricacies of masts and rigging, with the commands and maneuvers of a vessel sailing into combat. He had served on sloops, transports, and sleek frigates—the fast-sailing scouts of the fleet, each mounting thirty-two to forty-four cannon along its sides. He had risen to command a ship of the line (also called a line-of-battle ship): these two- or three-decked leviathans carried anywhere from sixty-four to one hundred twenty heavy guns each (though seventy-four was the standard count). In the battle of Ushant in 1778, he flew his flag on the *Robuste*, as a French squadron met the British in the English Channel, driving them off at the end of the day. In February 1781, he seemed the logical choice as Commander in Chief of France's Atlantic fleet.

He faced a formidable opponent in the West Indies: George Brydges Rodney, a sixty-two-year-old living legend of the Royal Navy. Ferocious, highly capable, and somewhat greedy, Rodney won glory in 1780 by breaking Spain's siege of Gibraltar. In a moonlit battle at Cape St. Vincent, he annihilated a Spanish squadron of nine ships. On May 8, 1781, Rodney joined forces with the ships under his second in command, Samuel Hood, and began a duel with de Grasse. The two fleets never quite managed to meet in battle (Rodney, short of money, became preoccupied with capturing prizes), but the French admiral succeeded in capturing Tobago on June 2.

On July 26, a frigate aptly named the *Concorde* sailed up to de Grasse's flagship as it floated at anchor off Cap Haitien. It carried a letter from General Rochambeau, requesting his assistance in operations against New York. De Grasse immediately decided to comply. He quickly penned a reply, telling Rochambeau and Washington that he would set sail with twenty-six ships of the line; he intended to make landfall at Cheseapeake Bay. And he would bring 3,000 troops with him—though the soldiers would have to go back to Haiti after October 15.

On August 14, de Grasse's letter arrived on George Washington's desk. The general, who could not speak French, had to have it translated; in all likelihood, he waited with rising impatience for the English version. When he finally read it, he could scarcely believe his good fortune. He held in his hands the key to winning the war.

One of Washington's great strengths was that he combined broad strategic insight with tactical courage and skill; he grasped the war as a whole just as well as he understood a skirmish or battle. And he had always known that Britain's most important advantage was its command of the sea. The enemy could strike where he wanted, as he did at Charleston two years earlier; and he could escape when threatened, as he did from Boston in 1776. The small fleet under de Barras helped, but it still could not match the British navy in American waters. De Grasse's impending arrival promised to change all that— and he was headed directly for Virginia, the very place where he could do the most good.

Washington immediately realized the approaching French fleet offered him a chance to trap Cornwallis and his 7,000 men—the largest British army then in the field.[113] But to do so, he would have to shift his entire army to Virginia; he would have to do it before Cornwallis or Clinton could react; and he would have to leave the states of New York, New Jersey, and Connecticut virtually unprotected. On top of that, he could not be sure that de Grasse would arrive in time, or stay long enough to prevent Cornwallis's escape by sea. The British fleet in the West Indies might well follow the French to North America, and drive de Grasse away.

Washington considered all this as he read de Grasse's letter; he knew the plan that now emerged in his mind was an enormous undertaking, and an enormous gamble. But the possibilities were too great to ignore. It was perhaps the only moment in the entire war when he would have control of the sea—and it would be a temporary and local control, giving him a narrow opportunity indeed. He could not let it pass by. He informed Rochambeau and dashed off a letter to Lafayette, begging him to keep Cornwallis trapped on the Yorktown peninsula for as long as possible.

The American commander and his staff immediately set to work on the immense volume of details surrounding the great movement south. The first order of business was deception: he had to fool Clinton—even his own men—into believing that he intended to attack New York from New Jersey. As Washington brought his army down

[113]Clinton had 12,000 troops in New York, but this force was more like a garrison than an active army.

from the highlands to the New Jersey plains, he ordered the repair of roads and bridges leading to New York; he had a large bakery built, as if to feed the army; rumors were leaked of an impending assault; he deployed a large part of the army for a three-column attack on the city. General Clinton was completely fooled—he hunkered down across the Hudson, preparing for the assault that would never come.

Washington's own men were fooled as well. One of them was Captain James Duncan, commander of a light infantry company under Colonel Alexander Hamilton; he kept a journal of the campaign, in which he recorded his own surprise at the sudden march south. Duncan's account leads a string of three selections below. The second comes from a letter written by Washington to Lafayette, who commanded the detachment hovering around Cornwallis in Virginia. Here Washington reveals his prodigious attention to detail, as he played the triple role of strategist, quartermaster, and diplomat. His skill in each category proved essential to his success. Unlike Clinton and Cornwallis, Washington never let the stress of command shake his presence of mind, his firm grasp of the necessities of his position.

But Washington's letter does reveal stress at something he could not control: the arrival of the two French fleets, under Barras and de Grasse. Barras's squadron included essential transports, needed to carry the army from Pennsylvania and Maryland to the lines outside Yorktown; it also carried the heavy artillery so necessary in a formal siege. But the admiral was blockaded in Newport by the British fleet under Admiral Thomas Graves. Even more important was de Grasse's much larger force, which (with twenty-six ships of the line) could cut off Cornwallis's escape route. Washington sent urgent dispatches by sea to the French naval commander, but he heard nothing back. If de Grasse did not arrive in the Chesapeake, the entire plan could prove a catastrophe.

A Secret Movement
by James Duncan

The army were never so universally deceived in regard to the operations of the campaign as at this time. New York was thought to be the object, and no maneuver [was] left untried to confirm this opinion, when all on a sudden, the army decamped from W. Plains, crossed the North [Hudson] river, and proceeded by a circuitous route to Springfield, in New Jersey, where, after a halt of a few days (in order the better to deceive the enemy), they took their route for Trenton, at which place the artillery stores with our regiment and some other troops embarked.

We were now no longer at a loss to know our place of destination. We arrived at Christiana bridge and from thence marched by land to the head of Elk, where the French troops with the rest of our army joined us in a very short time. Here we were delayed for 6 or 7 days, being busily employed in embarking ordnance stores of all kinds on board the vessels. In the meantime the French troops with some other corps of our army proceeded by land for Baltimore. The bay not being able to furnish a sufficient number of vessels, the Rhode Island regiment with ours was obliged to embark on board a number of flat-bottomed boats, which had been constructed at Albany and brought to this place. We set out on this arduous and very hazardous undertaking about September 15, and arrived at Williamsburg the 26th.

Plans for a Siege
by George Washington

HEADQUARTERS, PHILADELPHIA   SEPTR. 2ND, 1781

Nothing, my dear Marquis [Lafayette], could have afforded me greater satisfaction than the information, communicated in your two letters . . . of the measures you had taken, & of the arrangements you were making, in consequence of the intelligence I had given you.[114] Calculating upon the regular force under your immediate orders, the militia which has already been called for & may be expected in the field, the whole of the French army, and the American corps now marching with Major Gen. [Benjamin] Lincoln from the Northward, in addition to the land forces expected on board the Fleet, I flatter myself we shall not experience any considerable difficulties from the want of men to carry our most favorite project into execution.

The means for prosecuting a siege with rapidity, energy, & success, and of supplying the troops while they are engaged in that service (as they are more precarious) have been, and still continue to be, the great objects of my concern and attention. Heavy cannon, ordnance stores, & ammunition to a pretty large amount are now forwarding. General [Henry] Knox, in whose immediate province these arrangements are, who knows our whole resources, is making every exertion to furnish a competent supply, and will be on the spot to remedy every deficiency as far as the circumstances will possibly admit.

Having also, from the first moment, been extremely anxious respecting the *supplies* of the army (in which, I comprehend not only provisions of the bread & meat kind, &c., but also forage & means of transportation), I had written pressingly to the governors of Maryland & Virginia on that subject previous to the receipt of your favor of the 21st of August. I have since reiterated my entreaties, and enforced in the strongest terms I was capable of using, the requisitions for specific supplies made by Congress. . . . I hope & trust the efforts of these states . . . will be commonly great & proportionate to the magnitude of the object before us.

In order to introduce some kind of system & method in our supplies, to know with certainty what may be depended upon, and to put the business in the best possible train of execution, I shall send forward the heads of departments as soon as their presence can be dispensed with. I have spoken to the Surgeon General respecting hospital stores & medicines; all that can be done, will be done in that

[114]In response to Washington's orders, Lafayette had taken steps to prevent Cornwallis from escaping off the Yorktown peninsula, situated between the York and James rivers.

department. As to clothing, I am sorry to inform you, little is to be expected, except in the article of shoes, of which a full supply will be sent on. In my progress to the Southward, I shall take care, as far as practicable, to make all the arrangements necessary for the operation in view, and to impress the executives with an idea of the absolute necessity of furnishing their quotas of supplies regularly; as we have no other resources to rely upon for the support of the army, and especially as I am very apprehensive that a quantity of 1,500 barrels of salted provisions which I had ordered to be shipped under convoy of the Count de Barras, did not arrive in time for that purpose.

But my dear Marquis, I am distressed beyond expression to know what is become of the Count de Grasse, and for fear the English fleet, by occupying the Chesapeake (toward which my last accounts say they were steering) should frustrate all our flattering prospects in that quarter. I am also not a little solicitious for the Count de Barras, who was to have sailed from Rhode Island on the 23rd ult., & from whom I have neard nothing since that time. Of many contingencies we will hope for the most propitious events. Should the retreat of Lord Cornwallis by water be cut off by the arrival of either of the French fleets, I am persuaded you will do all in your power to prevent his escape by land.

The Fleet Arrives
by François-Joseph Paul de Grasse

AT CAPE HENRY   SEPT. 2, 1781

I received at the moment when I least expected it the letter which Your Excellency [Washington] has had the kindness to transmit to me. . . . I am as concerned as it is possible to be that I have not with me any other ships than my men-of-war, which are too large to be used for the transport of American and French troops from the river Elk to Chesapeake Bay, and four frigates only, which take the place of very small vessels, and are at this moment employed to guard the James river in order to prevent the retreat of Lord Cornwallis on the Carolina side. I have also a few ships blockading the mouth of the York river, and I am with the rest of my force at Cape Henry ready to engage the enemy's maritime forces, should they come to the relief of Lord Cornwallis, whom I regard as blockaded until the arrival of Your Excellency and of your army. The union of my three thousand men with the forces of the Marquis de Lafayette ought to take place at Jamestown the 5th of this month. My men are on the rivers in launches and canoes of the army and I expect their arrival tomorrow in the course of the day.

Lord Cornwallis is present at York where he is fortifying himself by land and sea. He is also holding the post of Gloucester on the other side of the river, and he has fortified the neck of the peninsula. He has the *Charon* of 44 cannons and several sloops of war, with the frigate the *Guadeloupe*, which ran to shelter the day of my arrival, pursued by men-of-war and frigates, which seized the *Loyalist*, a sloop of 22 cannons. I have in the river James the *Experiment*, of 44 cannons, the *Andromaque*, a frigate of 30, and three sloops of from 16 to 20 cannons, which I luckily seized the day previous to landing in this bay.

Your Excellency will perceive that with so few ships suitable for the different rivers that must be entered in order to attack the strong places of these regions, I am very poorly equipped for assisting [directly] in your plans. Happily, we have drawn up at that spot where I can be of use, but with no means for hastening the arrival of Your Excellency, and I am told it is impossible to find any in this immense river. . . . I shall devote my entire attention to the means of facilitating all the attacks you will judge proper to make on your arrival against the army of Lord Cornwallis. This is the only practical plan, since he is giving us the opportunity by the position he has taken in altogether abandoning Portsmouth on the river James. . . . The arrival of the squadron of M. de Barras, to whom I have written to come to join me, should be useful to us.

WASHINGTON NEED NOT have worried; the same day he wrote to Lafayette, expressing his fears about the French fleet, de Grasse was writing him the letter above from the waters off Yorktown. His

fleet had sailed into the Chesapeake on August 30, sealing off Cornwallis by sea; and the 3,000 soldiers he brought with him helped
blockade Cornwallis by land. Of course, the British general might still
have attempted a breakout by attacking Lafayette's smaller force, but
he felt bound by his orders to remain where he was; so he kept his
men at work, constructing a naval station for the powerful fleet he
expected any day.

Ironically, a part of that fleet had already arrived, only to depart
before de Grasse's appearance. The story of the naval operations in
those critical weeks was one of British error and misfortune, and
French valor and skill. Back in July, before de Grasse's departure from
the Caribbean, Admiral Rodney had sent two small ships to Admiral
Graves (the commander in American waters), warning that the French
might sail north. But American privateers[115] captured both of these
craft; meanwhile, Graves led his ships on a cruise to the waters off
Massachusetts—taking him away from the real theater of war.

Things grew steadily more complex—and more unlucky for the
English. Rodney fell ill and returned to Britain, taking three ships of
the line with him. His subordinate, Admiral Samuel Hood, sailed for
the Chesapeake on August 10 with fourteen ships of the line. He still
had no idea how many French ships were headed north; he felt that
de Grasse was taking perhaps half of his fleet, leaving the rest in West
Indian waters. Nor would Hood learn any more: the French captured
four British warships, all that came within scouting distance of their
fleet. Hood actually beat de Grasse to the Chesapeake, arriving there
on August 25; but seeing no sign of either the enemy or Admiral
Graves, he promptly left, sailing on to New York. Five days later, de
Grasse safely sailed in with twice as many ships as the British expected.

Washington's great plan—driven by opportunity, skill, and good
fortune—was coming together perfectly. In the first weeks of September, he had almost his entire army on its way to Virginia, where he
eventually collected some 16,000 troops against Cornwallis's 7,000.
The French fleet had arrived as promised, trapping the British by sea.

---

[115]Privateers were privately owned ships that carried government commissions,
allowing them to attack the enemy's vessels. Since the United States had only a few
warships, it relied heavily on privateers to inflict damage on Britain's merchant fleet.

All he needed was Barras's squadron from Newport, which included critical transports and the siege train of heavy artillery.

What were the British thinking as Washington's strategy unfolded? Once again, the words of the Commander in Chief open a window on the dark and jumbled attic that was Henry Clinton's mind in the autumn of 1781. In the passage that follows, Clinton reveals the critical factors that drove his planning—and his inertia. First, he and Admiral Graves had no idea that de Grasse was coming to North America with a powerful fleet, since every messenger craft had been captured by American privateers and French warships. As a result, he felt no need to stop Washington's march south, once he learned that there would be no attack on New York. The allied army, of course, was well on its way before Clinton learned of its destination; and his natural timidity made him fearful of a sortie against it. In addition, he distracted himself with plans against peripheral targets; he wanted to go anywhere, it seems, but where Washington was.

Finally, Clinton could not bring himself to believe that Cornwallis was in any real danger. If there was a single constant in British history, it was the superiority of the Royal Navy. Rarely in the annals of English warfare—and never in the American Revolution—had the British lost control of the sea. Certainly a distinguished general such as Cornwallis, at the head of 7,000 crack troops, could hold out until help arrived.

Naval Maneuvers
by Henry Clinton

The Minister directed me to support Lord Cornwallis and [a] solid operation in Virginia; the danger of which, without a covering fleet, I had constantly represented to him. He repeatedly and positively promised me a covering fleet; and when the Admiral [Samuel Hood] arrived with the naval reinforcements from the West Indies, he . . . convinced me that he had brought that covering fleet. Therefore, as Admiral Graves's squadron was acknowledged to be superior to that under Monsieur de Barras,[116] I could not but suppose that the arrival of Admiral Digby (hourly expected) would give us a most decisive naval superiority. . . .

Under these circumstances, and with these assurances, I never could have the most distant idea that Mr. Washington had the least hopes of a superior French fleet in the Chesapeake; and I consequently never could suppose that he would venture to go there. But if he should, I was satisfied . . . that I should be able to meet him there with every advantage on my side, by having the command of the waters of that bay—without which he could not possibly feed his army. . . .

I had not 12,000 effectives, and of these not above 9,300 fit for duty, regulars and provincials. But had I had twice that number, I do not know that, after leaving sufficient garrisons in the islands and posts . . . I could, as has been insinuated, have prevented the junction between Mons. Rochambeau and General Washington, which was made in the highlands, at least 50 miles from me; or that I could have made any direct move against their army when joined (consisting then of at least 11,000 men, exclusive of militia, assembled on either side of the Hudson) with any prospect of solid advantage from it. . . . [117] Nor could I, when informed of his march towards the Delaware, have passed an army in time to have made any impression upon him before he passed that river. But with my reduced force, any attempt of the sort would have been madness and folly in the extreme.

With what might possibly be spared from such a force, nothing could be attempted except against detachments of Mr. Washington's army, or (when reinforced in a small degree) against such of its distant magazines as might occasionally happen to be unguarded. Two of the latter offered, one against Philadelphia. . . . The other, much more

[116]Barras had only eight ships ships of the line in American waters. The British Admiral Digby was expected soon with additional ships for Graves's fleet.

[117]Clinton's entire narrative is extremely self-serving, but this comment surpasses the rest of the selection in that respect. If he had merely marched out against Washington, he would have slowed down (or perhaps stopped) the Franco-American army, merely by forcing it to halt and deploy for battle—no actual fighting would have been necessary. Washington carefully prepared his ruses to deceive Clinton to forestall just such an occurrence.

important, was against Rhode Island. I had discovered by intercepted letters from all the French admirals and generals, that Count Rochambeau's army had marched from Rhode Island to join Mr. Washington at White Plains; that their battering train and stores for siege were left at Providence under little more than a militia guard; and that their fleet remained in Rhode Island harbour with orders as soon as repaired, to retire to Boston for security. By private information, which I had at that time, I found also that the works at Rhode Island were in a great measure dismantled, and had only a few invalids and militia to guard them, and that they were both there and at Providence under great apprehensions of a visit from us.

From other motives as well as my own knowledge of these posts, I had the strongest reason to expect the fullest success to an attempt against them, and I therefore immediately proposed to Admiral Graves a joint expedition for that purpose; which he readily consented to. It was accordingly agreed between us, that it should be undertaken as soon as he could assemble his fleet, and a small reinforcement (hourly expected) should arrive from Europe. The reinforcement joined me on the 11th of August, and the Admiral (who had sailed on a cruise) having returned to the coast on the 16th, I immediately renewed my proposal.

The Admiral informed me in answer, that he was under the necessity of sending the *Robuste* to the yard to be refitted, and that he should take the opportunity while that was doing of shifting a mast or two in the *Prudente*; and when those repairs were accomplished, he would give me timely notice. The ships were not ready on the 28th; Sir Samuel Hood, however, arriving on that day, I immediately ordered the troops to be embarked; and going to the Admirals on Long Island, I proposed to them that the expedition should instantly take place; but receiving intelligence that evening that Monsieur de Barras had sailed on the 25th, it was of course stopped. Thus, to the Admirals' great mortification and my own, was lost an opportunity of making the most important attempt that had offered [in] the whole war.[118]

[118]Clinton's remark that an attack on Newport would be "the most important attempt that had offered [in] the whole war" is rather incredible; it would have accomplished little, in either military or political terms. It indicates clearly how muddled his strategy had become.

Early in September, to my great surprise (for I still considered our fleet superior), hearing that Mr. Washington was decidedly marching to the southward, I called a council of all the general officers, who unanimously concurred with me in [the] opinion that the only way to succour Earl Cornwallis was to go to him in the Chesapeake. . . .

His Lordship [Cornwallis], in his letter of the 22nd of August, [had been] pleased to say, "The engineer has finished his survey and examination of this place (York), and has proposed his plan for fortifying it; which appearing judicious, I have approved, and directed to be executed." And in the same letter, it was farther implied, that through the exertion of the troops, the works would probably be tolerably complete in about six weeks from that period. . . .

In short, I think his Lordship appears to have implied in all his letters (except that of the 17th of September, the day he heard from Lieutenant Conway of the navy, that Mons. de Grasse, by the junction of Monsieur de Barras, had thirty-five or thirty-six sail of the line) that he could hold out as long as his provisions lasted—which was, by his Lordship's own calculation, to the end of October at least.

From all these circumstances, I had flattered myself, that the works at York would have been tolerably complete by the 9th of October, the day Mr. Washington opened his batteries against them; and from the opinion given me by certain officers of rank, who had lately come from Lord Cornwallis at York, I was under no apprehensions for his Lordship before the latter end of that month, as I could not conceive that the enemy could possibly bring against him such a powerful battering train as would demolish his defences (such as I had reason to hope they would be) in so short a space of time as nine or ten days.

WHEN ADMIRAL HOOD arrived at New York, he later wrote, "I got in my boat and met Mr. Graves and Sir Henry Clinton on Long Island." His message to them was clear and emphatic: "You have no time to lose; every moment is precious. My arguments prevailed."

On September 1, Graves got his fleet out of New York Harbor, and the combined force of nineteen ships of the line set sail for Virginia.[119]

In the Chesapeake, the French frigate *Aigrette* sailed along the mouth of the bay, watching for Barras's ships. At eight in the morning on September 5, it sighted a fleet to the northeast—only it was the British navy. De Grasse and his men frantically prepared for battle: all nonessential material disappeared into storage or flew overboard; sailors walked along the decks, spreading sand to absorb blood; they strung nets to catch men, spars, and rigging that might fall from aloft; and they descended to the magazines to retrieve gunpowder and solid iron cannonballs—weighing twelve, twenty-four, even thirty-two pounds each. Many of the French sailors were still ashore, but de Grasse could not wait for them; with most of his ships undermanned, he sailed his fleet out to sea when the tide changed at noon.

As Graves sailed to Cape Henry with his fleet, he faced a distinct disadvantage in numbers. He had only nineteen ships of the line, ranging from sixty-four-gun vessels to mighty ninety-eight-gun monsters, while de Grasse had twenty-four warships, carrying 2,000 guns to Graves's 1,500. But he was bearing down fast on the French anchorage, while the enemy was slowly sailing out to sea, one by one. And the French van—the leading squadron—soon advanced far beyond the support of the main body of the fleet; it might take hours for the rest of the French ships to come up to aid it. With the wind at Graves's back, he had an opportunity to smash the larger enemy force in detail, by bringing his entire squadron against the five ships in the lead. If he had done so, he could have won a glorious victory, and freed Cornwallis's army.

But the English admiral did no such thing. He felt bound by the *Fighting Instructions*, the official manual of conduct for British naval officers. The central principle of the *Instructions* was that battle should be conducted in a line sailing parallel to the enemy line, to allow the full broadside of each ship in the fleet to fire in one great barrage. There was a certain logic to this idea, since a warship's cannons pointed almost exclusively to either side, and it was a handy rule of thumb for most commanders. But the *Instructions* were en-

[119]Quoted in W. J. Wood, p. 268.

forced rigidly in the Royal Navy, to the point of stifling improvisation; in 1744 and 1757, two admirals had been court-martialed—and one of them shot—for violating its strictures. Graves was not about to go against dogma to bunch up his fleet around the isolated French van.

So he waited until de Grasse straightened out his fleet. Then he ordered his ships to engage the enemy—only he bungled the orders, flying two different signal pennants from his flagship's mast at the same time, leaving most of the fleet in utter confusion. As a result, only the British van actually fought the enemy—Graves had inadvertently exposed his own force to destruction in detail.

The officer in command of the French van was Commodore Louis Antoine de Bougainville. He had once been an army officer; in fact, he had served in the French and Indian War, and he had suffered the humiliation of surrendering Canada to the British.[120] Since that time he had joined the navy, winning fame for circumnavigating the globe in the years 1766–1769. And now, as the leading British ships bore down on his division, he had a chance for revenge.

As the British ships approached, the French were able to rake them—to fire broadsides at the bows of the enemy vessels, when they could not respond with broadsides of their own. As the firing began, cannonballs smashed through the wooden hulls of Graves's ships, dismembering men and disabling cannons, causing lethal wooden splinters to fly through the air. When the British ships were raked, the French shot blasted down the length of the vessels, taking out men and guns along the way. But the French usually aimed at the enemy rigging, firing when their ships rolled upward on the ocean swells; this knocked down masts and sails, slowing or disabling the British ships.

Bougainville shouldered the bulk of the fighting; with skill and determination, he blasted the leading British ships to pieces. At one point he brought his flagship, the eighty-gun *Auguste*, alongside the British *Princessa*, until his men were firing their cannons from a dis-

---

[120]For Bougainville's own account of the last phase of the French and Indian War, see chapter 21 of *The Colonizers*, the previous volume in the *In Their Own Words* series.

tance of a few feet from the enemy. The English vessel was forced to flee; then Bougainville turned against the *Terrible*, knocking down its mainmast and splintering its hull. Other British and French ships battered away at one another, though none outdid Bougainville's own *Auguste*.

At half past six in the evening, Admiral Graves signaled his fleet to withdraw. The British had suffered 336 casualties; even worse, six of the nineteen ships of the line had been so badly damaged they could no longer fight. The French, on the other hand, had suffered a third fewer losses in men, and only four ships had to pull out of the line. Graves's timidity, Bougainville's heroism, and de Grasse's tactics of firing at the rigging had left the smaller British fleet largely crippled.

For four days the two columns of ships remained within sight of each other as they slowly sailed south; on the night of September 9, the French slipped away, returning to the Chesapeake. Graves took the opportunity to destroy the crippled *Terrible*; when he arrived at the Chesapeake himself, he discovered that Barras had arrived, giving de Grasse thirty-five ships against his own eighteen (five of which were almost helpless). The British admiral had been beaten; he sailed for New York, leaving Cornwallis trapped at Yorktown.

Historians have often called the battle of the Virginia Capes (as the affair of September 5 is known) a draw. They do so for two reasons. First, their heads have been filled with the smashing triumphs won by Admiral Horatio Nelson in later wars against the French—battles in which Nelson captured or destroyed dozens of ships at a time. In this clash, only one ship was lost, and it was scuttled a few days after the fighting. Second, naval historians tend to be British. They might well be uncomfortable with the fact that this was a French victory, in every sense of the word. De Grasse got the better of Graves in the fighting; more important, he accomplished his strategic objective—that of blockading Cornwallis. For once, the British had lost command of the sea.

Washington knew exactly how long that state of affairs would last: he had until October 15 or so to capture Cornwallis's army. After that, de Grasse was bound to return to Haiti with the 3,000 men he had brought with him. After some polite but urgent pleading, Washington won a promise of a few more days—a precious week or so to see the siege through to its completion. Even so, he had to push his attack with the utmost energy.

One of the men who served in that desperate operation was Captain James Duncan, the light infantry officer who was so surprised by the move away from New York to Virginia. In his journal, he recorded in remarkable detail the events of the siege. He reveals the gritty daily reality of the men who fought in the front lines, who dug the trenches, stood on watch, and formed the assault parties. From the first arrival of the main force outside Yorktown at the end of September until the final attack, Duncan's writing carries us inside the siege—a formal, highly technical operation, conducted according to scientific methods. The Americans had come a long way from the battle of Concord, when a swarm of militiamen descended on a column of British regulars; now their sophistication largely matched that of their French allies. Here, in the trenches around Yorktown, Washington's daring strategy reached its final climax.

Siege and Assaults
by James Duncan

I have said we arrived at Williamsburg the 26th [of September]; the 27th and 28th were detained at this place in making preparations for the siege, and on the 29th the allied army moved down toward York (distant from Williamsburg about 12 miles), and made a short halt about two miles distant from the enemy's outworks, when a few shots were fired from the French pieces at some of Tarleton's horses, who immediately dispersed.

In the evening we proceeded about half a mile farther and encamped for the night. In the course of the night three deserters came in with little or no intelligence that could be depended upon. On the morning of the 20th we had orders to approach the enemy's works. After marching a short distance we were ordered to load, and proceeded within half a mile of the enemy's works on the left.

One brigade of infantry was halted, while the First Brigade, commanded by General Muhlenburg, crossed a small morass and paraded in order of battle, marched a small distance in front; but [as] the enemy [was] not firing, they wheeled to the right and took their post in the line. A picket was now turned out (the better to favor reconnoitering parties), which advanced in front nearly halfway to the enemy, until they were obliged to retreat by the fire of a field piece from the enemy's works. (It was said his excellency, the commander-in-chief, was in front of this picket the whole time reconnoitering.)

The sentries were, however, continued at their posts and regularly relieved the whole day. One of the sentries was so unfortunate as to receive a wound on his foot from a cannon ball, which obliged the surgeons to make an immediate amputation of his leg. We sustained no other harm from their firing, although they frequently overshot us.

The remainder of the day was employed in reconnoitering the enemy; and toward evening the whole army encamped nearly on the ground they had before occupied. Before we proceeded it may be proper now to take some notice of the different corps and the arrangement of the army. The Marquis de Lafayette's division of L. [light] infantry, composed of Muhlenburg's and Hazen's brigades [to which the author belonged] on the right of the front line, and nearest the enemy; the Baron Steuben's division, composed of the Marylanders, Pennsylvanians, and Virginians on the left of the front line. The Jersey troops in the rear of the infantry, and the [New] York [troops] in rear of Steuben's division, with the park of artillery and sappers [engineers] and miners in the center, forming the second line; the militia forms the corps de reserve, and the French troops, commanded by Count Rochambeau, on the left of the whole.

We passed this night with little or no disturbance from the enemy, but guess our agreeable surprise when on the morning of the ensuing day (October 1) we found the enemy had evacuated all their front works, and retreated about half a mile. We knew no other way to account for this than that their works, being too extensive and weak, they were afraid of a storm [assault].

This morning, Colonel Scammel was unfortunately wounded and taken by the enemy, as he was too closely reconnoitering, and sent on parole to Williamsburg. No sooner was the enemy's works evac-

uated than they were taken possession of by our pickets, supported
by the whole army, who marched up for that purpose, and continued
on the lines a great part of the day, although the enemy at certain
times fired very briskly from their pieces. About 8 o'clock this morning the French grenadiers attacked and carried a small battery, with
the loss of four killed and six wounded.

Ten companies were ordered out early this morning for fatigue,
of which I had the honor to command one. Until 11 a.m. we were
employed in cutting and stripping branches for gabions [baskets to
be filled with dirt]. On being furnished with shovels, spades, pickaxes,
etc., we were ordered up to the lines, where we continued inactive
until about an hour before sunset. In the meantime, the engineers
were employed in reconnoitering the enemy's works, and fixing on
proper places to break the first ground. Let me here observe that the
enemy, by evacuating their works, had given us an amazing advantage, as the ground they left commanded the whole town. . . .

The engineers having fixed on and chained off the ground in two
different places to erect their works within point blank shot of the
enemy, the parties were called on. Five companies were ordered to
an eminence on the right and five to another on the left. It happened
to be my fate to be stationed on the left, a place the most dangerous
of the two, as it was nearest to the enemy, and more exposed to the
fire from the enemy's batteries.

We were now conducted to a small hollow near the ground. Five
men were ordered by the engineer to assist him in clearing away the
rubbish, staking out and drawing the lines of the work. This was in the
face of open day, and the men went with some reluctance; a little before this we had a shot from the enemy which increased their fears. At
dusk of evening we all marched up, and never did I see the men exert
themselves half so much or work with more eagerness. Indeed, it was
their interest, for they could expect nothing else but an incessant roar
of cannon the whole night. I must confess I too had my fears, but fortunately for us they did not fire a shot that whole night. I am at a loss
to account for it, for the moon shone bright, and by the help of their
night glasses, they must certainly have discovered us. We were relieved
about daybreak, and scarcely had we left the trenches when the enemy
began their fire on both works from three pieces.

OCTOBER 2—The works were so far finished in the course of the preceding night that the men worked in them this day with very little danger, although the enemy kept up an almost incessant fire from two pieces of artillery. A drummer, rather too curious in his observations, was this day killed with a cannon ball.

OCTOBER 3—Last night four men of our regiment, detached with the first brigade, were unfortunately killed (on covering party) by one ball; one of the men belonged to my own company (Smith), a loss I shall ever regret as he was, without exception, one of the finest men in the army.

A militia man this day, possessed of more bravery than prudence, stood constantly on the parapet and damned his soul if he would dodge for the buggers. He had escaped longer than could have been expected, and, growing foolhardy, brandished his spade at every ball that was fired, till, unfortunately, a ball came and put an end to his capers. This evening our brigade was ordered for an evening party, and in the course of the night, a deserter went to the enemy, informing them of our situation, in consequence of which they directed a few shots our way, but did no harm.

OCTOBER 4—This morning, on leaving the ground, the enemy were complacent enough to favor us with a shot, but did no execution. Fatigues were continued in the works as usual, and suffered little or no harm. This day's orders give us an account of Tarleton's defeat on the Gloucester side on the 3rd. He was attacked by Duke de Lauzun's legion and the militia grenadiers, commanded by Weedon. Tarleton lost 50 men, killed and wounded, and the officer who commanded his infantry killed, and himself badly wounded, with very little loss on our side.

OCTOBER 5—We had more firing from the enemy last night than any night since the commencement of the siege. . . .

OCTOBER 6—The parties did not go out, and nothing extraordinary happened this day.

OCTOBER 7—The regiments ordered for the extra duty were last night employed in drawing the line of circumvallation [to completely close off the British position]. This line extends to the river on each side of the town, and at all places nearly equally distant and better than 200 yards in front of the former works. The enemy discovered us, although the night was pretty favorable, but the chief of their fire was directed against the French. They were, no doubt, much astonished in the morning to find themselves so completely hemmed in on all sides, and trenches so deep that we could sustain little or no harm from their fire.

The trenches were this day to be enlivened with drums beating and colors flying, and this honor was conferred on our division of light infantry. And now I must confess, although I was fond of the honor, I had some fear, as I had no notion of a covered way, and more especially as I was posted in the center with the colors. We however did not lose a man in relieving, although the enemy fired much. The covered way was of infinite service. Immediately upon our arrival the colors were planted on the parapet with this motto: *Haec Manus inimica tyrannis.*[121]

Our next maneuver was rather extraordinary. We were ordered to mount the bank, front the enemy, and there by word of command go through all the ceremony of soldiery, ordering and grounding our arms; and although the enemy had been firing a little before, they did not now give us a single shot. I suppose their astonishment at our conduct must have prevented them, for I can assign no other reason. Colonel Hamilton gave these orders, and although I esteem him one of the first officers in the American army, must beg leave in this instance to think he wantonly exposed the lives of his men. Our orders were this night that if the enemy made a sortie and attempted to storm the trenches we were to give them one fire from the barquet, rush over the parapet, and meet them with the bayonet. . . .

OCTOBER 8—The fire this day was chiefly directed against the parties employed in erecting batteries. We were relieved about 12 o'clock and sustained no harm during our tour excepting two men badly wounded; but we had scarcely left the trenches when a man working on the parapet had his arm shot off. . . .

OCTOBER 9—Last night the troops in the trenches as well as the great part of this day, were busily employed in finishing the batteries, and about 4 o'clock this afternoon an American battery was opened, consisting of three 24-pounders, three 12's, and four 10-

[121]"This company is an enemy to tyranny." See Bobrick, p. 459.

inch mortars.[122] The enemy's fire was chiefly directed against this battery, and the others that were nearly finished.

OCTOBER 10—Last night the men were busily employed in finishing the batteries, and early this morning four more were opened against the enemy. . . . This afternoon our American bomb battery was opened of four 10-inch mortars. A flag came out with Secretary Nelson. He informs us our fire did great execution last night; that we had killed 11 or 12 of their officers, that his black servant was killed by his bedside, and that the first gun fired killed two commissaries as they were sitting at their wine.

OCTOBER 11—Last night commenced a very heavy cannonade and the enemy returned fire with no less spirit. Being apprehensive of a storm, they often fired in every direction. The largest of the enemy's vessels was set on fire by the bursting of a shell or red hot ball from some of our batteries, and communicated it to another, both of which were burnt down. They must have lost a considerable quantity of powder in the last, as there was an explosion which made a very heavy report.

The whole night was nothing but one continual roar of cannon, mixed with the bursting of shells and rumbling of houses torn to pieces. As soon as the day approached the enemy withdrew their pieces from their embrasures and retired under cover of their works, and now commenced a still more dreadful cannonade from all our batteries without scarcely any intermission for the whole day. We were relieved about noon this day, and went home very much fatigued.

OCTOBER 12—Last night we began the second parallel [trench] and extended it better than half round the enemy. This parallel is better than three hundred yards in front of the other, and close upon the enemy's right works. No sooner had the morning made its appearance and the enemy discovered our very near ap-

---

[122]The poundage indicates the weight of the ball fired by the cannon—the 24-pounder being exceptionally large, used in sieges, not on the battlefield. The mortar, too, was specifically for use in sieges: short-barreled, squat, largely immobile, it spat out a shell filled with explosives on a high arch. Before firing the shell, the gunners would light a fuse to cause detonation in the air above the enemy—a fine skill, and a highly dangerous operation (thanks to the risk of premature explosion). The howitzer was the lighter battlefield version of the mortar.

proach, than they commenced a very heavy fire from the batteries, and in the course of the day no little surprised us by opening five royals [big mortars], as we were in hopes they had no shells, by their not giving them on the first parallel.

OCTOBER 13—Last night we were employed in strengthening the line, and began a French battery and redoubt. We lost several men this night, as the enemy by practice were enabled to throw their shells with great certainty. About noon this day our division relieved the trenches, and about 2 o'clock advanced to the second parallel. . . .

OCTOBER 14—The enemy last night kept up a continual blaze from several pieces of cannon, of nine royals, and some howitzers. Early in the night the fire was chiefly directed against the French, who were just on our left, but about 10 o'clock our people [began] to erect a battery. They soon discovered us, and changed the direction of their fire. It happened to be our lot to lie in the trenches just in the rear of the battery, exposed to all their fire; and now were I to recount all the narrow escapes I made that night it would almost be incredible.

I cannot, however, but take notice of a remarkable and miraculous one indeed. About midnight the sentry called "A shell!" I jumped up immediately to watch the direction, but had no suspicion of its coming so near until it fell in the center of the trench, within less than two feet of me. I immediately flung myself on the banks among some arms, and although the explosion was very sudden and the trench as full of men as it could possibly contain, yet not a single man was killed, and only two of my own company slightly wounded. . . .

Our division was relieved about 12 o'clock, and on our march home two of our men were wounded by the bursting of a shell. About 5 o'clock this day we were again ordered for the trenches.

OCTOBER 15—I have just said we were ordered yesterday to the trenches. The French grenadiers were ordered out the same time and all for the purpose of storming two redoubts on the enemy's left. Our division arrived at the [rendezvous] a little before dark, where every man was ordered to disencumber himself of his pack. The evening was pretty dark and favored the attack. The column advanced, Colonel Guinot's regiment in front and ours in the rear.

We had not got far before we were discovered and now the enemy opened a fire of cannon, grapeshot, shell, and musketry upon us, but all to no effect. The column moved on undisturbed and took the redoubt by bayonet without firing a single gun. The enemy made an obstinate defense (but what cannot brave men do when determined?). We had 7 men killed and 20 wounded. Among the latter were Colonel Guinot, Major Barber, and Captain Oney. Fifteen men of the enemy were killed and wounded in the work, 20 were taken prisoners besides Major Campbell, who commanded, a captain, and one ensign. The chief [part] of the garrison made their escape during the storm by a covered way.

———

THE NIGHT ASSAULT succeeded brilliantly—as had everything else in this brilliant campaign. Duncan had gone in with a detachment under Colonel Alexander Hamilton; they had rushed through the abatis in front of the British redoubt, relying on their bayonets alone against the enemy inside. A short distance away, a French detachment carried out a similar attack, also capturing its objective, though at a higher cost in killed and wounded.

Cornwallis now realized that he had no hope. On October 16, he tried to ferry troops across the York River to his outpost at Gloucester, in order to break out—but a sudden storm halted this desperate effort. And de Grasse still lingered in the bay with his powerful fleet; Washington had convinced him to stay just a week or two longer than he had intended. On October 17, Cornwallis sent an officer through the lines with a flag of truce. The earl, he announced, wished to discuss terms of surrender.

Two officers had direct responsibility for the disaster now looming—and neither of them wanted to accept it. Since the beginning of the campaign, generals Henry Clinton and Charles Cornwallis had squabbled and squandered the summer away, refusing to make difficult decisions. Each blamed the other for tying his hands; and each shared in the misery of defeat, now fast approaching at Yorktown.

———

The Want of a Covering Fleet
by Henry Clinton

Lord Cornwallis was pleased to tell me that his letter of the 20th of October [concerning his surrender] was written under great agitation of mind and in a great hurry. No man could possibly feel for his Lordship, and his dreadful situation, more than I did. And I will venture to say, no man could be more anxious, or would have gone to greater lengths to succour him. Nor will this, I trust, be doubted, when it is recollected that the proposal first came from me for embarking six thousand men for that purpose on board an inferior fleet of twenty-seven sail of the line, including two fifties . . . and therefore putting the fate of the American war on the joint exertions of the fleet and army, to relieve that noble Lord and his gallant corps. I have to lament that these exertions could not have been made in time. . . . But, at the same time, that truth compels me to impute our misfortunes ultimately to the want of a covering fleet in the Chesapeake.

Defeat
by Charles Cornwallis

When the arrival of the French fleet, and the approach of General Washington, were known to Sir Henry Clinton, it will appear by the correspondence that his promises of relief in person were uniform, without giving me the slightest particle of discretionary power, different from holding the posts that I occupied. Every reader will therefore be competent to judge whether, under these circumstances, and as I could not but suppose that the Commander in Chief spoke from a perfect knowledge of his own resources and of the force of the enemy, it would have been justifiable in me either to abandon, by the evacuation of York, a considerable quantity of artillery, the ships of war, transports, provisions, stores, and hospitals, or, by venturing an action, without the most manifest advantage, to run the risk of precipitating the loss of them. . . .

Far less could I have ventured an action without the most evident advantage after the junction of General Washington [with Lafay-ette]—a decision which nothing could have justified but a certainty that I could not be relieved. In that case, I should have fought before I was hemmed in by the enemy's works, believing a victory, over a great disparity of numbers in the open field, to be possible, but a successful defence, without relief, in such a post, and against such an attack, to be impossible. . . .

[In the end,] the enemy's immense train of battering artillery had now nearly reduced our fresh earthen works to ruins. The attacks were conducted with so much caution, that we had no opportunity of making any material impression upon them. The batteries of the second parallel, which I knew in a few hours would compel us to surrender at discretion, were nearly completed; and I had then lost all hopes of relief.

ON THE EIGHTEENTH of October, officers from the two armies sat down to go over the terms of the British surrender. Washington did not negotiate over the fourteen articles; he issued them as an ultimatum. The next day, Cornwallis signed the agreement.

At two o'clock in the afternoon of October 19, 1781, the British troops marched to a field between the two lines, reportedly stepping to the tune "The World Turned Upside Down," played by their drummers and bandsmen. With the American troops on one side of them and the French on the other, they desposited their arms in a heap and gave themselves up as prisoners. Cornwallis remained in his headquarters; instead, he sent out Brigadier General Charles O'Hara to deliver the formal capitulation. O'Hara tried to surrender to Ro-chambeau, but the French general directed him to Washington, who pointed him in turn to his own subordinate, General Benjamin Lin-coln. The Americans captured 7,247 men, along with 840 sailors and 244 pieces of artillery.

The Yorktown campaign was the crowning glory of George Washington's military career. While his opponents squabbled with each other, lapsing into indecision and inertia, he had conceived a brilliant strategy, based on a rare opportunity for control of the sea. He had planned and executed a complex operation, secretly moving thousands of men and endless tons of supplies hundreds of miles, between two hostile armies. And he had carried out the siege itself with technical mastery, relentlessly pushing the attack. And with good reason: just five days after Cornwallis surrendered, Clinton finally arrived in the Chesapeake with twenty-seven warships and 7,000 troops.

As Benson Bobrick writes, the implications of the great victory were understood immediately almost everywhere. The morning after the news arrived in Philadelphia, Congress went together to church to give thanks. In Paris, King Louis XVI ordered a Te Deum to be sung in the cathedrals, and he called on the city's residents to put out lanterns in celebration. And in London, Lord North descended into a wild fit of despair. "Oh God! Oh God!" he cried. "It is over! It is all over!"[123]

---

[123]Quoted in Bobrick, p. 466.

14

TRIUMPH

It is the place of diplomats to defy reality—or at least to make it seem less real. If the parties to a negotiation simply agreed on the facts and wrote out treaties accordingly, there would be little need for diplomats at all. Victors in war, for example, would get their way; losers would accept defeat, and concede every point. But diplomats, like lawyers, try to shade and blur what seems to be clear; they downplay certain facts, emphasize others, and suggest the future may change the situation. A good diplomat can win back at the bargaining table much of what a bad general has lost on the battlefield. Or so British leaders hoped, in the wake of Yorktown.

The king, however, still wanted nothing less than victory. On November 28, 1781, George III scribbled his reaction to Cornwallis's defeat in a note to Lord North. "I have no doubt," he wrote, "when men are a little recovered of the shock felt by the bad news . . . that they will then find the necessity of carrying on the war, though the mode of it may require alteration."[124] After all, the British still held Savannah, Georgia; Charleston, South Carolina; and New York, New York. But even if George's forces had been driven out of America completely, he would not have receded. This inflexible king was now at his rigid worst; peace, he declared, would come after an American surrender, and not before.

But Britain had gone to war in the name of parliamentary supremacy, and it would now make peace because of that supremacy. The nation cried out for an end to hostilities; in March 1782, the House of Commons voted for a resolution declaring that all those who wished to use force to make the colonies submit were enemies of their country. Lord North understood that by repudiating the war, the Commons had repudiated him; on March 20, he resigned. North

[124]Quoted in Bobrick, p. 466.

was replaced by the staunch Whig Lord Rockingham—"heading a government," writes Robert Middlekauff, "that the king could hardly bring himself to acknowledge. Nor did the king like Rockingham— he could barely tolerate being in the same room with him—and insisted that Shelburne serve as an intermediary when the first minister had to be consulted. It was Rockingham's fate to rouse his monarch's disgust even as he saved him from disaster."[125]

William Petty Fitzmaurice, Earl of Shelburne, was the new secretary for the Southern Department; nominally he was responsible for the American colonies, a responsibility that was now largely an empty one. But not completely empty—in the spring of 1782, Shelburne helped start the first tentative negotiations for peace. In July, Rockingham died, and Shelburne emerged as first minister. Now the task of defying reality by diplomatic means fell squarely on his shoulders.

Congress was ready for Shelburne's overtures. On June 15, 1781, it had named a peace commission of five men: Thomas Jefferson, Henry Laurens, John Adams, John Jay, and Benjamin Franklin. Jefferson begged off in favor of overwhelming personal obligations. Henry Laurens was captured by a British warship while crossing the Atlantic; locked away in the Tower of London, he could play no part in the discussions. John Adams was already serving overseas, but before he could negotiate the peace, he had to secure a major loan from the Dutch. Jay and Franklin did not arrive in Paris, where the negotiations would be held, until June 23, 1782; Adams joined them at the end of October.

The American negotiators were not innocents at diplomacy; Adams had spent some time abroad, and Franklin could boast a number of years on the far side of the Atlantic. But the problems of securing a peace made the complications of the war itself seem simple. First, their nominal ally Spain behaved like a hostile party; before arriving in Paris, John Jay had languished in Madrid, waiting vainly for formal recognition as an American ambassador. The Spanish government was concerned with other matters—especially the recovery of Gibraltar and the island of Minorca from Britain; it also claimed vast amounts of land in North America, including Louisiana (ceded to it by France

[125]Middlekauff, p. 571.

in 1762) and a region east of the Mississippi called West Florida. It had not even recognized the United States as an independent country.

Next there was France—a real ally in the war, and a real problem in the peace negotiations. The foreign minister under Louis XVI, Charles Gravier de Vergennes, was a cunning, unscrupulous man, which meant he was well suited to handle France's foreign affairs. It also meant that the American negotiators could not, and did not, trust him. He had been the driving force behind France's entry into the war on the American side; but now that peace was at hand, he maneuvered to secure French interests at the expense of the United States.

John Adams in particular worried Vergennes; the Frenchman recognized his fierce independence and incorruptibility. So he turned to others who lacked those qualities, bribing John Sullivan, a Congressional delegate from New Hampshire. With the help of Sullivan and others, the French got Congress to vote for a letter of instructions to the American diplomats, telling them to follow the directions of the government in Paris.

Congress's instructions infuriated Adams, Franklin, and Jay; they knew very well that France's interests were not identical with America's. A key point in contention was the Grand Banks: Britain, France, and the United States all hungered for access to this rich fishery off the coast of Nova Scotia. The Americans wanted to secure a treaty that pushed the United States's borders all the way to the Mississippi, with the Great Lakes as the northern frontier; they also wanted free navigation of the Mississippi, to speed settlement of the interior. Vergennes feared that Britain and the United States would reach an agreement on these critical points before France itself was ready to end the war.

Vergennes still hoped for gains in the West Indies at Britain's expense. Fortunately for America, those hopes collapsed after the naval battle of the Saints, fought between admirals Rodney and de Grasse in the Caribbean on April 12, 1782. Rodney ignored the *Fighting Instructions*, broke through the French line of battle, and captured de Grasse's flagship; in the succeeding days, Admiral Hood captured six more ships of the line as he chased the retreating French fleet. Vergennes became more reasonable in the battle's aftermath—but not completely.

As Adams, Franklin, and Jay navigated the treacherous shoals of their allies' ambitions, they still had to face their real opponent, Britain. The British wanted peace, but they also wanted an advantageous agreement on the questions of the Grand Banks fishery, the northern and western borders of the United States, and control of the Mississippi. Most important, they wanted payment for all debts contracted before the start of the war, and they demanded compensation for American loyalists whose property had been destroyed or confiscated.

Congress refused to compensate the Tories. Indeed, it is difficult to grasp just how much the people who made the Revolution hated their royalist neighbors. The American Whigs or patriots saw the loyalists as traitors, as people who had aided the enemy—who *were* the enemy. In many states, they believed the Tories were actually responsible for the war itself. And Congress was largely incapable of making compensation. The real power of government rested in the state legislatures; Congress was still an ad hoc body with sharply limited powers and responsibilities.

As the American peace commissioners entered the negotiations, then, they stepped into the remorseless, byzantine world of European great-power politics. Friends and foe alike were looking to preserve their own interests at the expense of anyone who stood in the way—and they would stall, lie, and bribe as necessary. Fortunately, Shelburne had wisely dispatched Richard Oswald to Paris to conduct the negotiations for Britain. This seventy-seven-year-old Scot knew America quite well; he had lived there as a young man, and he had made his fortune in the transatlantic slave trade. Now, as a wealthy, elderly gentleman, he pursued peace at a steady, dispassionate pace, combining realism and sympathy for the American position. He even bailed Henry Laurens out of the Tower; the two were old business partners, and he may have known that Laurens was suffering from depression at the death of his son, an army officer, in August 1782 (Laurens did not, however, arrive in Paris in time to play much of a role in the negotiations with Oswald).

Perhaps the best account of these delicate discussions comes from the diary of John Adams. The passage below begins with Adams in the Netherlands, where he had just secured a loan for the United States of five million guilders (about £400,000); it follows his ride south to Paris, where he joined negotiations already under way. Interestingly, the ever-prickly Adams detected some tension between Franklin and Jay; he identified with Jay's earnestness, but he looked askance at Franklin's worldly realism in these affairs of state. And the lawyer from Braintree, Massachusetts, reveled in the respect now granted him in the great courts of Europe; indeed, he began to worry about being corrupted by the decadence and amorality of the Old World.

But such things worked themselves out rapidly; the three had other things on their minds. At first, Oswald had no formal commission to treat with Adams and his fellows—and they insisted on being recognized as representatives of the United States, which would imply a British acknowledgment of American independence. That problem would eventually be solved through vague diplomatic language, but the hard work of negotiation continued. Neither Adams, Franklin, nor Jay wished to bargain away in Paris what Washington and the American army had so brilliantly won at home.

Negotiations for the New Nation
by John Adams

SEPTEMBER 14, 1782. SATURDAY. THE HAGUE. Supped last night at Court, in the *maison du Bois*. M. Borcel told me he had been to Paris, which he quitted eight days ago. Mr. Franklin had been sick; it was at first reported that he had been struck with an apoplexy; then it was said he had a bilious colic, and afterwards a retention of urine, but that he had got well before he left Paris.

Fell into conversation naturally with Don Joas Theolomico de Almeida, Envoy extraordinary of Portugal. He said to me, "The peace is yet a good way off; there will be no peace this winter; there will be another campaign, and no peace until the winter following. Spain will be the most difficult to satisfy of all the powers. Her pretensions will be the hardest for England to agree to. As to the independence of America, that is decided."

I said to him, "It is reported that Portugal is about to open her ports to American vessels." "I have not yet received," says he, "any intelligence of that."

The Comte Montagnini de Mirabel, minister plenipotentiary of the King of Sardinia, asked what was the principle of the indecision of Great Britain. "Why don't they acknowledge your independence? They must have some intelligence that is not public." I answered, "I don't believe there is any principle or system in it. It is merely owing to their confusion. My Lord Shelburne, in compliance with the will of his master, refuses to do what all the world sees to be necessary."

"Perhaps," says the Comte, "they mean to annex certain conditions to the acknowledgment of your independence." "But," says I, "what if we should insist on an acknowledgment of our independence as a preliminary condition to entering into any treaty or conference?" "Ay," says he, "in that case you may have work enough." . . .

M. Borcel, the Baron de Lynden de Hemmen, and the President of the Grand Committee . . . told me that five copies of the treaties [concering the loan from the Netherlands] would be made out according to my desire, the English and Dutch side by side upon every page, and the treaty would be signed next week. . . .

OCTOBER 17. THURSDAY. Began my journey to Paris from the Hague; dined at Harlem, and drank tea at five o'clock at Amsterdam. . . .

OCTOBER 26. SATURDAY. We took a cutlet and a glass of wine, at ten, at Chantilly, that we might not be tempted to stop again; accordingly we arrived in very good season at the *Hotel de Valois, Rue de Richelieu*, where the house, however, was so full that we found but bad accommodations.

The first thing to be done in Paris is always to send for a tailor, peruke-maker, and shoemaker, for this nation has established such a domination over the fashion, that neither clothes, wigs, nor shoes made in any other place will do in Paris. This is one of the ways in which France taxes all of Europe, and will tax America. It is a great branch of the policy of the Court to preserve and increase this national influence over the *mode*, because it occasions an immense commerce between France and all the other parts of Europe. Paris furnishes the materials and the manner, both to men and women, everywhere else.

Mr. Ridley lodges in the *Rue de Cléry*, No. 60. Mr. Jay, *Rue des petits Augustins, Hotel d'Orléans.*

OCTOBER 27. SUNDAY. Went into the bath upon the Seine, not far from the Pont Royal, opposite the Tuilleries. You are shown into a little room which has a large window looking over the river into the Tuilleries. There is a table, a glass, and two chairs, and you are furnished with hot linen, towels, &c. There is a bell which you ring when you want anything.

Went in search of Ridley, and found him. He says Franklin has broke up the practice of inviting everybody to dine with him on Sunday, at Passy; that he is getting better; the gout left him weak; but he begins to sit at table; that Jay insists on having an exchange of full powers before he enters in conference or treaty; refuses to treat with D'Aranda, until he has a copy of his full powers; refused to treat with Oswald, until he had a commission to treat with the Commissioners of the United States of America. Franklin was afraid to insist upon it; was afraid we should be obliged to treat without; differed with Jay; refused to sign a letter, &c.; Vergennes wanted him to treat with D'Aranda without.

The [French] Ministry quarreled. De Fleury has attacked De Castries, upon the expenses of the Marine. Vergennes is supposed to be with De Fleury; talk of a change of ministry; talk of De Choiseul, &c. . . .

Mr. Ridley dined with me, and after dinner we went to view the apartments in the *Hotel du Roi*, and then to Mr. Jay, and Mrs. Izard; but none at home. Ridley returned, drank tea, and spent the evening with me . . . R. is still full of Jay's firmness and independence; has taken upon himself to act without asking advice, or even communicating with the Count de Vergennes, and this even in opposition to an instruction. This instruction, which is alluded to in a letter I received at the Hague, a few days before I left it, has never yet been communicated to me. It seems to have been concealed designedly from me. . . . [126]

Between two as subtle spirits as any in this world, the one malicious, the other, I think, honest, I shall have a delicate, a nice, a critical part to act. Franklin's cunning will be to divide us; to this end he will provoke, he will insinuate, he will intrigue, he will maneuver. My curiosity will at least be employed in observing his invention and his artifice. Jay declares roundly that he will never set his hand to a bad peace. Congress may appoint another, but he will make a good peace or none. . . . [127]

NOVEMBER 2. SATURDAY. Mr. Oswald, Mr. Franklin, Mr. Jay, Mr. Strachey,[128] Mr. W. Franklin, dined with me at the *Hotel du Roi, Rue du Carrousel*. Almost every moment of this week has been employed in negotiation with the English gentlemen concerning peace. We have made two propositions: one the line of forty-five degrees [as the boundary with Canada]; the other, a line through the middle of the [Great] Lakes. And for the bound between Massachusetts [Maine] and Nova Scotia, a line from the mouth of Saint Croix to its source, and from its source to the highlands.

NOVEMBER 3. SUNDAY. In my first conversation with Franklin, on Tuesday evening last, he told me of Mr. Oswald's demand of the payment of debts and compensation to the Tories. He said that their answer had been, that we had not power, nor had Congress. I told him I had no notion of cheating anybody. The question of paying debts, and that of compensating Tories, were two.

I had made the same observation that forenoon to Mr. Oswald and Mr. Strachey, in company with Mr. Jay, at his house. I saw it struck Mr. Strachey with peculiar pleasure; I saw it instantly smiling

[126]The instructions in question were from Congress, which insisted that the peace commissioners defer to the advice of the French in their negotiations with Great Britain. Jay, Franklin, and Adams himself realized that the interests of their French allies did not necessarily coincide with those of the United States, and they purposely ignored Congress's orders.

[127]Adams clearly indicates his suspicions of the worldly Franklin (who may have felt slighted at the arrival of Adams, as yet another partner in the delicate negotiations), and his admiration of the much more earnest Jay. But as he writes later on, the three soon resolved their differences.

[128]Strachey joined Oswald as a British negotiator, and pursued a tougher line during the talks.

in every line of his face; Mr. Oswald was apparently pleased with it too. In subsequent conversation with my colleagues, I proposed to them that we should agree, that Congress should recommend to the States to open their courts of justice for the recovery of all just debts. They gradually fell into this opinion, and we all expressed these sentiments to the English gentlemen, who were much pleased with it; and with reason, because it silences the clamors of all the British creditors against the peace, and prevents them from making common cause with the refugees.

Mr. Jay came in and spent two hours in conversation upon our affairs, and we attempted an answer to Mr. Oswald's letter. . . . I learn from him . . . [that] Vergennes also pronounced Oswald's first commission [from the British government] sufficient, and was for making an acknowledgment of American independence the first article of the treaty. Jay would not treat; the consequence was, a complete acknowledgment of our independence by Oswald's new commission under the great seal of Great Britain, to treat with the commissioners of the United States of America. Thus a system of temperate firmness has succeeded everywhere, but the base system nowhere. . . . [129]

O. [Oswald] proposed solemnly to all three of us yesterday, at his house, to agree not to molest the British troops in the evacuation, but we did not; this, however, shows they have it in contemplation. Suppose they are going against West Florida; how far are we bound to favor the Spaniards? Our treaty with France must and shall be sacredly fulfilled, and we must admit Spain to accede when she will; but until she does, our treaty does not bind us to France to assist Spain.

The present conduct of England and America resembles that of the eagle and the cat. An eagle sailing over a farmer's yard espied a creature that he thought a hare; he pounced upon him up in the air; the cat seized him by the neck with her teeth, and round the body with her fore and hind claws. The eagle, finding himself scratched and pressed, bids the cat let go and fall down. No, says the cat, I won't let go and fall; you shall stoop and set me down.

---

[129]Actually, Oswald's commission was written with diplomatic skill; the Americans interpreted it as a recognition of U.S. independence, while the British could claim it was no such thing, in the event that peace negotiations broke down and the war continued.

NOVEMBER 4. MONDAY. Called on Jay, and went to Oswald's, and spent with him and Strachey from eleven to three, in drawing up the articles respecting debts, and Tories, and fishery. I drew up the article anew in this form.

"That the subjects of His Britannic Majesty, and the people of the said United States, shall continue to enjoy unmolested, the right to take fish of every kind, on all the Banks of Newfoundland, in the Gulf of Saint Lawrence, and all other places, where the inhabitants of both countries used, at any time heretofore, to fish; and also to dry and cure their fish on the shores of Nova Scotia, Cape Sable, the Isle of Sable, and on the shores of any of the unsettled, bays, harbors, or creeks of Nova Scotia and the Magdalen Islands; and His Britannic Majesty, and the said United States, will extend privileges and hospitality to each other's fishermen as to his own."

Dined with the Marquis de Lafayette, with the Prince de Poix, the Viscount de Noailles and his lady, Mr. Jay, Mr. Price and his lady, Mrs. Izard and her two daughters, Dr. Bancroft, Mr. William Franklin. The Marquis proposed to me in confidence, his going out with D'Estaing, to the West Indies. But he is to go, a month hence, in a frigate.

Mem. All the forenoon, from eleven to three, at Mr. Oswald's, Mr. Jay and I—in the evening there again until near eleven. Mr. Strachey is as artful and insinuating a man as they could send; he pushes and presses every point as far as it can possibly go; he is the most eager, earnest, pointed spirit. We agreed last night to this:

Whereas certain of the United States, excited thereto by the unnecessary destruction of private property [by the British army], have confiscated all debts due from their citizens to British subjects, and also, in certain instances, lands belonging to the latter. And whereas it is *just* that private contracts, made between individuals of the two countries before the war, should be faithfully executed, and as the confiscation of the said lands may have a latitude not justifiable by the law of nations, it is agreed that the British creditors, shall, notwithstanding, meet with no lawful impediment, to recovering the full value, or sterling amount, of such *bona fide* debts as were contracted before the year 1775. And also, that Congress will recommend to the said States, so to correct, if necessary, their said acts respecting the confiscation of lands in America belonging to real

British subjects, as to render their said acts consistent with perfect justice and equity.

NOVEMBER 5. TUESDAY. Mr. Jay likes Frenchmen as little as Mr. Lee and Mr. Izard did. He says they are not a moral people; they know not what it is; he don't like any Frenchman; the Marquis de Lafayette is clever, but he is a Frenchman. Our allies don't play fair, he told me; they were endeavoring to deprive us of the fishery, the western lands, and the navigation of the Mississippi; they would even bargain with the English to deprive us of them; they want to play the western lands, Mississippi, and the whole Gulf of Mexico into the hands of Spain.

Oswald talks of . . . a plot to divide America between France and England; France to have New England. They tell a story about Vergennes, and his agreeing that the English might propose such a division, but reserving a right to deny it all. These whispers ought not to be credited by us.

NOVEMBER 9. SATURDAY. The Marquis de Lafayette came in and told me he had been to Versailles, and in consultation with him about the affairs of money, as he and I had agreed he should. He said he found that the Count de Vergennes and their ministry were of the same opinion with me; that the English were determined to evacuate New York.

After some time, he told me, in a great air of confidence, that he was afraid the Count took it amiss that I had not been to Versailles to see him; the Count told him, that he had not been officially informed of my arrival; he had only learned it from the returns of the police.

I went out to Passy to dine with Mr. Franklin, who had been to Versailles, and presented his memorial and the papers accompanying it. The Count said he would have the papers translated, to lay them before the King; but the affair would meet with many difficulties. Franklin brought the same message to me from the Count, and said he believed it would be taken kindly if I went. I told both the Marquis and the Doctor that I would go tomorrow morning.

NOVEMBER 10. SUNDAY. Accordingly, at eight this morning I went and waited on the Comte. He asked me how we went on with the English. I told him we divided upon two points—the Tories and Penobscot [the Maine boundary]; two ostensible points; for it was impossible to believe that my Lord Shelburne or the nation cared much about such points. . . .

The Comte said that Mr. Fitzherbert told him they wanted it [lands northeast of the Penobscot River] for the masts [to be made by logging the forests]; but the Comte said that Canada had an immense quantity. I told him I thought there were few masts there, but that I fancied it was not masts, but Tories that again made the difficulty; some of them claimed lands in that territory, and others hoped for grants there.[130]

The Comte said it was not astonishing that the British ministry should insist upon compensation to them, for that all the precedents were in favor of it; that there had been no example of an affair like this, terminated by a treaty, without reestablishing those who had adhered to the old government in all their possessions. I begged his pardon in this, and said in Ireland at least there had been a multitude of confiscations without restitution. Here we ran into some conversation concerning Ireland, &c.

Mr. Reyneval [Vergennes's secretary], who was present, talked about national honor and the obligation they were under to support their adherents. Here I thought I might indulge a little more latitude of expression than I had done with Oswald and Strachey; and I answered, if the nation thought itself bound in honor to compensate these people, it might easily do it, for it cost the nation more money to carry on this war one month, than it would cost it to compensate them all.

But I could not comprehend this doctrine of national honor; those people, by their misrepresentations, had deceived the nation who had followed the impulsion of their devouring ambition until it had brought an indelible stain on the British name, and almost irretrievable ruin on the nation; and now that very nation was thought to be bound in honor to compensate its dishonorers and destroyers. Reyneval said it was very true. . . .

NOVEMBER 11. MONDAY. Mr. Whiteford, the secretary of

---

[130]There was an immense migration of displaced loyalists into Canada; many settled in Nova Scotia.

Mr. Oswald, came a second time, not having found me at home yesterday, when he left a card with a copy of Mr. Oswald's commission, attested by himself (Mr. Oswald). He delivered the copy, and said Mr. Oswald was ready to compare it to the original with me. I said, Mr. Oswald's attestation was sufficient, as he had already shown me the original. He sat down, and we fell into conversation. . . .

We soon fell into politics. I told him that there was something in the minds of the English and French which impelled them irresistibly to war every ten or fifteen years. He said the ensuing peace would, he believed, be a long one. I said it would, provided it was well made, and nothing left in it to give future discontents; but if anything was done which the Americans should think hard and unjust, both the English and French would be continually blowing it up and inflaming the American minds with it, in order to make them join one side or the other in a future war. He might well think, that the French would be very glad to have the Americans join them in a future war. . . .

For my own part, I thought America had been long enough involved in the wars of Europe. She had been a football between contending nations from the beginning, and it was easy to foresee that France and England both would endeavor to involve us in their future wars. . . .

NOVEMBER 13. WEDNESDAY. This is the anniversary of my quitting home.

Three years are completed. Oh! when shall I return? . . .

NOVEMBER 15. FRIDAY. Mr. Oswald came to visit me, and entered with some freedom into conversation. I said many things to convince him that it was the policy of my Lord Shelburne, and the interest of the nation, to agree with us upon the advantageous terms which Mr. Strachey carried away on the 5th; shewed him the advantages of the boundary, the vast extent of land, and the equitable provision for the payment of debts, and even the great benefits stipulated for the Tories.

He said he had been reading Mr. Paine's "Answer to the Abbé Raynal," and had found there an excellent argument in favor of the Tories. Mr. Paine says, "that before the battle of Lexington, we were so blindly prejudiced in favor of the English, and so closely attached to them, that we went to war at any time and for any object, when they bid us." Now, this being habitual to the Americans, it was excusable in the Tories to behave upon this occasion as all of us had ever done upon all others. . . .

I replied, that we had no power, and Congress had no power, and, therefore, we must consider how it would be reasoned upon in the several legislatures of the separate States, in the course of [the] twelve or fifteen months it should be there debated; you must carry on the war six or nine months certainly for this compensation, and consequently spend, in the prosecution of it, six or nine times the sum necessary to make the compensation; for, I presume, this war costs every month to Great Britain a larger sum than would be necessary to pay for the forfeited estates. . . .

"Have you seen," says he, "a certain letter to the Count de Vergennes, wherein Mr. Samuel Adams is treated pretty freely?"

"Yes," says I, "and several other papers, in which Mr. John Adams has been treated so too. I don't know what you may have heard in England of Mr. S. Adams; you may have been taught to believe, for what I know, that he eats little children; but I assure you he is a man of humanity and candor, as well as integrity; and further, that he is devoted to the interest of his country. . . . What will he say when the question of amnesty and compensation to the Tories comes before the Senate of Massachusetts, and when he is informed that England makes a point of it, and that France favors her? He will say, here are two old, sagacious courts, both endeavoring to sow the seeds of discord among us, each endeavoring to keep us in hot water, to keep up continual broils between an English party and a French party, in hopes of obliging the independent and patriotic party to lean to its side. . . ."

NOVEMBER 18. MONDAY. Returned Mr. Oswald's visit. . . . We went over the old ground concerning the Tories. He began to use arguments with me to relax. I told him he must not think of that, but must bend all his thoughts to convince and persuade his Court to give it up; that if the terms now before his Court were not accepted, the whole negotiation would be broken off. . . .

"You are afraid," says Mr. Oswald today, "of being made the tools of the powers of Europe."

"Indeed I am," says I.

"What powers?" said he.

"All of them," said I. "It is obvious that all the powers of Europe will be continually maneuvering with us, to work us into their real or imaginary balances of power. . . ."

"I beg of you," says he, "to get out of your head the idea that we shall disturb you. . . . We can never be such sots," says he, "as to think of differing again with you."

"Why," says I, "in truth I have never been able to comprehend the reason why you ever thought of differing with us thus far. . . ."

NOVEMBER 20. Dr. Franklin came in, and we fell into conversation. . . . I asked, what could be the policy of this Court in wishing to deprive us of the fisheries and the Mississippi? I could see no possible motive for it, but to plant the seeds of contention for a future war; if they pursued this policy, they would be as fatally blinded to their true interests as ever the English were. Franklin said, they would be every bit as blind; that the fisheries and Mississippi could not be given up; that nothing was clearer to him than that the fisheries were essential to the Northern States, and the Mississippi to the Southern, and, indeed, both to all. . . .

I thought it was now a crisis in which good will or ill will toward America would be carried very far in England; a time, perhaps, when the American Ministers may have more weight in turning the tide of sentiment, or influencing the changes of administration, than they ever had before, and, perhaps, than they would have again. . . . Where would England be if the war continues two years longer? What the state of her finances? What her condition in the East and West Indies, in North America, Ireland, Scotland, and even in England? What hopes have they of saving themselves from a civil war? If our terms are not now accepted they will never have such offers from America; they will never have so advantageous a line; never, their debts; never, so much for the Tories, and, perhaps, a rigorous demand for compensation for the devastations they have committed.

Mr. Jay agreed with me in sentiment, and, indeed, they are the principles he has uniformly pursued through the whole negotiation before my arrival; I think they cannot be misunderstood or disapproved in Congress. . . .

NOVEMBER 23. SATURDAY. Mr. Jay called at ten, and went

out with me to Passy to meet the Marquis de Lafayette, at the invitation of Dr. Franklin. The Marquis's business was to show us a letter he had written to the Count de Vergennes on the subject of money. This I saw nettled Franklin, as it seemed an attempt to take to himself the merit of obtaining a loan [from France], if one should be procured. He gave us also a letter to us three, for our approbation, of his going out with the Count d'Estaing. He recites in it, that he had remained here by our advice, as necessary to the negotiations.

This nettled both Franklin and Jay. I knew nothing of it, not having been here; and they both denied it [that they had asked Lafayette to stay and help]. This unlimited ambition will obstruct his rise; he grasps at all, civil, political, and military, and would be thought of the *unum necessarium* in everything; he has so much real merit, such family supports, and so much favor at Court, that he need not recur to artifice. . . .

NOVEMBER 25. MONDAY. Dr. Franklin, Mr. Jay, and myself, at eleven, met at Mr. Oswald's lodgings. Mr. Strachey told us he had been to London, and waited personally on every one of the King's Cabinet Council, and had communicated the last propositions to them; they, every one of them, unanimously condemned that respecting the Tories, so that that unhappy affair stuck, as he foresaw and foretold that it would.

The affair of the fishery, too, was somewhat altered. They could not admit us to dry on the shores of Nova Scotia, nor to fish within three leagues of the coast, nor within fifteen leagues of the coast of Cape Breton. The boundary they did not approve; they thought it too extended, too vast a country, but they would not make a difficulty. . . .

I could not help observing, that the ideas respecting the fishery appeared to come piping hot from Versailles. . . . I related to them the manner in which the cod and haddock come into the rivers, harbors, creeks, and up to the very wharves, on all the northern coast of America, in the spring, in the month of April, so that you have nothing to do but step into a boat and bring in in a parcel of fish in a few hours; but that in May they begin to withdraw. We have a saying at Boston, that when the "blossoms fall, the haddock begin to crawl";

that is, to move out into deep water, so that in summer you must go out some distance to fish. . . . That neither French nor English could go from Europe and arrive early enough for the first fare; that our vessels could, being so much nearer, an advantage which God and nature had put into our hands; but that this advantage of ours had ever been an advantage to England, because our fish had been sold in Spain and Portugal for gold and silver, and that gold and silver sent to London for manufactures; that this would be the course again; that France foresaw it, and wished to deprive England of it, by persuading her to deprive us of it; that it would be a master stroke of policy if she should succeed, but England must be completely the dupe before she could succeed. . . .

Strachey said, perhaps I would put down some observations in writing upon it. I said, with all my heart, provided I had the approbation of my colleagues. . . .

Mr. Jay desired to know whether Mr. Oswald had now power to conclude and sign with us. Strachey said he had, absolutely. Mr. Jay desired to know, if the propositions now delivered us were their ultimatum. Strachey seemed loath to answer, but at last said, No. We agreed these were good signs of sincerity. . . .

NOVEMBER 26. TUESDAY. Breakfasted at Mr. Jay's with Dr. Franklin, in consultation upon the propositions made to us yesterday by Mr. Oswald. We agreed unanimously to answer him, that we could not consent to the article respecting the refugees, as it now stands. Dr. Franklin read a letter which he had prepared, to Mr. Oswald, upon the subject of Tories, which we had agreed with him that he should read, as containing his private sentiments. We had a vast deal of conversation upon the subject. My colleagues opened themselves, and made many observations concerning the conduct, crimes, and demerits of those people.

Before dinner, Mr. Fitzherbert came in, whom I had never seen before, a gentleman of about thirty-three; seems pretty discreet and judicious, and did not discover [reveal] those airs of vanity which are imputed to him. He came in consequence of the desire which I had expressed yesterday, of knowing the state of the negotiation between him and the Count de Vergennes, respecting the fishery. He told us, that the Count was for fixing the boundaries where each nation should fish; he must confess he thought the idea plausible; for that there had been great dissensions between the fishermen of the two nations. . . .

He said his principal object was, to avoid sowing the seeds of future wars. I said, it was equally my object; and that I was persuaded that if the germ of a war was left anywhere, there was the greatest danger of its being in the article respecting the fishery. The rest of the day was spent in endless discussions about the Tories. Dr. Franklin is very staunch against them; more decided a great deal on this point than Mr. Jay or myself.

NOVEMBER 27. WEDNESDAY. Mr. Benjamin Vaughan came in, returned from London, where he had seen Lord Shelburne. He says he finds the ministry much embarrassed with the Tories, and exceedingly desirous of saving their honor and reputation in this point; that it is reputation more than money, &c.

Dined with Mr. Jay, and spent some time before dinner with him and Dr. Franklin, and all the afternoon and evening with them and Mr. Oswald, endeavoring to come together concerning the fisheries and Tories. . . .

NOVEMBER 29. FRIDAY. Met Mr. Fitzherbert, Mr. Oswald, Mr. Franklin, Mr. Jay, Mr. Laurens, and Mr. Strachey, at Mr. Jay's, *Hotel d'Orleans*, and spent the whole day in discussions about the fishery and the Tories. I proposed a new article concerning the fishery; it was discussed and turned in every light, and multitudes of amendments proposed on each side; and at last the article drawn as it was finally agreed to. . . .

After hearing all this [the arguments from the Americans], Mr. Fitzherbert, Mr. Oswald, and Mr. Strachey retired for some time; and, returning, Mr. Fitzherbert said that, upon consulting together, and weighing everything as maturely as possible, Mr. Strachey and himself had determined to advise Mr. Oswald to strike with us, according to the terms we had proposed as our ultimatum respecting the fisheries and the loyalists. Accordingly, we all sat down and read over the whole treaty, and corrected it, and agreed to meet tomorrow, at Mr. Oswald's house, to sign and seal the treaties, which the secretaries were to copy fair in the meantime.

NOVEMBER 30. SATURDAY. ST. ANDREW'S DAY. We met

first at Mr. Jay's, then at Mr. Oswald's; examined and compared the treaties. Mr. Strachey had left out the limitation of time, the twelve months that the refugees were allowed to reside in America, in order to recover their estates if they could. Dr. Franklin said this was a surprise upon us. Mr. Jay said so too. We never had consulted to leave it out, and they insisted upon putting it in, which was done.

Mr. Laurens said there ought to be a stipulation that the British troops should carry off no negroes or other American property. We all agreed. Mr. Oswald consented.

Then the treaties were signed, sealed, and delivered, and we all went out to Passy to dine with Dr. Franklin. Thus far has proceeded this great affair.

The unravelling of the plot has been to me the most affecting and astonishing part of the whole piece. As soon as I arrived in Paris I waited on Mr. Jay, and learned from him the rise and progress of the negotiations. Nothing that has happened since the beginning of the controversy in 1761, has ever struck me more forcibly, or affected me more intimately, than that entire coincidence of principles and opinions between him and me.

In about three days I went out to Passy and spent the evening with Dr. Franklin, and entered largely into conversation with him upon the course and present state of our foreign affairs. I told him, without reserve, my opinion of the policy of this Court, and of the principles, wisdom, and firmness with which Mr. Jay had conducted the negotiations in his sickness and my absence, and that I was determined to support Mr. Jay to the utmost of my power in the pursuit of the same system. The Doctor heard me patiently, but said nothing.

The first conference we had afterwards with Mr. Oswald, in considering one point and another, Dr. Franklin turned to Mr. Jay and said, I am of your opinion, and will go on with these gentlemen in the business without consulting this Court [the French]. He has, accordingly, met us in most of our conferences, and has gone on with us in entire harmony and unanimity throughout, and has been able and useful, both by his sagacity and his reputation, in the whole negotiation.

I was very happy Mr. Laurens came in, although it was the last day of the conferences, and wish he could have been sooner; his apprehension, notwithstanding his deplorable affliction under the recent loss of so excellent a son, is as quick, his judgment as sound, and his heart as firm as ever. . . .

I have not attempted, in these notes, to do justice to the arguments of my colleagues, all of whom were, throughout the whole business, when they attended, very attentive and very able; especially Mr. Jay, to whom the French, if they knew as much of his negotiations as they do of mine, would very justly give the title with which they have inconsiderately decorated me, that of *"Le Washington de la négociation"*; a very flattering compliment indeed, to which I have not a right, but sincerely think it belongs to Mr. Jay.

———

THE AMERICANS WON—it was as simple as that. Adams, Franklin, and Jay accomplished a marvelous victory at the bargaining table, one that actually expanded Washington's triumph on the battlefield. Britain accepted the sovereignty and independence of the United States (of course); it granted Americans full rights to the Grand Banks fishery; it conceded generous boundaries for the new nation, stretching to the Mississippi and up to the Great Lakes; and it agreed that compensation for the Tories would be handled by state legislatures, at Congress's urging. France and Spain soon followed suit, and the final articles of peace were signed by all parties on September 3, 1783.

By then, news of the peace had long since reached American shores. The initial agreement signed by the peace commissioners on November 30, 1782, had been ratified by Congress, but the formal cessation of hostilities had to wait for France's own treaty with Britain. That was signed on January 20, 1783; a copy of that document arrived in Philadelphia on a French ship aptly named the *Triumph*. Congress began to discharge the troops, as British forces in Charleston, Savannah, and New York (now commanded by General Carleton) prepared for departure. On November 25, 1783, the last of the king's soldiers sailed out of New York Harbor, as General Washington rode into the city at the head of his troops.

As victory celebrations erupted up and down the continent, a few Americans stopped to consider the long, hard struggle now seen through to its conclusion. In the midst of events, it had been impossible for them to see things clearly; even now, after it was all over, it must have been difficult to grasp it all. Perhaps John Adams flipped open his diary to his entries just before the First Continental Congress: "We have not men fit for the times," he wrote then. "We are deficient in genius, in education, in travel, in fortune, in everything. I feel unutterable anxiety. God grant us wisdom and fortitude!" He and his fellows had proved himself wrong—or perhaps God *had* granted them wisdom and fortitude, in overwhelming measure.

When trouble first appeared in relations between the colonies and the government in London, only a prophet or a fool would have predicted the emergence of a united, independent American government before the end of the next decade. The thirteen colonies shared little beyond a common king and continent: the colonists had different folkways and religious convictions; they had little mutual trade or migration; and they had almost no centralization institutions. They thought of themselves as British, and they appealed to their rights *as Englishmen*.

Even so, the colonists shared strikingly similar political values, thanks in part to that English heritage and to their isolation across the Atlantic. Though they owed their allegiance to the crown, they enjoyed a large measure of self-government. They associated in fraternal organizations; served on local boards, commissions, and juries; fought elections for public office and colonial legislatures. The measures the British ministries took in the mid-1760s undermined this de facto self-rule across the eastern seaboard; their impact was felt down to the humblest townships in all thirteen colonies. The genius of John and Samuel Adams, and all the other "men fit for the times," was to direct this outrage, to give it an articulate voice, to recognize that all the colonies now had an overriding common cause.

A later generation of British colonial officials would learn to divide and rule in their overseas possessions; in the eighteenth century, however, the age of enlightenment, the king's ministers tried to rationalize American policy, covering all thirteen colonies with blanket taxes and regulations. In so doing, they polarized the Americans, giving them that common cause they had always lacked.

Perhaps the men who formed the ministries of the 1760s and 1770s were incapable of understanding the political sophistication of the colonists. They were aristocrats, after all, in a hierarchical era that valued birth and breeding. They suffered from a geographical arrogance as well: the British world revolved around London, the one great metropolis of the empire. From their point of view on the Thames, the outer fringes of England itself—let alone America—looked like a barbarous wilderness. They viewed Scottish highlanders as savages, and Irishmen as subhumans. They could scarcely imagine that American political leaders would translate their anger into precise arguments about the nature of government, that they could erect a unified body like the Continental Congress. And so, in arrogance, they pushed on with their measures, driving the rebels to further extremes, pushing them to make their arguments even sharper, giving them even greater unity.

The incomprehension of the British had grown more profound after war erupted. Nothing in England's history prepared the king's army for the American Revolution. It was simultaneously a formal war between regular armies; an irregular war against local militia; and an outright guerrilla war against disparate partisan forces. If it had been only a standard clash between organized armies, the redcoats would have done well; indeed, they were always at their best in pitched battles. If it had been only an irregular or guerrilla war, they also might have constructed a winning strategy—perhaps building networks of fortified posts, or driving in the population from the countryside. But the hybrid nature of the war created intense difficulties: British commanders had to watch both the American army in front and the partisans or militia rising up in their rear.

It would be a mistake, however, to think that the war was simply unwinnable for the British army. General Thomas Gage might have carried off an immediate triumph, if he had been given the forces he asked for early on. He recognized that a powerful strike at the very beginning of the rebellion might make the Americans recede. But the ministry recoiled from expending so much effort on the "rabble" across the Atlantic. And so it stumbled on, relying on a succession of indecisive or wrong-headed commanders: Howe, who pursued stationary cities, rather than the enemy army; Burgoyne, who conjured up fantasy strategies out of the map of North America; Clinton, who quarreled with everyone and fought almost no one.

Even these men achieved great successes along the way—successes that made patriots despair of ever winning the war. Clinton's capture of Charleston, for example, was a decisive victory, dealing a heavy blow to American arms and opening the way for a conquest of the South. Howe's capture of New York battered American morale; and when he marched to the gates of Philadelphia, John Adams quailed in his diary, "O, Heaven! Grant us one great soul! One leading mind would extricate the best cause from that ruin which seems to await it for the want of it."

So strange those words must have seemed to Adams, if he had stopped to read them again in 1783. By then it was clear to everyone that one great soul and leading mind had already appeared in 1777, in the form of George Washington. Yet Adams's despair in that dark hour serves as a reminder of the greatness of Washington's achievement. In almost every campaign and battle, he faced an enemy with more troops—and the British and Hessian regulars boasted discipline, training, and equipment that the Americans only began to match in the last years of the war. The king's officers were uniformly professional, from the lowest ensign to the commanding generals; Washington, on the other hand, always suffered from an uneven roster of subordinates.

But Washington carried through, rising to every occasion. With his ragged band of untrained citizen soldiers, he avoided battle except under the most favorable conditions—indeed, as Eric McKitrick and Stanley Elkins note, the term "Fabian strategy" entered the English language as a description of Washington's campaigns, which, like those conducted by the ancient Roman general Fabius against Hannibal, baffled the invading enemy. He knew that the existence of an organized army symbolized the American cause itself; he had to preserve that army, or the Revolution would be lost. At the same time, Washington combined prudence with daring, striking whenever an opportunity offered—sometimes taking great risks when he saw a chance to slice off an exposed British detachment.

His judgment in such matters was borne out by the course of the war. He knew he could not drive the British into the sea, but he had to strike back whenever he could, for two reasons. First, he had to wear down the British forces in the field, which were never very large in the first place. Second, he understood the political nature of the war; he had to win victories to boost American morale, tire the British out, and impress potential allies overseas. Sometimes, as Robert Middlekauff argues, he planned beyond the capabilities of his army, especially at Germantown; but he more than made up for such oversights with his calm, commanding presence on the battlefield, as he rallied his troops and directed counterattacks—often in the teeth of impending disaster. And at Trenton, Princeton, Yorktown, and (to a lesser extent) Monmouth Court House, his strategy of surprise attacks against isolated detachments succeeded splendidly.

Washington's performance was outstanding, sometimes even brilliant—but his genius was hidden by his very coolness, his constant self-possession. He was not given to flamboyance, like Burgoyne, or late-night gambling, like Howe, or hell-for-leather cavalry charges, like the one Cornwallis conducted at Monmouth Court House. He remained in full control of his faculties at all times, never cracking under pressure (as Gates did at Camden) or lapsing into confusion and inertia (as Clinton and Cornwallis did in the Yorktown campaign). That inner strength set him apart from almost all the other generals on either side. At the same moment that John Adams pleaded for "one great soul" to save America, that soul was preparing for the battle of Germantown, imparting his own perseverance to the army and the republic.

Washington's strength and selflessness would dazzle the nation once more, after the British troops departed in 1783. "The greatest act of his life," writes historian Gordon Wood, "the one that gave him his greatest fame, was his resignation as commander in chief of the American forces. Following the signing of the peace treaty and the British recognition of American independence, Washington stunned the world when he surrendered his sword to Congress on

December 23, 1783, and retired to his farm at Mount Vernon. . . .
This self-conscious and unconditional withdrawal from power and
politics was a great moral action, full of significance for an enlightened
and republicanized world, and the results were monumental. His re-
tirement had a profound effect everywhere in the Western world. It
was extraordinary, it was unprecedented in modern times—a victorious general surrendering his arms and returning to his farm. Cromwell, William of Orange, Marlborough—all sought political rewards
commensurate with their military achievements."

The nation had come far since the beginning of the great conflict,
when even Samuel Adams distanced himself from "levelling principles." The citizens of the new republic aspired to equality and liberty
beyond that of the corrupt, hierarchical world they had always known;
now they looked to the ancient Roman republic as their model, in
which public-minded leaders had acted for the good of their country,
not themselves. And Washington, Wood writes, "was the perfect Cin-
cinnatus, the Roman patriot who returned to his farm after his victories in war. Washington knew very well these classical Republican
virtues and tried to live his life by them."[131] ▶

Before Washington handed in his sword, he issued one last general order to his rapidly disappearing army. He looked back at the
astonishing events, and marveled that the country had survived
them—that they had all triumphed. And he celebrated the astonishing unity that had come over the thirteen colonies, the way that all
Americans had pulled together to create a nation. But most of all, he
expressed his thanks and affection for his men, who had carried on
through the worst conditions, the direst setbacks, until they achieved
victory.

[131]Gordon Wood, pp. 203–204.

Farewell Orders
by George Washington

HEADQUARTERS, ROCKY HILL, N.J.   NOV. 2, 1783

The United States in Congress assembled, after giving the most honorable testimony to the merits of the federal armies, and presenting them with the thanks of their country for their long, eminent, and faithful services, having thought proper . . . to discharge such part of the troops as were engaged for the war, and to permit the officers on furlough to retire from service . . . it only remaining for the Commander-in-Chief to address himself once more, and that for the last time, to the armies of the United States (however widely dispersed the individuals who composed them may be) and to bid them an affectionate—a long farewell.

But before the Commander-in-Chief takes his final leave of those he holds most dear, he wishes to indulge himself for a few moments in calling to mind a slight review of the past . . . and he will conclude the address by expressing the obligations he feels himself under for the spirited and able assistance he has experienced from them in the performance of an arduous office.

A contemplation of the complete attainment (at a period earlier than could have been expected) of the object for which we contended, against so formidable a power, cannot but inspire us with astonishment and gratitude. The disadvantagous circumstances on our part, under which the war was undertaken, can never be forgotten. The singular interpositions of Providence in our feeble condition, were such as could scarcely escape the attention of the most unobserving—while the unparalleled perseverence of the armies of the United States, through almost every possible suffering and discouragement, for the space of eight long years, was little short of a standing miracle. . . .

Every American officer and soldier must now console himself for any unpleasant circumstances which may have occurred, by a recollection of the uncommon scenes in which he has been called to act no inglorious part, and the astonishing events to which he has been a witness.

Events which have seldom, if ever before, taken place on the stage of human action, nor can they probably happen again. For who has before seen a disciplined army formed at once from such raw material? Who that was not a witness could imagine that the most violent local prejudices could cease so soon, and that men who came from the different parts of the continent, strongly disposed by the habits of education to despise and quarrel with each other, would instantly become but one patriotic band of brothers? Or who that was not on the spot can trace the steps by which such a wonderful revolution has been effected, and such a glorious period put to our warlike toils?

It is universally acknowledged that the enlarged prospect of happiness opened by the confirmation of our independence and sovereignty, almost exceeds the power of description. And shall not the brave men who have contributed so essentially to these inestimable acquisitions, returning from the field of war to the field of agriculture, participate in all the blessings which have been obtained? In such a Republic who will exclude them from the rights of citizens, and the fruits of their labors? In such a country so happily circumstanced, the pursuits of commerce and the cultivation of the soil will unfold to industry the certain road to competence. . . .

The Commander-in-Chief conceives little is now wanting to enable the soldier to exchange the military character into that of the citizen, but that steady, decent tenor of behavior which has generally distinguished not only the army under his immediate command, but the different detachments and separate armies through the course of the war. From their good sense and prudence, he anticipates the happiest consequences; and while he congratulates them on the glorious occasion which renders their services in the field no longer necessary, he wishes to express the obligations he feels himself under for the assistance he has received from every class—and in every instance.

He presents his thanks in the most serious and affectionate manner, to the general officers, as well for their counsels on many interesting occasions, as for their ardor in promoting the success of the plans he had adopted. To the commanders of the regiments and corps, and to the others, for their great zeal and attention in carrying his orders promptly into execution—to the staff for their alacrity and exactness in performing the duties of their several departments. And to the noncommissioned officers and private soldiers, for their extraordinary patience and suffering, as well as their invincible fortitude in action. . . .

And being now to conclude these his last public orders, to take his ultimate leave in a short time of the military character, and to bid a final adieu to the armies he has long had the honor to command— he can only again offer in their behalf, his recommendations to their grateful country, and his prayers to the God of armies.

May ample justice be done them here; and may the choicest of Heaven's favors, both here and hereafter, attend those, who under the divine auspices have secured innumerable blessings for others. With these wishes and this benediction, the Commander-in-Chief is about to retire from service—the curtain of separation will soon be drawn—and the military scene to him will be closed forever.

WASHINGTON TRULY BELIEVED that he had drawn "the curtain of separation" between his life and public service. And yet, ironically, he virtually guaranteed that he would be called again into the government, thanks to the very sincerity of his disinterest and the restraint of his ambition.

The war had ended; independence had been secured; but the Revolution continued. It was, as Gordon Wood writes, "the greatest utopian movement in American history. The revolutionaries aimed at nothing less than a reconstitution of American society. They hoped to destroy the old bonds holding together the old monarchical society—kinship, patriarchy, and patronage—and to put in their place new social bonds of love, respect, and consent. They sought to construct a society and governments based on virtue and disinterested public leadership and to set in motion a moral movement that would eventually be felt around the globe."[132]

That revolution would reach into countless spheres of public and even private life. Slavery would be abolished in half of the

[132]Gordon Wood, p. 229.

states; voting rights would be steadily expanded; guarantees of religious and political liberties, of freedom of speech, would soon be passed by legislatures up and down the continent. And delegates would soon gather in a convention to create a fundamental law for the republic, one that would guarantee all those things they had fought so hard for in the war of independence. They would call it the Constitution.